FOUNDATIONAL FICTIONS

LATIN AMERICAN LITERATURE AND CULTURE

General Editor
Roberto González Echevarría
R. Selden Rose Professor of Spanish and
Professor of Comparative Literature
Yale University

FOUNDATIONAL FICTIONS

The National Romances of Latin America

Doris Sommer

UNIVERSITY OF CALIFORNIA PRESS
Berkeley • Los Angeles • London

The Press gratefully acknowledges the support of
Amherst College in the publication of this book.

University of California Press
Berkeley and Los Angeles, California

University of California Press
London, England

Copyright © 1991 by
The Regents of the University of California
First Paperback Printing 1993

Library of Congress Cataloging-in-Publication

Sommer, Doris, 1947–
Foundational fictions: the national romances of Latin America /
Doris Sommer
p.   cm.—(Latin American literature and culture; 8)
Includes bibliographical references and index.
ISBN 0-520-08285-0
1. Latin American fiction—19th century—History and criticism.
2. Literature and society—Latin America. 3. Nationalism in
literature.   I. Title.   II. Series: Latin American literature and
culture (Berkeley, California); 8.PQ7082.N7S58   1991
863—dc20
90–44240
CIP

Printed in the United States of America

1   2   3   4   5   6   7   8   9

The paper used in this publication meets the minimum
requirements of American National Standard for Information
Sciences—permanence of Paper for Printed Library Materials,
ANSI Z39.48–1984 ⊗

Permission for quoted material and photographs
will be found at end of book.

*for Allen, who has taught
me so much.*

Contents

Preface

Love and patriotism have evoked or promised the same feelings for me—a simultaneous rush of belonging and possession—ever since my teenage fantasies of passionate bonding became confused with another longing to belong. I mention this emotional tangle because my effort to follow its contours is largely responsible for this book on the relationship between romance and national foundations in Latin America. I therefore feel obliged to share a bit of the intimate history behind my particular focus on the novel construction of a national intimacy. In tracing the turns of one erotic longing into another national one, I come back to a desire that must have begun when I was born without belonging anywhere. It was in something called a displaced persons' camp, a nowhere for nationals, so precisely and perversely utopian. Yet it was a site better than the camps my parents had visited in Poland a bit earlier. In fact, one of the misplaced jokes of my New York childhood (beginning at age four when the United States quota let in one more Jewish family) was to tell friends who asked why I wasn't going off to summer camp that my parents had been there, didn't like it, and decided not to send me.

My most acute memories of being dis-mis-placed and unidentifiable—exhilarating memories in their ontological emptiness—are of an adolescence dedicated to impersonating a range of national "beings," at the same time that I was trying to get a gender assignment in on time. Much later, on reading Benedict Anderson's aside about how modern subjects "can, should, will 'have' a nationality as he or she 'has' a gender," I thought back on playing at to be or not to be. For each language tried or foreign inflection of English mastered, there was another persona. My game was to see how long I could get away with "being" (someone else). It reached tragicomic hilarity when my college applications showed a blank for nationality, since I had nothing original to put down and had wrongly assumed I was automatically "naturalized" when my parents became citizens; so there I was on the dock of Brooklyn, all eighteen years of a young-adult self, swearing-in to "be" what could only be a fiction by then. A more illustrious immigrant, like Hans Kohn (author of *American Nationalism*, 1957), wasn't playing games. He was congratulating himself and us—"the wretched refuse of the teeming shore" where Liberty holds her lamp (a Lady and Light that were fogged over when our boat came in)—for arriving in America, where we were all equally free to be patriots as a matter of civic contract, not ethnic pedigree. But the America that interpellated childish me was no freely entered agreement; it was a cluster of accents with a hollow cultural center. (Need I say that *Zelig* is my favorite film?) Where I grew up, only children spoke English with an American accent, so the occasional adult who spoke that way (say, a teacher) seemed to lack the historico-cultural density that made our Italian, Hispanic, Chinese, Jewish parents so admirably adult—and so embarrassingly out of place. We all wanted desperately to be in place, for America not to be the contractual artifice that Kohn celebrated, but so full it could fulfill us. We wanted it as much as Italians in Argentina wanted to be gauchos, as much as Hungarians in Brazil wanted their children to bear indigenous names. We wanted national fulfillment as much as we wanted to "be" in love, hardly stopping to worry that the wanting was greater than any possible payoff. And yet I already knew enough to feel as relieved as Kohn that irrational patriotism was unlikely here, so that be-longing alternated undecidably with cosmopolitan skepticism. In general, differences in evaluating nationalism may have less to do with which position is right or wrong than with the positionality one occupies: as an aspirant to national identity, for example, or as a disenchanted national. Critiques are made, it seems, from centers of uncontested nations, and disaffection presupposes a romantic prehistory. But my double positionality as a would-be American and a European has-been kept desire and dread in deadlock. The relief was that others were straddling too; un-American as I was, I was no more so than anyone else.

No wonder I learned Spanish early on; it was so familiar and so safely not. Thanks to identifying with/in Spanish, I could belong to America (and vice versa) not as the Other, but as

Another. Spanish kept my alterity in a paradoxically stabilizing schizophrenia and assuaged the immigrant self-hatred by revealing it as structural, repeated, iterable, perhaps essential to Americanism both here and to the South. There, immigrant teenagers often learned to desire their countries and each other by reading national novels. In the next pages I will say that I came to those nineteenth-century books out of curiosity for the tradition new Latin American novelists were so loudly denying. I should add that it was also after writing *One Master for Another: Populism as Patriarchal Rhetoric in Dominican Novels* (1984), where I sensed that *Enriquillo,* the centerpiece of a national tradition, was typical of an entire Latin American canon. I don't mean to contradict that personal scholarly history, but only to add, along with that archi-American Whitman, "This hour I tell things in confidence, / I might not tell everybody but I will tell you" (*Song of Myself,* 19). It is that this nineteenth-century canon speaks to the passionate investment I/we have in nationalism. This may turn out to be a tautology if, as I will suggest, the books construct Eros and Polis upon each other.

Before I venture this speculation in the second part of the introductory chapter 1, I will offer a more narrative and descriptive first part to suggest why it makes sense to read these particular books together and what makes them so hard to resist. Chapter 2 sketches some points of contact between James Fenimore Cooper and his Spanish American admirers, for whom he was a model, or perhaps another pretext for their own plagiarized authenticity. Chapters 3 to 8 explore particular examples of nineteenth-century romances, their projections of national conciliation through lovers' yearnings across traditional racial and regional barriers. The cases, though, are far from inclusive, since on the one hand some of the twenty-one countries did not produce a standard midcentury novel but rather "borrowed" continental classics; and on the other, including each of the classics would have been unwieldy. Chapter 9 reads two twentieth-century reformist novels as populist revisions of romance, that is to say defensive supervisions of transgressive affairs. Their contemporary is a novel written by a woman, to whom I give the last word in chapter 10, where her appreciation for linguistic and historical disencounters comments coyly on the programmatic fictions that helped to found Latin American nations.

Regarding my references to primary texts, readers will note that quotes appear consistently in English. Where two page numbers appear in parentheses, the first refers to the Spanish text and the second to the English translation; a single reference means that the quoted passage was omitted from the translation and that I have provided it (unacknowledged translations in the notes are mine as well). Consecutive versions in Spanish and English in the body of these essays would have produced a possibly unpleasant reading rhythm between repetitions that are redundant to some and opaque to others. And since an exclusive use of Spanish would have distanced some readers, I reluctantly chose English. Unwilling, though, entirely to excise the Spanish originals in essays attentive to their charms, I opted to include both versions at least in the longer quotes set off by easily visible spaces.

I could not have written this book without the step-by-step encouragement and advice from Andrew Parker, or without the initial skepticism from Antonio Benítez Rojo, an ideal reader who gradually exacted from me the text his reading demanded. They both have my heartfelt gratitude. I would also like to especially thank Benedict Anderson and Sylvia Molloy for inspiration and encouragement, along with Allen Kaufman, Scott Mahler, Tulio Halperín Donghi, Roberto González Echevarría, Eve Kosofsky Sedgwick, Homi Bhabha, Nancy Armstrong, Josefina Ludmer, Jean Franco, Donna Guy, Stewart Voss, Heloisa Buarque de Hollanda, Antonio Cornejo Polar, George Yúdice, Rocardo Piglia, Elizabeth Garrels, Efraín Barradas, Neil Larsen, Norman Holland, Leonard Tennenhouse, Iván Jaksic, Valeria de Marco, Roberto Schwarz, Adolfo Prieto, Julio Ramos, Rubén Ríos, Silviano Santiago, Michael Kasper, Ginny DuCharme, Greta Slobin, Betty Tsafrir, Julius Sommer, Adela Sommer, and Anna Kaufman, all of whom generously offered support and suggestions.

For permission to publish material that appeared in earlier essays, I am grateful to several publishers. "Plagiarized Authenticity: Sarmiento's Cooper and Others" originally appeared as a chapter in *Do the Americas Have a Common Literature?*, edited by

Gustavo Pérez Firmat (Durham, N.C.: Duke University Press, November, 1990). "Irresistible Romance: The Foundational Fictions of Latin America" appeared in *Nation and Narration*, edited by Homi Bhabha (London: Routledge, 1990). An earlier version of the essay "Allegory and Dialectics: A Match Made in Romance" appeared in *boundary 2*, vol. 18, no. 1 (1991), and is reprinted with the permission of Duke University Press.

"Foundational Fictions: When History Was Romance in Latin America" appeared in *Salmagundi*, no. 82–83 (Spring-Summer, 1989):111–141. "Sab c'est moi" appeared in *Hispamérica*, no. 48 (December, 1987):25–38. This essay also appeared in *Genders*, no. 2 (Summer, 1988):111–126, and is reprinted with the permission of University of Texas Press. "El mal de *María*: (Con)fusión en un romance nacional" appeared in *Modern Language Notes* (March, 1989):439–474.

1
PART I
IRRESISTIBLE ROMANCE

por encima del distanciamiento del título, de la
fortuna y del color de la piel . . . está la atracción
de los sexos, el poder irresistible del genio de la
especie.

—*Matalaché*, Enrique López Albújar

AN ARCHEOLOGY OF THE "BOOM"

When Gabriel García Márquez, Carlos Fuentes, Mario Vargas
Llosa, and Julio Cortázar, among others, apparently burst onto
the world literary scene in the 1960s, they told us categorically
and repeatedly how little there was worth reading in earlier
Latin American fiction.[1] Only now, they said, was the continent
gaining cultural independence by Calibanizing the range of
European traditions, mere raw material in purposefully naive
American hands.[2] Content, perhaps, with this vindication of our
scant information about Latin America, an English-language
public hardly suspected the Boom's substantial pre-texts: a
whole canon of great novels that elicited disingenuous dismissal
by writers who anxiously claimed to be literary orphans at
home, free to apprentice themselves abroad.[3] This book is written for that unsuspecting public, and also for a generation of
Latin Americans who, with justified enthusiasm for the Boom,
may have taken the dismissal too literally.

Although some critics argue that the Boom was merely a
promotional explosion, hardly a literary phenomenon at all, the
new novels do show distinct family resemblances, enough in fact
to produce a checklist of characteristics. These include a demo-
tion, or diffusion, of authorial control and tireless formal ex-

perimentation, techniques apparently aimed at demolishing the straight line of traditional narrative.[4] The epic subtexts about Latin American development that can be read back through the debris now become risible simulacra. If all this sounds like denial, it was. New novelists tried to laugh off the appeal of positivist and populist projects that had, by then, run aground and made history stumble when it should have been going forward. Looking back at Latin American history after reaching a precipitous end, to find that end no longer meant purpose, evidently produced giddiness. In several countries national productivity had in fact been rising from the middle of the nineteenth century to the populist period of Import Substitution Industrialization during World War II when, for a change, foreign powers were too busy to stunt local growth by supplying manufactured goods. But after the war imports flooded the markets again, and Latin American history no longer seemed progressive, no longer a positivist national biography of maturation that was overcoming some childhood or chronic illness. When Western Europe, but especially now the United States, was again free to meddle in Latin American internal affairs and to step up the production and exportation of goods, populist optimism waned. Along with it, the linear logic of economic developmentalism twisted into the deadend of perpetual underdevelopment, while patriotic storylines wilted into the vicious circles that Carlos Fuentes found typical for the new novelists.[5]

Yet the more they protested indifference to tradition, the more they would send me back to the persistent attractions that caused so much resistance. What was it, I would ask, about the notoriously obsolete programmatic brand of Latin American fiction that haunted the Boom? What burden of narrative habits or embedded assumptions could account for so round a repudiation? The attraction is practically visceral and is provoked, I believe, by a rather flagrant feature that has nevertheless gone unremarked. It is the erotic rhetoric that organizes patriotic novels. With each obsessive effort to be free of the positivist tradition in which national projects (were) coupled with productive heterosexual desire, a continuing appeal is reinscribed in the resistant Boom. The straight lines of "historical" novels can fairly be reconstructed from the efforts to bend them. What would account for the tragicomedy of self-defeating repetition in, for example, *One Hundred Years of Solitude,* or for the frustration and shame in *The Death of Artemio Cruz,* if not the bad fits between developmentalist assumptions and Latin American history? And we can deduce, for another example, that "positive" reality was a reigning literary ideal from the important departure that the proto-Boom style of magic realism represented.[6]

The Boom's parodies, its fine ironies and playfulness, are the kind of endless denial that is bound to produce the opposite effect of an admission, so that its vicious narrative circles comment on a writerly frustration as well as on disappointments with developmentalism: the more national romance must be resisted, the more it seems irresistible. One way out of circles, it seemed, was the collapse staged by Mario Vargas Llosa at the end of *Aunt Julia and the Scriptwriter* (1977); an earthquake levels the baroque confusion between Vargas Llosa's scandalously modern romance with a scriptwriter's allegedly "realist," ever-escalating, and mutually invading soap operas until the once multiple but now cumulative and mangled project falls on his, their, our, heads.

For those who survived this Boom, including most of its authors, it evidently was not the collapse of history. Time passes and pendulums swing. Some writers who had written circles around history in the sixties and seventies began to experiment with new versions of historical narrative.[7] This return of a repressed tradition may arouse some curiosity about the fictions the Boom deliberately left behind, perhaps even a capacity to understand and to *feel* the passionately political quality of Latin America's earlier novels. They had, among other things, the charm of promise that has since turned to bitterness at the perceived fraud. We may also notice that the Boom's playfully pessimistic terms were largely accepted as literarily mature, which is perhaps to say flattering to a First World's taste for the postmodern, the almost narcissistic pleasure of having one's ideal notions of literature mirrored back.

My readerly paradox, taking denial as a symptom of unresolved dependence, would not only send me back to the foundational fictions that the Boom was resisting, but also to an entire tradition of resistances. The paradox borders on a typical irony of writing (in) America, where successive generations may deny literary resemblances to the point that denial itself constitutes a resemblance. If the new novelists imagined themselves suddenly born into full maturity, other American writers had imagined the same.[8] Jorge Luis Borges jokes about the repetitive circularity and the impossible pride of starting anew in "The Wall and the Books," about the emperor of China who built the Great Wall and burned all books written before his reign only to sense that a future emperor would erase his epoch-founding work with another new beginning. Borges, the American writer, is evidently amused but also fascinated by a tradition written in erasures of the past.

To appreciate this countertradition of repeated denials, it is important to remember how epoch-making nineteenth-century "national novels" seemed for generations of readers. The concept of the national novel hardly needs an explanation in Latin America; it is the book frequently required in the nations' secondary schools as a source of local history and literary pride, not immediately required perhaps but certainly by the time Boom novelists were in school. Sometimes anthologized in school readers, and dramatized in plays, films, television serials, national novels are often as plainly identifiable as national anthems. As for the foundational bonds between this literature and legislation, ties that seemed "unacknowledged"[9] in Shelley's England, they were no secret in Latin America. One stunning acknowledgment is the page-long list, by the turn of the century, of Hispano-American writers who were also presidents of their countries.[10] A comparable list for lesser offices might seem endless. And despite important parallels, North American writers who were establishing a national literature might assume a metapolitical posture, an apparently disinterested critique that was rare for the South. Latin Americans seemed more integrated into partisan struggles and less available for transcendent social criticism.

By the end of the century, when economic prosperity and "scientific" state policies produced an intellectual division of labor, the literary pendulum had swung writers away from affairs of state. This tended to relieve literati from political responsibilities and freed them to develop the preciousness of *modernismo*, largely in poetry, or it exiled narrators to the pessimist borders of "naturalism." But in 1941 when Pedro Henríquez Ureña delivered his now classic Harvard lectures on "Literary Currents in Hispanic America," it was obvious that the pendulum had swung back to engagement for many of the continent's writers. The younger generation was split between the poetic vanguard of Borges and early Neruda, who inherited the "splendid isolation"[11] of the modernists, and an exalted or rebellious neoromanticism that gradually led back to the "old habit of taking part in political affairs,"[12] though most of these writers seemed no longer to hope for political leadership. Typically, they wrote from a "nativist" or reformist opposition in order to sway opinion about, say, race relations or economic policy. Many dedicated themselves to reform through education, as had Domingo F. Sarmiento and the many positivist nation-builders who followed. Nevertheless, to cite only three examples of the tradition's resilience after the premature eulogy in the Harvard lectures, by 1948 novelist Rómulo Gallegos became Venezuela's first freely elected president; in 1962 novelist and story writer Juan Bosch won a landslide victory in Henríquez Uieña's native Dominican Republic, and in 1990 Mario Vargas Llosa almost won a campaign for the presidency of Peru.

Henríquez Ureña's periodization of committed, precious, vanguard and reformist writers is, of course, very rough. But like so much he wrote, a wealth of detail justifies the boldness. So I won't presume to improve on his scheme, only to add that half a century later it seems that historical romances and romanticized history continue to burden a resistant tradition. By *romance* here I mean a cross between our contemporary use of the word as a love story and a nineteenth-century use that distinguished the genre as more boldly allegorical than the novel.[13] The classic examples in Latin America are almost inevitably stories of star-crossed lovers who represent particular regions, races, parties, economic interests, and the like. Their passion for conjugal and sexual union spills over to a sentimental readership in a move that hopes to win partisan minds along with hearts.

To show the inextricability of politics from fiction in the history of nation-building is, then, the first concern of this study. I am certainly not the first to notice this connection. Leslie Fiedler, for one, uses it to launch his study of the ethical and allegorizing penchants in American novels.[14] And more recently, Benedict Anderson pointed to the continuities between nation-building and print communities formed around newspapers and novels.[15] However astute and provocative these analyses are, though, I cannot manage to make them suggest why Latin America's traditional novel is so relentlessly attractive.

My own suggestion constitutes the second concern here. It is to locate an erotics of politics, to show how a variety of novel national ideals are all ostensibly grounded in "natural" heterosexual love and in the marriages that provided a figure for apparently nonviolent consolidation during internecine conflicts at midcentury. Romantic passion, on my reading, gave a rhetoric for the hegemonic projects in Gramsci's sense of conquering the antagonist through mutual interest, or "love," rather than through coercion.[16] And the amorous overtones of "conquest" are quite appropriate, because it was civil society that had to be wooed and domesticated after the creoles had won their independence.[17] The rhetoric of love, specifically of productive sexuality at home, is notably consistent, taken for granted in fact, despite the standard taxonomies that like to distinguish foundational novels as either "historical" or "indigenist," "romantic" or "realist."[18] It will be evident that many romances strive toward socially convenient marriages and that, despite their variety, the ideal states they project are rather hierarchical. Nevertheless, the question of degree and even of style will make all the difference in considering the mixed political and esthetic legacy of romance.

To paraphrase another foundational text, after the creation of the new nations, the domestic romance is an exhortation to be fruitful and multiply. Exhortation is often all we get though, along with a contagious desire for socially productive love and for the State where love is possible, because these erotico-political affairs can be quite frustrating. And even when they end in satisfying marriage, the end of desire beyond which the narratives refuse to go, happiness reads like a wish-fulfilling projection of national consolidation and growth, a goal rendered visible.

FLESHING OUT HISTORY

Romantic novels go hand in hand with patriotic history in Latin America. The books fueled a desire for domestic happiness that runs over into dreams of national prosperity; and nation-building projects invested private passions with public purpose. This was no simple matter of one genre giving the other a hand, because the relationship between novels and new states has a Moebius-like continuity where public and private planes, apparent causes and putative effects, have a way of twisting into one another. "(T)hese fictions have helped, from the very beginning, to shape the history which has engendered them," as Djelal Kadir has put it.[19] Romance and republic were often connected, as I mentioned, through the authors who were preparing national projects through prose fiction and implementing foundational fictions through legislative or military campaigns.[20]

For the writer/statesman there could be no clear epistemological distinction between science and art, narrative and fact, and consequently between ideal projections and real projects. Whereas today's theorists of history in the industrial centers find themselves correcting the hubris of historians who imagine themselves to be scientists, the literary practice of Latin American historical discourse had long since taken advantage of what Lyotard would call the indefiniteness of science[21] or, more to the point, what Paul Veyne calls the undecidability of history.[22] In the epistemological gaps that the non-science of history leaves open, narrators could project an ideal future. This is precisely what many did in books that became classic novels of their respective countries. The writers were encouraged both by the need to fill in a history that would help to establish the legitimacy of the emerging nation and by the opportunity to direct that history toward a future ideal.

Andrés Bello, the Venezuelan poet, legislator, grammarian, and educator who became one of Chile's most important cultural arbiters, suggested the necessary connection between fiction and history in an essay he called "Historical Method."[23] The apparently conservative defender of standardized Spanish (whose widely adopted *Gramática* did more to preserve the continent's coherence than did Bolívar's political ambitions)[24] was polemicizing here against what others (mis)took as modern historiography. In their passion for progress, Bello alleged, young radicals like José Victorino Lastarria and Jacinto Chacón were leading themselves and their students astray by courting foreign models, French models in this case, which focused on the "philosophical" patterns of history.[25] To replace Spanish habits with French fads made no sense to the judicious old man. In France it might well make sense to develop a "scientific" history—meaning codifiable in predictable rules—on the basis of painstaking inquiry and documentation, the kind of preliminary work yet to be done for the Americas. Not that it was invalid to search for the "spirit" of events, but that it was inappropriate or hasty on a continent where even the most basic historical data were lacking. Instead, Bello supported a narrative option that would delay explanations until after the facts were in, perhaps indefinitely. "[W]hen a country's history doesn't exist, except in incomplete, scattered documents, in vague traditions that must be compiled and judged, the narrative method is obligatory. Let anyone who denies it cite one general or particular history that did not start this way." Then the cautious chronicler does something daring: he advocates self-consciously personal (even self-interested) narrative over the pretense of objectivity. One writer's worries, another's colorful memories or fabulous legends, all seemed to deliver more autonomous and more accurate pictures than those offered by a still unformed "science" of history. "Do you want to know, for example, what the discovery of America was like? Read Columbus's diary, Pedro de Valdivia's letters and those of Hernán Cortés. Bernal Díaz will tell you much more than Solís or Robertson."[26] It is easy to see that Bello's endorsement of the narrative method in history could be construed as more than simply a defensive modesty that falls short of explanations. Without the presumption of scientific truthfulness, narrative had a freer hand to construct history from private passions. So, we can extrapolate a paradoxical boldness from Bello's warnings: narrative becomes necessary, not only because the gaps in our historical knowledge make more "modern" methods unfeasible, but also because the filler can then be taken for an origin of independent and local expression. Perhaps this is why Bello's essay has been renamed and often reprinted as "Cultural Autonomy of America."

Other Latin Americans might have been reading into Bello's authorization of narrative in history when they went so far as considering narrative to *be* history; and several issued calls to literary action as part of the nation-building campaign. In 1847 the Argentine future historian, general, and president, Bartolomé Mitre, published a manifesto promoting the production of nation-building novels. The piece served as prologue to his own contribution, *Soledad,* a love story set in La Paz shortly after the wars of Independence. In that prologue, he deplores the fact that "South America is the poorest region in the world when it comes to original novelists." More than an esthetic deficiency, this signals social and political immaturity, because good novels, he says, represent the highest achievement in any nation. So, in the idealist spirit of enlightened reform that assumed rational legislation could effect rational behavior, it followed for Mitre that good novels could promote Latin American development. Novels would teach the people about their history, about their barely formulated customs, and about ideas and feelings that have been modified by still unsung political and social events. They would be what they already were in Europe and in Cooper's America: "a loyal mirror in which man contemplates himself as he is with all his vices and virtues, and which generally wakens profound meditation and healthy criticisms."[27] Then, with perhaps feigned but nonetheless fitting humility, Mitre offers his own story as a mere stimulus for others to write.

José Martí, another notable propagandist for nation-building novels—along with Alberto Blest Gana and Ignacio Altamirano to whom we'll return in chapter 6—admired European novels.[28] But Martí worried that their ironies and pessimism would do more harm than good at home.[29] America needed edifying and autonomous stories, the kind Manuel de Jesús Galván wrote for the Dominican Republic (*Enriquillo,* 1882) and to which Martí responded in a rapturous letter: "How sublime Enriquillo is, so much like Jesus! And his Mencía is a bride more perfect than Fray Luis ever imagined! . . . This is no historical legend [Galván's subtitle] but a brand-new and enchanting way to write our American history."[30] By contrast, he fretted over the sorry state of literary dependence elsewhere in the Americas, in Mexico for example: "Can there be a national life without a national literature? Can there be life for local artists in a scene always taken up by weak or repugnant foreign creations? Why in this new American land should we live an old European life?"[31]

All this assumes that literature has the capacity to intervene in history, to help construct it.[32] Generations of Latin American writers and readers assumed as much. But since the 1960s, since Latin America's post-Borgesian Boom in narrative and France's self-critical ebullience in philosophy and literary studies, we have tended to fix on the ways that literature undoes its own projects. This is, of course, a healthy antidote for our centuries-long habit of ignoring or dismissing the gaps and the absences that partly constitute literature.[33] To notice this shift in emphasis, though, is also to acknowledge that earlier writings/readings managed the tensions differently.[34] In the particular case of Latin America's nineteenth-century "historical" novels, the nagging insecurities that writing produces only peek through the more patent and assertive inscriptions. Tensions exist, to be sure, and they provide much of the interest in reading what otherwise might be an oppressively standard canon. But what I am saying is that those very tensions could not be appreciated if the overwhelming energy of the books were not being marshaled to deny them. When the job of writing America seemed most urgent, the question of ultimate authority was bracketed in favor of the local authors. They didn't necessarily worry about writing compensatory fabrications as fillers for a world full of gaps. Empty spaces were part of America's demographic and discursive nature. The continent seemed to invite inscriptions.

Given this imagined lure to write and the enthusiastic responses just sampled, some critics have wondered at the late appearance of novels in Latin America. The most obvious reason is probably the best one: Spain had proscribed the publication, and even the importation, of any fictional material in the colonial dispositions of 1532, 1543, and 1571. Whether for its own Catholic utopian vision of the new world, or for reasons of security, Spain tried to police the creole imagination. But the rapid repetition of edicts and the surviving records of a lively business in forbidden fiction show with what frustrated insistence Spain tried. The unwieldy, literally unmanageable bureaucracy of the empire was a network in Dr. Johnson's sense, that is a system of holes held together by a string. Administrative negotiations and economic deals regularly slipped through, along with fiction from Spain, including *La Celestina, Lazarillo de Tormes, Orlando Furioso, Amadís de Gaula, Belianís de Grecia, El Caballero del Febo, Comedias* by Lope de Rueda, most notably abundant copies of *Don Quijote* from its first 1605 printing on, and followed by books like the satire *Fray Gerundio de Campazas* (1758) by Padre José Francisco de Isla, the translator of *Gil Blas*.[35] There were also imaginative excesses written inside the colony, in texts that negotiate the ban on fiction by way of decorous paraliterary genres, including the travelogue, (auto)-biography, and history.[36]

Defiantly fictional novels as such started to appear along with and as part of the movement for emancipation that was triggered in 1808 by Napoleon. His threatened arrival in Lisbon sent the Portuguese court packing to Brazil, where in 1822 the visiting monarch decided to go home and the creoles insisted on substituting him with their own emperor and their own empire. Napoleon's army did force the abdication of Charles in Spain; it exiled his heir Ferdinand VII, and gave the colonists a legitimate excuse to rebel. There was a venerable Spanish norm that granted her subjects local self-rule in the event of a failure in the monarchy. And through this handy Spanish framework, which was made to accommodate French and English republican philosophy, France's usurpation made Americans responsible—so they alleged—for popular sovereignty. What is often considered the first novel published in the Spanish-speaking New World was a good example of the cultural and political amalgam. *El periquillo sarniento* (1816, completed 1830) by Mexico's José Joaquín Fernández de Lizardi has a Spanish picaresque shape and an enlightened spirit, a book that seems to come at the end of a literary tradition running from *Lazarrillo* to Lesage rather than to initiate a new one. What was novel about Lizardi's work was the very fact that it was scandalously imaginative and that it earned a small but heterogeneous readership, despite the public's preference for short and informative newspaper articles over the books they associated with colonial power. Part of his writerly challenge was to create "a public who could not help liking his novel," as Umberto Eco says of Manzoni.[37]

More modern novels, sometimes called romances, came at midcentury, after independence had been won (everywhere but Cuba and Puerto Rico), civil wars had raged for a generation, and newspapers had become the medium for serialized European and American fiction.[38] The local romances did more than entertain readers with compensations for spotty national history. They developed a narrative formula for resolving continuing conflicts, a postepic conciliatory genre that consolidated survivors by recognizing former enemies as allies.[39] In the United States, it has been argued, the country and the novel practically gave birth to each other.[40] And the same can be said of the South, as long as we take consolidation rather than emancipation to be the real moment of birth in both Americas. Perhaps, then, in addition to the colonial ban on fiction there was another reason for the late appearance of romantic novels; it is their pacifying project. National romances would have been politically and socially premature before the mid-nineteenth century. That was when leadership passed into the hands of young men who were trained to respect Natural reason in the postcolonial liberal schools. They were also trained to desire Nature's most passionate alliances in the novels they read so ardently.

ROMANCE REALIZED

After three centuries of Spanish imperial politics, inquisitorial Catholicism, and economic monopoly, Nature meant a general relief from counterproductive constraints. The wars of Independence, fought roughly from 1810 to 1825, were led by

American-born whites, the creoles who were routinely denied the best administrative jobs and often coveted business opportunities too. Private initiative had few outlets in the empire's unnatural "corporatist" state, in which groups rather than individuals were recognized in a rather strict hierarchy of color and caste.[41] The new societies experimented with liberalism adapted from examples in Great Britain (Bentham was a great favorite), the United States, and also France; that is, they experimented with a representative constitutional government (constitutional monarchy for some) that banished the "artificial barriers" to individual initiative and expression. Latin American nation-builders, privileged as they were, selected what they would from liberalism. They wanted, for example, unrestricted international trade yet refused to abolish tariffs. They got rid of Spain's monopolies (sometimes to fall prey to England) yet held on to domestic cartels, land entailment, and coercive labor systems. For those who were typically called "Conservatives," liberalism often ended with the elimination of Spanish and Portuguese intermediaries. "Nevertheless, in the period from independence to the late nineteenth century, it did come as close as anything to serving as a dominant ideology," with the result that the area was far more egalitarian after independence than before.[42]

In the third quarter of the century, as if synchronized, countries were clearing away the special privileges, including church rights to land and taxes, left over from the colony. Between 1851 and 1854, slavery was abolished in Venezuela, New Granada, Ecuador, Peru, Argentina, and Uruguay. Other countries (except for Brazil and Cuba) preceded or followed within a few years. The refusal of authoritarian habit and the increased private initiative might have added up to a loss of state power, but there were gains from appropriated church lands and jurisdictions, buoyant foreign trade, and from passing civil and business codes to regulate private decisions.

Another place to notice this peak of liberal reform and optimism is in the midcentury novels that were daring to realize the romantic and utilitarian dreams of the European genre. The Latin American elite wrote romances for zealous readers, privileged by definition (since mass education was still one of the dreams) and likely to be flattered by the personal portraits that were all the rage in bourgeois painting and in narrative local color, the *costumbrismo* that became a standard feature of the novels. Perhaps as much in Spanish America as in the Spain that Larra spoke for, the function of costumbrismo was "to make the different strata of society comprehensible one to another," that is to promote communal imaginings primarily through the middle stratum of writers and readers who constituted the most authentic expression of national feeling.[43] Identifying with the heroes and heroines, readers could be moved to imagine a dialogue among national sectors, to make convenient marriages, or at least moved by that phantasmagorical ideal. Despite their variety, the romantic conciliations seem grounded in human nature, variously interpreted in this optimistic period but always assumed to be rational and constructive. Erotic passion was less the socially corrosive excess that was subject to discipline in some model novels from Europe, and more the opportunity (rhetorical and otherwise) to bind together heterodox constituencies: competing regions, economic interests, races, religions.[44] In Europe too, love and productivity were coming together in the bourgeois household where, for the first time in the history of the family, love and marriage were supposed to coincide.[45] But America was Europe's ideal, imaginary,[46] realm for the bourgeoisie's project of coordinating sense with sensibility, productivity with passion. It was, to cite the specific example of Jeremy Bentham, a realizable utopia, the place where his reasonable laws (solicited by American admirers like Bolívar, San Martín, Rivadavia, and del Valle) could bring the greatest good to the greatest number.[47] This America aspired to a modernity metonymized from the other, Northern, America. And no one was more dedicated to the possibility than the transplanted Europeans whose dreamwork was making them American. Theirs was the space to fulfill the desires of a corrupt and cynical Old World, the space where domestic "novels" and ethico-political "romance" could marry.

We might remember that after winning independence, the creoles hoped for internal conquests. The uncompromising and heroic militarism that expelled Spain from most of America was now a threat to her development. What America needed now were civilizers, founding fathers of commerce and industry, not fighters. Juan Bautista Alberdi, whose notes for Argentina's 1853 constitution became a standard of political philosophy throughout Latin America, wrote that, "glory has ceded its place to utility and comfort, and military heroism is not the most competent medium for the *prosaic* needs of commerce and industry" (as if to say the prose of domestic fiction should now replace grandiloquent epic verse).[48] He and Domingo F. Sarmiento agreed, if on little else, on the need to fill up the desert, to make it disappear. What sense was there in heroically reducing warm bodies to dead ones, when Alberdi pronounced that in America, "to govern is to populate."[49] Few slogans have caught on and held on so well as this one. Husband the land and father your countries, he was saying. They have already yielded and now they must be loved and worked.

Alberdi didn't stop at slogans. He glossed them with practical programs for increasing the population, not only through the immigration policies for which he is remembered but also through marriages between industrious Anglo-Saxons and Argentina's "army" of beautiful women, eminently equipped for the eugenics campaign to "improve" local and "inefficient" Spanish stock. In chapter 3 I'll return to the dalliance Alberdi prepares between affairs of the heart and affairs of state. During the twenty years that Alberdi was matchmaking through these political *Bases,* luring the sword-wielding Joshuas of Independence to reform their tools into Isaiah's ploughs, we have seen that novelists were also reforming one thing into another: valor into sentimentalism, epic into romance, hero into husband. This helped to solve the problem of establishing the white man's legitimacy in the New World, now that the illegitimate conquerors had been ousted. Without a proper genealogy to root them in the Land, the creoles had at least to establish conjugal and then paternity rights, making a *generative* rather than a *genealogical* claim. They had to win America's heart and body so that the fathers could found her and reproduce themselves as cultivated men. To be legitimate, their love had to be mutual; even if the fathers set the tone, the mothers had to reciprocate.

For barely more than a generation, roughly from 1850 to 1880, romances were projecting civil societies through patriotic heroes who were remarkably feminized. Almost Werther-like, without losing reason to passion, idealized young men shared enough delicate looks and sublime feelings with idealized young women to create intimate bonds with them. Their brand of productive heroism, in fact, depends on it after death-dealing machismo became a thing of the past in many countries, at least in those that produced lasting "national novels" of consolidation.[50] We will notice Daniel Bello's lovely hands in *Amalia,* the feminine fragility of Rafael San Luis in *Martín Rivas,* and the heroes' penchant for tears throughout. This gender (con)fusion also produced remarkably principled and resourceful romantic heroines who stand up to police, conspire to escape oppression, and rescue their refined heroes.[51] The equally admirable male and female lovers counterpoised in romance threaten to upset the top-down logic of hegemonic projects for hundreds of suggestively democratic pages, before the women dutifully submit to their men. And although the young women readers who would be drawn to these sentimental novels were arguably being trained in the limiting virtues of republican motherhood (sometimes by pseudonymous men such as Guatemala's José Millas who signed "Salomé Gil"), the books should complicate our notion of the feminine ideal at midcentury, specifically the assumption that domestic passions seemed trivial to patriotic imaginings.[52]

The French and English models, admired so by Latin Americans, were improved or corrected by disciples, since the tragic—extramarital and unproductive—love affairs that the masters called romance were risky bases for national constructions. Just as Sarmiento's respect for Europe's cities goaded him to imagine Argentina surpassing them, American novelists saw their laconic or future history as a chance to bring Old World flirtations to happier or more promising conclusions.[53] Bartolomé Mitre, for example, presumed to outdo Rousseau in *Soledad,* where a young bride reads and identifies with *Julie* in order to avoid spending time with her aged royalist husband. The desire she learns from reading is about to launch her on an adulterous adventure with an unworthy visitor. But she is saved from the double bane of boredom and betrayal when her cousin and childhood sweetheart comes home as a hero of Independence.

He stays to marry her after the repentant old husband blesses the couple and conveniently dies. Julie's impossible and incestuous dream to combine propriety with passion comes true for Soledad.[54]

Martín Rivas by Alberto Blest Gana (Chile, 1862), is one more of several cases where the romance is set right. It rewrites Stendhal's *The Red and the Black* by having the provincial secretary Martín actually marry his boss's genteel daughter. Probably indebted to Balzac's wish-fulfilling allegories where ideal marriages between legitimacy and power can at least be imagined, Blest Gana's book celebrates the wish fulfilled.[55] In these American versions (as in Europe's more conventional love stories and in what one might call "Americanized" utopias such as George Sand's *Indiana*),[56] love is sentimental; it is neither a jaded *Bovarysme* that desires to desire, nor is it romantic in the sense of the unrequitable and unilateral that describe important European literary affairs of the same period, or of any period according to René Girard. Futility, Girard says, is constitutive of desire: "Romantic passion is . . . exactly the reverse of what it pretends to be. It is not abandonment to the Other but an implacable war waged by two rival vanities."[57] When, for example, Stendhal's aristocratic heroine finally admits her passion for Julien, the struggle for recognition between them ends and his ardor cools, just as she had once become indifferent with his declaration of love. This instance of what Girard calls triangulated desire (imitative of the desire imputed to an idealized, more successful rival and therefore cut short once the heroine prefers the hero) seems familiar too from more recent Latin American novels written during the brilliant phosphorescence of national projects. *Hopscotch* and many of Cortázar's short stories come to mind, especially "Manuscript Found in a Pocket." Here, subway romances begin with a triangulated flirtation as protagonist and prey both fix on her reflection in the car window, and they end with despair and relief every time the escalator disappears a new conquest.[58]

The nineteenth-century national novels insist on simplifying the triangle; they straighten and flatten it out into a dyad where no mediation is necessary or even possible for lovers who know they're right for each other. Tensions that inevitably exist and

drive the story on are external to the couple: the counterproductive social constraints that underline the naturalness and
the inevitability of the lovers' transgressive desire. Triangula-
tion is produced, then, in a strangely fecund rather than frustrating way, since the lovers must imagine their ideal relationship through an alternative society. Once they project that ideal
as an image that looks like a wedding portrait, their union—
rather than the rival who comes between Girard's lovers in
order to join them—becomes the mediating principle that urges
the narrative forward like a promise.

Mere erotic power play was decidedly un-American during
those formative years. The object is not to tease but literally to
engender new nations, just as it was during the exaltedly optimistic moments of the French Revolution. "Now is the time
to make a baby," read one of its slogans.[59] Fathers of nations
couldn't afford to simply lord it over mothers if they hoped to
produce legitimate bourgeois children. And whereas Europe's
favorite romances risked the sterile trap of narcissism,[60] American domestic desire tries to keep the lovers interdependent. If
authors such as Rousseau and later Balzac, along with the
Richardson of *Clarissa,* showed the strains and finally the cracks
in the ideal of the bourgeois family, the Latin Americans tended
to patch up those cracks with the sheer will to project ideal histories backward (as a legitimating ground) and forward (as a
national goal), or with the euphoria of recent successes.

The successes should not be underestimated.[61] They sometimes have more than a metaphoric relationship to the project
of coordinating love and marriage in the foundational novels.
The marriage metaphor slips into, or out of, a metonymy of
national consolidation if we stop to consider how marriages
bridged regional, economic, and party differences during the
years of national consolidation. I am referring to data specifically about Argentina, Chile, Mexico, and Central America
which suggest a pattern for other countries too.[62] If the love
matches in *Amalia* (1851), binding the agricultural interior to
the commercial port city, and in *Martín Rivas* (1862), where
Chilean mining interests marry commerce in the capital, or in
Mexico's *El Zarco* (1888) about a mestiza's unconditional love
for the Indian hero, are indications of historical accuracy be-

cause they coincide with data on regional alliances, economic diversification, and racial coalitions, other novels may also reveal something about the project—and also the process—of bourgeois consolidation through literal and figurative marriage. In the nineteenth century, notable families were both public and private affairs, making strategic bonds that were stronger than merely political affiliations. They filled the "relative vacuum of sociopolitical structures" to construct a social organization preliminary to public institutions including the state itself.[63]

Before Independence, these were typically merchant families.[64] With the new republics and the constitutional separation of powers in the 1820s and 1830s, the next generation seized the opportunity to coordinate executive, legislative, military, and financial powers through the existing structure of personal alliances. Those respectable citizens (*gente decente*), whose excessive decorum or deficient drive resisted the opportunities, demoted themselves, in effect, to become clients of the "notables" and would later figure in oppositions to the oligarchic state, in the Mexican Revolution for example. At midcentury, while state institutions were being invented, rather bold family bonds (in which marriageable women often represented investment, or risk, capital) were also the springs of new and dynamic economies.[65] The merchants who lent money (formerly an ecclesiastical business) to promote the circulation of capital, to diversify from commerce into industries, and for government spending made private deals with consistently public consequences. And even in the third generation, when state institutions were being established, principal families continued to coordinate their diversifying interests through leadership in banks, government, army, and schools. These private deals were apparently more flexible, relatively informal, and open to the racial and class mobility described (or imagined in phantasmagoria of conciliation) by national romances, than were the fourth-generation contracts. These were made after public and ideally impersonal institutions had solidified, and after the liberal optimism of founding fictions was replaced by grimly deterministic positivism. For several countries, cross-over dreams had by the 1880s become the nostalgic stuff of an originary prehistory (see chap. 8), not a project of alliances. Once the family network congealed, economic and political deals were struck between oligarchic men, not through the risky inclusions called marriage.[66]

It would seem, to follow the historians, that families were a stabilizing force, a "cause" of national security. But we may also reckon the high seriousness attributed to family ties as a possible "effect" of the nation. Without the goal of nationhood, alliances and stability would be perhaps less transparently desirable than they were. Seen from either angle, the mutual dependence of family and state in Latin America (the reciprocal allegorization to be considered in part II of this chapter) could and sometimes did mitigate the tension between private and public allegiances which has dogged Western political philosophy. From Plato, whose solution in *The Republic* was to abolish the family along with its divisive gender roles, and Aristotle, for whom the public man/private woman distinction was useful so long as it was hierarchical, through, for example, the English contract theorists and Rousseau's more radical but still incomplete dismissal of family as the natural model for society, political philosophy has had to consider what was "natural" about the family. One result has been so much debate about nature that the concept is continually exposed as a social construction.[67]

And the variety of "natural" families celebrated in national romances offers such radically different social programs that to say the novels are romantic reconciliations may register only their general contour. Read individually, the foundational fictions are very different indeed. It seems difficult, in fact, to talk of the books' commonality when the projects they advocate are so varied, ranging from racism to abolitionism, from nostalgia to modernization, from free trade to protectionism. In *Amalia* (José Mármol, 1851), civilization, associated with the city-based free-trading and Europeanizing Unitarian Party, opposes the barbarism of gaucho-like Federalists who dominated the interior, just as the white skin of the intercity lovers contrasts with the dark skin of untutored Federalist masses. *Martín Rivas* (Alberto Blest Gana, 1862) attempts to mitigate oppositions by matchmaking across class and regional lines. Determined to convince Santiago's banking families that their disdain for the "radical" mining bourgeoisie in Chile has been less pleasant and less profitable than fiscal cooperation would be, the son of a ruined miner finally marries the banker's daughter.

But mitigation depends on more radical change in tragic Cuban novels, written before Independence and with hopes perhaps of raising multicolored armies to win it. Failure to bring the racial (love) affair to a happy ending accounts for the tragedy of *Sab* (Gertrudis Gómez de Avellaneda, 1841) in which the racially amalgamated hero (also Cuba) is desperate for the love (and legitimacy) his creole mistress could give him. Sab's hopes are obscured by the dazzle of a blond English rival who marries the mistress and proves how indifferent foreigners are to both women and slaves. Compared to these bold tones, the frustration in *Cecilia Valdés* (Cirilo Villaverde, 1882) is endemic to a system of subtle color coding which the lovers never un-learn. Racial difference produces exploitative privilege in one and a vengeful yearning for privilege in the other. Racial disen-counters are also the cause of tragedy in *Birds Without a Nest* (Clorinda Matto de Turner, 1889)—an important Peruvian novel I refer to only briefly[68]—this time between Indians and whites. By contrast, those relations are the hope of national regeneration in Mexico's *El Zarco* (Ignacio Altamirano, 1888), where an Indian hero learns to love his mestiza admirer during the same years that Mexicans were learning to admire their In-dian president Benito Juárez. And though color never seems at issue in *María* (Jorge Isaacs, 1867), Latin America's most popular nineteenth-century novel, racial distinction haunts the book in the fissured identity of originally Jewish María, a figure for the incestuous self-destructive aristocracy *and* for the ra-cially unassimilable blacks.

Brazilian slavocrat José de Alencar was evidently writing about blacks too when he wrote about conveniently submissive Indians. *O Guaraní* (1857) is Brazil's possible idyll once Indians and Europeans learn to love each other; and *Iracema* (1865) is a more pessimistic Pocahantas-like story where the indigenous princess makes the greatest sacrifices for her Portuguese lover. In a similar sleight of hand, writing a simulacrum that stuck as a racial reality, *Enriquillo* (Manuel de Jesús Galván, 1882) re-places rebellious blacks for peace-loving and long-extinct natives who become putative ancestors for today's "Indian" masses in the Dominican Republic. Spain's first conquest in the New World becomes a love story here between an indigenous prince and his mestiza cousin (the Chactas who gets his Atala), fights to protect her honor, and finally defers to Charles V's magnanimous authority. By an inverted displacement, *Matalaché* (Enrique López Albújar, 1928), significantly subtitled *Novela retaguardista,* would substitute long-emancipated black slaves as personae for the Indian peons who concerned him in order to highlight continuing racial abuse and the redemptive capacity of crossover-romance.[69] As a rhetorical solution to the crises in these novels/nations, miscegenation (an unfortunate translation for *mestizaje,* which is practically a slogan for many projects of national consolidation) is often the figure for pacification of the "primitive" or "barbarous" sector. Yet sometimes the terms of desired amalgams slip from synecdochal figures for different races to metaphoric representations of color-coded factions among the creole elite. The legitimating alliances announced by the racial alchemy may therefore have less to do with race relations than with the political flirtations between "liberal" dark horses and "conservative" ruling sectors. This can be argued for Brazil's romances as well as for Ecuador's *Cumandá* (Juan León Mera, 1887), where the Indian heroine turns out to be the missionary's lost daughter, and probably for Uruguay's *Tabaré* (Juan Zorrilla de San Martín, 1888), in which the lovable Indian hero, possibly associated with imperializing Brazil, must be resisted if white civilization is to survive.

With *Doña Bárbara* (Rómulo Gallegos, 1929), the authoritarian father who had stepped aside during nineteenth-century negotiations takes the center again. This anti-imperialist novel was neither ready for conciliation nor desperate enough to defer sovereignty as *Enriquillo* had done. Instead, it apprentices the hero to the "un-naturally" powerful woman he will replace. Her irresponsible eroticism is not only immoral, it is as unpatriotic as was the lechery of villainous men in the earlier romances, men like Mariño (*Amalia*), Loredano (*O Guaraní*), Ricardo (*Francisco*), Valenzuela (*Enriquillo*), repeated in Bárbara's ally Mr. Danger. They are almost always the brutish bosses, macho rather than manly and lustful rather than loving.

In militant "populist" revisions like this one, where romance's gender confusion is cleared up as a matter of national defense, a sensuous and resourceful woman is degenerative by definition (the characters of Doña Bárbara and Zoraida in chap. 9).

If the difference between masculinity and machismo is somewhat vague, the vagueness should suggest at least one trap in romance. In its revised expressions, possibly as a response to the dour positivism that followed the fictive amalgamations of midcentury, nationalist romance valorizes virility as a self-evidently male attribute while it tries to distinguish between good and bad men. By the time a new imperialism threatens to overtake what national alliances there have been, the erotic figuring of politics often loses the flexibility that facilitated founding partnerships. In *Doña Bárbara,* the father's comeback makes sharing power seem unpatriotic or economically irrational. From the 1920s on, nativist or populist novels that share similarly defensive features would coincide with the popular fronts of newly founded Communist parties (and of right-wing populism?). And, to some degree, the patriarchal culture of populism is prepared in narratives that recast foundational romances to bring the soldier-citizen back into history. He had been the hero of the wars of Independence, and even of the civil wars that followed. Then the fighters had been called home to be fathers; manly independence had given way to the negotiated domesticity of notables who had traded diplomatic daughters in cross-sectoral alliances to secure the peace. But the men could not stay home long, not after the shocking 1898 intervention of the United States in Cuba's war of Independence, recast as the Spanish American War for Cuba and for Puerto Rico as well. And the geopolitical reality of U.S. control makes a new homecoming seem remote. Spain had finally given up her fight in the Americas and gone home; but the United States assumes that the Americas are home. Populism, therefore, has an important narrative career in Hispanoamerica, and a long afterlife even when the political culture changes its name.[70]

One might assume that the diversity of national contexts and the range of partisan programs in nineteenth- and twentieth-century patriotic novels overload any common structure to the point of crushing it. Chile's vertical integration, Cuba's racial integration, Argentina's color-coded campaigns, Colombia's retrograde idyll, Ecuador's Jesuitical paternalism, Venezuela's vamp-raiding, what possible ground could join them? One very general answer is America, the space for Bolivarian dreams of continental unity. This would explain, for example, how Andrés Bello could write about Chile and sustain an argument about cultural autonomy for the continent; and why Mitre set his story in Bolivia while writing about his native Argentina; or why Cuban Martí celebrated a Dominican novel as the model for American writers in general. But the answer I have been getting at is rather more specific than the goal of developing neighborly nations on Pan-American principles. The novels share a particular kind of intimacy. Read together, they reveal remarkable points of contact in both plot and language, producing a palimpsest that cannot derive from the historical or political differences that the novels address. The coherence comes from their common project to build through reconciliations and amalgamations of national constituencies cast as lovers destined to desire each other. This produces a surprisingly consistent narrative form that is apparently adequate to a range of political positions; they are moved by the logic of love. Whether the plots end happily or not, the romances are invariably about desire in young chaste heroes for equally young and chaste heroines, the nations' hope for productive unions.

To call their books romances is, then, hardly to understate a public function. In the United States, at least, the label has traditionally distinguished an ethico-political character of our most canonical books of fiction. And in Latin America, romance doesn't distinguish between ethical politics and erotic passion, between epic nationalism and intimate sensibility. It collapses the distinctions. In Spanish America the two are one, Walter Scott and Chateaubriand in the same pot-boilers, *pace* Georg Lukács.[71] In *The Historical Novel* (1937),[72] Lukács set historical Scott apart from sentimental Chateaubriand by an unbreachable esthetic and political distance. During the Popular Front Lukács was reducing his own earlier distinction between epic and novel in order to defend the novel's construction of social coherence as no less binding than that of epic.[73] Novels, he now maintained, could be just as objective and historical. And

Scott came closest to the "great historical objectivity of the true epic writer" (Lukács, 34) who respects and even celebrates historical necessity as progress (Lukács, 58). Chateaubriand, by contrast, "chopped and changed his material at will" (Lukács, 290), "tr[ying] hard to revise classical history in order to depreciate historically the old revolutionary ideal of the Jacobin and Napoleonic period" (Lukács, 27). Like other sentimentalists, he was writing the nostalgic tales we might now call romance when, Lukács implies, he should have been writing novels. Scott looks ahead; Chateaubriand looks back; Scott's heroes are average participants in historical change; Chateaubriand's are uniquely sensitive victims of history. How could the two possibly be reconciled?

The possibility seems even more remote from our Anglo-American tradition of criticism that opposes novel to romance in terms that now appear to be inverted. Novel was the domestic genre of surface detail and intricate personal relationships, whereas romance was the genre of boldly symbolic events. The tradition probably originated with Dr. Johnson's definition of romance as "a military fable of the middle ages; a tale of wild adventures in love and chivalry," whereas the novel was "a smooth tale, generally of love." But Walter Scott adjusted these definitions in his own article on romance (1823), stressing the novel's "ordinary train of human events [in] the modern state of society."[74] That is to imply its lesser status, fit more for ladies than for robust men. Scott claims, and is largely granted, significance as a historian because he is a "romancer," concerned not only with the "marvelous and uncommon," but also with the extrapersonal and social dimensions of a collective past.

In the United States writers like Hawthorne and his admirer Melville picked up this distinction and insisted they were writing romance dedicated to America's mission.[75] Cooper, at least, suggested the connection between the public good and private desire when he boasted that the special quality of romance was that it aimed to deal poetic justice all around and thus achieve a higher truth than any available from chronicles where too many heroes marry the wrong girls.[76] And Fiedler noticed that apparently male romance and female novels keep very close company.[77] Perhaps any distinction would be moot, since all

U.S. fiction of the nineteenth century can be called some variety of romance.[78]

Even Lukács, who in the service of the Popular Front theorized the opposition between "heroic" history and lachrymose legend, showed despite himself how the genres attract each other in practice.[79] Lukács admitted that the novels of what one might call underdeveloped European countries could not repeat either Scott's middle-of-the-road modernity or his celebration of past events. These were possible for Scott only because England had already achieved its "progressive" bourgeois formation. And the happy outcome of English history produced an entire class of heroes. But for countries such as Germany or Italy, where bourgeois unification was frustrated, so too was the project of writing celebratory Scott-like novels. As in Latin America, European foundational fictions sought to overcome political and historical fragmentation through love. Lukács points to the strategy but doesn't call attention to the recurring pattern or to its relevance even for Scott. "Thus, while Manzoni's immediate story [in *The Betrothed*] is simply a concrete episode taken from Italian popular life—the love, separation and reunion of a young peasant boy and girl—his presentation transforms it into a general tragedy of the Italian people in a state of national degradation and fragmentation." The story of Manzoni's lovers grows into "*the* tragedy of the Italian people as a whole" (Lukács, 70). Gogol, too, concentrates on the downfall of the Cossacks in the romance of *Taras Bulba*. It is the tragedy of one of the hero's sons who, in love with a Polish aristocratic girl, becomes a traitor to his people" (Lukács, 74).

Latin American "historical novelists" found themselves in a similarly premodern situation, although, to follow Benedict Anderson, we should add that they did so before many Europeans and offered models in fiction as well as foundation.[80] Therefore, Latin American histories during the nation-building period tend to be more projective than retrospective, more erotic than data-driven. Viewed from the margins, then, Scott's "middlebrow" exemplarity becomes inimitable.[81] Scott was a model of what a fully integrated national culture could be, just as the extraordinary heroes of Latin American romance were. But to work for his willing heirs, Scott first had to get between the book covers with Chateaubriand, or Rousseau, or Stendhal. It was their ardent sentimentalism that helped to flesh out the histories that lacked usable, that is, constructive and flattering, data.

To marry national destiny to personal passion was precisely what made their disciples' books peculiarly American. On the one hand, little seemed to determine the direction of historical discourse from the middle to the end of the nineteenth century, since, as Andrés Bello seemed to complain, basic data were lacking. But on the other hand, and this is my point, not just any narrative filler would have done. The glee I surmise in Bello's exhortation to imagine the past surely owes to the opportunity he perceives for projecting an ideal history through what Northrop Frye calls the most basic and satisfying genre, romance.[82] What better way to argue the polemic for civilization than to make desire the relentless motivation for a literary/political project? To read on, to suffer and tremble with the lovers' drive toward marriage, family, and prosperity, and then to be either devastated or transported in the end, is already to become a partisan.

PRETTY LIES

What contemporary novelists can no longer take seriously, it seems, is the interested imaginings of empty spaces. Where nation-builders projected an unformed history on a beckoning empty continent, new novelists trace the historical density on a map full of mangled projects. *A Hundred Years of Solitude,* just to take one masterful example, is no less driven by history than were the earlier novels. It recounts the long century of Colombia's vexed history staged as a series of erotic alliances among principal families. But these are families that fight one another, mistake foreign interest for mere curiosity, and resist the talented outsiders whom romance should have invited in. The great Boom novels rewrite, or un-write, foundational fiction as the failure of romance, the misguided political erotics that could never really bind national fathers to mothers, much less the *gente decente* to emerging middle and popular sectors. And no novel disintegrates more programmatically than does *The Death of Artemio Cruz* (1964), by Carlos Fuentes.[83]

At first, Artemio seems like a classic father, less because he was an officer in Pancho Villa's army (Zapata was clearly too radical an option for him or for the liberal heroes of romance) than because he was a lover. Artemio loved Regina; he braved battles in order to be with her. And she reciprocated, getting ahead of the army to prepare a cozy spot and a warm meal for her man, as did so many other *soldaderas* of the Revolution. As they made love they thought back on the idyll of their first meeting, sitting on a beach, watching their double portrait in the water. So magic a memory, and so self-serving a vanishing act for the originary scene of rape. The imagined idyll was

> esa ficción . . . inventada por ella para que él se sintiera limpio, inocente, seguro del amor . . . esa hermosa mentira. . . . No era cierto: él no había entrado a ese pueblo sinaloense como a tantos otros, buscando a la primera mujer que pasara, incauta, por la calle. No era verdad que aquella muchacha de dieciocho años había sido montada a la fuerza en un caballo y violada en silencio en el dormitorio común de los oficiales, lejos del mar.[84]

> [a fiction that she had conjured up that she (*sic*) might feel clean and innocent and sure of love . . . her pretty lie. . . . It had no trace of truth. Neither did the truth: it was not true that he had gone into that Sinaloan pueblo just as he had gone into so many others, ready to grab the first woman who incautiously ventured outside. It was not true that a girl of eighteen had been thrown helplessly across his horse and carried back to the officers' dormitory to be violated in silence.][85]

Later, under fire, Artemio faces the fact of his cowardice. But before there is time to invent his own pleasing fiction, perhaps about a consuming love for Regina that made death unthinkable, she dies and Artemio turns deserter and opportunist.

If his desertion is an ethical disappointment for the reader, it does not compare with the erotic failure, in this unraveled romance, to make the next conquest. When the Revolution ends, he tries to win Catalina Bernal, the daughter of a rich landowner who blesses the uneven match in order to insure his holdings by joining forces with the revolutionary victors. Catalina refuses, or is unable to make up the requisite romantic lies that would legitimate the union. She suspects Artemio's treachery against her brother. She is hurt by her father's acquiescence when she herself is proud enough to resist. But mostly she is unsure about how heartfelt interested love can be. Whereas *Doña Bárbara* showed only traces of guilt in the marriage between Bárbara's mestiza daughter Marisela and civilized Santos, a marriage that tries to cover over the history of usurpation and civil war with a lawful union, *Artemio Cruz* makes the guilt relentlessly self-conscious. Here, the foundational love affairs of romance are revealed as rapes, or as power plays that traffic in women. If only Catalina would do for Artemio what Marisela had done for Santos, we may sigh. The pair seems perfect: a beautiful aristocratic girl and a resourceful boy from the provinces with heroic credentials. Fuentes arouses and makes us confront the habits of romantic longing we have learned from national romance. But if she had given in, would Artemio have become more honest or admirable in reconstructing Mexico on a popular base? Or would he merely have seemed more genuine while reproducing the class structure that equally shameless exploiters bequeathed to Catalina's more elegant father?

Readers keep few illusions about Artemio's possible career in a country that "institutionalized" the revolution as a strategy of containment.[86] It is possible that the pretty lies of national romance are similar strategies to contain the racial, regional, economic, and gender conflicts that threatened the development of new Latin American nations. After all, these novels were part of a general bourgeois project to hegemonize a culture in formation. It would ideally be a cozy, almost airless culture that bridged public and private spheres in a way that made a place for everyone, as long as everyone knew his or her place.

1

PART II
LOVE AND COUNTRY:
AN ALLEGORICAL SPECULATION

It is worth asking why the national novels of Latin America—
the ones that governments institutionalized in the schools and
that are by now indistinguishable from patriotic histories—are
all love stories. An easy answer, of course, is that nineteenth-
century novels were all love stories in Latin America; but it just
begs the question of what love has to do with the requirements
of civic education. The novels weren't immediately taught in
public schools, except perhaps in the Dominian Republic where
Enriquillo appeared rather late and where the number of students may have been limited enough for an adequate production of books.[1] In other cases, serialized or sentimental novels
were at first hardly academic or even proper literature, to judge
by their exclusion from the first national literary histories. Written at the same midcentury moment as the novels and with
largely the same legitimating impulse, their authors had comparable political credentials but more classical criteria than the
novelists. Literary historians selected a kind of elite prehistory
for the "progressive conservative" consolidations that were stabilizing the new states,[2] but they omitted perhaps the most
useful renderings of those oxymoronic consolidations: the romances that celebrated or predicted an identification between
the Nation and its State.[3] The programmatic centrality of novels
came generations later; precisely when and under which particular circumstances in each country are questions that merit
a different study.[4] But in general, one can surmise that after
renewed internal oppositions pulled the image of an ideal nation away from the existing state, like a mask pulled from the

30

masquerader, after nationalism could be understood as a political movement against the state,[5] nineteenth-century novels apparently promised the ministries of education a way of covering over the gap between power and desire. The books, so immediately seductive for elite readers whose private desires overlapped with public institutions, might reinscribe for each future citizen the (natural and irresistible) foundational desires for/of the government in power.

My musing here about why erotics and politics come together—in school no less—begins by noting that it happened practically everywhere in Latin America. A particular novel may be celebrated in its national tradition as autochthonous, characteristic, and somehow inimitable; yet we have seen that each romance shares far more than its institutional status with others. The resemblances may be symptomatic of nationalism's general paradox; that is, cultural features that seem unique and worthy of patriotic (self-)celebration are often typical of other nations too and even patterned after foreign models.[6] Almost like sexual intimacy, that which seems most private turns out to be embarrassingly public knowledge.[7]

In this section I would like first to consider *why* eroticism and nationalism become figures for each other in modernizing fictions and then to notice *how* the rhetorical relationship between heterosexual passion and hegemonic states functions as a mutual allegory, as if each discourse were grounded in the allegedly stable other. For examples of the perhaps constitutive connection between private and political passions, one can certainly turn to any of the following chapters. But here I want to speculate on what may account for the generic coherence that individual readings will necessarily miss.

From our historical distance, both romantic love and patriotism can be mistaken for natural givens, although we know them to be produced, perhaps, by the very novels that seem merely to represent them. To acknowledge this possibility is also to ask whether what may have passed for effects of the greater culture in the novel (for instance, the representation of romantic love or of conciliatory nationalism) may indeed be partial causes of that culture. If heroes and heroines in mid-nineteenth-century Latin American novels were passionately desiring one another across traditional lines and desiring the new state that would join them, they were hardly representing timeless or essential affections. Those passions might not have prospered a generation earlier. In fact, modernizing lovers were learning how to dream their erotic fantasies by reading the European romances they hoped to realize.

The appropriateness of European fiction for Latin American founders may perhaps be read backward too (in a reflex learned from Benedict Anderson),[8] meaning that the appropriateness suggests a cultural overlapping that should be as easily identifiable from Latin America as from Europe. Therefore, my rather local observations about a particular moment and genre in Latin America tempt me to hazard some conjectures about more general implications. Is it possible, for example, that outside of Latin America, too, political passion was being grounded in erotics? Had sexual desire as the shorthand for human association become "the explanation for everything," as Foucault said it had?[9] The claim is hardly hyperbolic or even original. By 1865 in England, John McLean's influential *Primitive Marriage* considered "sexual attraction the underlying principle of all social formations," thus agreeing with other early texts of cultural anthropology including those by Herbert Spencer who would be so popular among Latin American positivists.[10] Alternatively, if there were no erotic or sentimental investment in the state, if our identities as modern sexually defined subjects did not take the state to be a primary object and therefore the partner on whom our identity depends, what could explain our passion for "la patria?"[11] Is it also possible that the romances are themselves synecdoches of the marriage between Eros and Polis that was taking place under the broad canopy of Western culture? I hesitate to say bourgeois culture because it may be as much the child as the maker of the match. Nancy Armstrong's provocative work on England, *Desire and the Domestic Fiction: A Political History of the Novel,* is wonderfully suggestive here: "Rather than see the rise of the new middle class in terms of the economic changes that solidified its hold over the culture," her reading "shows that the formation of the modern political state—in England at least—was accomplished largely through cultural hegemony," primarily through the domestic novel.[12] This is possibly true for Latin America as well, where, along with constitutions and civil codes, novels helped to legislate modern mores. But unlike the English books that empowered the language of feminine domesticity by "disentangling" it from masculine politics, Latin American novels took advantage of the tangle to produce a secure knot of sentimentalized men.

The broad possibilities I am suggesting for readings of these novels are not (merely) an effort to suggest that Latin Americans may have general lessons to teach. The possibilities also derive from a suggestive coincidence between two significant books—one about desire, the other about nationalism—that have no apparent investment in each other's project. They are Michel Foucault's *The History of Sexuality* and Benedict Anderson's *Imagined Communities*. Together they will help to map out a context for passionate patriotism. Despite the books' different points of departure, their lines of inquiry intersect at two evident places. One is on the matter of timing: the end of the eighteenth century when the fundamental discourse originates (sex for Foucault and patriotism for Anderson).[13] The other coincidence is a denial: each historically marked discourse claims to be timeless and essential to the human condition (Foucault, 105; Anderson, 14). However paradoxical and provocative their observations (respectively that sexuality is a function of the power structure that appears to repress it, and that nationalism is always a modeled but not inauthentic phenomenon), Anderson's and Foucault's timing is rather conventional and unlikely to arouse skepticism.[14] Could there be some mutual significance to the overlap? To find out, Anderson and Foucault might be invited to a tête-à-tête, or a heart to heart, that would begin with their respective quandaries.

For Foucault the problem is why we so endlessly discuss what we say is repressed, which leads him to show how the "prohibition" against discussing sexual "irregularities" has spawned an array of institutional discourses for its control. The pathologies didn't exist before the authorities invented and deployed them. Perhaps for his own strategic purpose of foregrounding "marginal" sexualities and arguing, no doubt correctly, that they have been both the motive and the effect of juridical and clinical power, Foucault tends to elide what we could call the "other" sexuality and the "other" discourse. He seems almost indifferent to the most obvious deployment of bourgeois sexuality, the legitimate conjugal variety without which there could be no perverse difference, as indifferent as he was to the best-selling genre of bourgeois discourse, the novels that did so much to construct the heterosexual hegemony in bourgeois culture.[15] Foucault defends this relative silence on the majority phenomenon by saying that it was itself discreet and decorous: "The discursive explosion of the eighteenth and nineteenth centuries caused this system centered on legitimate alliance to undergo two modifications. First, . . . heterosexual monogamy . . . was spoken of less and less. . . . It tended to function as a norm, one that was stricter, perhaps, but quieter. On the other hand, what came under scrutiny was the sexuality of children, mad men and women, and criminals" (Foucault, 38). Yet we know that heterosexual love was being scandalously exhibitionistic from the concern caused by masses of young women who read sentimental novels. The absence of an *ars erotica* in the West does not necessarily signal discursive boredom with heterosexuality, as Foucault assumes, since we can boast an incredibly voluminous literature of courtship and titillation. Romantic novels seldom invite us into the bedroom, it is true, but they succeed very well at inciting our desire to be there. Because Foucault limits his range of discourses to the medico-juridical systems that exercised power rather directly, he understands desire to be the product of a power network that appears repressive. Had he included the novel, desire would also have been seen as the effect of a less paradoxical kind of training, something like an apprenticeship to republican parenthood. The exclusion helps to explain why his almost defensive insistence that power can be experienced in positive terms lacks really convincing illustrations. The "spirals of pleasure and power" that professionals and wards derived from each other (Foucault, 44–45) could not have had the broad appeal of the power that enthralled readers who wanted to possess or be possessed by the heroes and heroines of novels.

To stand Foucault's observation on its head, we could say that alongside the ubiquity of "perversion" in Western Europe there is a more obvious and public discourse of "normal" conjugal love. It must have had an enormous appeal to have kept all the other discourses in business. Not so much an emotional appeal (without minimizing that) but more importantly a legitimating appeal, which is Foucault's point. But what monumental body needed legitimation so desperately as to account for the kind of public sex appeal that the novel evidently had? What was the defensive impulse that generated the spirals of power and plea-sure in other discourses? I can think of only one body inclusive and insecure enough: the tenuously constructed antimonarchi-cal state that needed (or would need in the "underdeveloped" European cases we saw with Lukács) a self-legitimating dis-course and found one in erotic desire. Sexual love was *the* trope for associative behavior, unfettered market relationships, and for Nature in general. If the traditional hierarchies were to be legitimately deposed, the ideological ground had to shift; and the natural ground as it was redefined was not only human-ity's intrinsic acquisitiveness, but also its productive desire, the socially harnessable urge for heterosexual companionship and family. For some reason, Foucault writes off the republican pursuit of legitimacy by making bourgeois states curiously con-tinuous with monarchies. Although not exactly silent on the construction of modern states, he shifts gear after describing the rupture in the history of sexuality and accounts for re-publics with a rather seamless genealogy (Foucault, 115). The modern state, he argues, is not qualitatively different from the monarchy; one inherited a juridical system practically intact from the other. "At bottom, despite the differences in epochs and objectives, the representation of power has remained un-der the spell of monarchy. In political thought and analysis, we still have not cut off the head of the king" (Foucault, 88). Objections to monarchs were basically objections to their abuse of perfectly reasonable laws. Why, then, does Foucault in-sist that the new (universal) class invented a new (universal) language?

> The bourgeoisie made [sex] identical with its body, or at least sub-ordinated the latter to the former by attributing to it a mysterious and undefined power; it staked its life and its death on sex by mak-ing it responsible for its future welfare; it placed its hopes for the future in sex by imagining it to have ineluctable effects on gener-

ations to come; it subordinated its soul to sex by conceiving of it as what constituted the soul's most secret and determinant part. (Foucault, 124)

The guidebooks to that inner sanctum were largely the novels that Foucault ignores. They tended to banish alternative sexualities and construct legitimate models. Even so, an erotic education—whether natural or no—was officially off limits for young girls, not because it taught perversion, but evidently because it made even legitimate sex seem like fun. Novelists tried to insist that their work was "history" not fiction; and therefore not idle or fuel for fantasies.[16] But the protestations of innocence became as much a rhetorical come-on as the sentimental plots. Foucault's readers can already guess what this "repression" did for sales. In the nineteenth century everyone was reading the forbidden texts, which is one reason the Mexican Ignacio Altamirano, among many others, was using them for patriotic projects. "Novels are undoubtedly the genre that the public likes best," he wrote in 1868; "they are the artifice through which today's best thinkers are reaching the masses with doctrines and ideas that would otherwise be difficult to impart."[17]

Thanks to Foucault, some homophobic ground has been cleared away in discussions of sexuality; and now we can afford to notice how strategically laconic he was about heterosexuality and the novel. What remains curious, though, is the way he seems to take for granted the concept of "state power" on which he grounds so many arguments about policing sexuality and controlling populations (e.g. Foucault, 25). Is it conceivable that the state derived some of its power from its positive attractions as the guarantor (or promisor) of rights, services, and national pride, and that, like some jealous lover, the state punished disloyal affections? Yet Foucault's hypothesis doesn't really acknowledge a seductive moment in state-celebrated sexuality (as the motivation both for engendering more patriots and for securing their embrace), as if all institutional stimulations were indirect or repressive.[18] To sum up, Foucault's love of paradox, his arguably eccentric focus, and the seductive rhythm of his own powerful discourse cannot but produce pleasures for the reader. But these as well as his important insights are generated around a cluster of blindspots, including heterosexual exhibitionism, the novel, and the invention of modern states.

Some of these are what Benedict Anderson sees best. One organizing question of his book is precisely how nation-states were constructed, and his speculations take him directly to the "fictive" discourse of newspapers and novels. Specifically, he asks how we can account for the passionate charge of nationalism even, or most especially today, in marxist regimes that should have gotten beyond the limits of national bourgeois culture. In part it is because nationalism is not "aligned" to abstract ideologies such as liberalism or marxism but is mystically inflected from the religious cultural systems "out of which—as well as against which—it came into being" (Anderson, 19). A certain spiritual investment in Christendom was deflected to a limited territory and therefore intensified, once the hegemony of Latin fragmented along the borders of secular administrative vernaculars. The fissures deepened after the local bourgeoisies developed vernacular print capitalism.[19] The imagined community of a nation, he suggests, inherits or appropriates a spirit of sacrifice that would be unimaginable from the kind of cost-benefit calculations that self-conscious ideologies assume, and that Foucault apparently assumes when he wonders at the insanity of masses of people dying to save the "people" (Foucault, 137). Nationalism makes it possible for "so many millions of people, not so much to kill, as willingly to die for such limited imaginings" (Anderson, 16). Limited, because the modern state is "fully, flatly, and evenly operative over each square centimetre of a legally demarcated territory," very different from monarchies which "were defined by centers" and where "borders were porous and indistinct" (Anderson, 26).

The fullness and uncompromising visibility of these new states—which were at the same time particular and universally proliferated in the West—brings to mind a different kind of body being constructed simultaneously. While nations were being embodied, their borders meticulously drawn and their resources territorialized, so too were the sexual bodies that attract Foucault's attention. For the early period of bourgeois consolidation Foucault notes that sex was forced into a productive economy that distinguished a legitimate realm of sexuality inside a clearly demarcated conjugal relationship and "banished" the casual pleasures of polymorphous sexuality (Foucault, 36). At the borders "the isolation, intensification, and consolidation of peripheral sexualities . . . *measured the body,* and penetrated modes of conduct" (Foucault, 48, my emphasis). Therefore, Foucault understands his project to be a "history of bodies" (Foucault, 152)—ungendered bodies that don't betray the long-standing convention that makes territory female—much as Anderson's is a study of national bodies. As if they assumed that the other's discourse were their own stable grounding, Foucault charts sexual bodies as sites of national production and governmental surveillance, while Anderson wonders at the libidinal attachment we have to bodies politic. The eighteenth century is not only remembered for the rationalizing sex (Foucault, 23–24) but also for drawing maps as the logos (locus too?) of desire. In a double paradox, repression was producing desire while diffuse empires were spawning patriotic passion for the local territory.[20] Yet Foucault doesn't wonder about how the nation is engendered, and Anderson doesn't mention that the definite contours of the new (national) bodies were making them the objects of possessive bourgeois desire.

Because of its relevance for Latin American national romances, I should point to the very different values Foucault and Anderson can imagine for territorialization. For Foucault it is always constraining, as when he makes the link between state-supervised sexuality and racism. "The works, published in great numbers at the end of the eighteenth century, books on hygiene, etc., improving the lineage bear witness to . . . the correlation of this concern with the body and sex to a type of 'racism'" (Foucault, 125; cf. 26). But Anderson notices the redemptive potential attributed to the national body and contemplates a map of interlocking bodies far beyond Foucault's Western Europe. He remarks that state-supervised sexuality had been seen as the "solution" to racism, sometimes with similarly nefarious results. His striking example, typical for Latin America, is Pedro Fermín de Vargas's suggestion that the way to *exterminate* the lazy degenerate Indians of his early nineteenth-century Colombia was to intermarry with them and grant them property through land (Anderson, 21). Miscegenation was the road to racial perdition in Europe, but it was the way of redemption in Latin America, a way of annihilating difference and constructing a deeply horizontal, fraternal dream of national identity. It was a way of imagining the nation through a future history, like a desire that works through time and yet derives its irresistible power from *feeling* natural and ahistorical. "The fact of the matter is that nationalism thinks in terms of historical destinies, while racism dreams of eternal contaminations, transmitted from the origins of time through an endless sequence of loathsome copulations: outside history" (Anderson, 136).

Unlike Foucault's dour tracing of sexuality to a priesthood of moralizers and pseudo-scientists, Anderson locates the production of nationalism precisely in the space of our democratically shared imagination, the private space of novels that links us serially and horizontally through a "print community." Newspapers, of course, were the hub of market and political information for an ascending bourgeoisie, but they would have been inconceivable, Anderson suggests, without the preparation of a print community through books, specifically novels. Novels pioneered what Walter Benjamin called "homogeneous, empty time," measured for everyone on the same calendar so that it linked an entire society through simultaneity. This is radically different from figural or "messianic" time in which there is no "meanwhile" but only a paratactic relationship to revealed truth.[21] So, instead of considering novels (often published serially alongside the news) to be a function of newspapers, Anderson argues that newspapers derived from novels, that in the profound "fictiveness" of their kaleidoscopic juxtapositions among people and events newspapers were in effect "one-day best-sellers" (Anderson, 39). And the imagined communities of readers produced by these fictive juxtapositions became modern nations. It was a process that Anderson brilliantly argues took shape first among the linguistically homogeneous elites of the New World who became practical models—in nationalism's loopy trajectory—for the Europe that first imagined modern nations (Anderson, 49, 78–79). It may therefore not be too presumptuous to maintain here that Latin

American novels seem to be "correcting" European romance or at least putting them to good, perhaps exemplary, use by realizing their frustrated desires.

But those desires are precisely the issue on which Anderson is strangely silent. He values the novel, like the newspaper, for its synchronicity, its *horizontal* and democratizing commonality of time, rather than for its dynamism through time which he leaves fundamentally "empty." Therefore the overview of colonial Mexican society in Fernández de Lizardi's picaresque *Periquillo sarniento* (1816) seems ideologically indistinguishable from the romantic novels that would soon take over the newspaper columns (Anderson, 35). Those novels were trying to pull calendar time forward, by spacing the readings in consecutive issues of the paper, but mostly by constructing a desire for certain narrative developments. We can read out of Anderson's observations that in addition to sharing news items, print communities were being consolidated because everyone who read the paper was either laughing or (usually) panting and crying over the same installment of the serialized novel. Yet he doesn't discuss the passions constructed by reading novels, or their ideal gender models that were teaching future republicans to be passionate in a rational and seductively horizontal way.

This is where Foucault comes in. He points to the locus of modern social investments as the sexual body, which can be interpreted perhaps to be a national body as well. It is also where Anderson himself makes a suggestive aside while discussing the passion of patriotic feeling. After he accounts for it through the analogy with religion, Anderson mentions the equal centrality of our sexual identities (almost parenthetically and without development) in an observation about how universal both nationality and discrete genders are today. "[I]n the modern world everyone can, should, will 'have' a nationality, as he or she 'has' a gender" (Anderson, 14). Said inversely, everyone not only "has" a nationality and gender in the same imagined way, but these imaginings constitute us as modern subjects. Unlike the competitive comparison between nationalism and religion, the interchangeability between nation and sex here is mutually reinforcing. And it is possible, through their overlapping analogies to religion, to see sex and nation helping each other to displace earlier attachments. At least this mutual incitement of love and country is felt in the Latin American novels that helped to train generations of patriots in the appropriately productive passions of liberal intercourse.

By assuming a certain kind of translatability between romantic and republican desires, writers and readers of Latin America's canon of national novels have in fact been assuming what amounts to an allegorical relationship between personal and political narratives, a relationship that my reading is bound to repeat. Allegory is a vexed term, but unavoidable to describe how one discourse consistently represents the other and invites a double reading of narrative events. So if I shuttle back and forth from reading romantic intrigues to considering political designs it is because everyone else was doing the same.

The difficulty with the term *allegory* here is that the shuttling is not a simple matter of round-trips to the same two points or lines but is more loomlike in that the thread of the story doubles back and builds on a previous loop. Love plots and political plotting keep overlapping with each other. Instead of the metaphoric parallelism, say between passion and patriotism, that readers may expect from allegory, we will see here a metonymic association between romantic love that needs the state's blessing and political legitimacy that needs to be founded on love. Walter Benjamin provides a lead out of this terminological impasse through his unorthodox matchmaking between allegory and dialectic, a lead that detours back from Fredric Jameson's rather conventional and Paul de Man's acetic allegories.[22]

Not long ago, Jameson discovered the possible charms of contemporary "third-world literature," thanks to allegory. "All third-world texts are necessarily, I want to argue, allegorical, and in a very specific way: they are to be read as what I will call *national allegories*."[23] We will miss the interest of third-world literature, Jameson says, by missing the allegory, "a form long discredited in the west and the specific target of the Romantic revolution of Wordsworth and Coleridge, yet a linguistic structure which also seems to be experiencing a remarkable reawakening of interest in contemporary literary theory" (Jameson, 73). With this gesture, Jameson joined a number of critics who bemoan allegory's fall from favor and who individually attempt to redeem and appropriate the term, as if there were a "repressive hypothesis" about allegory that insures it as the topic of our critical interest.[24] If we would but learn how, Jameson exhorts us, we could get beyond the rather unremarkable surface narrative to "an unveiling or deconcealment of the nightmarish reality of things, a stripping away of our conventional illusions or rationalizations about daily life" (Jameson, 70). This reading lesson is a gratifying acknowledgement for some of us and a welcome reminder for others about the way many people still read and write, so that it will not do to simply dismiss the relationship between nation and allegory.[25] But Jameson both affirms too much by it (since clearly some "third-world" texts are not "national allegories") and too little (since "national allegories" are still written in the First World, by say Pynchon and Grass among others). I also wonder if Jameson's assumption that these allegories "reveal" truth in an apparently transparent way, rather than construct it with all the epistemological messiness that using language implies, doesn't already prepare him to distinguish too clearly between Third and First World literatures. Even he strains at the borders by including Dostoyevsky with Proust and Joyce as a purveyor of First World literary satisfactions.

In any case, the texts that concern me here date from a period before that vexed geo-literary breakdown, before Jameson's guilt-ridden worry over our readerly disappointments with "underdeveloped" literature (Jameson, 65). When Latin America's national novels were being written, there were no First and Third Worlds but only an Old World that was producing model texts and a New World where those texts were grist for the nation-making mill. Perhaps this choice of novels accounts for my admittedly unorthodox but not wholly original appropriation of the term *allegory*. Following Walter Benjamin, when he identified baroque allegory as the vehicle for time and dialectics, I take allegory to mean a narrative structure in which one line is a trace of the other, in which each helps to write the other, much as I took Anderson and Foucault to imply traces of each other's discourse. A more standard interpretation describes allegory as a narrative with two parallel levels of signification. These are temporally differentiated, with one revealing or "repeating" the anterior level of meaning (either trying desperately to become the other or looking on from a meta-narrative distance at the futility of any desire for stable meaning). Jameson's sense that the personal level reveals the priority of the political seems safely within this interpretation. But he ventures beyond it with the observation that the static structure could be "set in motion and complexified were we willing to entertain the more alarming notion that such equivalences are themselves in constant change and transformation at each perpetual present of the text" (Jameson, 73). Had he wanted to track the change from one moment to the next, Jameson might well have taken Benjamin's clue, as my working definition tries to do when I describe the allegory in Latin America's national novels as an interlocking, not parallel, relationship between erotics and politics.

The combination of allegory and dialectic will no doubt be oxymoronic for readers who begin with standard definitions, but it was the basis for Benjamin's effort to salvage allegory for historical writing, and probably to salvage history itself from the late-Romantic love of immediacy so dear to Nazi culture. Benjamin's essay on "Allegory and Trauerspiel," in *The Origin of German Tragic Drama* (1928),[26] is a polemic against the Romantic critics who preferred symbol over allegory. This was the same as preferring a "resplendent but ultimately non-committal knowledge of an absolute" over the consciousness that language, like allegory, functions in time as a system of conventions (Benjamin, 159–160). He explains in a proto-postmodern way that allegory is alive to the dialectic between expression and meaning because it is "a form of expression, just as speech is expression, and, indeed, just as writing is" (Benjamin, 162). Allegory works through the gaps, whereas "organic" symbols sacrifice the distance between sign and referent and resist critical thinking in order to produce more awe than irony.

Benjamin was apparently impatient with what he considered the Romantics' philosophical laziness. With the symbol they had short-circuited the apotheosis of the beautiful, even sacred, individual. "In contrast the baroque apotheosis is a dialectical one," because its subject could not stop at the individual but had to include a politico-religious dimension, "that worldly, historical breadth," which is "dialectical in character" (Benjamin, 160, 166). His prime example of the allegorical dialectic is the relationship between human history and nature, which was of course the Romantics' favorite instance of symbolic correspondences. But Benjamin takes care to point out a strategic difference between the figures: in symbol, nature is a hint of eternity and seems independent of culture; in allegory it is a record of human history and decay (Benjamin, 167). This dialectical record is what distinguishes modern secular allegory, initiated with baroque literature, from the medieval variety in which nature is the immutable background for the history it contains (Benjamin, 171). Yet Benjamin evidently had difficulty maintaining the distinction by 1938 when he wrote notes for an essay on "Baudelaire as Allegorist"; there he identifies the poet as a straggler of the seventeenth-century "allegorical way of thinking" yet adds that Baudelaire had excluded (baroque) dialectics from this notion of history.[27]

Benjamin's distinction between medieval and baroque allegories may therefore have seemed negligible to Paul de Man, or he may deliberately have omitted the historical difference, along with Benjamin's respect for dialectics, for his own "new new critical" purposes.[28] If I pause to mention de Man it is to clear some theoretical space, because his version of allegory as the inevitable failure of words to attain meaning (surprisingly conventional in its strictly parallel structure and ironically reminiscent of Romantic enchanted timelessness) has become so general as to practically cancel Benjamin's dialectical departure.[29] Years after the *Trauerspiel* book, de Man would begin "The Rhetoric of Temporality" (1969)[30] by apparently reviving Benjamin's preference for allegory's pause over symbol's rush. Yet de Man was declaring a polemic from his very title, which disappears the historical temporality Benjamin associated with allegory as a fiction of rhetoric. The battle cry is time, but the stakes are dialectics.

Curiously, though, Benjamin had never made his dialectic count for anything constructive. It moves only downward and backward into an infinite regression in which "history does not assume the form of the process of an eternal life so much as that of irresistible decay. . . . Allegories are, in the realm of thoughts, what ruins are in the realm of things" (Benjamin, 177–178).[31] Irresistible, too, would be the corollary tragic sense of life for those of us who tend to suffer more from allegorical double vision than from symbolic ex/implosions. But before we are overcome by comforting pessimism, we might consider the possibility that it depends on Benjamin's ambivalent farewell to theological allegory when he claims that human, historical, time is only an opportunity for distance from nature, for decay. In Benjamin's essay (as in de Man's), allegory is the trajectory of a philosophically felicitous failure, the recurrent waking from an endless dream of absolute presence.

If however we care to willfully misread Benjamin in order to sustain the possibility of mutually constructing terms without looking back at the crumbling structure of bad fits, we may get a sense of how the foundational fictions work. My reading consciously delays the ultimate questions of meaning, because I am more concerned to suggest *how* these books achieved their persuasive power than to determine *if* they had any right to do so. The foundational fictions are philosophically modest, even sloppy. Lacking the rigor that would either keep levels of meaning discrete or show how that was impossible, these novels hypostatize desire as truth and then slide easily between them. With the exception, perhaps, of *María,* these novels are not trapped in unproductive impasses. They do not actively worry about any incommensurability between Truth and Justice, the aporia that de Man locates in Pascal,[32] because they know themselves to be performing and seducing.[33] Their object is to win at love and at politics, not to anchor the narrative or to reckon the cost of winning. Content to construct personal and public discourses "upon each other in a circle without end," as Pascal had described his own mundane allegorizing,[34] with no stable philosophical ground to either violate or desire, foundational novels are precisely those fictions that try to pass for truth and to become the ground for political association.

If the novelists had closely followed a popular model such as Rousseau they might have worried about what they were doing. Rousseau had fretted over the "referential error" of the word love. He sensed that love was not the cause of desire but desire's effect. "Love is a mere illusion: it fashions, so to speak, another Universe for itself; it surrounds itself with objects that do not exist or that have received their being from love alone; and since it states all its feelings by means of images, its language is always figural."[35] And figure masquerades as reality once "Pathos is hypostatized as a blind power . . . , it stabilizes the semantics of the figure by making it 'mean' the pathos of its undoing . . . the figurality of the language of love implies that pathos is itself no longer a figure but a substance" (de Man, 198–199). But the nation-building novelists didn't fret. The possibility that hypostatized passion would be taken for empirical reality was hardly a "danger" at all but precisely their opportunity to construct a legitimating national culture. Whereas Rousseau's *Julie* counterpoises passion to piety in a way that must have seemed too classical to Latin American writers from the middle of the nineteenth century on, they were making a virtue of love. For Rousseau erotic passion may well have been pathological; for them it was the cure to the pathology of social sterility.

Despite their admiration for fashionable French and English styles, we noted that Latin Americans dared to adjust imported patterns. Balzac's Chilean disciple explicitly accommodates the master to local material in *Martín Rivas*: "The French . . . say: l'amour fait rage et l'argent fait mariage, but here love makes both: rage et mariage."[36] This "improvement" does not mean that the national novels represent any literary advance over a work like *Julie*; on the contrary, they are far more conventional. The genre has all "the stock characters in a situation of sentimental tragedy, persecuted by the social inequities of wealth and class and by the caprices of a tyrannical father" that *Julie* puts into question. They are closer in spirit to what de Man said about "*Werther* or the Mignon chapter in *Wilhelm Meister* or *Sylvie*," than to *La nouvelle Héloise*, which "would be a very different (and a much shorter) text . . . if the narrative had been allowed to stabilize" (de Man, 215). More predictable, and understandably less challenging to read, these novels set up a dialectic between love and the state—as does *Julie* in the first part—but never stop, as Julie does, to turn around (in the Augustinian sense of converting)[37] and look back.

They look relentlessly forward, like the mortals Benedict Anderson leaves with their backs to Benjamin's nostalgic Angel of

History (Anderson, 147) and so do not draw desire into the regress of loss that seems inevitable in allegory.[38] Instead, they set desire into a spiral or zigzagging motion inside a double structure that keeps projecting the narrative into the future as eroticism and patriotism pull each other along. Rather than rue their artificiality, these novels celebrate their own handiwork as revolutionary departures. There is no crisis associated with the loss/castration that triggers the telling. Instead the loss opens a space because it is the father who has been castrated, not the hero of the piece. I am suggesting that some allegories, such as the ones I'll consider in the following chapters, may have no preexisting and eternal level of referentiality, but—like Nietzsche's point about the fiction of empirical moorings—make themselves up, all the while attempting to produce an illusion of stability.

If I read a double and corresponding structure between personal romance and political desiderata, it is not with any priority of either register. I am suggesting that Eros and Polis are the effects of each other's performance, something like the Marquis de Sade's explanation of sexual desire as the effect of another's commotion (although the analogy would certainly have scandalized the Latin American founders).[39] Erotic interest in these novels owes its intensity to the very prohibitions against the lovers' union across racial or regional lines. And political conciliations, or deals, are transparently urgent because the lovers "naturally" desire the kind of state that would unite them. For example, histories still debate about the political portrayal of Juan Manuel de Rosas. Was he a bloodthirsty and vindictive barbarian who singled out Argentina's intelligentsia for terror and torture? Or was he a sophisticated defender of Argentine cultural and economic autonomy, no more bloody than his equally extravagant opponents who wanted to Europeanize the country as soon as possible? If we "know" from reading *Amalia* that Rosas was an unscrupulous dictator, our knowledge is to a considerable degree a political articulation of the erotic frustration we share with Amalia and Eduardo. And we feel the intensity of their frustration because we know that their obstacle is the horrible dictator.

In national romance, one level represents the other and also fuels it, which is to say that both are unstable. The unrequited passion of the love story produces a surplus of energy, just as Rousseau suggested it would,[40] a surplus that can hope to overcome the political interference between the lovers. At the same time, the enormity of the social abuse, the unethical power of the obstacle, invests the love story with an almost sublime sense of transcendent purpose. As the story progresses, the pitch of sentiment rises along with the cry of commitment, so that the din makes it ever more difficult to distinguish between our erotic and political fantasies for an ideal ending.

What I find ingenious, indeed brilliant, about this novel productivity is that one libidinal investment ups the ante for the other. And every obstacle that the lovers encounter heightens more than their mutual desire to (be a) couple, more than our voyeuristic but keenly felt passion; it also heightens their/our love for the possible nation in which the affair could be consummated. The two levels of desire are different, which allows us to remark on an allegorical structure; but they are not discrete.[41] Desire weaves between the individual and the public family in a way that shows the terms to be contiguous, coextensive as opposed to merely analogous. And the desire keeps weaving, or simply doubling itself at personal and political levels, because the obstacles it encounters threaten both levels of happiness. These obstacles are almost always a social convention or a political impasse; that is, they are public and interpersonal rather than some intimate and particular differences between the lovers. The fact that the lovers almost never quarrel probably has something to do with the vestigial aristocratic character of these romances; its heroes and heroines appear on the scene full blown, immutable and easily distinguished from the masses of servants and supporters. Romantic heroes don't develop in the way we expect from the heroes of novels; instead they move the narrative as a magnet moves unanchored metals, selectively and at the center. When novels were imported by Latin Americans, the genre suffered some sea changes, along with its companion ideology of liberal democracy.[42] The Latin American elite wanted to modernize and to prosper, yes; but it wanted at the same time to retain the practically feudal privilege it had inherited from colonial times. Logically, a functioning aristocracy by any name might prefer to represent itself in the in-

corruptibly ideal terms that Northrop Frye finds characteristic
of romance, "the structural core of all fiction."[43] In Latin America's newly won bourgeois excess, Frye's heroic heroes, villainous villains, and beautiful heroines of romance are dislodged,
unfixed. They cross class, gender, and racial stereotypes in ways
unspeakable for European romance. Yet Frye's observations
about masculine and feminine ideals here are to the point;
they point backward to medieval quest-romances where victory meant restored fertility, the union of male and female
heroes.[44] One might say that modernizing romances too are
written backward, progressing like religious or mythical discourse from a sacred given and reconstructing a trajectory
toward it. The narrative begins conceptually from a resolution
of conflict, whether that resolution is realized or not, and serves
as a vehicle for love and country that seem, after the fact, to
have preexisted the writing. For some evidently cautious and
controlling reason, its heroes are not the self-reflexive, naive,
and developing protagonists that European theorists expect
in the novel. Instead, they are unerringly noble, by birth and
talent. Non-white lovers are more often than not indigenous
or imported princes, like Sab's mother, Alencar's Guaraní, Enriquillo, Tabaré, and the African lovers in *María*.

To mention the "aristocratic" quality of Latin America's bourgeois heroes is meant to reinforce an observation about a particular narrative lack in their stories. It is the lack of personal
antagonism or intimate arguments between lovers (except perhaps for the erotic power struggle in *Martín Rivas*), the stuff
that sentimental romance is apparently made of. The only
problems here seem external to the couple. That they can
thwart the romance, fuels our desire to see it flourish. So it is
not only desire that doubles itself on public and private levels
here; it is also the public obstacle that deters (and goads) the
erotic and national projects. Once the couple confronts the obstacle, desire is reinforced along with the need to overcome the
obstacle and to consolidate the nation. That promise of consolidation constitutes another level of desire and underscores the
erotic goal, which is also a microcosmic expression of nationhood. This zigzagging movement describes a kind of allegory
that works primarily through metonymic associations between

the family and the state rather than through the parallelism of metaphoric analogy which seems so standard for allegory.[45] There is no insistence here on translating from one discourse to another, say from the Good Shepherd in standard Christian allegory to God himself. In these sentimental epics, one meaning doesn't merely point to another, unreachably sublime, register; it *depends* on the other. The romantic affair *needs* the nation, and erotic frustrations *are* challenges to national development. By the same token, requited love already *is* the foundational moment in these dialectical romances. This is one reason for my not including here Alberdi's far more conventional allegory *Peregrination of Light of Day, or Voyages and Adventures of Truth in the New World* (1871), with its standard translatability already visible in the title. The main reason, though, may be a result of the first: the book was simply not so popular nor (therefore) so institutionally promising as to help reinforce love of country. Alberdi may have borrowed his title from Eugenio María de Hostos's *The Peregrinations of Bayoán* (Puerto Rico, 1863), an intriguing attempt at Pan-Caribbean (amorous) alliance which is hardly so schematic as Alberdi's "travails of truth." Yet *Bayoán* is rather heavy-handed about announcing distinct allegorical registers, and its contradictory affairs with politics and passion founder in the rather un-American competition between erotics and duty. Whether or not the conventionally allegorical and puritanical features of Hostos's sentimental and political peregrinations kept *Bayoán* off the canonical list of national romances I take up here, it can hardly have had a similar career. Which country would it celebrate or project? Which existing government could it have supported, when Bayoán's dream was precisely international, beyond the future institutions that might have required it?[46]

Of course the allegories will appeal rhetorically to some legitimating a priori principle. Being a justification for modern and anti-authoritarian projects, that principle is often Nature that has been conveniently redefined since the days of enlightened Independence as interactive rather than hierarchical. If erotic desire seemed to be the natural and therefore eternal grounding for happy and productive marriages (including national families by extension) it was thanks to these redefinitions. Nature was no longer the classical realm of predictable law but the realm of flux where energy could meet obstacles and turn frustration into excess. It was a world that produced angels and monsters, not clockwork. The allegories will strain at points against these redefinitions. For one thing the writing elite was loathe to give up its hierarchical privilege to conciliatory projects, and for another compelling characters may exceed or somehow miss an ideally assigned meaning.

But the observation I am making is far more fundamental than any demonstration of the allegory's partial failures. I am simply registering the incredible measure of its success. In many cases, the double dealing romance actually helped to give a cognitive expression and an emotive mooring to the social and political formations it articulates. The historical romances became national novels in their respective countries, a term that refers not so much to their market popularity, although to be sure many of these novels were immediately popular, but to the fact that they became required reading by the first decades of the twentieth century. Perhaps their promise of a nationalizing embrace was particularly appealing after massive immigration in some countries seemed to threaten a cultural core, and after Latin American regimes decided on patriotic programs for economic and civic development as responses to the Depression and to competing "foreign" ideologies. These states, in other words, tacitly accepted the nineteenth-century pot-boilers as founding fictions that cooked up the desire for authoritative government from the apparently raw material of erotic love.

2
PLAGIARIZED AUTHENTICITY: SARMIENTO'S COOPER AND OTHERS

Poor Cora! Why must James Fenimore Cooper kill her off in *The Last of the Mohicans* (1826)? After lingering so long on her heroism, generosity, resourcefulness, and sheer ethical strength (not to speak of the physical attractions that fix Cooper on Cora) her death seems entirely undeserved. And poor us. Why make Cora so admirable only to deny us the continuing fantasy of possessing, or of being, her? This is especially distressing in a romance, or sentimental novel, which should typically unite hero and heroine after making them overcome apparently insurmountable odds.

One of the problems here is that she is not the heroine at all. Nor, much less, is the Mohican Uncas her hero. Cora is a woman marked by a racially crossed past that would have compromised the clear order Cooper wanted for America. And this is precisely why, tragically, he has to kill her off: to stop us short in our sentimental sidetracks and to leave us only the legitimate lovers who must command our lasting sympathy. They are childlike Alice, Cora's half-sister, and her dashing English suitor, Major Heyward.

I should confess right away that my responses to Cooper, romantic heartbreak alternating with practical resignation, are marked by my own past as a reader of Cooper's Latin American heirs. They reread and rewrote him, either to defend Cora's death as a necessary sacrifice or to redeem her as America's more colorful and more convincing heroine. Given the inevitable years and books that have intervened between Cooper and me, I cannot help but read him through these writers, just as

Jorge Luis Borges read *Don Quijote* through Pierre Menard's rewriting. Like Menard in Borges's story, the Latin Americans produced contemporary texts with each rereading of Cooper. Borges tells us that, "Cervantes' text and Menard's are verbally identical, but the second is almost infinitely richer. (More ambiguous, his detractors will say, but ambiguity is richness.)"[1] When Cervantes wrote, for example, that history is the mother of truth, he was merely a "lay genius" offering rhetorical praise for history. But when Menard rewrites it, Borges finds that "the idea is astounding. Menard, a contemporary of William James, does not define history as an inquiry into reality but as its origin. Historical truth, for him, is not what has happened; it is what we judge to have happened." Borges comes to understand that this brilliant updating of the text should not be surprising because, even if Menard's own fetishized version ironically wants to reinscribe a textual stability denied to Cervantes, the very practice of rewriting has already opened up the possibility for further tamperings. This leads his posthumous reviewer to contemplate that,

> "Pensar, analizar, inventar . . . no son actos anómalos, son la normal respiración de la inteligencia." . . . Menard (acaso sin quererlo) ha enriquecido mediante una técnica nueva el arte detenido y rudimentario de la lectura: la técnica del anacronismo deliberado y de las atribuciones erróneas. Esa técnica de aplicación infinita nos insta a recorrer la Odisea como si fuera posterior a la Eneida. . . . Esa técnica puebla de aventura los libros más calmosos.[2]
>
> ["Thinking, analyzing, inventing . . . are not anomalous acts; they are the normal respiration of the intelligence." . . . Menard (perhaps without wanting to) has enriched, by means of a new technique, the halting and rudimentary art of reading: that of the deliberate anachronism and the erroneous attribution. This technique, whose applications are infinite, prompts us to go through the *Odyssey* as if it were posterior to the *Aeneid*. . . . This technique fills the most placid works with adventure.][3]

Why not, then, read Cooper through the Latin American writers who read him? Each reading is original, because none really is, since the very pretense of originality is mocked by the endless succession of rereadings. Said another way, originality is precisely what is unstable, that which decomposes and recomposes itself with every reading. The lesson to be learned from Menard's perhaps involuntary destabilization of writing, including his own, is that even if we *could* succeed in bracketing all the texts that have come between Cooper and us we would be fetishizing his novel by assuming that "thinking, analyzing, inventing" are discrete activities. And worse, perhaps, we would miss a series of "adventurous" Latin American revisions.[4]

Cooper himself might well have objected to these exploits when it came to exploiting *The Last of the Mohicans.* All such liberties would surely confound his foundational project, a book that became America's "gymnasium of the heart" according to a century and a half of autobiographical testimony by "politicians, businessmen, and soldiers—but also those who became her historians, preachers, writers."[5] To be fair, few nation-builders would have welcomed other writers to tinker with their constructions. Nor could they have appreciated the controlling charm of Walt Whitman's injunction to "stray from me," a liberating gesture that of course insures a paradoxical obedience by granting the right to disobey: "yet who can stray from me"?[6] And Cooper seems particularly defensive about his founding text for America. Tampering was tantamount to meddling with providence, because Cooper's pretext for writing was (to defend) God's own creation, the pristine and natural lines of America. It denounces no traces of writing but reveals a perfect creation that a spiritual elite may inherit. More true certainly than "cowardly" written histories, whose absent authors avoid criticism,[7] and truer even than the Bible, in which God's intentions are colored by fallible human language (Cooper, 107), America's wilderness is His transparent writing. When David Gamut misses Hawk-eye's reference to the only book worth reading, the scout explains,

> 'Tis open before your eyes, . . . and he who owns it is not a niggard of its use. I have heard it said that there are men who read in books to convince themselves there is a God. I know not but man may so deform his works in the settlements, as to leave that which is so clear in the wilderness a matter of doubt among traders and priests. If any such there be, and he will follow me from sun to sun, through the windings of the forest, he shall see enough to teach him that

he is a fool, and that the greatest of his folly lies in striving to rise
to the level of One he can never equal, be it in goodness, or be it
in power. (Cooper, 138)

Yet, the very novel he gives us to read shows that Cooper is his
own Menard, taking timeless nature as a pretense for adventurous historical embellishments. If God has already written, who
is man to overwrite the creation until nature spells civilization?
This contradiction certainly seems to nag Cooper as he reduces
the divine work to writerly raw material. Only the Author's for-
bearance, and the Puritans' mission to make God's signs visible,
can hope to resolve it. Cooper seems alive to the problem and
makes visible efforts at writing an extension of nature, thus to
provide his heroes with a legitimating prehistory. But extending, interpreting, writing, inevitably produce supplements. And
in Cooper they convert an alleged static plenitude into the ani-
mated project of endless rewritings.

The fact that Latin Americans rewrote Cooper's books in
so many *ways* assumes a reason *why* they gave him so much
attention. Why did they? Domingo Faustino Sarmiento (1811–
1888) gives more than a clue. Probably the foremost author
of the Argentine nation as journalist, ideologue, general, and
president, Sarmiento provided an argument for Cooper's use-
fulness to other national authors which practically set off a
Coopermania among them. His reasons were evidently powerful enough to make Sarmiento refer in great detail to Cooper's
novels at the beginning of *Facundo* (1845), translated by Horace
Mann's wife as *Life in the Argentine Republic in the Days of the Tyrants*.[8] Something about Cooper's writings warrants the Argentine's review of several scenes from *The Last of the Mohicans* and
from *The Prairie* (1827) in order to launch his own book, a
book that seems to have little to do with fiction and less to do
with North America. Or was the connection, perhaps, Cooper's
emblematic value among European readers as *the* American
writer of his day? These admirably civilized readers admired
him, and this is Sarmiento's argument, because Cooper had
developed a formula for writing about America that took advantage of her originality and that should therefore be taken
as a model of New World writing. It amounted to "removing

the scene of the events he described from the settled portion of the country to the border land between civilized life and that of the savage, the theater of war for the possession of the soil waged against each other, by the native tribes and the Saxon race" (Sarmiento, 24, 25).

THE DOUBLE-CROSS: RACIAL AND GENDER CROSSINGS CROSSED OUT

This is one hint that Sarmiento understood Cooper's sign for the natural, legitimate hero and heroine as, rather, a lack of sign, a pristine blankness in the original sense of whiteness, which leaves fair Alice and Heyward unblemished.[9] Unlike Cora, whose dark hair and dignified manner denounce a complicated history, and unlike Uncas whose race is marked by his savage coloring, no mark or trace of a compromising past, no "cross" of blood, burdens Alice or Heyward. They not only survive more colorful Cora and Uncas but also, presumably, prosper and populate the innocent and benign America. Inheriting her by virtue of a mutual love that bears no crosses of the past, they set out together, he to inscribe himself on, and she to be inscribed along with, an equally untraced wilderness.

The heroine of the piece is, then, also America, both mother and consort to the founding white fathers. By the same token, seen from its flip side, women can offer the legitimate ground for society only if they seem unmarked and nonhistorical, as America appeared to the settlers who called her a wilderness. Rhetorical figures like the "virgin forest" and her "bosom" are so standard here that one may miss the vanishing act of a language that vaporizes woman by substitution. Cooper's romance gives a domestic cast to what has been called America's pastoral dream and helps to relieve some ambiguity or guilt over the white man's conquest of a Virgin Land.[10] What could be more legitimate than courting and winning a virgin? If man's penetration threatened to destroy the wilderness, certainly this was not true once conquest was figured as mutual love. Or was it? The domestic conquest of women was not entirely benign, as we see from Cora's case. How could it be, when, for apparently ethical and historical reasons, women should be inert terrain for human activity?[11] Those who can serve do not act. And those who cannot serve are eliminated.

Reducing the female to a blank page, the better to bear man's inscription, means, for example, that Cora will not do. Her flaw is not only a racial slippage but also a certain gender indeterminacy evident in her manly dignity (Cooper, 119). Along with her, Uncas is victim to this founding romance, not only because he threatens to complicate Cora's racial crossings, but also because his masculinity has room for the grace and sensitivity associated with women. Both characters cross over the rigid racial and sexual divides, although readers have more often noted Cooper's defense of racial purity than his simultaneous policing of gender boundaries. Misgivings about miscegenation spill over into misogyny. I do not mean to ignore the pained ambiguity that one senses each time this exterminating angel waxes critical of pure whites, or each time Cooper prefers women with histories. On the contrary, I want to underline the pain, the cathartic sacrifice of social impurities, that became necessary if the nation was to be established in the clearest possible terms.

One might imagine, from reading Michel Foucault, that Cooper's defense of racial and gender purity is consistent with an eighteenth-century "map" or "grid" of knowledge. Foucault understands the classical *épistéme* to posit a universal plenitude, every part of which fits neatly into a table of categories; any spillovers from one category to the other were simply errors or symptoms of the temporary limits of human knowledge. Science, in one form or another, was taxonomic. Yet Cooper either shows that this view of the eighteenth century is unnecessarily static or that he is caught between a classical affirmation of knowledge and the daring nineteenth-century pursuit of new categories. Taxonomies, Foucault continues, were giving way to histories, and attention shifted from static parts to unstable organisms, changeable combinations that disturbed and finally dismantled the meticulous grids of classical knowledge.[12] Charles Brockden Brown was already dabbling with cross-overs in *Arthur Mervyn* (1799), where the hero's marriage to a Portuguese-Jewish widow makes social order seem possible through inclusion rather than elimination.[13] But he worried along with Cooper about the appropriateness of certain mixes for America. Various Europeans might combine, as they do in Cooper's *The Pioneers* (1823), but cautiously.

In the more defensive *Mohicans* written three years later, both Sarmiento and his straying Latin American readers would find an endorsement of their alternative assumptions about order and progress. On the one (Sarmentine) hand, each of the characters in the novel can be located on a stable graph of utility in language (French being inferior to English, for instance); musicality and religiosity (David Gamut's excess in contrast to Iroquois paucity); domestic practices (the cooking Mohicans and the raw-eating Iroquois); and gender (Alice's ideally infantile femininity, Heyward's masculinity, and the confused categories of Cora and Uncas). These hierarchies function more to set up a grid of values than to motivate the novel. Motivation comes precisely from a commitment to keep the categories pure, against the disturbances in gender and, more conspicuously perhaps, against racial amalgamations. It's bad enough here to be an Indian or even a Frenchman, but much worse to be a mixture that upsets the neat rungs of the racial ladder. That is why Hawk-eye keeps insisting, rather defensively, that he is a man without a cross (of blood); but Chingachgook, too, is bound to call himself "an unmixed man" (Cooper, 37).[14] As for Cora, her tragedy is announced by the fact that she is the product of a leaky grid of blood. Her blood was so rich that it "seemed ready to burst its bounds" (Cooper, 21). It stains her; makes her literally uncategorizable, that is, an epistemological error.[15] Heyward agrees that this is "unfortunate," because even though there is no blame in Cora, there is a blemish that "obscures" her worth (Cooper, 308). By contrast, Alice is pure, named for truth itself and for the mother who sacrificed her youth to remain true to Munro.

But on the other (romantic novelist's) hand, Cooper's novel seems ready to explode the classical prisonhouse of knowledge by way of its most vital and most admirable characters. Through them, America and the nineteenth century practically promise to be the place and time for new possibilities and unplotted histories. If America is different from Europe, as Cooper's and Sarmiento's nationalism must insist that it is, surely her children should subject Old World categories to a new reflexivity and to new combinations. How could it be otherwise, if instead of the historicized Nature of Europe, America was a Wilderness, an unknown and surprising land? Therefore, along with their map of civilization, Cooper and Sarmiento give us guides to the unknown, a scout named Hawk-eye and an entire class of *mestizo* Argentine pathfinders. And alongside these quintessentially "American" characters whose rustic nobility dares to straddle social categories, we get a combination of "masculine" dignity and "feminine" sensuality in Cora.

We do not get them for long, however, as Sarmiento is quick to recognize. Cooper introduces these anomalous figures as if to pledge that America can be original by providing the space for differences, variations, and crossings. But then he recoils from them, as if they were misfits, monsters. If Hawk-eye seems redeemable inside the gridwork of a classical reading because, unlike the gauchos, he is a man without a cross, he is finally as doomed as they are by Cooper's obsessive social neatness. Hawk-eye disturbs the ideal hierarchies that Sarmiento and his Cooper have in mind, because neither birth nor language can measure his worth. And Cooper leaves the scout behind as surely as his characters leave their cross-over identities after the carnival-like masquerade of the final rescue scenes. Chingachgook can no more remain a beaver than Heyward can be a buffoon, or Alice an Indian. And Cora, already exposed as impersonating a white maiden, can hardly remain the beloved of a Mohican. At her funeral Munro asks Hawk-eye to comfort the mourners with the promise that "the time shall not be distant when we may assemble around [God's] throne without distinction of sex, or rank, or color." The more "natural" man objects: "To tell them this . . . would be to tell them that the snows come not in the winter" (Cooper, 411). To be beautiful, vital, virtuous, and resourceful was not enough for Cora. Rather, it was too much for any woman.

Some readers weep along with the Indian maids. Sarmiento may have wept too, but with the grateful cathartic tears that felt the profound injustice but also the "necessity" of what had already become a policy of Indian removal or genocide in both the United States and Argentina. For Sarmiento, Cooper's dedication to progress made the sacrifice inevitable. Surely, Cooper could not have been serious about imagining that America was already the rational and uncorrupted given order of things. Instead, she was merely available for men to impose clarity and rationality. Apparently loyal to the eighteenth-century épistéme, Cooper seemed to defend the purity of her natural wilderness, just as he insisted on the transparent simplicity of his virginal heroine. But what he really wants, on Sarmiento's reading, is to defend the nature of society, for inchoate nature to embrace civilization. This reader is untroubled by the possible paradox of loving the wilderness to death,[16] or by the related paradox of loving virgins like Alice. Love a virgin and she stops being one; inhabit the pristine wildness of America and you've civilized it. The violation of the purity that seems to legitimate America may be a problem for some North American readers, but it was precisely what Sarmiento wanted: to engender civilized settlers who would conquer the still overpowering land.

He had no pretense of preserving the virginity or totality of America; quite the contrary. Empty spaces were the problem itself: "Its own extent is the evil from which the Argentine Republic suffers." The country's demographic and discursive nature was an emptiness that "threatened to invade her entrails" (Sarmiento, 9; 1)[17] and that invited man's writing and the supplement they could produce together. That meant, of course, bodies to populate the pampa and modern systems of production and exchange. But Sarmiento's immediate supplement was, in fact, his native overwriting of "exotic" texts, travelogues and voyagers' accounts that provided the only pampa he knew.[18] As for the danger that objections to nature could be construed as blasphemy, Sarmiento arrogantly quips that, "We should lodge a *complaint against Providence* and ask it to correct the land's configuration" (Sarmiento, 12; 6. Mrs. Horace Mann's pious mistranslation reads: "This would be to complain of Providence and call upon it to alter physical outlines."). Sarmiento and his Cooper then proceeded to take providence in hand; he resents the awe-inspiring land, so immense and empty that it was uncontrollable. The indistinct horizon on an endless pampa may inspire the American sublime and may be a source of national pride—as in Sarmiento's reverie about the American subject whose gaze "sinks into that shifting, hazy, undefined horizon; the further it withdraws from him, the more it fascinates and confuses him, and plunges him in contemplation and doubt" (Sarmiento, 26; 27). But that same obdurate landscape defeats reason and industriousness.

More specifically, it mocks him in the figure of an overwhelming tease, a taunting and tempting virgin who doesn't quite have the shape of a woman, because no one has yet been able to make a woman of her. Unlike Cooper's wilderness, Argentina's pampa is chaste only in the most technical sense. Demanding to be admired wild and shapeless as she is, the land lies ready for the man who dares to make her productive. She "flaunts her smooth, infinite, downy brow without frontiers, without any landmarks; it's the very image of the sea on land, . . . the land still waiting for the command to bring forth every herb-yielding seed after its kind" (Mrs. Mann's chaste translation gives "downy" as "velvet-like," while the Spanish word *velludo* is unmistakably associated with pubic hair) (Sarmiento, 10–11; 2). The American sublime may well be that conflicted response to the combination of responsibility and inadequacy, the duty to intervene and the helplessness before an enormous hermetic body. In any case, Sarmiento is saying that Argentina needs the manageable, recognizably demarcated body that a modern subject could love, because his real passion was for progress.

That is why the Land's unproductive consorts, Indians and gauchos so indolently at peace in unredeemed nature, had to be erased from the national project. They were racially unfit, in Sarmiento's proto-positivist language, for associative behavior. Learning about European positivism in Latin America was like learning that people spoke in prose. It was already a habit of thought that had developed, as it had in Europe, from certain disappointments with revolutionary idealism. Very broadly, positivism in Latin America is an often eclectic tradition that combines a reverence for positive or "scientific"—meaning here empirical—data along with the assumption that the emerging social sciences should take the physical sciences, mostly biology, as their models. Social ills were duly diagnosed and remedies were prescribed. Herbert Spencer's organicism was especially popular and coordinated with a Comptian schema of the progressive stages of history.[19] Since growth meant modernization and Europeanization, the most extreme ideologues advocated a combined policy of white immigration and Indian or black removal, whereas others settled for redeeming the "primitive" races through miscegenation and ideological whitening. Cooper's nineteenth-century Latin American readers either defended Sarmiento's categorical position or, as we'll see below, developed a more conciliatory and romantic one.

SELF-AUTHORIZED DISCIPLES

The book that Sarmiento wrote to follow his praise for Cooper's novels seems dutifully to follow the master's lead. In *Facundo,* Sarmiento was in fact writing America through her racial and cultural conflicts; and he produced what is probably the most widely read and influential of any book Cooper may have inspired. Yet my point here will be that Sarmiento's backing up Cooper is quite subtle, even paradoxically self-advancing. By setting up Cooper's America as a model for Argentina, Sarmiento will hardly sacrifice his own particularity or his country's; he is far too cunning an author simply to subordinate either himself or the nation he hopes to lead to another's authority. Sarmiento was in the habit of giving strong readings, or as Sylvia Molloy astutely points out, translating others' work, an operation she shows was related to plagiarism.[20] I will be suggesting that in the case of his Cooper, and in multiple cases from *Recuerdos de Provincia* (1850), Sarmiento's apparently deferential gesture, his respectful naming of masters and models, is merely a strategic distancing. It constitutes the second move in a maneuver that works like a boomerang, ultimately circling back with the spoils of borrowed authority. The first step, logically, is to wield the rhetorical boomerang, to assume full control, announce the pursuit, and predict the prize.

Everyone who reads Spanish American literature, or history, or politics, knows what Sarmiento is pursuing in *Facundo.* He practically tells us what the prize is in the book's subtitle, *Civilization and Barbarism.* This opposition constructs a normative difference between what Argentina should be and what it now is, between productive control and desultory excess, a difference that amounts to a program for accomplishing one by eliminating the other. Sarmiento evidently reviles Agentina's present excess as unproductive waste. He does so repeatedly and passionately, every time he mentions a gaucho who butchers a cow just to eat its tongue, or a regional caudillo like Facundo Quiroga who sacrifices whole armies to his personal glory and scores of women to his lust.

Yet excess is precisely what characterizes Sarmiento's writing about it in this exorbitant text, half fiction, half biography, half political history, half manifesto, a generically immoderate book that obviously adds up to much more than one.[21] He is writing inside what he might have called the American idiom, as well as against it, writing *in* conflict as well as about it. Sarmiento is founding a peculiarly American political rhetoric by resisting, simultaneously, his anarchic environment and the unnatural constraints of European genres that would distinguish between poetry and politics and that keep missing the specificity of American life.[22] *Facundo* spills over standard generic categories and even seems to be written out of Sarmiento's writerly control; it reads like a feverish product of an inspiration that never condescended to an editing job. On rereading the very title, we may notice that the equivalence introduced by the colon makes both opposing terms of the subtitle curiously apposite to the name Facundo.[23] Alberdi must have been among the first to notice that this two-faced book argued for and against the same questions.[24] An explosive rhetorical pressure keeps threatening to blow up (in both senses of exaggerating and destroying) his initial dichotomy of civilization versus barbarism, and the ones that follow from it: the future versus the past; Europeans versus Indians; settlers versus nomads; and generally, deliberation versus passion. These oppositions tend to cross out/into each other until Sarmiento himself admits how useless it may be to keep them straight. One notorious example is his treatment of "savage" dictator Rosas, who is credited with having accomplished the national unity that his civilized Unitarian antagonists only dreamed of. Their improvement on Rosas would certainly not be to level his top-down style but to replace him at the top with a more legitimately elite leadership.[25] Far from wanting to destroy this authentically Argentine "barbarian"'s work (just because some defensively dichotomous definition would make barbarians incapable of real work), Sarmiento wanted to appropriate it, in the same way that he wanted to appropriate whatever was salvageable in Argentina's special character. (No wonder that Alberdi thought the book should have been called *Faustino* instead of *Facundo*.)[26] The country's originality, after all, was the justification for Independence and for the patriotism that Sarmiento must attribute to himself in order to win support for his own leadership.

His paean to that originality comes very early on, long before he gets to Rosas, and even before the bulk of the book where he sketches out the figure of the national tyrant in Facundo's minor regional lines. It comes in the first section, after Sarmiento rushes his reader through the vast, empty expanse of the country left barren by nomadic gauchos and Indians, an emptiness that mutely invites him to write on it. Chapter 2 is where Sarmiento pauses at his own dichotomy as he stops, with some pride, to consider the "Originality and Peculiarities of the Argentine People." Mrs. Mann ends her chapter title there, but Sarmiento had added a list of untranslatable types: "El Rastreador. El Baqueano. El Gaucho malo. El Cantor." This early double take about laudable Argentine peculiarities in Sarmiento's apparently single-minded campaign for civilization is, as I said, itself a peculiarly Sarmentine move. He shows his American self to have non-European tastes, values, structures of feeling. Different from Europeans on the one hand and from native nomads on the other, Americans are also extensions of both; they are culturally doubled and different from themselves, a violent excess. Therefore, a truly American literature would necessarily be unorthodox by European standards; it would attend to "scenes so peculiar, so characteristic, and so far outside the circle of ideas in which the European mind has been educated, that their dramatic relations would be unrecognized machinery outside the country that developed these surprising customs and original characters" (Sarmiento, 24; 24).

Those inimitable Argentine characters occupy Sarmiento in this second chapter, where his legitimacy as a specifically Argentine leader must be established. And yet Sarmiento's literary model for describing the indigenous drama and the extravagant actors is, as I already said, the North American Cooper. How strange that Sarmiento should refer to a foreigner precisely when he is celebrating what is most homespun and characteristic. It is as if the difference between domestic self and imported other didn't matter when it came to marketing his national political identity. One explanation Sarmiento offers is that he senses the stirrings of a local, properly American esthetic in Cooper's work, a barbarous esthetic of the sublime (probably taken more from travels in the United States, like Chateaubriand's, than from Cooper)[27] that was both deferential to and contemptuous of Europe. "The natural peculiarities of any region give rise to customs and practices of a corresponding peculiarity, so that where the same circumstances reappear, we find the same means of controlling them invented by different nations" (Sarmiento, 25; 25). But to offer this explanation, Sarmiento has had to tailor Cooper to fit Argentina; he purposefully ignores the differences in terrain among Cooper's novels, which by Sarmiento's own determinist logic (roughly, that geography was destiny) should have mattered. Whereas Cooper's wilderness is a womblike enclosure in *The Last of the Mohicans*, *The Prairie* shows a blinding expanse. And this expansive landscape is the one that Sarmiento chooses to universalize for America. "To arouse the poetic sense . . . we need the sight of beauty, of terrible power, of immensity of extent, of something vague and incomprehensible; . . . Hence it follows that the disposition and nature of the Argentine [and North American?] people are poetic. How can such feelings fail to exist, when a black storm-cloud rises, no one knows whence, in the midst of a calm, pleasant afternoon, and spreads over the sky before a word can be uttered?" (Sarmiento, 26; 27).

It is very possible that Sarmiento's apparently eccentric national identity, meaning that it seems mirrored through Cooper's America, was programmatic for a man who wanted to modernize his country by "Europeanizing" or "North Americanizing." What interests me here, as I said, is less the degree to which Sarmiento may be borrowing from Cooper's originality than the way he manages to invert the terms and perhaps even the implied debts. He manages through a double-dealing logic that begins, as we saw, by announcing programmatic oppositions between civilization and barbarism, then proceeds to defer to a model of writing about American oppositions, a model endorsed, significantly, by a European (that is, exoticizing) standard that allegedly glorifies conquest of the land. She had resisted domesticating inscriptions, for Cooper as much as for Sarmiento, because Mr. Right and his writing tool hadn't come along yet. To whose authority would the virtuous, or stubborn, Land yield? Whom would she allow to inscribe his name, to produce a landmark? Certainly not the Indians. They had their chance and were obviously unequal to the challenge, mostly because they were cast as "nomads" in the discourse of America ever since the sixteenth-century settlement of Roanoke and Shakespeare's *The Tempest*. And since civilization meant stable settlements for the Europeans, the Indians were practically synonymous with barbarians. From the European "discovery" through the period of imperialist rivalries and internal conquests, the Americas were named and renamed after the fathers who fought on and over her. Cooper traces one such history of conflict over what, for now at least, is called Lake George. The Jesuits had given it the "title of lake 'du Saint Sacrement.' The less zealous English thought they conferred a sufficient honor on its unsullied fountains when they bestowed the name of their reigning prince," both having blotted out the "original appellation of 'Horican'" (Cooper, 12).

If Cooper was indeed convincing himself that America was worthy of love because she was pristine and untouched by history, it must have been to establish her legitimacy as wife. To acknowledge her former consorts might have been to cast doubt on the permanence of her current ones. Cooper, in fact, manages with one hand to write the land's "erotic" prehistory with the Indians and the French and to erase it with the other. Like Alice, whose family history leaves no mark of experience, the landscape around Lake George remains a wilderness because it shows no trace of rivalries and intrigues. These became the history of her suitors, but not hers. "Forts were erected at the different points that commanded the facilities of the route, and were taken and retaken, razed and rebuilt, as victory alighted on the hostile banners" (Cooper, 13). Perhaps her innocence, her wildness, allowed her to resist their efforts to brand her.[28] In any case, the traces of successive inscriptions would have been problematic for Cooper, if he hoped to convince us that the wilderness was pure and virginal. The Father may be willing to share his virgin child with a worthy husband, so that they might be fruitful and multiply. But her chastity and the transparency of her language cannot survive the marriage.

With far less show of guilt or nostalgia, Sarmiento performs a similar *ninguneo,* the "nobody-ing" of a threatening somebody.[29] Calling the Indians and the mestizo gauchos "American Bedouins" in *Facundo* (Sarmiento, 14; 10)[30] is enough to eliminate them from history, since "there can be no progress without permanent possession of the soil, or without cities" (Sarmiento, 18; 15). This would be embarrassing enough for today's readers if nomadism really canceled "conjugal" rights to the land. After all, the Old Testament promised land to the patriarchs and the prophets, so dear to the Puritan settlers, and so inspiring to Sarmiento (Sarmiento, 8; 15). Their nomadic life was the only spiritual safeguard in a world of decadent settlements. But recent work shows that the North American Indians he gleefully saw exterminated were not invariably nomadic. In fact, the Algonkin word for the land area known now by the pristine name of "Virginia" meant "densely populated." Algonkins typically lived in towns, to which the English settlers would flee periodically when their own resources failed them.[31] The obviously winning suitors are the Europeans, the ones who know how to write on smooth surfaces. Sarmiento does not mince words, because he casts himself here as none other than Mr. Right, writing an epic of (pro)creation; and he can attribute no less to his putative model, Cooper.

Step three in Sarmiento's roundabout rhetorical trajectory is, then, to close up the distance between imported models and local manufacture. His Cooper evidently supported the extreme racist position that backed Sarmiento against some critics at home.[32] If he had paused to consider that Cooper's struggle for the land probably had as much to do with his own rearguard defense of "feudal" rights in New York State (besieged by the anti-rent legislation of the democratizing "masses") as with

Monroe's Indian removal policy formulated in 1824, Sarmiento might have admired him even more.[33] It was as easy for the Argentine as for the New Yorker to conflate the "anarchic" propertyless classes with "savages." Unfortunately for Cooper, the "masses" were winning some ground, while the more obliging Indians continued to lose it. Jane Tompkins underlines how typical Cooper's guilt-ridden celebration of that loss was in those years. "Between the War of 1812 and the Civil War, Americans wrote seventy-three novels dealing with Indian-white relations. . . . With few exceptions, the white hero and heroine marry at the end, the bad . . . Indians are killed, and the good Indian either dies, or dies out."[34] These blood-purging novels lament the sacrifice, as Sarmiento apparently laments it in the second chapter of *Facundo,* but not so loudly that readers could miss the barely muffled gasp of relief.

Sarmiento's Cooper is uncannily close to a marxist Cooper, like the one Lukács remembers through Gorky, one who bids a mournful but necessary farewell to the primitive world that capitalism replaces.[35] Neither Lukács nor Sarmiento could afford to worry themselves over Cooper's possibly ambivalent position between classical, clearly defined, signs and romantic evolutionism.[36] Sarmiento "knew" that Cooper was a modern man dedicated to progress and change. And he also "knew" that progress depended on keeping the signs clear; it depended on distinguishing Indian from white and male from female, so that in the battle for America the best man would win. His Cooper was not only tidying up the sloppy signs that exceeded ideal categories. He was also setting the American record straight by clearing up the space that previous settlers had scribbled on, before the ideal English writers appeared. So, unlike the average North American reader, and unlike the Latin American novelists who would follow, Sarmiento doesn't allow sentimentality to distract him. He assures us that genocide is the necessary condition for progress; and he affirms that this is the deepest and the most significant message of Cooper's novels.

And right after he establishes Cooper as the model for literary and military exploits that Argentina would do well to imitate, Sarmiento makes his final, fourth, move in his magisterially circular logic. He boldly questions the master's own originality by noting that Cooper's "descriptions of practices and customs . . . seem plagiarized from the Pampa." Notice that he says "plagiarized," not inspired, or suggested, or even copied. What could Sarmiento possibly have meant with that word? Is he simply telling us that the North American experience is notably similar to that of South America? If that were the case, then why not point out the relationship from the other direction and say that the South shows similarities with the North? This would maintain the chronological (and ontological) order between Cooper's text and Sarmiento's commentary, between center and periphery. In other words, why not say that the pampa seems like a copy of the prairie? After all, it is rather obvious from the very fact of his references to Cooper, not to mention Sarmiento's national catching-up projects, that the United States provided the model for Argentina and not the other way around. Of course his comment could pass for an offhand or ironic way of emphasizing the similarities and thus establishing the possibility that Argentina could develop just like the United States did. It might pass for levity, perhaps, if it were not for the nature of the details from Cooper's novels that Sarmiento finds so appropriate(able) and that immediately precede the remark about plagiarism. Those details, which I mentioned as the measure of Sarmiento's admiration for Cooper and which we should consider now, represent some significantly predictable scenes for the Argentine reader:

> Cuando leía en *El último de los Mohicanos,* de Cooper, que Ojo de Halcón y Uncas habían perdido el rastro de los Mingos en un arroyo, dije: "Van a tapar el arroyo." Cuando en *La Pradera,* el Trampero mantiene la incertidumbre y la agonía mientras el fuego los amenaza, un argentino habría aconsejado lo mismo que el Trampero sugiere al fin, que es limpiar un lugar para guarecerse, e incendiar a su vez, para poderse retirar del fuego que invade sobre las cenizas del que se ha encendido. . . . Cuando los fugitivos de *La Pradera* encuentran un río y Cooper describe la misteriosa operación del Pawnie con el cuero del búfalo que recoge, "va a hacer la *pelota,* me dije a mi mismo: lástima es que no haya una mujer que la conduzca," que entre nosotros son las mujeres las que cruzan los ríos con la *pelota* tomada con los dientes por un lazo. El procedimiento para asar una cabeza de búfalo en el desierto es el

mismo que nosotros usamos para *batear* una cabeza de vaca o un lomo de ternera. En fin, otros mil accidentes que omito prueban la verdad de que modificaciones análogas del suelo traen análogas costumbres, recursos y expedientes. No es otra la razón de hallar en Fenimore Cooper descripciones de usos y costumbres que parecen plagiadas de la pampa.

[When I came to the passage in Cooper's *The Last of the Mohicans*, where Hawkeye and Uncas lose the trail of the Mingos in a brook, I said to myself: "They will dam up the brook"; when the trapper in *The Prairie* waits in irresolute anxiety while the fire is threatening him and his companions, an Argentine would have recommended the same plan which the trapper finally proposes,—that of clearing a space for immediate protection, and setting a new fire, so as to be able to retire upon the ground over which it had passed beyond the reach of the approaching flames. . . . When the fugitives in *The Prairie* arrive at a river, and Cooper describes the mysterious way in which the Pawnee gathers together the buffalo's hide, "he is making a *pelota*," said I to myself, "it is a pity there is no woman to tow it," for among us it is the women who tow *pelotas* across rivers with lassos held between their teeth. The way in which a buffalo's head is roasted in the desert is the same which we use for cooking a cow's head or a loin of veal. I omit many other facts which prove the truth that analogies in the soil bring with them analogous customs, resources, and expedients. This explains our finding in Cooper's works accounts of practices and customs which seem plagiarized from the pampa; . . .] (Sarmiento, 25–26; 26)

Sarmiento can tell, before Cooper informs him, how the most characteristically American characters will (or in the case of the Pawnees, should) behave. And this sustained display of foreknowledge has a peculiar effect. It suggests that the real Cooper was Sarmiento himself, especially if the redundancy of publishing what the Argentine public already knew could have occurred to him. Sarmiento practically boasts of having anticipated many of Cooper's pages before he read them. And one can just imagine how he read, almost preparing textual ambushes and traps for poor Cooper, to see if the revered American author could get out of his own tight spots with the right American solutions.

Perhaps already sensitive to his reputation as an inveterate braggart, Sarmiento slyly evades any renewed imputations of arrogance by removing himself from the comparison with Cooper. Sarmiento was not, he implies, competing with or, much less, improving on Cooper. Cooper's copying was not of Sarmiento at all, but of the pampa, since the plagiarism that he attributes to Cooper is not of a particular text, or even of the pampa's foremost interpreter: Sarmiento himself. Cooper's greatness is having deliberately imitated the Land, God's creation, the divine text that the American says he respects. And Sarmiento's attribution of a divine inspiration for Cooper's plagiarism is even more crafty than the calculated modesty of staying out of the comparison. It safeguards the model's value as an American artist. If Cooper, plagiarist that he was, were not also valuable as the honorably mimetic portrait-maker of American reality, he would be no good to Sarmiento as a point of departure or as a mentor.

Sarmiento's doubletake here is to reduce the stature of his model and to keep him as a model at the same time. It responds to a characteristic double-bind for some national authors in Latin America; that is, a certain reticence to share authority, even with the models who bestow it on their disciples and who, therefore, must be respected as legitimate. In Sarmiento's exemplary case, Cooper is as much an opportunity to improve on the model as to improve himself. If it were not for Cooper's success, and for the success of the country he helped to found, what foundation would Sarmiento have for writing America? And if Sarmiento let himself become a simple copy of Cooper, or if the pampa were an imitation of the prairie, where could his own authority come from, and where the very sovereignty of his country? The military strategist in Sarmiento surely understood that the best defense is sometimes an offensive move. So, in a tactic designed to free himself and his country from the ignominious charge of being mere copies (which he was more than willing to acknowledge in his arguments for modernization in this same book), Sarmiento fires the first shot at Cooper. Of course, he aims to do very little damage, because without his opponent as counterpart, without the mirror that would reflect back a legitimate American name, Sarmiento could not have hoped to make a name for himself.

What does he hope to accomplish, then, by sowing a seed of doubt about the North American model's originality, suggesting that it might be the copy of his own imitation of Argentina? He hopes, I am suggesting, to harvest an irrefutable originality that is well rooted in a stable landscape of precursors. And Sarmiento's desire for unquestionable authority is so great that instead of simply cannibalizing Cooper's text as a subtext, as a pretext of his own work (a consumption that would make conspicuous the model's priority), Sarmiento prefers to toy with it, as if time and linearity were illusory, and as if a reader could be the greatest authority of someone else's text.

This displacement or metaleptic inversion between text and commentary, and also between master and disciple, will repeat itself in *Recuerdos de provincia* (1850), where at one revealing point Sarmiento makes the paradigmatically circular and self-serving assertion that "to my progeny I am my own successor."[37] In general, the book's self-reflexive logic, meaning here that it is twisted always to reflect well on its author, needs to propose a revaluation of plagiarism. It does this quite explicitly through mention of Deacon Funes, about whom Sarmiento writes, "he has been burdened too long with the charge of plagiarism, which for me turns into something far from a reproach, but rather a sure sign of merit,"[38] the merit of erudition and good taste. This indulgence bordering on enthusiasm for plagiarists frees Sarmiento from having any qualms about plagiarizing his own biography from Benjamin Franklin's. "No other book has done me as much good as this one." "I felt I was Franklin"—he says, immediately to ask himself rhetorically and a bit defensively, "and why not? I was very poor, just like he was, a diligent student like he was." That is, a veritable "Franklincito" before discovering his own person in somebody else's book. A little later he adds, "prodding myself on and following his footsteps, I could one day become as accomplished . . . and make a name for myself in American literature and politics."[39] Sarmiento's staged adulation here is probably meant to dramatize his endorsement of Franklin's book for Argentine school boys. In general, Sarmiento instructs us in one of the appendices—which lists some of his publications and promises others—that "Biography is the most original kind of book that South America can produce in our times, and the best material we can offer history." It is the genre, according to him, to which *Facundo* belongs, and also the *Provincial Memoirs* we are reading, both being personal stories about exemplary persons.

But Sarmiento's celebration of Franklin's achievements may also be providing a measure for the celebrant's even greater success. He must already have felt the satisfaction of outdoing Franklin, both in literary accomplishments and in the brilliant political career that these very *Recuerdos* helped to assure. While he was writing them, as a kind of narrative curriculum vitae or political self-portrait,[40] he was also circulating a photographic portrait with the caption, "Sarmiento, future president of Argentina."[41] If his cautiously respectful diminution of Franklin seems a daring appropriation, Sarmiento had anticipated it in his lines about Cooper; and he had also gone arguably further in an earlier chapter of the *Recuerdos*. It is the one dedicated to Domingo de Oro as the "model and archetype of the future Argentine."[42] But this future model is past history for prophetic Sarmiento who concludes on the next page, "De Oro's life is proof of the way I understood his rare eloquence." How do we disentangle the subject from his representation here? How do we know where priority resides? In the prophecy, in the proof?

This tactical inversion will already be familiar to us through Pierre Menard's work. If it seems a bit anachronistic to misread Sarmiento via Borges, it is at least a strategy that both teach us. It would be almost perverse to miss reading Sarmiento as Cooper's and Franklin's and Oro's Menard. If we had attempted respectfully to stabilize some of his sources as Cooper's novels, Franklin's biography, and Oro's life we would have been mistaking "thinking, analyzing, inventing" as discrete activities. And if we care to be even more anachronistic, we could mention that Jean Baudrillard makes a similar observation about production in the "postmodern" world, an observation that should have little relevance for a nineteenth-century writer who found that his country was already behind the times. Alleging that Western culture used to be or to feel itself more solidly grounded, Baudrillard complains that all we can produce today are simulacra, copies of models that are themselves inauthentic. Even what we call reality is nothing more than a series of fictitious constructions, neither more nor less genuine than their "re-presentations."[43]

Baudrillard begins his meditation with a gesture that has evidently become stylish in French philosophy. He begins with a Borgesian parable, the one about the cartographers who are so determined to make a scientifically exact representation of reality that they produce a map as big as the empire. He starts with Borges in order promptly to discard the model, condescendingly charging that Borges's irony depends on a naive notion of the Real, on an empire that precedes the map.[44] Baudrillard thus reads without mentioning Borges's proverbial circularity, the textual whirlwind that blows away any pretense of stable originality and that is so notorious among his French fans. Whether or not this reading does justice to Borges's thought, one must agree that Baudrillard's is a strategic reading (in the same way that Sarmiento strategically misreads Cooper). It would be rather out of character for the theorist of simulation and of the failure of referentiality to refer respectfully to the authority who gave him the base for theorizing. Baudrillard evidently opted for intellectual orphanhood, perhaps in order to dramatize his own theme: the impossibility of lineage and of the relationship between origin and following. If everything is (and all of us are) inauthentic, it would be absurd to follow in anyone's footsteps.

But it was not absurd for Sarmiento who preferred a different option. I say option, because I imagine in my necessarily Menardian reading that he had several to choose from. One was to resign himself to renouncing originality, with the same ironic and haughty modesty that Baudrillard and Borges no doubt affected. Another was to assume absolute, practically divine, originality, as Sarmiento does in *Mi defensa* (1843) and, by an apparent rhetorical slip, as he does once in *Recuerdos*. "When I had finished this work [a book on pedagogy], I could say in my rejoicing that I had produced something worthy: *et vidi quod esset bonum*. Then I applauded myself."[45] A third option was what I am calling the boomerang effect: to attribute originality and the authority it implies to someone else, so that they may be snatched out of the model's hands in a lightning game of "now you see it, now you don't." If the strategy Sarmiento followed with Cooper is characteristic, and it seems to be, given the subsequent uses he made of Funes, Franklin, and Oro among others, he clearly preferred this last choice. He proposes models, cuts them down to manageable size, and glories in their presumed (or explicit) approval, even when they have doubtful credentials. The chapter on de Oro, for example, criticizes the model's misdirected shrewdness that ends up clearing the political obstacles to Rosas's victory. Yet the chapter ends by quoting in its entirety a letter of recommendation that Oro had sent the author.

Sarmiento distances himself from his models only enough to outdistance them, not to dismiss either them or their offer of legitimacy. The ambiguity is really ingenious here for someone who may have "known" history to be a fiction, a simulacrum. If he did, it was always as an opportune fiction for the writer who dared to invent it. Sarmiento succeeds in attributing to himself the authority and the privilege of a foundational thinker. At the same time his claim to legitimacy is based on implied approval by an established origin, established just to make sure, by the very fact that he considers it a model. *Facundo,* after all, had something to do with Cooper's exemplary status among Latin Americans who admired, imitated, and adopted him as the first among (North) American narrators.

PIERRE MENARD'S COOPERS

Menardian readers that they were, though, Latin American novelists followed neither the foreign model nor the Argentine purveyor too closely, unless of course, following Sarmiento means learning a Whitmanian step that strays enough to find comparably opportune uses for Cooper. They also learned (and further bequeathed) the disciple's backstep, putting model behind copy: "You're like the Romantic writers," Marito incautiously remarked to their scriptwriting heir in *Aunt Julia.* "In point of fact, *they're* like *me.* . . . I've never plagiarized anybody."[46] These romantics were national authors, in the same multivalent sense that describes Sarmiento. They will occupy us in the following chapters, so that short mentions may suffice here as we consider the possible repercussions of Sarmiento's praise for Cooper. As novelists they were generally bound to challenge Sarmiento's assumptions about the didactic and socially constructive potential of exemplary single lives.[47] Writing novels was already a statement about the collective, or coupling, nature of nation-building. If one of the main goals of Argentina's national program was to populate the deserted pampa, if for the modernizing bourgeois culture that South America's elites were trying to adopt sexual desire had indeed become what Foucalt characterized as "the explanation for everything," heroic biographies would hardly be (re)productive enough.[48] Typically, the novelists presumed to "correct" Cooper, or at least to read him correctly. Most of them knew, for instance, that the author of *The Last of the Mohicans* really preferred, or should have preferred, Cora as America's archetypal mother. Rather than keep America racially pure, a Latin-Americanized and romantic Cooper was warning his compatriots that their country's hope for peace and progress should not be sacrificed to an ideal of purity as anachronistic and self-destructive as military heroism. National consolidation needed the reconciliation of differences, not their exclusion. The hegemonic project of the dominant class had to win the support of other interests for a (usually) liberal national project that would benefit them all, just as the hero of romance won the heroine through love and practical concern for her well-being. A white elite, often in the large port cities, had to convince everyone, from landholders and miners to indigenous, black, and mulatto masses, that liberal leadership would bridge traditionally antagonistic races and regions in a new prosperity.

In political practice, Argentines were evidently far less jealous husbands than was Cooper. In the introductory chapter, we saw that prudent Juan Bautista Alberdi recognized his own national shortcomings and made a virtue of the necessity to share his patrimony with foreigners. (To import Anglo-Saxon studs in order to develop a superior and manageable breed, one might say in the cattle-breeding logic that prevailed.) Sexual love would do the rest, once Argentina's army of desirable women conquered the white would-be conquerors. But Cooper, convinced of his own superiority, had seen no advantage to amalgamation. After all, he *is* the Anglo-Saxon Prince Charming whom the swarthier Argentines want.

Is it possible that the erotic or fairy-tale rhetoric that I am attributing to the political theorist Alberdi comes from contemporary Latin American novels rather than from his own juridical discourse? Is it also possible that I have been reading Sarmiento's Cooper as an advocate for enlightened inscription, or the civilizing kiss, through this same literary tangle of romance and nation-building? Perhaps Sarmiento was insensible to the love story between the land and the men who would make her prosper. The drama of seduction may be superfluous to a man accustomed to commanding. If I am caught in a rhetorical jumble, it owes as much to a tradition of Latin American writing as to my belated reading. Sarmiento became the pretext for so many other Pierre Menards in Latin America. Nevertheless, to defend this possibly misplaced "romantic" reading of Sarmiento, I should point out the inevitable resonance of *romance* for today's reader. Referring to Cooper as a *romancista*, might simply have been a gallicism for "novelist"; and Mrs. Mann duely translates it both as "romancer" and "novelist" (Mann, 24). The difference between these terms is an Anglo-American, not a Romance language, tradition.[49] But when Sarmiento uses *romance* in a sarcastic remark about Facundo's abuse of his girlfriend ("No es éste un lindo romance?" [Isn't this a fine story / romance?]) (Sarmiento, 126), the word acquires the precocious quality of love story, even though that meaning probably came a century later, perhaps from Hollywood. Through a conscious anachronism, then, I find myself reading Sarmiento's epithet as acknowledging the erotic core in Cooper's work.

The national novelists certainly read it as erotic. Their Cooper allegorized Sarmiento's pseudo-scientific rhetoric about civilization and barbarism, white settlers tackling the pampa, into a story of requited love. Therefore, the ideal national marriages were often projected in romances between whites and Indians (the title characters of José de Alencar's Brazilian *O Guaraní* [1857] and *Iracema* [1865], are examples), or mestizas inspired no doubt from Chateaubriand's *Atala* (such as Manuel de Jesús Galván's Doña Mencía in *Enriquillo* [Dominican Republic, 1882] and Marisela in *Doña Bárbara* [Venezuela, 1929] by Rómulo Gallegos). The ideal of *mestizaje,* so pejoratively rendered in English as miscegenation, was based in the reality of mixed races to which different virtues and failings were ascribed, and which had to amalgamate in some countries if anything like national unity was to be produced. Unity, in positivist rhetoric, was not so much a political or economic concept as it was biological. José Vasconcelos gave probably the most famous and utopian formulation in *Raza cósmica* (1925), written after the Mexican Revolution when Indian masses forced themselves into any consideration of nationalism and progress. But as early as Simón Bolívar's famous discourse at Angostura, Latin Americans have at least rhetorically assumed a racially mixed identity. "It is impossible to correctly determine," said the Liberator, "to which human family we belong. . . . Born all of the same mother, our fathers [are] of different origins and blood."[50]

Only an atypical novel like Jorge Isaacs's *María* (Colombia, 1867), his swan song for the slavocracy, could afford to revive Cooper-like pessimism about mestizaje. Like double-crossed Cora, the originally Jewish María was born in the West Indies (Jamaica) and, though perfectly innocent and admirable, she too bears a blemish of racial difference. It is a Jewish stain and serves as a sign for the more troubling differences between blacks and whites. As in *Enriquillo* and in *O Guaraní,* the real threat that darkens a plantation society becomes unspeakable to Isaacs. Instead, he seems to be saying that no amalgamation, however innocent and sincere, can be productive in the aristocratic society he yearns for. Although more programmatic, perhaps, Uruguay's *Tabaré* (1888), by Juan Zorrilla de San Martín, is atypical too for its sacrifice of racial difference in the person of the mestizo hero. The blue-eyed Indian is as out of place in either white or native society as was Cooper's tragic culturally mestiza Ruth, the captive of *The Wept of Wish-Ton-Wish* (1829). More Latin American writers by far, however, tended to be programmatic in a more synthetic way. When the lovers in romance are both white, they probably come from mutually hostile areas, as in José Mármol's *Amalia* (1851), where the hero is a Buenos Aires boy and his heroine a childless young widow from provincial Tucumán. Far from being put off by his heroine's past, as an unassimilated Cooper might have been, Mármol admitted that Argentina had an unproductive history that national romance would cure. And Alberto Blest Gana's *Martín Rivas* (1862) joins the son of a bankrupted mining entrepreneur in the north of Chile to the daughter of the Santiago usurer who had acquired the mine. The hero finally convinces Santiago's bankers that getting together would be mutually satisfying, at the same time that Chile's elite sectors were making political and financial deals. Where racial and regional differences keep lovers apart, as in Cuba's abolitionist novels, *Francisco* (1839) by Anselmo Suárez y Romero, *Cecilia Valdés* (1839; 1882) by Cirilo Villaverde, and *Sab* (1841) by Gertrudis Gómez de Avellaneda, the blame for personal and national tragedy falls on archaic and un-American habits of social ordering. The implied or explicit program for change saves these novels from the ruthlessness of Sarmiento's Cooper and from the pessimism of Isaacs's tragedy. This is not to say that racism and economic partiality ceased to exist among the novelists. To see prejudice at work, one has only to observe that Indian and mestiza lovers appear in books like *O Guaraní* and *Enriquillo* so that blacks can disappear, or that *Amalia*'s Tucumán remains a background producer for the trade decisions made in Buenos Aires. Hegemony, after all, is not an egalitarian project but one that legitimates the leadership of one social sector by winning the consent of others. Romance had, therefore, to give a loving cast to national unity, not necessarily to equalize the lovers.

The Latin Americans must have been relieved to see that Cora Munro was redeemed at home after the defensive nervousness about gender and race coding relaxes; that is, after the man's work is done and the West is won. She comes back to be celebrated in the late and "decadent" period of dime novels. Cooper himself paved the way by freeing at least one legitimate heroine, Ellen Wade in *The Prairie* (1827), from the noble birth that confers inhuman paralysis on his women,[51] and especially in "self-reliant" Mabel Dunham of *The Pathfinder* (1840). In fact, Cooper's dime-novel-writing Menards of the North became fond of celebrating half-breed heroines and even of displacing the traditional genteel heroes with the savage women protagonists. The great difference from South America is that the mass production of Western novels, starting with Beadles's literary industry in 1858, was less an enterprise to establish an American consciousness and national project than to mine that earlier effort in order to supply the growing market for sensationalism. The Amazon cum heroine of the end of the century, according to Henry Nash Smith, is one exemplary innovation that marks the decay of dime-Westerns that learned to pander to an American public hungry for ever more gratuitous adventure.[52] But if we read more sympathetically, these ungenteel heroines encode the return of the repressed Cora. Cooper may have been compelled to doom her because she was too able and too full of surprises for the benighted hero's taste. Her self-motivation complicated his rights to motivate her and, by extension, to manipulate the land. But for his Menards to the South, Cooper may also have preferred her. In that case, his novel is a tragedy, along the lines of Isaacs's *María* and Cuba's heart-rending antislavery novels. To prove the tradition's profound preference for Cora they could point to her domestic line of descendants: the straight-shooting, hard-drinking, Calamity Janes who get their men one way or another.

I am suggesting, perhaps provocatively, that gender-crossing is as endemic to foundational romances in Latin America as are racial and regional crossings. Even in a later, defensive, "populist" romance such as *Doña Bárbara,* written when men were men and women women, again, the apparently ideal hero has a paradoxical lesson to learn from women. He has to fall helplessly in love with the right one in order to maintain his masterly control.

These romancers understood why Cooper had to make impressionable Heyward, rather than the ideally male Hawk-eye, a founding father. They also felt the tragedy of sacrificing as graceful and sensitive a man as Uncas, whom Alencar revives to be the hero of *O Guaraní.* Some readers, including Sarmiento, may have thought that Cooper's ideal America was based on precise gender and racial categories, but Latin American romancers recognized the unproductive distance that ideal opposites have to maintain in order to stay pure. If a lover at all, Hawk-eye is in love with the equally pure wilderness, which is as sublimely simple as Alice, or with impassive Chingachgook, D. H. Lawrence's choice. In fact, their mutual affection is most convincing if we consider the two men bound together through their equal respect, rather than erotic love, for nature. Their very chaste version of homosocial desire[53] takes the form of a ménage à trois where nobody really violates anybody else. Nobody makes children either. This categorical purity is one reason why Natty must shun Judith Hutter in *The Deerslayer* (1841). What other readers have called his chastity is also his pride in being a "man without a cross," as free of feminized, domestic inclinations as he is of Indian blood. North American readers may be concerned with what appears to be the unresolved dual allegiance to civilization and to barbarism that plays itself out through Hawk-eye's contradictions. He of course betrays Chingachgook by acting as scout for the other men, those who "civilize" the wilderness, marry virgins, and turn them into mothers. But the Cooper whom Latin American romancers read (into) calmly kissed Hawk-eye's ideal and obsolete masculinity good-bye, just as they had turned their backs, during this peaceful moment, on heroic Bolívar and San Martín.

Their impressive chain of reading and writing Cooper surely began from a particular text. But after Sarmiento's playful remark about plagiarism, after noting that it is he who makes Cooper a landmark in South American literature, we should wonder whose text is originary. Is it Cooper's, or is it Sarmiento's appropriation? Is it the father who makes the son, or is it thanks to the son that the father recognizes himself as such? With this simile, I want to suggest the Oedipal character of this inversion between model and commentator, aligning it therefore with a strategy that Beatriz Sarlo and Carlos Altamirano have identified so convincingly in *Recuerdos de provincia*. I am referring to Sarmiento's repeated denial of his paternal lineage and of his father's personal importance. The son seems to have engendered himself upon the body and the genealogy of his mother, whose identity is sometimes and purposefully confused with that of the motherland. The superfluous father is infantilized, or feminized, which amounts to the same thing, so that Sarmiento can replace him in the familial text.[54]

But despite a possible parallel between his father and Cooper (or any other model in *Recuerdos*) Sarmiento's rivalry with adoptive mentors allowed for something different from denial, something that must have been an inspiration for other national authors. It allowed him to subordinate the master, gently and without eliminating him, so as not to lose the legitimacy of the master's approval that Sarmiento attributes to himself. This difference (which Tulio Halperín Donghi also suggested when he contrasted the self-creation of *Mi defensa* with the respect for lineage in *Recuerdos*)[55] suggests a pattern for the strategy that I have been trailing here. It may be parallel to parricide, but it is cunningly restrained. I mean Sarmiento's practice of making plagiarism count for the most efficient originality by inverting the priority between model and revision.

Happily for authorized imitators like Sarmiento, and for their Menardian readers, imitation often surpasses the model, even as it constitutes the model as such. It is, to sum up, doubly foundational: first by establishing the origin, and second by improving on it. And if this displacement tends to cast doubt on all pretension of originality, the liberating side of doubt for latecomers to writing and to history is that it leaves unresolved the question of priority between master and pupil. Sarmiento turns out to be a proto-Borgesian priest who unites the two with a Moebius ring for which inside and outside, origin and trajectory, are only illusions of perspective. After this marriage, it would be rather mean-spirited to remind Cooper of his distance from Argentina, as mean-spirited as reminding Sarmiento of his debts as a disciple.

3

AMALIA: VALOR AT
HEART AND HOME

"On the night of the 4th of May, 1840, at half-past ten o'clock, a party of six men crossed the inner courtyard of a small house on the Calle Belgrano, in the city of Buenos Aires" (Mármol, 11; 1).[1] Readers of José Mármol's *Amalia* (1851, serialized in Montevideo's *La Semana*) may remember this ominous first sentence. The date makes it ominous, marking Rosas's stepped-up terror against the traditional elite, and so does the conspiratorial lateness of the hour. Five of the six men are, in fact, conspiring to join the resistance in Montevideo. The sixth, their guide, turns out to be an infiltrator who delivers them to the *Mazorca*, Rosas's death squad. This betrayal, and the rest of Mármol's rambling novel about the terror and the frustrated campaigns against it, practically require readers to venture a political interpretation that amounts to partisanship. For many, *Amalia* is a Manichean tract that was duly suspended in 1852 from a second printing in the columns of *El Paraná* during the post-Rosas climate of "neither winners nor losers";[2] it was both a long pamphlet against Federalism, which advocated a loose association of semi-autonomous provinces, and a paean to the Unitarian ideal of centralized rule under the intellectual and commercial elite of Buenos Aires.[3] The city had a taste of Unitarian rule under Bernardino Rivadavia, the utopian thinker who was elected president of the United Provinces in 1826. He provided some respite in Argentina's civil wars (the "decade of anarchy" 1820–1830) and a promise of relief from colonial patriarchy in public and private spheres.[4] But Rivadavia's victory was illusory in a country where the interior regions resented their subordination to the center. His resignation in 1827 brought chaos back, and Argentines wanted nothing so

much as a strong leader. By 1829 they got him when Juan Manuel de Rosas, a rancher from the Province of Buenos Aires and
the "Restorer of Law," was elected governor of the province.
In 1835 he was invested with almost absolute power, which by
1840 he exercised remorselessly, until his fall in 1852.

But another political interpretation of that first sentence of
Amalia becomes possible if we notice that beyond the obvious
threat announced by the precise timing, danger lurks in the
location. I am not referring merely to the contrast between
civilized interior space that the conspirators leave and the savage streets where all but one is killed, although David Viñas is
quite right to note an ideological coding throughout the novel
that pits an enlightened private sphere against barbarous public
life.[5] To underline his point we could add that, at some level,
the Unitarians understood their mission as "domesticating" the
wild outdoors, and at another the exiles who managed to escape
also wanted to come home, to be domestic.

What interests me here is the particular street that Mármol
chose as the danger zone, la Calle Belgrano. Once we learn that
the foiled emigré whom the text has singled out for admiration
is also named Belgrano, we may suspect an additional threat to
Unitarian hegemony. It is as serious as the Federalist reaction:
the threat of static and self-contained centering that literally has
no future. This "youth with the sword," whom we have been
admiring as much for his phallic epithet as for the melancholy
dark eyes set off by his handsome pale face (Mármol, 12), turns
out to be a nephew of Manuel Belgrano (Mármol, 26; 22),
the Unitarians' foremost hero of Independence and the namesake of the street. The illustrious surname repeated as young
Eduardo stands in the name and the place of his forefather
seems to redound to the glory of the Unitarian cause. But there
is more than a hint of incestuous habit or sterility in this closed
circuit. What possible room is there for history or any narrative
if Belgrano the man could remain on Belgrano the street in an
inherited noble and military pose? In what follows, Rosas's men
untie the tangle of name and place like a Gordian knot. The
violence is lamentable, but it is also Mármol's opportunity to
narrate, to dislodge Belgrano from the narrowly Unitarian
struggle and enlist him for a more flexible project.

Eduardo's battle against the *mazorqueros* is practically super-human: they circling him with butchers' knives aimed at his head like some menacing coalition of barbarians converging on a civilized center, and he opening breaches in their alliance while heading for town. Finally faint as a result of blood lost from a thigh wound, Belgrano is literally about to lose his head when suddenly the last assassin falls, joining the circle of dead Federalists with Eduardo surviving at their center. The savior in this miniature rehearsal of the civil wars is his best friend, Daniel Bello. He has stolen behind the assailant and dealt him a mute blow with a mysterious weapon. He then spirits Eduardo home, not his own or his friend's, but off to a home in a distant suburb where Daniel's widowed cousin Amalia lives. That is, away from the center where Belgrano's redundant and suicidal habits were leading him, toward a peripheral haven. As the only survivor of the attack, Eduardo will be hunted down by the police. And they will find him, Daniel warns, if Eduardo refuses to exchange his social meaning based on (aristocratic) origins for a new meaning based on domesticity. Going home, it appears with growing clarity, is not a return at all but finding where the woman is.

Much later, Bello will reveal his weapon, calling it a *casse-tete*, which translates in Spanish as *rompecabezas*, literally a head-breaker but also a puzzle and perhaps a pun on its threat of permanent disaggregation. The detail is important, because the neologism evidently associates Bello with the Francophile opposition to Rosas. This admiration for France was not only typical for young intellectuals, modeling themselves after French romantics; it was also a response to France's punitive blockade of Buenos Aires (while Rosas continued to traffic with England to the point of stifling home industry)[6] and to her promises of support for the resistance. Daniel's Francophilia is detailed in long scenes of a clandestine trip to Montevideo where our hero tries to negotiate alliances among exiled leaders and French sympathizers, scenes that recreate Juan Bautista Alberdi's frustrating negotiations.[7] But the weapon itself, with its wicker (*mimbre*) handle connecting two ropes tipped by iron balls and covered by a fine net of soft leather, turns out to be uncannily familiar. I am not referring only to the visual

joke it produces when Amalia's curiosity about Daniel's hidden
tool finally makes him expose what looks like artificial genitals
(*miembro*):

> —¿Qué arma es ésa, Daniel, que usas tú y con la que has hecho a
> veces tanto daño?
> —Y tanto bien, podrías agregar, prima mía.
> —Cierto, cierto perdona; pero respóndeme; mira que he tenido
> esta curiosidad muchas veces.
> —Espera, déjame terminar este dulce.
> —No te dejo ir esta noche sin que me digas lo que quiero.
> —Casi estoy por ocultártelo entonces.
> —¡Cargoso!

> ["What is that weapon which you use, Daniel, and with which you
> have at times done so much harm?"
> "And so much good, you might add, cousin."
> "True, true, forgive me. But answer my question; it is one that I
> have often before desired to ask you."
> "Wait, let me finish this piece of candy first."
> "I shall not let you leave the house tonight until you tell me what
> I wish to know."
> "I am almost inclined to hide it from you, then."
> "Tease!"] (Mármol, 391; 274)

The joke, so characteristic of Mármol's flair for dialogue but
perhaps lost on generations of required readers,[8] is of course
prepared earlier on the same page, when Daniel hopes out loud
that Eduardo has given up his unwieldy sword for something
less troublesome, to which Eduardo condescends, "I do not use
mysterious weapons, sir." "That may be," Daniel retorts, "but
they are more effectual, and above all more comfortable."
  The familiarity I am referring to is also the structural and
strategic similarity between this new and improved phallus and
the gaucho's traditional lasso, or *bolas*. The device is a triple
rope tipped by three hard balls that wrap around the victim's
legs. Structurally Daniel's weapon displaces power from the
rigid center (that Eduardo still prefers) to a multiple periphery,
just as the bolas do, the difference between two balls and three
being one measure of the plurivalence achieved once phallocen-
trism gives in to dissemination. And strategically, Daniel's dis-

creet masculinity, borne close to the heart in his breast pocket (and turning upside down Freud's quip about the heart being at the genitals) is more potent than Eduardo's sword, much as the ensnaring bolas are. (They had, in fact, made the Unitarian cause hopeless after General Paz's horse was caught in the whirling ropes of Rosas's gaucho troops.)[9] The analogy is ambiguous to be sure. It may even leave the reader incredulous at the transgression of a French signifier, *casse-tete,* pointing to a "barbarous" signified. Nor do we easily imagine that elite ends (saving Eduardo) are served by popular means (gaucho equipment). But this lack of imagination, Alberdi was arguing, had more to do with a doctrinal narrowness he associated with Sarmiento than with the country's political economy. Gauchos, after all, should hardly be eliminated in a clean sweep of barbarism by civilization, since they were the rural workers who produced the nation's wealth and who kept its cities in business.[10] Nevertheless, more and more Argentine intellectuals after 1840 tormented themselves because "Americanism," the rallying cry for so many heroes of Independence and the bond that might have conciliated Centralists and Federalists, now appeared to be in stark contradiction to national "progress."[11]

By the time Bello exposes his intriguing instrument, we know that he is Mármol's sign for excess and transgression, a trace of Argentina's young intelligentsia that had tried to rise above (or maybe to step aside from) the paralyzing standoff between Unitarians and Federalists. The Generation of 1837, as they were known, galvanized around Esteban Echeverría, who had returned from Paris in 1830 with Hugo's blasting of convention and Saint-Simon's utopian prophesies still ringing in his ears. From their war of position against both traditional parties, these youths imagined Argentina as a community with no party but *la Patria,* no regime but the thirty years of Independence. "From the heights of these supreme facts, we know not what Unitarians and Federalists are . . . , plebeians and gentlemen, old and young, capital and provinces . . . mean-spirited divisions that we see disappearing like smoke before the three great unities of the People, the Flag, and Argentine History."[12] Mostly children of Unitarian families, they wanted to recognize the Federalist other in themselves, hoping that they could produce a spark of reciprocity among the Federalists in power. Their elders, like Mármol's Eduardo, were skeptical that any good could come of this ignoble straddling. Yet it described the Unitarian posture as well, according to Bello's self-defence and self-implication; duplicity was endemic to a city that thought it should be a nation.[13] "Eduardo, I am a son of Buenos Aires, whose people are the most fundamentally inconsistent and mutable in all America; . . . that's why they chose despotism: for the perverse pleasure of being inconstant to liberty. And that's what you think too, Eduardo" (Mármol, 188).

The group was officially inaugurated in June of 1837, when it began to meet in Marcos Sastre's bookstore.[14] There members would read and discuss works by Cousin, Guizot, Lerminier, Quinet, Villemain, Saint-Simon, Leroux, Lamennais (whose *Paroles d'un croyant* read like a theology of liberation),[15] Mazzini, Tocqueville, among so many others.[16] It was at this literary salon that Echeverría presented drafts of what would become his *Dogma Socialista*, a selective compilation of French utopian socialism, which became the group's ideological platform.[17] Part of its practice, logically, was to interpolate the traditional antagonists. So the cultural arbiters of Rosas's government, Pedro de Angelis and Felipe Senillosa, were warmly invited to join the salon. They did so but soon left. And early in 1838 Rosas had the bookstore closed. His relative tolerance up to that point ended abruptly when he banned even the publication of "women's" journals such as Juan Bautista Alberdi's *La Moda*. The fashion magazine was correctly suspected of fronting for the unmanly Europeanized "fops"; it was a coy screen in both senses of hiding and showing,[18] a womanly voice as the men's public organ.[19] Alberdi didn't hesitate to describe himself as feminized, although the suggestion of homosexuality would have been an outrage.[20] The ban shocked him, because this youth from the province of Tucumán stubbornly believed in conciliation between the nation's intellectual center and the interior heartland. That is why his journal regularly published Federalist slogans and appeals to Rosas.[21] Once those failed, Alberdi was among the first to leave Buenos Aires. "If ever Echeverría's group dreamt of a conciliation in which it would become the *brain* for Rosas's formidable political *arm,* the dream was now abandoned."[22]

The members now formed as the clandestine "Asociación de Mayo"; since they couldn't win Rosas over to them, they would conspire to win power over him.[23] And they continued to leave one by one as the terror mounted. They went to Montevideo, Santiago de Chile, La Paz. One particular group, "the five-man club," whose contacts with the army included the officer who denounced them, bears more than a coincidental relationship to the party of would-be emigrés at the beginning of Mármol's novel.[24] In exile, the "proscripts" published newspapers and generally agitated politically. This time it was not for rapproachment but for Rosas's defeat.

Only Echeverría stayed as long as possible, before he finally fled to Montevideo, penniless and reduced to selling his books. But before he went very far, he stayed for a long while at "Los Talas," the ranch outside of Buenos Aires that he shared with his brother. (In a similar move, Daniel Bello removes Amalia and her ward to "the solitary house" toward the end of the book.) "Emigrating," Echeverría would say, "is making yourself useless to your country."[25] Like him, Mármol's heroic homebody knows that the struggle is within, inside the self/other and inside the city that practically was the country. Bello, like so many Argentines he represents, kept waiting for something to happen in Buenos Aires; no one could understand why General Lavalle's liberating army never reached home. Although alliances with the provinces were important for the struggle and ultimately for national consolidation after Rosas, Lavalle's provincial campaigns merely stretched the resistance too thin and kept missing the mark. Rosas and his few trusted supporters were in the capital.

But Mármol (1818–1871) himself had to leave in 1840, after spending some months in the dictator's dungeon. He was well received by the exiles already in Montevideo, although Mármol was too young to be an original member of the Asociación de Mayo. By then, political flexibility with the regime was evidently impossible. Except for Alberdi and a very few others, any conciliation with Federalists seemed misguided. The Gen-

eration of 1837 had managed to hypostatize an ideological
middle road and then to recognize the illusion. That meant
giving up the Romantic promise that the popular, untutored
charm of "Americanism" could be the handmaid of progress.
The political loss was very real. It led to a renewed intransi-
gence among Argentina's intelligentsia, a stubbornness that
would later cause, among other things, General Mitre's refusal
to join other provinces in ratifying the 1853 Constitution
drafted by Alberdi. Buenos Aires would rebel against the provinces and win.

Of the original Generation of 1837 only Alberdi maintained
some balance through the terror and later on. Only he published scathing criticisms of entrenched, monolithic (not to say
unitary) postulations such as Sarmiento's *Facundo* (1845), where
the terms *civilization* and *barbarism* achieved their unfortunately
paradigmatic clarity. It was Alberdi who kept Echeverría's early
principles of the *Dogma Socialista* alive enough to draft a practical proposal for the new constitution after Rosas's defeat. It
stipulated, among other things, that the political capital of the
country should not be in Buenos Aires, which was de facto the
economic center; this was to prevent a Unitarian tyranny that
well-meaning Federalists justly feared. To Alberdi's legislative
balancing act, Mármol would add a literary one, his mercurial
hero.

Hardly an orthodox Unitarian and certainly not a sincere
Federalist, Daniel Bello is an unstable mix, a lamb in wolf's
clothing, the gentleman who does not hesitate to show Federalist bravado. Sarmiento's *Recuerdos* had drawn a less duplicitous
but quite as exorbitant a figure in Domingo de Oro, the enlightened Federalist whose political target was the tyrant but
whose strategy backfired: forcing negotiations between Rosas
and his rivals only cleared the road to terror. His resemblance
to Bello is notable:

(S)alido de una de las familias más aristocráticas de San Juan, ha
manejado el lazo y las bolas, cargado el puñal favorito como el
primero de los gauchos. . . . Pero estas predilecciones gauchas en
él son un complemento, sin el cual el brillo de su palabra habría
perdido la mitad de su fascinación; el despejo adquirido por el roce
familiar con los hombres más eminentes de la época, . . . la

seguridad del juicio adquirido en una edad prematura, y las dotes que traía ya de la Naturaleza, toman aquel tinte romancesco que dan a la vida americana las peculiaridades de su suelo. . . . Oro ha dado el modelo y el tipo del futuro argentino, europeo hasta los últimos refinamientos de las bellas artes, americano hasta cabalgar el potro indómito; parisiense por el espíritu, pampa por la energía y los poderes físicos.

[Hailing from one of San Juan's most aristocratic families, he used to wield lasso and bolas, carrying his favorite dagger with the best of the gauchos. . . . But these rural preferences complemented his polished discourse, which otherwise would have lost half its charm. The easy manner acquired from associating with the most eminent men of the period, . . . the sure judgment so precociously his, along with Nature's generous endowments, take on in him the romantic hue that the peculiarities of American soil can give. . . . Oro presents the model and archetype of future Argentines: European down to the last refinements, and so American he can mount a wild horse; Parisian in spirit and Pampa in his sheer energy and physical capacities.][26]

Once terror grips the city, Bello can give the slip to police as long as he does, practically until the end of the book, thanks to his talent of course. But it is also thanks to the Federalist credentials of his adoring father, like the credentials of several historical Federalists whose sons—Rafael Corvalán, the Quiroga brothers, Alejandro Heredia, Vicente Fidel López—joined the conspiracy.[27]

Don Antonio Bello era un hombre de campo, en la acepción que tiene entre nosotros esa palabra, y al mismo tiempo hombre honrado y sincero. Sus opiniones eran, desde mucho antes que Rosas, opiniones de federal; y, por la Federación, había sido partidario de López primeramente, de Dorrego después, y últimamente de Rosas, sin que por esto él pudiese explicarse la razón de sus antiguas opiniones . . . sin embargo, tenía un amor más profundo que el de la Federación; y era el amor por su hijo. Su hijo era su orgullo, su ídolo y, desde niño empezó a prepararlo para la carrera de las letras, para hacerlo *dotor*, como decía el buen padre.

[Don Antonio Bello, himself a good Federalist, was at the same time honorable and sincere. Long before Rosas he had supported the Federation. . . . Nevertheless, he had a profounder affection than that which he entertained for the government—his love for his son. His son was his pride, his idol, whom from a boy he had trained for the profession of letters—to be a *dotor,* as the good man used to say.] (Mármol, 37; 35–36)

This inverted familial hierarchy, privileging a rebelliously intellectual son over a father associated with dictatorial power, is one measure of the constitutive transgression in this foundational fiction. For a contrast, one may think of the defensive Argentine novels of the 1920s and 1930s often called *mundonovista* and which I prefer to call populist. Whereas *Amalia* assumes a social chaos in the absence of legitimate power, and therefore sets about to construct a legitimate nation/family from the elements in flux, the populist novels insist nervously on safeguarding an already established patriarchal structure. Unruly sons devastate that order, almost as much as do the sensual women who incite them.[28] For Mármol, though, sons and lovers make their own families. And an indulgent father seems to wink at his appreciative son as they go through the obligatory steps of an Oedipal conflict that has already been resolved through love.

A divine prankster like Hermes, Daniel continually risks his life to protect his friends and to build the resistance. But he is never so foolish as to risk it for some feudal and inflexible notion of honor and masculinity. This makes him different from Mármol's apparently ideal lovers, the impeccably correct "youth of the sword," and his ministering angel of a hostess. Belgrano would jump at any chance to defend his and Amalia's good names, if Bello's restraining arm did not save him from noble but stupid suicide. And Amalia is flat enough as a character to announce to the police who have searched her home that, yes, she is a Unitarian and proud of it (Mármol, 295; 255). Proud but not very smart is what readers think, after Bello has taught us how to think.

This strategically promiscuous double-crosser is as willful as Rosas himself.[29] From the beginning, Daniel insists on having full command. "Let me take full control here" (Mármol, 28). Against Eduardo's objections, Bello explains almost patronizingly, "You've got more talent than I, Eduardo, but there are certain cases where I'm worth a hundred times more than you"

(35). And his tactics are tyrannically crafty. Daniel will insinuate to his ever-loyal servant Fermín that any carelessness might get him drafted into the army. In a paroxysm of loyalty, the servant blurts out that rather than betray Daniel, "I would let myself be killed" (41; 41). He will also blackmail the madame of a local whorehouse into hosting clandestine meetings: "Remember that the slightest indiscretion on your part, without costing me a hair would cost you your head" (100; 113). Her repetition of Fermín's response is just what Bello wants. "My life has been in your hands for a long time past, Señor Daniel; but even if that were not the case I would die for the least of the Unitarians" (100; 113). This is precisely the kind of response that Rosas elicits from his own henchman: "I would sacrifice my life for your Excellency" (60; 66).

Cunning Daniel is the very image of Rosas, described by many as monstrously sly,[30] but an image inverted. Whereas Daniel multiplies himself to cover all fronts at home and in the world, Rosas cleverly stays under cover in his most public appearances, at the battle front:

> ¿Dónde dormía Rosas? En el cuartel general tenía su cama, pero allí no dormía.
> En la alta noche se le veía llegar al campamento, y el héroe popular hacía tender su recado cerca de sus leales defensores. Allí se lo veía echarse; pero media hora después ya no estaba allí. ¿Dónde estaba? Con el poncho y la gorra de su asistente, tendido en cualquier otra parte, donde nadie lo hallase ni lo conociese. (Mármol, 414)

> [Where did Rosas sleep? He had his bed in the main barrack, but he didn't sleep there.
> In the dark of the night he would come to the encampment, and the hero of the people would lay down his pack near his loyal defenders. You could see him lie down; but a half hour later he was no longer there. Where was he? Under the poncho and cap of some assistant, stretched out in the most unlikely spot, where no one would find him or know him.]

The hero's portrait and its negative manage to confuse allies as much as enemies, as if they were figures for a Lacanian phallus that continually plays hide and seek with our desire to know it.

When, for example, Daniel's old teacher Don Cándido appeals to him for protection, because even innocent apolitical subjects are not safe from the Mazorca, Bello senses an opportunity. Rather than console Cándido, he prefers to use the effect of official terror to force the nervous old man into spying for the conspiracy. "Daniel laughed," as he began to scheme, while "Don Cándido was staring at him and racking his brains to understand what his disciple was up to" (Mármol, 145). This manipulation cannot but recall Rosas's interview with the English ambassador (68–80; 74–94). After several exchanges that leave him "truly perplexed and unable to comprehend what Rosas was after (74; 85), Mr. Mandeville congratulates himself on finally understanding and then pledging what Rosas wants from him, namely military support against the resistance. But Rosas takes care not to lose his advantage. The Englishman gets a reply that is calculated to convince his government that it would be acting only in self-interest; any debt of gratitude for the tip could be collected by Rosas. "'Do what you choose. All I desire is that you should write the truth,' said Rosas, with a certain air of indifference, under which the minister, if he had been at this moment less enthusiastic, might have perceived that Rosas had now begun to act a part" (77; 89). Here is an Argentine outscheming and outtalking the Englishman, whose people exercised what critics called a virtual commercial monopoly in Argentina and who probably taught Rosas something about the relationship between shrewdness and power. If his success betrays some patriotic pride on Mármol's part, enough pride for readers to guess who Daniel Bello's instructor might have been, then the writer's manipulation will not be lost on us.[31]

Bello, like Rosas, gets results. That is why he is the real hero of the piece. But unlike the tyrant, whom Sarmiento was crediting at the same time for finally establishing Buenos Aires as supreme, Mármol's hero doesn't merely hide an elite effect behind a "barbarous" sign, although he does that too. He also manages to occupy the distance between the antagonistic signs, the distance that Rosas's terror needed in order to construct itself as a campaign against the Other. Bello fills in the space and so cancels the polar opposition, as the conciliatory youths of 1837 had tried to do. At the same time, Bello suggests the extent to which Rosas had already canceled oppositions by forcing the federation behind the capital.[32] Rather than merely a trespasser, I prefer to think of Bello as one of those puzzles in which differently marked spaces can be shifted into many combinations because one square is missing and open. Zero becomes the magic cipher, the empty space that makes possible the manipulations that Belgrano's integral figure cannot conceive.

Our puzzle of a hero shifts more than party lines; everything about him seems doubled or contradictory, including his gender. Besides the guile that might typically be associated with women (his beloved Florencia becomes a double) and that Sarmiento disparagingly attributed to Rosas, Daniel is also physically feminized. "The whiteness of his lovely hands could have made any coquette jealous" (Mármol, 96). And, if women are admirable in this novel, and they are, it is because they are as independent and courageous as men should be. Amalia is free to help Belgrano because, as she says, "I am independent; I lead a solitary life" (29; 25). Then she confronts the police chief with this generalized role-reversal: "In Buenos Aires only the men are afraid; the women know how to defend a dignity which the men have forgotten" (295; 255). Victorica already knew, of course, that the most persistent enemies of the regime were the university students and the women (66). (See also p. 299: "Only God knows, surely, how many noble Argentine women have sacrificed themselves"; and p. 411: "Without any dispute or historical doubt, the women of Buenos Aires showed a moral valor, a firmness and dignity of character . . . that the men were far from exhibiting.") By the time the young men of Buenos Aires are disdained for acquiring "effeminate habits" (401; 291), the adjective may no longer point to women but precisely away from them.

By contrast to this vogue for unisex virtue, racial distinctions seem indelible in this novel. In fact, one of the few clearly programmatic differences between Rosas and his rivals was on the question of white immigration from Europe. He objected to it, whereas opponents were convinced it was Argentina's most urgent need. Sarmiento and Alberdi agreed (despite acrimonious disputes about everything from federal projects to spelling conventions)[33] that the country's racially inferior stock of Spaniards and Indians needed to be improved by Anglo-Saxon immigrants. Sarmiento's biological determinism was somewhat attenuated by his faith in mass education and modern institutions in general, but Alberdi was implacable.[34] So were others, such as Juan María Gutiérrez, the "Generation"'s literary historian: "Those who invoke democracy to the exclusion of good birth, misunderstand both. No matter how many turns society may take, it will never alter the fundamental laws of nature."[35] Like his ideal citizens, Mármol's are flawlessly white, and in the case of Florencia Dupasquier, half French. Among even reformed Unitarians, such as Daniel represented, the half-Spanish half-Indian gaucho produced a practically visceral revulsion that extended by association to Federalists in general. (The narrator describes the infiltrator Merlo as "a man of the people . . . connected to . . . the gaucho by antipathy to civilization" (Mármol, 13; 4). Fermín is also called a gaucho; but carefully set apart as a white one (34; 30). And although the novel never mentions Indians, since it hardly ventures outside the capital, Argentines dealt with them in much the same way as did North Americans; that is, largely by extermination campaigns for territorial expansion, like the one Rosas led in 1833 to prop up his waning popularity.

The fate of Argentine blacks may, however, be less familiar than the history of Indian removal. During the wars of Independence, in which Argentina repeatedly came to the aid of her sister states, African slaves were drafted in large numbers. The creole elite that launched those wars, even the constitutional monarchists who projected a Conservative continuity to avoid anarchy, may not have imagined how uncontrollable that mobilization would become. The very privileges creoles were fighting for could be lost to their former slaves, because the military importance of blacks and mestizos guaranteed a series of reforms that the Unitarian elite begrudgingly conceded after the fighting.[36] Rosas knew how to exploit the resentment of Argentina's masses. One result of the elite's reconquest of power after 1852 (and after it adapted Alberdi's proposal for enlightening Federalism through European immigration more than mass education) was that blacks seem to have disappeared entirely. This time the "genocide" is—quite remarkably—a "textual" campaign; the government apparently made a decision to be color-blind and to eliminate the category for blacks in the national census.[37] This recalls Florencia's purposeful blindness when she hardly deigns to notice the black women in María Josefa's house (Mármol, 85; 96). They won recognition elsewhere. Rosas had eyes and ears for their enthusiastic support and their practically seamless spy network of workers and servants of the city. The first thing Daniel requires of Amalia when she agrees to hide Belgrano, for example, is to fire her black servants. Later, the lovers are spied upon and denounced by another black working woman. Yet Daniel's apparently color-fast social text leaves some room for attractive shades when the colors bleed and cross over; that is, when black is whitened. "In the lower classes the mulattoes only are to be trusted, because of the tendency which every mixed race has to elevate and ennoble itself" (29; 25).

Daniel's sympathies are not always predictable; nor are his lessons all in duplicity. A recurring self-reflexiveness keeps his enchanting game from deteriorating to cant. But Belgrano is puzzled by his friend's indefinite nature and general lack of scruple. This disappointment, or criticism, gives Mármol an opportunity to defend an entire esthetico-political project, one that he shared with other Romantics of his generation even though most of the others had long since retreated. The project would fail, Mármol suggests, if its goals were mistaken as merely "ideological"; it was at the same time a cultural reformation based on a Romantic appreciation of nature in flux, a notion that denied the classical grid of knowledge on which so many misfired Rivadavian schemes had hung. Daniel's reply is worth quoting:

No hay nada, mi querido Eduardo, que se explique con más facilidad que mi carácter, porque él no es otra cosa que una expresión cándida de las leyes eternas de la Naturaleza. Todo, en el orden físico como en el orden moral, es inconstante, transitorio y fugitivo; los contrastes forman lo bello y armónico en todo cuanto ha salido de la mano de Dios; . . . (Mármol, 187)

[There is nothing, my dear Eduardo, that is more easily explained than my erratic character, because it's nothing more than a candid

expression of the eternal laws of Nature. Everything in the physical
world and in the moral order is inconstant, transitory and fleeting.
It is contrast that creates beauty (lo bello) and harmony in everything that issues from God's hand.]

Purposefully unstable, Bello objects to the anarchic personalism
that, for example, keeps General Paz from joining forces with
Lavalle and keeps the exiles in Montevideo absurdly vying for
supremacy inside the cafés. Is there a suggestion here that an
older generation of arrogant Unitarians might learn something
about association and coalitions from virtuous Federalists?
There is no dearth of them in the book, from Daniel's father,
to Police Chief Victorica, whom Mármol thanks in a footnote
for his kindness while the author was Rosas's prisoner (Mármol,
291), and especially Manuelita Rosas, whom Mármol helped to
promote as an almost mythic figure of eternally feminine kindness, both in this novel and in his biography of her.[38] Daniel
dismisses some gossip that Amalia hears at the Federalist Ball
like this: "Those are malicious inventions. . . . Mrs. Rolón is the
best of the Federalist circle; her generous heart is always open
to everyone" (191). In any case, political opposites live together
in Daniel Bello. It is a marriage of convenience, no doubt, but
a delicate bond of respect and affection blesses the union.
Clearly Mármol has forced an unequal balance between the
partners, but Bello is nonetheless a model for national cohesion.

  He is also the agent, insofar as he gets Belgrano and Amalia
together. The crossover artist is a natural go-between. And marriage, a figure for the institutional basis of government that Sarmiento defended (not personal exemplarity) would provide social stability.[39] Bonds of love (not the sword of justice) would
make this Romantic generation succeed where its classical elders did not. "Our new politics needs the element of affection,"
as Gutiérrez put it, "it needs to thrust away the threatening dagger by now as classical as the sword of Justice. Now is the time
for much love."[40] In his serialized love story launched from
Montevideo, the sentimental frame of Mármol's daily interventions in Argentina's political deadlock does far more than keep
us reading and panting from installment to installment. This is
not to say that the panting is extraneous to the intervention.

On the contrary, it ensures it by constructing our desire for a particular kind of sexuality that crosses over. As soon as Bello removes his wounded, almost castrated, friend from town to Amalia's home where he could acquire a more modern sexuality, we suspect that Mármol's geographic decentering is itself a strategic, conciliatory move. And when we learn that the lovely Amalia hails from further still, the interior city of Tucumán, the weight of association pulls our hunch into the sure nod of recognition. Amalia's inevitable love affair with the Buenos Aires boy will signal a national rapprochement between center and periphery, or at least between modern history and Arcadian pastoral. Tucumán was the old colonial capital, when Spain was more concerned with getting Peruvian gold and silver out to the Atlantic coast than with encouraging commerce from the port of Buenos Aires. After Buenos Aires declared independence in 1810, Tucumán was where the United Provinces declared their independence in 1816.[41] Tucumán was also the first important center to renounce Rosas once he institutionalized terror, as Mármol takes care to remind us. "By a decree passed on the 7th of April, 1840, the Chamber of Representatives of Tucumán had withdrawn from Rosas their recognition of him as Governor of Buenos Aires" (Mármol, 43; 45). It was, in other words, already in the centralists' orbit, pleasantly provincial but hardly the rival Córdoba had been.[42]

The affair between "la bella tucumana" and General Belgrano's nephew, takes on programmatic proportions, even if we forget that Juan Bautista Alberdi, the one "tucumano" among the Romantics in the capital, Mármol's admirer in Montevideo[43] and roommate in Río,[44] became the architect of national conciliation. This Alberdi dated his own birth along with the birth of his nation (as did Sarmiento), as if they were inseparable, mutually dependent twins.[45] Mármol may even have attempted a kind of lopsided parity between the cities by dedicating the second part of the book to Amalia and beginning with a description of Tucumán, that tropical womblike interior paradise, just as he had begun the first part with a bachelor's Buenos Aires. True, the description is deferred and is mediated by quoting an English observer. I am not suggesting that Mármol's ideal relationship between the male and female figures is one of equals but merely noting the more obvious and promising point: that the gender-coded cities *could* be related in a seductive hegemony of the loving capital over its ministering province, very different from the dictatorial isolation that weakened both sites of civilization.

Rosas had little use for political seductions. Those whom he could not mold by artfulness, he simply eliminated. And while his empire tottered on the ruins of local popularity and international opinion, he became ever more deaf to special pleadings and warm requests, so deaf that he refused to hear his closest allies intercede for Camila O'Gorman. The twenty-year-old daughter of a solid Federalist family in the capital was also a personal friend of Manuelita. In December of 1847, the girl had run off with a young priest, Uladislao Gutiérrez, nephew of the governor of—where else?—Tucumán. To be fair, Rosas first tried to cover up the embarrassment, but Montevideo's emigré newspaper, the *Comercio del Plata*, made much of it with carping jokes about the morality of liberal Federals.[46] The lovers were then pursued and nothing, not even Camila's eight months of pregnancy, could save them from the execution that was never forgiven by the tyrant's most intimate associates.[47] Writing barely three years after the enduring scandal of this punctilious punishment for passion, Mármol must surely have sensed and exploited his readers' readiness to embrace less extravagant but equally outlaw lovers. And he must have anticipated that a delayed tragic climax would nourish the public's fantasies for the runaway couple before opening sentimental wounds that still festered with political outrage.

Understandably, if Mármol was indeed rewriting Camila's story as a hegemonic allegory, his romance would reroute the lovers to make her hail from the voluptuous interior and him from the heady capital. Yet the love story between Ms. Tucumán and Mr. Buenos Aires takes very little space in this more than 500-page novel. It does occupy the center of the book, though. And it is precisely at the center, somewhat decentered thanks to Bello (and also perhaps to Rosas who was clever enough to be a provincial from the central province), that they could have hoped to make their love last. The bulk of the novel is a wonderfully unorthodox jumble of intrigues, drawing-room dialogues, detailed descriptions of interiors and clothing worthy of the opposition "fashion" journals, historical documents, and character studies of historically identifiable agents.[48] All this loosely coordinated into a plot about Daniel Bello's personal contest of strategy against personalist Rosas. The tension builds toward an unbearable pitch that irresistibly quickens the pulse. Or is the throbbing a function of the love song that Mármol has been playing in harmony with the life and death theme? In fact we want much more than survival for individual heroes. We want them to survive because we increasingly desire their institutional and mutual union: Daniel's union with Florencia but, even more passionately, Amalia's union with Belgrano. These two finally marry near the end. But barely one hour later she is widowed again when the "barbarous" police storm her house. Belgrano and Bello hold them off with unbelievable heroism and success, but not long enough for Bello's Federalist father to arrive and turn the police away. The two friends *could* have been saved by his conciliatory presence. The tragedy was not inevitable; it was rather a miscalculation.

Perhaps that is why the loose ends of that final scene play on the reader's mind like some kind of possibility or a promise. Belgrano is dead, to be sure, but from the very beginning we knew that he was an anachronism and began to say our good-byes. The greater loss is Daniel, our model of future Argentines, who seems mortally wounded. Yet instead of pronouncing a narrative dead-end over his body, the narrator ends with this ambivalent meditation on the (il)legitimacy of Federalism and paternal authority: "his father, who by a single word (Restorer) had suspended the dagger which the same word had raised to be the instrument of so much misfortune and crime" (Mármol, 529; 416). Don Antonio arrives to fill a power vacuum in the city that Rosas, like the Unitarians, had abandoned to make war in the provinces. He arrives instead of the liberating army led by Lavalle, who lacked either the nerve or the timing to intervene. Buenos Aires is an empty center waiting for the *real* father to come home and to restore order. The title of Restorer is still legitimate, even if Rosas doesn't merit it. The place of the name of the father is still intact; it's the last word. If Daniel's cunning had not already reproduced Rosas's manipulations for us, if good Federalists were not already portrayed as equal to good Unitarians, this word itself would establish the overlap between the apparent antagonists in *Amalia*.

Probably surviving them all is Amalia, the title character whose name bears some resemblance to Argentina's. Admittedly she is heartbroken at Eduardo's death, but the very fact that their love was consummated, in Amalia's first surrender to passion, promises an afterlife to the novel. It promises a baby, perhaps to replace the one Rosas killed in Camila's womb. Orphaned as a girl (the colony so long ignored by Spain?), Amalia married her first husband out of respect for her mother's choice and the need for protection (Rivadavia's sterile Unitarianism?). But in her rapture with Eduardo she tells him what the new husband must already have found out: it was her first celebration of love, "mi primer himeneo" (Mármol, 522). They fairly melt into each other, this tucumana and the porteño, maybe to produce a child who is a little of both.

If I am deliberately stretching this possibility so thin that it barely covers my own fictitious construct, it is to tease out the connections between Mármol's novel and the original ideals of Argentine Romanticism. As the esthetic and political battle cry of the young men who met in Sastre's store during 1837, Romanticism defied the enlightened, classical habits of thought that led Argentina to Independence but were now anachronistic. Those habits had become obstacles to national consolidation and progress. "What barbarians!" Miguel Cané fulminated against the old guard. "Not to be romantic in the nineteenth century is not to be patriotic, or progressive, or Christian, or human!"[49] The struggle against categorical purity was at once ideological and esthetic in Victor Hugo's vastly popular formulation. "Romanticism, if it is militant, is the same thing as liberalism in literature."[50] Classicism, the youths charged, had kept Argentine literature at the standstill of imitation and had locked Argentine politics into a standoff between Unitarians and Federalists. Rivadavia's enlightened policies of the 1820s aimed to Europeanize the country but had misfired on the American frontier. Enlightened thinking did not, for example, account for Rosas's popularity. The Francophile Romantics

noted, with an ironic lapse of reflexivity, that ideas could not
simply be imported.

Old habits were literally sterile, compared to Alberdi's national project, for example: it was to dominate the "desert," not
by eliminating "barbarians" but by increasing population. This
revisionary of Argentine consolidation, who used to weep over
the passionate pages of *Julie* held under his desk in Latin class
and who used to insist that his notorious weakness for women
and dances answered to strict doctor's orders, understood very
well the mechanism for increasing population.[51] And if the nascent future I read in(to) Mármol's conclusion is a projection,
Alberdi's project may have engendered it. At least one remarkable section of his *Bases* for the new constitution practically
reads like a manual for lovers. In good bourgeois form, it recon-
ciles affairs of the heart to affairs of state. With other "pre-
positivists," Alberdi observed that as children of Spaniards,
Argentines are racially disabled for rational behavior, whereas
Anglo-Saxons were naturally hard working and efficient. So
Argentina should attract as many Anglos as possible.

The problem was that the state recognized no religion but
Catholicism and, without a legal sanction for intermarriage, the
Protestants who would inevitably desire Argentine women
would have no choice but to debase the women they could not
resist and to produce illegitimate children.[52] Another problem
for Argentines was how to maintain political power while encouraging foreigners to make fortunes. Alberdi showed how
the double jeopardy could be neatly contained, if only Argentina would grant religious freedom. The result would be, argues
this political matchmaker, that *romance* would literally conquer
all. It would effect a parity between prosperous husbands and
irresistible wives. And more than that, it would produce legitimate, homegrown inheritors of local power and foreign capital.

> Necesitamos cambiar nuestras gentes incapaces de libertad, por
> otras gentes hábiles para ella, sin abdicar el tipo de nuestra raza
> original, y mucho menos el señorío del país; suplantar nuestra ac-
> tual familia argentina, por otra igualmente argentina, pero más
> capaz de libertad, de riqueza y progreso. ¿Por conquistadores más
> ilustrados que la España, por ventura? Todo lo contrario; conquis-

tando en vez de ser conquistados. La América del Sud posee un
ejército a este fin, y es el encanto que sus *hermosas y amables mujeres*
recibieron de su origen andaluz, mejorado por el cielo espléndido
del nuevo mundo. Removed los impedimentos inmorales, que
hacen *estéril* el poder del bello sexo americano y tendréis realizado
el cambio de nuestra raza sin la pérdida del idioma ni del tipo nacional primitivo.[53]

[We need to replace our citizens with others more able to profit
from liberty. But we need to do this without giving up our racial
character, or, much less, our political control. . . . Should we, perhaps, bring in more enlightened conquerors than the Spaniards?
On the contrary; we will conquer instead of being conquered.
South America has an *army* for this purpose, its *beautiful and amiable
women* of Andalusian origin and improved under the splendid sky
of the New World. Remove the immoral impediments that *sterilize*
the power of America's fair sex and you will have effected the
change in our race without losing our language or our racial
character.]

Amalia could certainly have been one of those women,
although her conquest of the center is the precondition for
future, farther-reaching enchantments. Her charm inscribes
erotic desire as a "natural" grounding for any dialectic of political conciliation and economic growth. Amalia need not be
convincing or complex as a character in order to be central to
this national romance. It is enough that she is desired and that
political obstacles stand in the way of that desire, repeatedly
redirecting erotic energy to political conciliation. Her love story
becomes a foundational fiction because it projects the kind of
liberal social intercourse between regions and parties that could
establish a legitimate public family.

The same ardor with which the Generation of 1837 hoped
to thaw congealed categories of alliance did manage to melt
traditional literary barriers. The prudish distances between literary genres, registers of language, and classical unities were
overcome in the frenzy of Romantic transgressions. There was
a will to hybridization, surprises, unorthodox juxtapositions.
Echeverría launched this "revolution" with *Elvira o la novia del
Plata* (1832), but his "epic," *La cautiva* (1837), really blasted
open a new American literary terrain. It celebrates the "com-

mon" hero—in fact celebrates the far more heroic heroine—
and inscribes popular regionalisms without setting them off by
quotation marks or italics.[54] If these exceed standard Spanish,
the Romantics pointed out that their language was Argentine,
not Spanish. In the continuing polemic with the classicists, Juan
María Gutiérrez joined Alberdi in celebrating more excesses
yet. "In Paris everything is French, in Madrid everything
Spanish. But Buenos Aires is the place where everything has
come, is coming, and will come, thank God, from France, from
Spain . . . from all the civilized nations." The whole world's linguistic habits overlap to constitute an Argentine language.[55]

Now Mármol's style might seem conservative by contrast.
David Viñas, for one, notes with a combination of scorn and
embarrassment that *Amalia* is a stylistic see-saw of glaring contrasts: a spiritualized, practically ethereal language that floats
like a halo around the heroes, especially the heroines; and a
dogged attention to the carnal, almost bestial, immediacy of
the villains.[56] Of course Viñas is right. No reader today can miss
Mármol's knack for caricature, his unproblematized and flagrant racism, or his passion for (imported) luxury that is practically synonymous with civilized virtue and fills whole pages
with interior decorating and fashion news. More elitist at times
than his fellow travelers, and apparently sharing the schematic
and binary clarity that prevailed again after 1840, Mármol even
shows himself to be a monarchist, like Manuel Belgrano. The
hero of Independence had for years shopped around for a
European prince to head the new state in order to avoid setting
up a republic that might threaten the local elite with a tyranny
of the masses (Mármol, 338).

I cannot but grant all these dichotomous and regressive features in *Amalia*. But it is a long and also a wonderfully complicated, even contradictory, adventure in form. It is, to use a
Bakhtinian and economical word, a novel. In contrast to the
stunning ideological casualties suffered by the Generation of
1837, very little had yet been ventured or lost on the esthetic
front. Despite the romantic gesture of embracing local scenes
and signifiers into his texts, Echeverría's work retains a rigidly
binary logic. Between 1838 and 1840, he wrote *El matadero,* an
almost naturalistic story about a gang of butchers who attack

and—with a *mazorca* or ear of corn—"rape" a Unitarian who
passes by (a snob, more like Eduardo than like Daniel). This
was after Echeverría had lost hope of getting beyond traditional
dichotomies.[57] The story is evidently more pessimistic than was
La cautiva, probably because during the terror it seemed natural
to displace the barbarian from the Indian frontier right into the
center of the Argentine body politic. But the earlier work never
really got beyond the dichotomies either. Noé Jitrik asks, for
example, how any political reconciliation might be possible
when the characters of the poem are figured either as barbarous
Indians or as their civilized victims. After reifying the enemy
what can the writer do? "Do you exterminate him or try to assimilate him? Yet after proposing these alternatives, is assimilation possible?"[58]

Many others tried their hand at romantic fiction. Among
them were Juana Manuela Gorriti and the future general and
president Bartolomé Mitre. Like Mármol in *Amalia,* they wrote
ideological pronouncements in sentimental fiction. What is it
about his book, then, that makes it Argentina's uncontested first
great novel?[59] To follow Benedict Anderson's lead, we could
note that Mármol's care in dating and timing his novel has significant nation-building significance. We might recall *Amalia*'s
initial sentence and the insistence on keeping the reader up to
date. Anderson brings our attention to this kind of "calendrical
time" that provided the frame for national narratives through
newspapers and novels and allowed for a simultaneity of related
events, joining reader and writer in a shared social moment.
But on recalling *Amalia,* we may also remember that other fictions timed and dated themselves precisely and were, moreover,
written by far more credible leaders of the Liberal resistance.
El matadero, for example, begins with a tongue-in-cheek rejec-
tion of the epic time in America's first chronicles: "Although I
am writing a history, I won't start with Noah's ark and the
genealogy of his descendants, the way our first Spanish historians of America used to do."[60] Then he dates the story during
the meat shortage of the 1830s. Mitre's *Soledad* (1847), takes
place directly after the Independence war in Bolivia. And many
of Gorriti's stories mark their precise moment. Probably the
easiest and the best reason for *Amalia*'s institutional success is

that it is a better and longer-lasting piece of entertainment, keeping readers of *La Semana*'s installments at a pitch of hopeful anticipation until the very eve of victory against Rosas.

Another reason may be that unlike Mármol, passion and politics often compete for the reader's sympathy in other writers. For Gorriti, to cite one telling example, the possible contest seems almost irrelevant, because both desire and power belong to the male world, as capable of producing horror as of winning glory. Her alternative is a spiritualized celebration of "female" self-denial; that is, of Christian love possible only in the victims of history. Gorriti's own marginalization from the ideological and strategic debates among aspiring agents of Argentine history is repeatedly rehearsed and universalized in her stories of the incompatibility between women and men. So, far from blurring traditional gender distinctions, as Mármol does, Gorriti underlines them. The alternative to machismo for her is not flexibility but a countervailing ideal of *marianismo*.[61] Nevertheless, her heroines are sometimes caught between personal desire and spiritual duty; that is, the femaleness is vulnerable not only because it is victimized by men but because it can be complicitous with them. Gorriti's ideal reader is never confused about what the right choice is; she knows, as well as does Racine's classical and prebourgeois reader, that sexuality can pervert female virtue into destructive power. In the story "El tesoro de los incas," for example, an Indian princess reveals the secret of Cuzco's treasure to the Spaniard who has seduced her. Rosalía pays for her sin once the colonial authorities learn of the treasure; they torture her and her family, finally killing them, in the hope of learning the secret.[62] This is one of Gorriti's warnings against succumbing to desire across national and class lines. Another is "Un drama en el Adriático," about a Venetian noblewoman in love with an Austrian officer in the occupying army. After learning that her incredibly solicitous and loving brother is conspiring for liberation with other patriots, she betrays them to her lover, but not without an interior struggle that readers are expected to resolve on the side of patriotism as against passion. The point is that in choosing her lover she loses the struggle and causes a general loss for both sides. The desperate Italians prefer anything to ignominy, including the cataclysmic mass suicide that brings the Austrian victory down with the victims.[63] By contrast, a "winning" heroine is she who chooses to lose in love. Clemencia, for instance, the ideal title character of "La hija del mazorquero" (Manuelita?) sacrifices everything, including romantic fantasies about the Unitarian she had saved, and finally her life. Her brutal father mistakes the girl for the Unitarian's lover and slits her throat. This is the story with a "happy" ending. "Her virgin blood found favor before God, and like a new baptism He cast the divine light of salvation on the sinner now redeemed."[64] Love, in what can only be called a fervently Catholic and even colonial model, amounts to self-sacrifice. The womanly ideal here is the Virgin Mary or even Christ himself, someone who can wipe the slate of history clean, not the prudent bourgeoise whose passion produces children to fill up the empty spaces.

As for Mitre's precocious novel, it shows the teenage title character struggling against her passions in desperate efforts to avoid the old royalist she was forced to marry. One distraction in the solitude of her bedroom is reading, which provokes as many problems as pleasures because Soledad is reading Rousseau's *La nouvelle Héloise*. From one forbidden chapter to the next, she grows dangerously attracted to an insincere visitor who would have played a parody of St. Preux to Soledad's Julie. She is saved from this false passion when her cousin and childhood sweetheart returns from the wars, aborts the rendezvous, and saves her virtue. Then cousin Eduardo patiently waits for the superfluous husband to obligingly die, so that he and Soledad can marry. Without an informed reading partner, Soledad had obviously gotten Rousseau all wrong. She managed to notice that *Julie* constructed a particular kind of illicit desire between two youths who were separated by the young woman's father (her mother in Soledad's case) and the older man she obediently married. But she, or Mitre, missed Rousseau's equally powerful construction of womanly virtue as the apparent constraint on passion that, in fact, produces it. Julie and St. Preux could not have loved so intensely if they had not struggled so passionately against love. Perhaps, though, Mitre's misreading is more purposeful than naive, suggesting along with some of Gorriti's stories that female desire needs manly control. In the first place, the military hero is privileged and, like Mitre himself, would take credit for defending (public) virtue; and in the second, he finesses the conflict between Soledad's passion and her virtue by denying her the liberty to be conflicted.

Although *Soledad* "corrects" its tortured and pessimistic European model by among other things returning vir-tue to the hero and suggesting that America is the free space for modern love and bourgeois productivity, a space where aristocratic fathers such as Julie's were eliminated with the colony, Mitre's happy ending is rather airless. Like Echeverría and Gorriti, Mitre also rehearses the rearguard Unitarian opposition between "us" and "them." That is, it contrasts the civilized young lovers who are already related as cousins with the barbarous, feudal outsider who (like Rosas) is a lecherous and sentimentally illegitimate husband. There is no conciliation here, only a consolidation. And this hasty narrative closure by Mármol's or Alberdi's standards seems to predict General Mitre's hostile response to the 1853 constitutional demand to move the capital into the interior. It also underlines the divide between "our" kind of Europeanizing novels that Mitre's Prologue calls for and "their" *gauchesca* poets in vogue at the time. That kind of "oral" literature was evidently a contradiction in terms; instead Mitre preferred the books that novelistic heroes and heroines were reading, European books. From the imposed distance of exile, he and other Argentine novelists had turned their backs to the pampa and were striking Romantic poses in Europe's direction.[65]

The only really comparable book to *Amalia* was Vicente Fidel López's *La novia del hereje o la inquisición de Lima*, published serially in 1846 and issued as a book in Buenos Aires along with *Amalia* in 1854.[66] Writing from exile in Chile, this founding member of Sastre's salon performed some of the same narrative seductions that made Mármol so powerful. Through its lengthy and complex intrigue set in Peru's inquisitorial sixteenth century, López's novel assigned contrasting cultural and ideological backgrounds for his star-crossed lovers; it went so far as to make the Liberal a "heretic," that is a Protestant Englishman. His marriage to the daughter of the viceroy's first minister, and their escape to England where the couple produces a family, bring Mármol's themes to a happy finale. But this very resolution may satisfy rather than engage the reader politically. *La novia* is about a past perfect world whose resolution of problems is a given, whereas *Amalia*'s world is indefinite, unsettling. The tried and true practice of Scott-like historical novels that dress contemporary issues in medieval garb produces, as the Scottish aristocrat may have intended, a ready-made ending. Mármol, by contrast, keeps the ends of history untied. His preliminary "Explicación" admits that the book is only masquerading as a historical novel. "By a calculated fiction," the author imagines that several generations have intervened between contemporary events and the writing. The calculation pays off by making Mármol our contemporary, equally distant from the events. By absenting himself from the history he does more than project a possible relief from horror; he also gives himself a narrative "presence" for future generations of readers.

It may be, however, that other factors intervene in the comparative success of these books, factors external to their relative merits in combining convention with Romantic excess. López, the historian who acknowledged how intimately novels consorted with history, even more than Mitre did, ended up on the losing side of the struggle between Alberdi and Mitre.[67] The son of a prominent Federalist, López defended Alberdi's constitution as the only stable and equitable means of consolidating a divided country. Mitre, of course, did not. And the new government established in Buenos Aires after Mitre's victory appointed José Mármol to the Senate, not Vicente Fidel López, while it promoted *Amalia*'s celebrity as the foremost novel.

Whatever the circumstances, the celebrity was surely justified. *Amalia* is a startling esthetic departure that finally gave form to the passions of Argentina's early Romantics. That form was the novel, in the most flexible, hybrid, and "non-generic" use of the term. It provided an erotics of unity, exiled the all-too-admirable heroes to strut in the margins, and allowed the text to be a porous body in which every kind of writing is admissible. Mármol's personal success, including the appointment to the Senate, where he spoke eloquently and frequently if not always to the point, and his semiretirement as director of the National

Library, came largely from the success of patriotic verses he hurled against Rosas. But some contemporaries must have noticed in the novel a design for the new Argentine citizen, honorable in the last instance but elastic enough to associate with others, even opponents. For many it was *the* novel of triumphant Argentine liberalism. Yet today it is read more as a period piece than as a founding text. The novel's project, so the reading goes, was to depose Rosas. Once that was done, so was Mármol's politics.

Instead of *Amalia*, it is now *Martín Fierro* (1872) which people call Argentina's "epic." The long narrative poem written in gaucho dialect by José Hernández developed an already-existing genre of politically conciliatory poems that, as Josefina Ludmer masterfully shows, constructed a national voice by appropriating the language of "authentic" but notoriously shiftless Argentines for patriotic and economically rational projects.[68] In some ways, this poem is a swan song. Hernández wrote it when the gauchos had all but disappeared because of government policies, both military and economic. They were forcibly conscripted into armies sent to fight Indians in wars that may well have been aimed at a double extermination; and they were confined to narrowing spaces between modernized, privatized ranches on a once vast pampa. Martín Fierro's story is about these abuses, how they make him into the criminal and vagabond that whites expect gauchos to be, and about his flight from white settlements. But in part II called "The Return," (1879) the poem shows the gaucho's resignation to the new order and to its small mercies. Like the politically Promethean hero of *Amalia*, and like some leaders of Argentina's post-Rosas government, Martín Fierro would rather live compromised than die fighting for an impossible idea of liberty.

There is certainly good reason to read Hernández's poem as Argentina's epic. But there is no less reason to read *Amalia* as epic. Both narratives struggle through the conflicts of Argentina's middle period in order to show the room and the need for reconciliation. The difference between each book's claim to foundational status is qualitative; that is, a difference in the kind of political sympathies they develop. Both Mármol's conciliatory neo-Unitarianism and Hernández's reformed Federalism aimed to consolidate a nation rather than to defend provincial autonomy; and they provided more common ground than did the original antagonist parties. But their coming together means, of course, that they come from different positions. And in post-Rosas politics, the older ties and projects were more often left suspended than left behind. Policy debates on the virtues of European immigration or protectionism could be so partisan and passionate that they would become extraparliamentary and continue, again, on the battlefield. Hernández himself opposed the elite liberalism of Mitre and in 1870 participated in a revolution led by a provincial caudillo.[69]

Considering that *Amalia* and *Martín Fierro* coincide in projecting a national unity after devastating years of division, to choose one as *the* country's epic is like taking a particular partisan stand; it is to renew the debates about what kind of unity Argentina should achieve. One choice crosses male- and female-coded cities, a capital lover with a provincial beloved; the other crosses class boundaries between rural men as ranchers adapt their peons' language for a project of mutual understanding and legitimation. (Neither choice imagined a simultaneous move across gender and class lines.) One book excludes masses of mestizo and black workers through a linguistic seesaw between spiritual heights and blood-drenched lows; the other excludes women and the citified (feminized) men associated with foreigners who cannot keep the language's or their own gender assignments straight and who are therefore useless to Argentina's community of heroes and herdsmen.[70] The novel calls gauchos "barbarians"; the poem mocks all others as literally barbarous strangers, making itself at home in Argentina's homespun style. If these "epics" face one another like mirror images gesturing from opposite directions toward a patriotic threshold, the reader who calls one image reality and the other a reflection is, in fact, declaring what side of the mirror he or she is on. To remember the political significance that contemporary readers gave to *Amalia,* and the fact that *Martín Fierro* became a national epic only half a century after it was published, is also to remember that these readings are historical as well as partisan. Mármol's admirers, an elite class of literate Argentines returning from exile to take control at home, undoubtedly agreed with the positions taken in his book. At least they could choose between hegemonic bonding and indulgent paternalism in his inconsistent formulations. He was, therefore, an overnight success. But Hernández had to wait. Not that he wasn't immediately popular; he was, both with city people who could safely indulge their nostalgia for the vanishing gauchos and with the very gauchos themselves who lingered on for a short while as they recited his poem. Hernández was popular, but not seriously regarded as an artist, and certainly not an artist of national stature, until Leopoldo Lugones started a literary polemic in 1913 by proclaiming *Martín Fierro* to be Argentina's epic. He hoped that celebrating its local particularity would safeguard Argentine culture from the socialist and anarchist "corruption" of foreign immigration.[71] Since then, the claim has seemed less extravagant than self-evident, especially after the literary populism of the 1920s when, for example, a young Jorge Luis Borges helped to found a journal called *Martín Fierro,* after generations of immigrant children have identified themselves as Argentine through that poem, and after the long Peronist period when Rosas himself was becoming a symbol of nativist patriotism.[72] Nevertheless, Lugones knew that he was being polemical by favoring "Americanism" over progress in a country still dominated by Sarmentine liberalism. He may even have been surprised at his own success in promoting the poetic exaltation of autochthonous mestizo culture over Argentina's favorite novel, the genre that bourgeois Europe liked best.

4

SAB C'EST MOI

Gertrudis Gómez de Avellaneda could well have said something like Flaubert's quip about Bovary, because the Cuban writer evidently identified with the hero of her abolitionist novel, *Sab* (1841). Sab is a mulatto slave hopelessly in love with his young white mistress and on the verge of rebellion, precisely the kind of explosive (self)portrayal that allows the novelist to construct a paradoxical, interstitial, and ultimately new or American persona. In other words, it was never easy to identify "la Avellaneda," or Gertrudis the Great as she is also called, in conventional or stable terms. Born in Cuba in 1814 to an impoverished Spanish aristocrat and a wealthy creole mother, and more or less settled in Spain from 1836 until her death in 1873, her national allegiance and the glory that she brings are still disputed by both countries. And although feminist readers of Spanish American literature are giving her the kind of attention that amounts to a gender-specific claim on her work,[1] Avellaneda has always figured in the canonical, overwhelmingly male mainstream of Hispanic literature.[2] Neither Old World nor New World, neither a woman's writer nor a man's, Gertrudis was both, or something different; she was Sab.

Her identification with him is obviously not autobiographical. Neither is it simply mimetic in the sense of representing the writer's characteristics and passions.[3] As daring as this particular example of what might be called a spiritual mimesis is, given the fact that novelist and protagonist differ in apparently every conceivable way including gender, race, and class, the general literary practice is rather common and would by itself have been far less noteworthy than what Avellaneda does here. The stunning thing about this self-portrait is that it identifies author with apparently helpless slave through their shared productive func-

114

tion, their literary labor conditioned in both by the need to subvert and to reconstruct. The obscure slave represents the privileged novelist because both vent their passions by writing and because their literary slippages destabilize the rhetorical system that constrains them.

Sab writes at the end of the book, after his pitiful story of humiliation and loss. Exhausted and on the verge of death, he writes a long letter about Carlota, the chestnut-haired mistress and childhood playmate whom he loves desperately. And while writing "Sab's letter," probably in 1839, Avellaneda is also writing a long autobiographical letter to the one man whom she was passionate about and who managed to ignore her during a lifetime.[4] In Sab's letter, Avellaneda's hero declares his love for the unsuspecting girl and explains the other interests that had been motivating the narrative. Sab's name at the end of the letter serves as the signature for an entire novel that seemed to be a simple story about a slave who is ignored, misunderstood, and passive in the face of unequal social relationships. (The literature on Sab as "noble savage" is rather predictable.)[5] But the letter shows him as the writer of his own story and the only one who could fulfill Carlota's dream. Her dream was to marry Enrique Otway, the handsome son of an opportunist English merchant. Until she reads Sab's letter, Carlota is naive about Enrique's wavering interest in her (depending on how he assesses her dowry) and about her stoic cousin Teresa's infatuation with the same blond idol. Now Carlota learns that Enrique almost broke his engagement to her, after realizing that the dowry was indeed depleted; and she finds out that Sab had restored her wealth by slipping his winning lottery ticket into her mail. She also realizes that Sab then literally killed himself and his mount while racing on horseback to call Enrique back with the news of her good fortune.

The letter is written, as I said, afterward, while Sab is dying, and it is addressed to Teresa for safekeeping. She takes it into the convent where she chooses to live out her short life, and Carlota marries the man who soon proves, even to her, that he was unworthy of love. About to die, Teresa reveals the letter to Carlota. Thanks to Sab, whom she now recognizes as a soulmate, Carlota finally learns how much women and slaves have in common. "Oh women! Poor, blind victims! Just like slaves, they patiently drag their chains and lower their heads under the yoke of human law" (221).[6] Her faith in love (and liberation) revives, though, with the rest of Sab's letter. In it, Carlota manages to reread her romance in light of what could have been.

In other words, the end discovers Sab as the agent and the authority of the very story that portrayed him as a defenseless object of history. The signature authorizes the novel and leaves no doubt regarding his constructive role in the book. Already absent by the time he signs off, Sab makes himself present to Carlota, his mistress and ideal reader; he can present himself candidly by writing. In the same way, Avellaneda makes herself present to Cuba in a book written far away, from the absence that paradoxically makes possible the passionate supplement called writing. Sab, as much as she, writes from beyond hope. But much earlier than this signature, we suspect that Sab writes, directs, and manipulates everything we are reading. It is Sab, after all, who directs Enrique Otway to Carlota's house at the very beginning of the book; and it is he who decides to save the unworthy rival after Enrique falls unconscious in a storm. Later, Sab is the one who provides a guided tour through the treacherous caves of Cubitas where his master's family planned an outing to impress Enrique. And it is Sab again who interchanges people's fates by displacing lottery tickets. Finally it is Sab who determines their destinies by racing to stop Otway from embarking for Europe.

Throughout, Sab produces his story. Gertrudis did the same, within the limits that circumscribed them both. Only he, along with her, has enough command of the narrative to sound out the most intimate secrets of other characters, of Enrique for example.

> Yo he sido la sombra que por espacio de muchos días ha seguido constantemente sus pasos; yo el que ha estudiado a todas horas su conducta, sus miradas, sus pensamientos . . . ; yo quien ha sorprendido las palabras que se le escapaban cuando se creía solo y aun las que profería en sus ensueños, cuando dormía: yo quien ha ganado a sus esclavos para saber de ellos las conversaciones que se suscitaban entre padre e hijo, . . . (154)

[I have been the shadow that has constantly repeated his steps for many days now; I the one who has all the time been studying his conduct, his way of looking, his thoughts . . . ; I am the one who has surprised the words that escaped him when he thought himself alone and even the ones he offered up in daydreams, and when he slept: I am the one who has won over his slaves in order to know the conversations that take place between father and son.]

The productive confusion of gender, and also of race and class, that the identification between Sab and Gertrudis implies is among the liberating linguistic disencounters that this novel achieves. But the best example is perhaps the description of Sab himself. In the very first scene, when Otway stops Sab to ask for directions to Carlota's house, the slave is introduced through a series of negations or absences. He is not a landowning peasant, although by his appearance he could easily be mistaken for one; nor does he have an easily identifiable color.

No parecía un criollo blanco, tampoco era negro ni podía creérsele descendiente de los primeros pobladores de la Antillas. Su rostro presentaba un compuesto singular en que se descubría el cruzamiento de dos razas diversas, y en que se amalgamaban, por decirlo así, los rasgos de la casta africana con los de la europea, sin ser no obstante un mulato perfecto. (23)

[He didn't look like a white creole, neither was he black nor could he be taken for a descendant of the first inhabitants of the Antilles. His face presented a singular composition in which one could discover the crossing of two different races, an amalgamation, so to speak, of African and European features that doesn't add up, however, to a perfect mulatto.]

It is as if the inherited signs of a European language could not catch up with an elusive American referent. Before describing him in positive terms, the text first has to erase or cross out a certain ethnocultural linguistic space in order to compose a new sign. Sab, and by association Avellaneda, is different, somehow foreign to established categories of representation. In the next paragraph, Avellaneda recomposes the very same signifiers she has just destabilized, or liberated, in an almost incoherent way when she describes Sab's color as "a yellowish white with a tinge of black in the background" (24). The autonomy of each racial signifier was negated a few lines earlier only so that they could be amalgamated here. Sab is a new incarnation of an extinct aboriginal "Cuban," one who exceeds or violates the strict racial categories that have made slavery work. The reader, and Otway, are practically blinded to the existing social relationships by the lightness of Sab's skin. And it is this racial indefiniteness, this new shade of social meaning, that may be among the most radical features of the novel.

Despite the apparent incoherence of this exhaustive catalogue of colors, Sab is recognized as a typical resident of central Cuba, both by Enrique Otway and by the reader. The incoherence, in other words, owes to a certain linguistic obsolescence rather than to mistaken perceptions. The novel begins, then, with an aporia between language and experience, a ruse that would be repeated, significantly, in more than one canonical woman's novel. A particularly loving example, one I cannot help but mention, is Teresa de la Parra's nostalgic series of vignettes about plantation life in Venezuela called *Las memorias de Mamá Blanca* (1929). As will be seen in the last chapter, the playfully deliberate aporia between Snow White's name and her color, among many others, allows for the conciliatory effect of humor and affection.

The result in both *Sab* and *Memorias* is an awareness that our reality suggests its imaginary form, to borrow Lacan's terms, but that it still lacks a symbolic expression. If reality had an expressible form, if we could imagine an adequate sign that would represent Sab, a sign that would name this nameless pariah in the slave-holding language of the "parvenus,"[7] that sign might be, perhaps, Cuban. Then we would recognize him to be as legitimate and autochthonous in this New World as were the indigenous, or as Spanish says it, the "natural" masters of the island. In fact, the term "natural child," meaning bastard in the established language and attributed to both Sab and Teresa, takes on a legitimating value by association, because the orphaned Sab is spiritually related to the aboriginal masters through his adoptive mother Martina, an old slave who insists she is Indian royalty.

If we ask ourselves how Avellaneda could identify with so

complex a character, one so difficult to locate between negation and excess, her motives announce themselves in a cluster of possibilities. And all of them are bound up with the need in both subjects to transgress the symbolic order, the order of the father, in their effort to construct an identity. Before I try to specify the nature of their excess or transgression, it is probably worth noting that the reigning patriarchal order in this novel is itself in profound crisis. No character here can be considered a legitimate or effective father. Don Carlos de B., Sab's master and Carlota's father, is in general incapable of ordering anything; he is too sweet or naive, or simply too lazy, to provide continuity and cohesion for the symbolic realm. His moribund son, the only one in a house full of daughters, underlines Don Carlos's nullity as a progenitor and gives their tasteful slavocratic world a definite expiration date. It is easy to see that Enrique's crass and foreign father, Jorge Otway, is just as problematic. Despite his energy and occasional financial coups, the man is too calculating and graceless to be a legitimate model. And his son is even less promising because he turns out to be Jorge's clone, lacking the will to confront his father with alternative values. By comparison, despite the fact that Sab combines the contrasting virtues of disinterested sweetness and energetic dedication, he cannot aspire to be a father. What Sab lacks is any claim to legitimacy in the patriarchal symbolic order, precisely because he has no father and no patronym, because there is no space in his language in which he could occupy the place of the name of the father.

In this social vacuum, "author-ity" can pass on to new hands, feminine and/or mulatto hands. Except for Martina, there are no mothers either, no one but Sab's "indigenous mother" to hold out the promise, or the memory, of an alternative order to the slavocratic patriarchy. She, the mistress of Cubitas, is an inspiration for wresting a kind of independence from bondage. From the space of his social exile Sab can wrest a kind of independence too; the space allows him to construct a different "artificial" order that can recognize his natural legitimacy. And this is exactly what the slave does when he plants a garden in the middle of the plantation. The text tells us that Sab breaks this new ground in order to provide Carlota with an ideal space

for intimacy and daydreaming. But the miniature Eden, carved
out of the rival slavocratic system and composed of the most
surprising combination of flowers and shrubs from the master's
turf, must surely have given Sab another kind of personal satisfaction. He, at least as much as Carlota, needed a spot for
recreation.

> No había en Puerto Príncipe en la época de nuestra historia, grande
> afición a los jardines: apenas se conocían: acaso por ser todo el país
> un vasto y magnífico vergel formado por la naturaleza y al que no
> osaba el arte competir. Sin embargo, Sab que sabía cuánto amaba
> las flores su joven señora, había cultivado vecino a la casa de
> Bellavista, un pequeño y gracioso jardín. . . . No dominaba el gusto
> inglés ni el francés en aquel lindo jardinillo: Sab no había consul-
> tado sino sus caprichos al formarle. (70)

> [Gardens were certainly not in vogue in the area of Puerto Príncipe
> during the time of our story. They were hardly known at all,
> perhaps because the entire country was a vast and magnificent nat-
> ural bower, against which art did not dare to compete. Neverthe-
> less, knowing how much his young mistress loved flowers, Sab had
> planted a small and charming garden near the house at Bella-
> vista. . . . No English style nor French style dominated that lovely
> spot; Sab had consulted nothing but his own whims in forming it.]

There, in that little independently organized world, Sab's ideal
mistress and reader most enjoys herself. Consequently, it is
where her truest lover feels accomplished and happy.

In an analogous piece of work, and from the space of her
literary marginality, Gertrudis managed to compose a *doppel-
gänger* out of traditionally incompatible characteristics. In his
fissured totality, Sab turns out to be more pleasing than disturbing, more angel than monster, just as Sab's garden has an
Edenic, rather than an artificial (English or French), quality.
Sab, whose allegedly African name has no masculine or feminine marking in Spanish, is at the same time pacifist and rebellious, reasonable and passionate, practical and sublime, violent
and delicate, jealous and generous. He is, in sum, so integral a
combination of opposites that any hope of disentangling his
characteristics becomes illusory. Their possible origins in another traditional and binary linguistic system no longer seems

to matter. Sab is new, as natural and attractive as the garden he planted in the interior and liberated space of the plantation. In a like manner, Gertrudis constructed a new self between the crossings-out of a patriarchal language that would have identified her simply as a woman and white.

Gertrudis Gómez de Avellaneda understood that in order to write something new one had first to violate an earlier text, to open a space for oneself. The fact that this novel recognizes that writing implies a necessary violence should not surprise us. In one form or another, the notion was almost a commonplace of romantic literature. In *Sab* the violence is directed above all against the rhetorical system that organized races into a rigid hierarchy of color, from lightest to darkest. The unnameable but familiar mixture that Sab represents is not the only dilemma that the novel makes this order confront. Another misfit is Enrique Otway whose pure-blooded whiteness amounts to blinding good looks that are presented in contrast to his contemptible character (154). In fact, his very whiteness stands out against the subtle shades of his Cuban context like a foreign interruption that threatens to dissolve the tropical harmony.

At the same time that *Sab* abandons the strong colors that could tragically divide Cubans against themselves, the novel also relaxes an implied binary system of gender coding. It shows the porousness and the strategic availability of signs, for example the signs "male" and "female."[8] If Enrique is a disappointing man to the extent that he is unable or reluctant to feel a sublime and disinterested passion for Carlota, Sab is heroic, one might say, to the extent that he is passionate and sentimental. He can correspond to the depth of women's feelings, to Carlota's intensity and to his adoptive mother's affection. That is, he is heroic to the extent that he is feminized. Gender coding relaxes on the other side as well, with Teresa, a woman who gives up romantic infatuation for principled passions. Carlota's illegitimate cousin and the family's penniless ward, Teresa is the only one who understands Sab's sublime feelings and catches it like a liberating fever. She offers to run away with him, away from his frustrations and from her misguided longing for Otway. We admire her for the reserve and emotional control that cannot be confused with the shyness or coyness that a patriarchal language might require of women. But more than anything else, we admire her for the novelty of a fictional woman who falls in love with the abstract principles that Sab represents. Nevertheless, Avellaneda doesn't insist on establishing a balance between male and female characters. The regular coincidence here between the feminine and the admirable is borne out by a dramatis personae in which all the women are noble (heightened to an almost comic level in the "Indian princess," Martina), while the men range from the feminized ideal of Sab to the ineffectual Don Carlos and the opportunist Otway Senior.

This ironic association of vir-tue with women, as well as the insistent parallels that Avellaneda establishes between the condition of women and that of slaves, has led to various and eminently justified feminist readings of *Sab*. But for the purpose of specifying the feminist nature of this novel, it seems important to remember that the characters and much of the erotic struggle in the text are *typical* of the period. Or they became typical once other Latin American novels repeat, or independently invent and vary, her fissured characters. Those novels will create a context around this early one, making Avellaneda's daring project part of a legitimate canon. This doesn't minimize the effect of the novel. On the contrary, it makes the impact felt globally in the continent. Although some readers choose to focus on what makes Avellaneda's novel particularly feminist, arguing that she is writing against the male tradition (and even that she uses abolitionism as a code for the more radical feminism),[9] I am more concerned to show that she was at the vanguard of what would become the standard male canon and to suggest that the canon itself is remarkably feminized.

Even if we wanted to read Avellaneda as a lone rebel, we might find it impossible, by now, to bracket the later nineteenth-century novels through which we inevitably read hers. Our approach to her is necessarily like Borges's reading of Menard's *Quijote*. It is contaminated, or enriched, by layers of intervening readings. For some readers today, affected as we almost unavoidably are by feminist and more generally poststructuralist lessons in reading, nineteenth-century romantic novels produce an uncanny sense of familiarity and contemporaneity. The Latin American canon of romantic novels seems to wage a consistent struggle against classical habits of oppositional thinking. Instead of keeping race, class, gender, and cultural differences pure, the "historical" romances that came to be considered national novels in their respective countries married hero to heroine across those former barriers. After the wars of Independence and the civil wars that followed in many Latin American countries, insisting on pure categories became literally self-destructive. If nations were to survive and to prosper, they had to mitigate racial and regional antagonisms and to coordinate the most diverse national sectors through the hegemony of an enlightened elite; that is, through mutual consent rather than coercion. Even the most elitist and racist founding fathers understood that their project of national consolidation under a civil government needed racial hybridization. Of course for some, such as Argentina's political architects Sarmiento and Alberdi, the plans did not project a union of whites with blacks (and much less with Indians), but rather the marriage between Hispanics, allegedly incapable of liberty and progress, with Anglo-Saxons who could take advantage of the economic opportunities that the creoles kept missing. Still, Argentine consolidation, after Buenos Aires's centralism struggled against the interior's insistence on federating power, was posed more in interregional than interracial terms. Clearly, though, this kind of political embrace as well as the color-coded variations of national amalgamation implied a certain exclusivity, principally of sectors that would not fit the enlightened plans: these sectors were the Indians and gauchos in Argentina; the blacks in Galvan's *Enriquillo* (Dominican Republic, 1882); and in the Cuba that Avellaneda represented, the ideally excluded sectors were the creole "sugarocracy" and the English interlopers.

Unlike the militant populist novels that would follow, where heroes measure their manliness against imperialist or dictatorial contestants for their country's love, the early novels celebrated a domestic, sentimental, and almost feminized brand of heroism. Instead of the caudillo, or local boss, whose power came from being at the top of a rigidly patriarchal pyramid of supporters, the sentimental and bourgeois hero of the times developed more lateral relationships with fellow citizens. He exercised a freedom of (market) choice, for example, by picking his romantic partner; and he conquered her by love, always aware that she enjoyed the same kind of freedom. Consequently, the bond between the two, that is the hegemonic structure that coordinates diverse interests by appealing to their mutual benefit, seems to dispense with the need for military or any other type of coercive power. Instead, the love affair replaces power with desire, as if power and desire were two radically different things.

The obvious question with regard to *Sab* is what Avellaneda's Cuba has to do with this post-Independence esthetic and the related mandate to call an internal truce after the civil wars. Cuba in the 1830s was many decades away from achieving independence, let alone reconciling differences at home after Spain had left. It was also far from abolishing slavery, as Spain's other colonies had done after independence, and therefore far from creating at least the legitimate space for racial amalgamation. In some ways, Cuba represents the mirror image of Brazil, the other apparently anomalous and long-lasting slave society. Neither country fits the general Latin American pattern of Independence in the 1810s and 1820s followed by civil wars that ended by midcentury. Cuba was among the last colonies that Spain lost at the end of the century, whereas Brazil, long independent from Europe, was a sovereign monarchy at home. Yet both countries were slavocracies until the end of the century, when Cuba rid itself of Spain and Brazil became a republic. If slavery created a bond between them, it also should have distanced them so much more from countries where slavery had been abolished, at least officially, with early independence. Therefore, it is most significant that Cuban and Brazilian national romances look so much like the others. It suggests a cultural and even political coherence in the literary/political project to reconcile oppositions, to embrace the other, that goes deeper than the historical differences among the countries.

This is remarkable, I cannot help repeating, because Cuba was still at odds with Spain; it was preparing militarily and culturally for a series of struggles that would last for decades. Nevertheless, the conciliatory genre of romance in this and other abolitionist novels seems to have seduced even the Cubans. Perhaps romance takes over because internal unity would be necessary for the fight against Spain. Romance between previously segregated sectors might ideally create the national unity among whites and blacks, ex-masters and ex-slaves, that the war for Independence would need. In Cuba, in other words, abolitionism becomes a *condition,* not a result, of independence. The fact that *Sab* makes a second appearance during the Independence struggle (in 1871, the same year that Avellaneda expunges it from her respectable *Complete Works*), and serialized in a Cuban revolutionary journal in New York, suggests how important an ideological weapon this novel must have been.[10] Even if its romantic project were insufficient to the goal of establishing mutual love between the races, the rigid and irrational distinctions that belonged to the old order would have to be toned down before independence could be a safe alternative for Cuba's white minority. The threat of slave uprisings, and lessons from Haiti's revolution, surely had something to do with the departure of Avellaneda's family from Cuba in 1836.

Critics are probably right to point out that *Sab* represents a perhaps feminized and radicalized version of the "noble black lover" theme so popular in romantic literature. From Aphra Behn's *Oroonoko; or the Royal Slave* (1688), through Victor Hugo's high romantic version in *Bug-Jargal* (1826), where for the first time love tragically (and violently) crosses race and class lines, to the abolitionist novels written in Cuba, black heroes were conquering white audiences.[11] Part of their heroic appeal, no doubt, was the cathartic effect they produced when they lost, inevitably, to unjust but unmovable laws of the state. In the context of contemporary Cuban abolitionist novels,[12] Avellaneda's variation amounts to dislocating the dramatis personae of the tragic genre, perhaps following Hugo's revolutionary move.[13] One specific dislocation makes her invert the expected racial identities between lover and beloved. Spanish American novels that describe interracial affairs have often been a loving or eroticized version of the white man's burden. They describe an active lover who is both male and white (the liberal bourgeoisie) and the yielding object of his galvanizing attention who is often a mulatta (the masses to be incorporated in a hegemonic project). Examples that come to mind range

from Cuba's canonical *Cecilia Valdés* (1839, 1882) by Cirilo Villaverde, to one of the most important populist novels, Venezuela's *Doña Bárbara* (1929) by Rómulo Gallegos.[14] When the lover
is a slave, his beloved is usually a slave too. But, as Mary Cruz
notes in her prologue to Avellaneda's novel, Sab is the only
"man of the enslaved race" who dares to desire a white woman.[15]

This evidently scandalized or terrified the Spanish authorities
in Cuba, as well as powerful groups of merchants and planters
who dominated the sugar economy of the island,[16] since the
book was banned almost immediately. It is difficult to know,
however, whether *Sab* scandalized them any more than did a
contemporary novel such as Suárez y Romero's *Francisco,* which
could be published only posthumously and abroad. Its delayed
publication date may have had something to do with the fact
that *Francisco* is an open denunciation of slavery. The fatal love
triangle that frames the narrative, involving a noble black slave,
the mulatta slave who reciprocates his love, and the lascivious
white master who stops at nothing to possess her, seems almost a pretext for the novel's relentless and detailed review of
slavery's institutionalized horrors. Throughout, Suárez underscores Francisco's Christian meekness. In *Sab* the censure is
more subtle and the response more violent. Slavery is not its
most urgent problem; the problem is rather a general system
of unequal, binary, esthetic, and social relationships between
light and dark, men and women, masters and servants.[17]

This difference in focus—from racial bondage to racist bonding—is refined in far greater detail and over many more pages
in *Cecilia Valdés* and helps to account for its claim as Cuba's
national novel after the period of abolition (1880–1886).[18] The
story is familiar even among Cubans who never read the novel,
for one reason, because it became popular literally as a revue,
a staged musical by Gonzalo Roig.[19] Understandably, the nation
constituted after the formal institution of slavery is replaced by
more delicate and daunting discriminations may identify more
with Villaverde's tragic rehearsal of elaborately exclusive habits
than with Avellaneda's projection of unity. His cast to the color
scheme, therefore, deserves more than passing mention in this
chapter dedicated to the other less pessimistic, more rebelliously feminist novel.

Hardly anyone in *Cecilia Valdés* escapes the charge of racism, not the mulatta or her white lover, and certainly not the white narrator. A first, far shorter version, published contemporaneously with abolitionist novels in 1839 but inoffensive enough to appear in Cuba and then in Spain, had featured a predictably idealized heroine, the omniscient author who knew her worth, and little of the flair for provoking self-doubt that distinguishes the four-part novel of 1882.[20] In it, the narrator continually calls attention to his own social blinders by delaying information long after it is news to us. It is delayed, a bit transparently and with a studied clumsiness that leaves the teller tellingly benighted because, for one thing, there is no free-thinking Teresa here who knows enough to listen to blacks. As in *Sab*, it is the slaves who can tell this story about Cecilia, the daughter of an unknown white gentleman and a mulatta who goes mad when her lover removes the baby to an orphanage. That first tragedy is reversed too late to save the mother, but Cecilia gets to grow up partly in her grandmother's house where she learns that any white husband is preferable to a black one, and partly on the street where she falls in mutual love with Leonardo Gamboa, the spoiled son of a Spanish slaver who—horrors!—happens to be her father too. Neither one knows that their affair is incestuous, nor that their conflicting expectations—love for him, marriage for her—will clash violently. To underline the potential for perverse productivity in the incest theme, Leonardo's youngest sister is Cecilia's double, so that if he and Adela "were not flesh and blood siblings, they would have been lovers" (Villaverde, 57).

The other woman in Leonardo's life is Isabel Ilincheta, elegant, correct, a fitting counterpart to independent and candid Cecilia. Isabel seems in excess of standard good-girl heroines; in fact she is more the hero, modeled perhaps after Villaverde's independentist wife.[21] It is Isabel who runs her father's business—growing coffee rather than the more labor-intensive sugar; and her womanly good looks don't interfere with a markedly virile appeal.[22] The fact that Leonardo can profess love for both women, for his incestuous and finally narcissistic sibling substitute as well as for the ideal fiscal match of Isabel's coffee with his sugar, even boasting that many more women have room in his heart, augurs the schizophrenic and irrational destiny of desire here. The campaigns of amorous conquest, the intrigues and jealousies, the doubts that Isabel feels about joining an insensitive if not brutal slave-owning family, are all set against a detailed backdrop of an inhuman system, inhuman because it denies human rights to blacks and because it makes monsters of their masters. The tragedy comes to a circular climax when Cecilia and her lover set up house together, have a baby girl, and separate once bored Leonardo feels ready to marry Isabel. Cecilia complains about the betrayal to her desperate mulatto admirer, a tailor's apprentice by day and a musician by night, which makes him doubly promising as the purveyor of an autonomous Cuban style.[23] The pattern traced here for fashioning a nation from competing colors and tastes evidently cuts Leonardo out after he betrays Cuba's characteristic beauty. As a result of her admirer's murderous outrage against Gamboa, Cecilia is left as mad as her mother was, and her baby is left quite helplessly orphaned.

This is a novel about impossible love, not because blacks and whites should not love each other—after all, they are mutually attractive and produce beautiful children—but because slavery makes it impossible. As Havana's frustrated mayor puts it, "In a country with slaves . . . morals tend . . . toward laxity and the strangest, most monstrous and perverse ideas reign" (Villaverde, 279). Romance and convenience don't coincide in this country that is not quite American, nor even a country yet, just as they did not coincide in aristocratic, hierarchical Europe. We know that Gamboa Sr. married his wife for money and then looked elsewhere for love, and that Leonardo, admiring and even loving Isabel for her useful virtues, remains romantically irrational. He undercuts—or overextends—his affections because archaic privilege exceeds his individual bourgeois self. Father and son are seduced as much by the absolute power of their racial and sexual advantage as by their partners' charms. This is no modern and rational free market of feeling where unprotected desire could produce social growth,[24] but a bastion of colonial custom where erotic protectionism nurtures desire in surplus of social need.

The novel, then, poses the problem of racial exploitation

whose other face is self-annihilation. The marriage contract to reproduce the family within domestic confines is here as transparently fictional and as easily violated as was the 1817 agreement that England had wrested from Spain to stop importing slaves, a promise that should have forced the reproduction of a labor force at home. Beyond a metaphoric relationship between broken conjugal contracts and contraband slaves, we saw that Havana's moralizing mayor senses a link of cause and effect between social dissolution and slavery. The brutality allowed by prospects of new imports, and the unproductive privilege it fostered, he said, corroded society's most sacred values: "familial peace and harmony" (Villaverde, 282). The family might not be quite so threatened by extramarital affairs, on which the men look with indulgence, were it not for the secrecy imposed by the conflicting code of bourgeois marriage contracts. It is secrecy that puts Leonardo at risk of incest. He will not be guilty with Adela because their relationship is clear; but Cecilia's parentage is an explosive secret, a debilitating blindspot where the rule of masters' privilege (double-)crosses modern family ties. Both the narcissism and the secrecy point to the moral contradictions of a slave society that assumes it can be modern. Neither the sugar industrialists—whose irrational excesses produce slave rebellions, suicides, and English interventions—nor the interracial lovers can make a stratified society coincide with bourgeois pacts. The tragedy, as I said, isn't caused by interracial romance but by the secrecy that obscures the slipperiness of racial categories.

The fine divide between exogamy and incest goes unattended, largely because of a certain reluctance to attend to the information slaves command. One informant is María de Regla, Adela's beloved black nurse now exiled to a sugar plantation. She eventually gets a hearing from the girl, joined by her mother and sister, at the end of part III, chapter 8, when she "connects the dots" in what had remained a studiously spotty story. This slave is also the one who provided Cecilia with a mother's milk and knows who the father was, which explains her removal from the house in Havana; the one who witnesses the self-annihilating heroism of a field slave who swallows his tongue to make his forced silence felt; the one who now keeps the ladies of the house listening for hours about the nefarious effect of slavery when black families are separated and sold off in pieces; the Hegelian slave whose storytelling power over the enchanted mistresses comes from the knowledge gained in the work only she was fit to do. Once her welcome assault on their bedroom frees the novel's narrative flow, the reader may feel an uncomfortable self-doubt in retrospect. Not about the evidently incestuous plot she points to and which begins to unravel from the very beginning of the novel; any one of us can enjoy the self-congratulatory pleasures of getting the point long before the punchline. I mean the self-doubt or self-censure that María de Regla provokes in us readers when she authorizes some information that we may have resisted when it came from a then-questionable source, her husband Dionisio.

In part II, chapter 17, the lonely and bitter man, separated from his wife for twelve years, had crashed a formal dance restricted to free "colored" artisans and had been rebuffed there by Cecilia. Enraged, Dionisio blurted out what we partially know and she suspects: that she and her lover are already too intimately related and that her enslaved nursemaid was banished to the sugar plantation where Gamboa Sr. would be safe from her knowledge; in short, that because of this haughty and thoughtless mulatta who was about to consummate her own disaster, Dionisio and his wife were leading disastrously lonely and humiliating lives. It's not the information that may make us uncomfortable, especially not when it's repeated by a nonthreatening female slave in the conventionally sentimental (s)pace for reading novels; it is rather thinking back on the scene of refusing to know, Cecilia's refusal, that of her admiring companions and, also perhaps, of her readers. Villaverde sets the trap of racially restricted listening by keeping Dionisio anonymous for a while, all the while he remains an aging too-black man, dressed in ill-fitting finery and forcing himself on the Cuban Venus. Borrowing standards of good taste—as well as entire pages—from his society articles for *La Moda* where, arguably, fashion news was meant to customize a particular national style (as in Alberdi's case),[25] Villaverde's novel counts on certain assumptions of etiquette that would censure the aggressive outsider for inappropriately coveting the barely bronzed object of general desire. Surely the free men documented by invitation, and by the narrator's biographical references, are likelier to get her attention. Isn't Cecilia's caution, if not her disdain, understandable? What possible significance could Dionisio's string of insults and recriminations have? She worries about it for a bit, at least until the next dance; and María de Regla reminds the reader to worry too, about why Dionisio, the source of knowledge, the appropriate teller of the story, cannot be appropriately heard. In this novel, as in *Sab*, it is the slaves who know and tell, if the masters will only listen to slaves whose mastery of standard Spanish should itself have been an eloquent promise of social coherence. And by drawing a distinction between blacks who know and whites or mulattoes who refuse to, Cirilo Villaverde cannot confuse himself with an omniscient informant, as Avellaneda had done when she signed Sab's name to the end of her book. Instead, Villaverde's signature appears at the beginning, on the initial title page, via his own initials (and credentials?), C. V., which also can stand for Cecilia Valdés.[26] He is Cecilia, deluded like her, unwilling but obliged to divorce desire from destiny, more white than black but, as Leonardo Gamboa remarks about his own privileged color, definitely Cuban in its indefinite origins. "My mother really is a Creole, and I can't vouch for her blood purity" (Villaverde, 38). The confusion doesn't produce a new autochthonous archetype, as it did in *Sab,* but an impossibly precarious hierarchy in which the mulatta's desire to move up coincides tragically with her white lover's taste for slumming. Compared to the bold abolitionist pronouncements of *Sab,* the politics in *Cecilia Valdés* is insidiously subtle, because color coding is shown to be so culturally constituting that the lovers never really unlearn it. Instead one yearns for racial privilege while the other plays on it.

With Villaverde's hindsight, we might assume that the Spanish censors of *Sab* were more concerned than they needed to be about its subversive potential. However, even if the novel wouldn't radically alter centuries of insidious habit, the prose patrol was probably right to fear for a peculiar institution from which slave traders and slaveholders were getting rich. After all, rebellious blacks would be among the most impassioned freedom fighters of Cuba's Ten Years' War (1868–1878) for independence. The book was stopped at the very dock in Havana as the censors surely worried about its potentially destabilizing effect on the slavocracy.[27] That is, the effect produced by seeing a slave invested with the power implied by desire and with the legitimacy that accompanied romantic passion, a combination of forces that took the white elite as its object. His excess of desire always threatens to spill over into a bloody explosion. By contrast, a canonical novel like Brazil's *O Guaraní* (1857) by José de Alencar, constructed around a similar erotic investiture of the subaltern class, caused little concern among slavocrats at home. Here the Indian protagonist adores his blond blue-eyed Portuguese mistress. But he adores her as the living image of the Virgin, not as an object of human desire, a passion experienced only by the less ideal characters. Like *Francisco*, this book refuses the radicalizing power of *Sab*, both because the Guaraní can feel no self-interest and because Alencar (antiabolitionist that he was) preferred to cast his sublime lovers in racially pure categories (even though the categories were bound to mix in the productive afterlife of his racial romances). *Sab*'s enduring charge of radicalism surely owes something to Avellaneda's success in making the racial categories themselves, along with gender assignments, the fragile objects of writing. She destabilizes oppositions from the beginning, by offering us a racially and generically mixed ideal in Sab; and she uses that ideal composite of selves to create a mirror effect for the ideal reader of Sab's letter; that is for Carlota, Cuba's sensitive, white elite that has been blinded by European esthetic and social habits. Sab is already a projection of national consolidation. As such, he goes much farther than simply taking the first denunciatory step in the struggle for blacks' and women's social equality. As a literary construction, who is nevertheless already a familiar type to the Cuban reader, Sab crosses over the very terms that constitute(d) the inequality.

I was suggesting above, that this Cuban romance, like others elsewhere, tends to reconcile tensions, and so it differs from populist, anti-imperialist novels of the 1920s, 1930s, and 1940s. These insist on distinct boundaries between self and other, legitimate and illegitimate ownership of national resources. Yet my suggestion may be a flagrantly Menardian anachronism. I may be reading *Sab* so much like a typical example of the canon that I can overlook a significant variation, one that links this book precisely with the populist novels that would follow. The point is that *Sab* distinguishes clearly between "legitimate" Cuban protagonists, both black and white, and "illegitimate" foreigners, the Otways. Like the first Spaniards who left traces of blood in the caves of Cubitas where Sab is the tour guide and Martina the living memory, these Englishmen came to Cuba only to exploit its wealth; that is, to marry her for her money.

Avellaneda's characterization of the Englishmen as social parasites is somewhat surprising in the general historical context of her book. She wrote it during a moment when the leading circle of Cuban abolitionists, who used to meet in Domingo Del Monte's living room, was allying itself with England.[28] England, after all, was the world power that did most to abolish the slave trade in those years. Predictably, this alliance made Del Monte's group the object of enmity and repression for Cuba's slaveholding authorities, which included the Creole sugarocracy and the Spanish merchants and slave traders. But in Spain the resistance to abolition and to England went much farther. It went as far as defending Spanish national or imperial sovereignty. During the first decades of the nineteenth century, the English were using the kinds of political and military means to stop the slave trade that actually threatened Spain's stability.[29] Needless to say, they also infuriated Cuban sugar growers for whom the Del Monte group was an annoying extension of English power.[30]

It also seems that English intervention hardly pleased Gertrudis Gómez de Avellaneda. She evidently held out some hope that Cuba could gain freedom without "selling herself" to England. In addition to being just as much a Spanish Liberal as she was a creole abolitionist, Avellaneda had other, more local reasons for belonging only marginally to Del Monte's Anglicized group. In the first place, she was neither from Havana nor from anywhere else in the western part of the island where sugar embittered the lives of far too many slaves. Her social and intellectual world was not polarized between sugar's power and abolitionist resistance. Avellaneda's country was elsewhere; it

was the "Little Cuba" at the margin of plantation society, to the
east of Havana and Matanzas.[31] It is "Cubita," represented time
and again in *Sab* (either in the womblike caves associated with
Martina or in the garden that Sab planted in the middle of the
plantation) as the small world whose master was the legitimate
Cuban, the feminized, mulatto, protagonist.

I will not insist that Carlota represents Cuba, or "la Cuba
chiquita," with her name beginning and ending like the island's
and the depleted dowry that still attracts mercenary lovers (40,
142). But I will suggest that her romance with Enrique Otway
parallels the misguided affairs that were bonding some sentimental Cubans to their English "allies" and others to conservative Spaniards. The alliances, Avellaneda is saying, are
one-sided. The English, as much as the Spanish slave traders
and merchants, are using Cuba for their own purposes. But
Cuba is getting nothing in return, nothing, that is, but the
useless and unproductive prestige of Old World elegance. A
pale and indolent Spain, like Otway, owes its life to the very
population that it excludes from its society—not only blacks but
also, to some extent, Cuban colonial subjects.

Certainly Avellaneda would not include all Spaniards in her
implied criticism. It must not have been easy always to predict
who would fit into the "us" and "them" categories of this proto-
populist opposition. After all, she herself was a Spaniard both
because of her father's family and then largely by choice. She
was Cuban more as a matter of sentimental allegiance. As if to
dramatize the opportunities for a personal construction of national identity, Avellaneda gives young Otway more than one
chance to make the switch from foreign opportunism to national sentiment. Virtue, in the form of passion for the other,
tempts him, but not enough to be saved as a New World hero.
"Under her power, despite himself, he felt his heart race with
an unknown emotion" (88). Enrique *could* have chosen to love
Cuba, as Avellaneda had, but his split and finally traditional
loyalties make his romantic flight with Carlota miss its liberating mark. Perhaps because of his years, Enrique seems more
capable of sincere feeling than does his father; and the youth
is almost redeemed through love. As in other romances, a generational difference suggests a possible political and sentimental

gap. In *Amalia* (Argentina, 1851), *Martín Rivas* (Chile, 1862), *Enriquillo* (Dominican Republic, 1882), and *Soledad* (Bolivia, 1847), parents often represent values that their children recognize as anachronistic or un-American. But the tragedy here is that Enrique is finally reconciled to his father. Carlota's lover is unmanned because he short-circuits the Oedipal circle and becomes his father's clone rather than his rival. And Cuba's birth is delayed because clones cannot hope to engender anything new.

The real man here is, of course, Sab, or Avellaneda herself, as passionate as Carlota and as principled and selfless as Teresa. S/he is the more manly, as we said, because s/he is womanly. And s/he is the more Cuban because, as already suggested, in a parallel move away from binary gender terms, Sab's racial and historical character is already so intimate an amalgamation of terms that it has produced a unique, "autochthonous" type.

The novel hints, at least, that continuing intimacy between the already Cubanized sectors would advance the colony's consolidation into a nation. Sab himself represents a product of that intimacy and the ideal harbinger of national authenticity. His desire for Carlota is also a desire for greater national solidarity. It is no revolutionary dream but, as the novel suggests, merely the hope of legitimating a family relationship that is already intimate. The match is less unthinkable than possibly redundant or even incestuous. In that first scene, when Sab meets Otway, he explains that he never knew who his father was; it was a secret that his mother would not reveal. The only thing Sab did know was that his guardian, Don Luis, prepared for death by having a long and secret conversation with his brother, Don Carlos. Since then, Carlota's father has cared for Sab almost like a son (29–30). A conversation between Enrique and Carlota corroborates the insinuation of family relationship, although for some reason Sab doesn't seem to have gotten the point (52). In any case, since Sab and Carlota are probably cousins, the intimacy of possible "incest" at this safe remove might have provided an ideal family consolidation in the nation-building project. Incest here is not the unproductive dead-end of love, as it would become with the threat of sibling incest in pessimistic novels like *Cecilia Valdés, Aves sin nido* (Peru, 1889), and even

One Hundred Years of Solitude (Colombia, 1967). Rather it was proof that Cubans had been loving Cubans productively for a long time. For pre-independentists like Avellaneda, *Sab* is no warning against some unnatural and secret passion. It is an opportunity for consolidation.

This kind of cousin-to-cousin love is the norm in many of the foundational novels that followed, as for example in *Soledad, María* (Colombia, 1867), *Amalia* (at another remove), *Enriquillo,* and *Doña Bárbara.* In this nation-building scheme that depended on marrying powerful and conflicting interests to each other, the possible match between Sab and Teresa is doomed from the beginning. Even if Sab had overcome his own self-limiting ideal of love and responded to the warmth he inspired in Teresa, their union would not have delivered the kind of hegemonizing stability that Carlota's recognition could promise. Teresa's history does not intersect with Sab's; instead it runs parallel. She is as illegitimate and economically dependent as is the slave (36). Whereas Carlota could have supplemented Sab's generic Cubanness and prudent industriousness with the aura of a broadly acknowledged legitimacy, Teresa could only encourage him to turn his back on Cuba: "Leave these lands, leave them and search for another sky" (159). She would have fixed him in another, ghettoized terrain, somewhere beyond a potentially amalgamated redefinition of the nation.

Read backward from the self-defeating racism that lingers in *Cecilia Valdés,* Avellaneda's knowing promise of a coherent Cuba may seem partial or strained, based on partial knowledge and straining with more will than conviction. Avellaneda has Teresa offer herself to Sab, but never really to tempt him; nor can his freedom to leave Cuba solve anything at home. These narrative dead-ends, along with Sab's preference for self-sacrifice over struggle, all point to an ideological pause in the novel's motivation. Despite the space that Sab and Avellaneda manage to liberate inside the discourse that traps them, as writers they are bound together by the classic double-bind. In the first place, Sab and Gertrudis continue to be united in their admiration for a schematic heroine whose adorable qualities themselves, her innocence and naiveté, keep her from recognizing Sab's worth. Carlota begins to love him only after she is no longer really Carlota anymore, but the embittered and disillusioned Mrs. Otway. The romantic affair that should have liberated Sab seals his tragic fate. The very language that channels his feelings makes sure that those feelings will be absent to his ideal reader until it is too late. In the second place, Sab also refuses to love himself through his textual double, Teresa. He refuses because he aspires to the recognition of his mistress, because he does not want to break with the binary generic categories of ideal romantic love. Carlota is not only his childhood playmate and the object of his incestuous fantasies; she is also the incarnation of an ideal and uncontaminated sign. Her name is woman.

But for Sab or Teresa there are no names adequate enough to make them feel legitimate. There are no new categories in the language of a slave society. Neither Sab nor Avellaneda coin any. Could this be because of some irreparable breach in their language? Or is it because of Avellaneda's fear of falling into excessive verbal violence, the same horror that Teresa had of Sab's fantasies of revenge?

> He pensado también en armar contra nuestros opresores los brazos encadenados de sus víctimas; arrojar en medio de ellos el terrible grito de libertad y venganza; bañarme en sangre de blancos. (147)

> [I too have thought about arming our chained and victimized bodies against our oppressors; of casting among them the terrible cry of liberty and revenge; of bathing in the blood of white men.]

No doubt Avellaneda preferred not to follow Hugo's lead in making his black hero a leader of the slave rebellion in Haiti; she rather chose to imagine the possibility of a peaceful and legitimate marriage of signs inside the existing order of things. Avellaneda must have felt safer about writing the old works in new combinations so that they would only look incoherent, because the idea of inventing new and revolutionary names evidently seemed more violent than constructive.

5

O GUARANÍ AND IRACEMA: BRAZIL'S TWO-FACED INDIGENISM

"Tupí or not Tupí, that is the question." Oswald de Andrade asked it, tropicalized English and all, in his "Cannibal's Manifesto" of 1928. He and other Brazilian Modernists writing for the *Revista de Antropofagia* were straining toward a new kind of literary independence, one that would replace the ornamental, more-Christian-than-thou Indian of Romantic nativism with the genuine cannibal. "We were never catechized. What we performed was Carnival. The Indian dressed as Imperial Senator. . . . Or appearing in the operas of Alencar, full of good Portuguese feelings."[1] And Oswald's more famous and less bristly contemporary, Mário de Andrade, was subtle enough to dedicate the first version of *Macunaíma: The Hero Without Any Character* (1928) to the now past master, Alencar.[2] Like his Indians, the modernist version was open to Europeans, but mostly at the mouth. He was a figure for using foreign texts, not so much as models but as ingredient. Brazilian writers, modernists proclaimed, were cannibals, Tupís. They were direct descendants of the most authentic Brazilians, the Indians who never resisted Europeans so well as when they found them delicious. Even the anthropophagous joke cooked up from Hamlet's crude question derives its bite from being open to English. (Or is the joke entirely English, reducing Hamlet's ontological void to a decision about voiding?)[3] If the outsider was inevitably inside, at least he should be there in digestibly American terms. To consume or not to consume; the Shakespearean echoes of the question give the only possible answer. In a country given to multiple and repeated cultural invasions, the modernists decided to make their consumption conspicuous. What choice was there, when a lesser appetite would have meant giving up in the name of autonomy a varied culture that was already Brazilianized? It would have meant defining the national "by subtraction," as Roberto Schwarz recently put it,[4] and by being left Tupí (alas, already Anglicized) with no alternative.

The question is why Tupí constitutes so stubborn a remainder of the subtraction. Why does an Indian identity survive in a culture that keeps killing off the real thing? Oswald de Andrade was probably asking this all along, while he demonstrated the impasse of asserting his nativism in a borrowed European language. The aspiring Tupís were already at the mercy of the English, just as the Indians had been at the mercy of the first Portuguese adventurers and Jesuits. If anyone was eaten up, it was the "cannibals" themselves. There was nothing pristine even about the Tupí language; calling it that, and alternatively the *lingua geral,* was an invention of the Jesuits who regularized a number of dialects under the name of Tupí so that they could proceed to replace it with Portuguese. They more often failed than not, first because the Indians often preferred to retreat to the jungle or to commit suicide than remain confined to the stable life of the missions; and second because the conquerors were impatient to clear the land—of Indians when necessary. The result was practically genocidal wherever the colonists chose to settle.

Andrade's pun, in other words, plays on more than the inevitable Europeanization of Brazilian culture; it plays on the tenacity of Brazil's "Indian" identity even though the country was founded on Indian removal. The joke is not only on Brazilians who claim native roots; it is also on the skeptics who may imagine these roots to be "false" as a national mooring, simply because they are produced by the desire to claim them. Simulacra, after all, can be taken for real cultural horizons, if there are willing takers. And there have been many, at least since Alencar's ever-popular indigenist romances, even if modernists like Andrade poked fun at the masquerade. So his rhetorical but also insoluble question is a dramatization not only of cultural hybridization but also of the necessary "Indianization" of Brazilian culture. If exclusive nativism is at an impasse, pure cosmopolitanism was in the same straits.

During his lifetime, José de Alencar (1829–1877) was already venerated as the father of Brazilian literature. Although most critics persisted in ignoring him, Alencar had the singular distinction of actually being read by his contemporaries, even in remote outposts of the country, and of being paid for the books they bought.[5] In one of the many public eulogies at his death, the *Diário Oficial* called him the "apostle" of Brazilian literature who eloquently proved what the combination of love of literature and love of country could create;[6] another called his death "a national calamity."[7] Today Alencar is no less conspicuous than he was then; and Afrânio Coutinho can echo earlier enthusiasts by reaffirming Alencar as the patriarch both of national literature and of Brazil's hybrid cultural identity.[8] Alencar was no mirror of society, Silviano Santiago says, but a lantern whose evenly distributed glow from the elite center produced the unifying effect called nationality.[9] His twenty-one published novels, another twenty to thirty at some stage of writing, and a dozen plays, gave his avid public ever more reason for admiration.[10] The vast production was, Alencar explained in the preface to *Sonhos d'Ouro,* a project to portray the entire country from the earliest conquest, through colonial times, to the present. The novels included regionalist and urban novels set in contemporary Brazil as well as the "historical" encounters between whites and Indians. There was more than the public remembers, according to Antônio Cândido, because in addition to the Alencar of boys' stories (heroic exploits generally in the past), and of girls' stories (idealized urban romances of the present), there is a third, "adult" Alencar of psychologically complex novels about mature men and women.[11] There was so much that Alencar's work, like the Bible, is a collection of foundational books too heterogeneous to build on together. So the first gesture of the exegete and cultural arbiter is to select, to be partial to some books over others. As for Alencar's general public, it always chose his two crossover historical romances between Indian and white lovers.[12] One is *O Guaraní* (1857), published serially in *O Diário do Rio de Janeiro* of which Alencar became editor-in chief a year earlier. The other is *Iracema* (1865), which competes as Brazil's national novel. These romances have been practically sacralized through frequent re-editions, adoption in school curricula, Carlos Gomes's opera *Il Guaraní* (1870; in Italian, naturally), multiple movie versions (the only examples on record of a novel being filmed four or five separate times),[13] and the countless Brazilian children named for Alencar's artificial Indians.[14] The obsessive repetition may have more to do with a need to reaffirm a Brazilian-ness based on interracial love than with the books' literary charm. Yet they are charming, despite critics who refuse to take these centennial best-sellers seriously.[15] "With all the unconvincing falseness of their romantic Indigenism, the fact is that the people [*o povo*] don't find them false, but rather love them and accept them as perfect."[16]

The title character of *O Guaraní* is Peri, a king of that gentle nation (Alencar 1857, 73; 169) who like Abraham "has left mother, brothers, and the land where he was born" (Alencar 1857, 89; 211) to follow a new deity.[17] The goddess is Cecilia, a blond, blue-eyed mistress to whom he is willingly enslaved; and the cult he founds is a mixture of Mariolatry and white supremacy. Ceci is loved by everyone in the fortresslike estate to which her father Dom Antonio de Mariz had removed his family in 1582 when Rio became a Spanish possession. As the novel begins, she is apparently responding to the love of gallant Alvaro, a soldier at the fortress. More willful but just as naive as *Sab*'s Carlota, Ceci ignores both the reason for Peri's devotion and the passion her mestiza "cousin" (really Antonio's illegitimate daughter) Isabel feels for the Portuguese suitor. The amorous tangle straightens out, though, once the white idols acknowledge their preference for Indian and mestiza lovers, for selfless and heroic Peri on the one hand, and for panting, irrepressibly sensual, Isabel on the other (Alencar 1857, 25; 40, and 108–109; 263–264). The affair between Alvaro and Isabel ends tragically in miscalculations and a double suicide (Alencar 1857, 196; 503). But Peri and Ceci are saved from multiple dangers. One was Ceci's haughty mother who would have banished Peri were it not for her truly noble husband whose defense, a bit like Las Casas's defense of Enriquillo, is that the Indian is "a Portuguese gentleman in a savage's body" (Alencar 1857, 34; 64). A happy inversion, no doubt.

But a foreigner was more dangerous by far than the skin-deep antagonisms between Indians and Portuguese. "The Italian," Loredano, an ex-Capuchin employed along with Alvaro as a soldier at the fortress, was planning to abduct Ceci to rape her, killing anyone who might stop him. Then he would pillage a silver mine that a repentant adventurer had revealed to the false priest. "Loredano desired, Alvaro loved, Peri adored her" (Alencar 1857, 39; 78). There is a paradigmatic scene of that peculiar triangular yearning, staged around the precipice under Ceci's bedroom window. The scene is a *mise-en-abîme,* as it were, a more didactic than dizzying condensation of the novel's tensions. It shows three men poised around the gaping void in order to look into the window that overlooks the drop. Watching unseen from a branch outside the window, "the Indian saw the two men, who placed respectively to his right and to his left, seemed to be expecting something" (Alencar 1857, 40; 80–81). Only he escapes the gaze of desire on the right hand and murderous hostility on the left. The undervalued slave, Peri (or Sab), knows as much as his omniscient author. He knows that Loredano watches Alvaro approach the building and strain his body up to the window sill to leave the bracelet he has brought for Cecilia. He also knows that Loredano will wait until his rival leaves to approach from the other side and push the gift into the chasm.

Many chapters later, Peri is the only one who can retrieve the purloined present, much as Sab retrieved Carlota's fortune (lost by father and husband) when he displaced his winning lottery ticket in her drawer(s?). Like that quintessentially Cuban mix of color and gender, Peri too knows how to satisfy the woman he loves. It is not Old World military prowess that makes him come up with the prize, nor less still Dupin-like astuteness that would have been foreign to his sublime American simplicity, but Peri's feline, almost female, agility and different kind of knowledge. This child of nature knows how to survive a descent into the sharp rocks, the damp vegetation and the serpents that infest what amounts to a "vagina dentata" under Ceci's window (Alencar 1857, 228–229). When he surfaces with the string of pearls, unharmed and happy to have pleased his mistress, a relieved Ceci may already suspect that her object of desire is Peri, not Alvaro's lost jewels. After Peri delivers them, Ceci is quick to lose them again, this time to Isabel, the woman who can make a man of Alvaro. And when he discovers the bracelet on her tawny wrist, Alvaro senses that this errant emblem of his manhood belongs there.

Ceci had already made a real (civilized) man of Peri when she gave him the pistol that belonged to her father. "This [firing] arm, which comes from the lady, and Peri will be one single body," pledges the slave in a characteristically self-estranged third person (Alencar 1857, 74; 170). That new and improved body of his, bound to Ceci thanks to the pistol, helps Peri lead the escape from the final and cataclysmic danger. It is the war Aimoré Indians are waging against Dom Antonio's fortress in revenge for the Indian girl who was thoughtlessly killed by his son. The aging and desperate Antonio urges his legitimat(ing) daughter and the indigenous king to escape together before he blows up his own indefensible position. In the calm that follows, chaste but quickly melting glances between Peri and Ceci suggest that Brazil is far from being destroyed; it is about to be born.

More explicit is the lush sensuality of *Iracema,* even in the brief presentation I can offer here. This novel inverts *O Guaraní*'s color assignments of hero and heroine, and so resumes the pattern of chronicles that record endless meetings between white conquerors and easy Indian conquests. No hint of coercion mars the poetic prose of this romance, at least no coercion by the blond soldier Martim. Princess Iracema loves him at first sight and, Pocahantas-like, saves him from tribesmen at war with his allies. Iracema is a priestess who had consecrated her virginity to the cult of the Jurema potion, but her contact with Martim proves headier medicine. Iracema administers the Jurema to Martim who hopes thereby to remember his fiancée clearly enough to resist the virgin "of the honey lips." Yet the potion brings Iracema so clearly into focus that the vision turns out to be flesh and blood, a fantasy of love realized. "The warrior more than once sighed forth her name, and sobbed as though to summon another loving lip. Iracema felt her soul escaping to merge itself in a fiery kiss" (Alencar 1865, 21; 17).[18] Later, under her father's hospitable roof, "the virgin, trembling like the Sahy-bird fascinated by the serpent, bent her yielding form and reclined upon the warrior's bosom" (Alencar 1865, 33; 44). The lovers are then forced to flee, as Atala had flown with Chactas and as Cumandá would flee with Carlos during the feast of the flowers. And although Martim's love and the child she expects would have compensated for Iracema's loss of home and family, their idyll ends when Martim becomes restless, spending ever longer periods away at war. When Moacyr is born he literally sucks life from her, and Martim understands his loss as he departs with his son to recruit new settlers for the spot where he buried Iracema.

If in Brazil itself Alencar's enormous project to write a nation has been more or less streamlined in the country's memory to highlight these two romances, abroad there is understandably an even greater tendency to inherit a limited, easily manageable Alencar. In North America, for example, Samuel Putnam introduces him like this: "That the author of *Iracema* and *The Guaraní* did succeed in attaining a very real kind of greatness: an impersonal sort of immortality in the hearts of his countrymen, no one can deny." "He was their idol. They laughed and wept and shuddered with his heroes and heroines and named their children after them."[19] Comparing Alencar to his friend and admirer Machado de Assis[20]—as many critics do, often to show that the ironic and precociously modern Machado was incomparably better—Putnam points out that Machado's very originality meant that his work could not be confused with a collective memory, as Alencar's was. The confusion, if we may call it that, is what Brazil's most popular sociologist, Gilberto Freyre, celebrated in Alencar; that is, his largely successful effort to make the Amerindian past a natural foundation for Brazil's future.[21]

This is just what Brazilians longed for while Alencar was writing and apparently thereafter: an undeniably local cast to the founding moment of Brazilian history. Their preference for Alencar's idealized Indians may be, among other reasons, a response to the cultural politics of a country avid for traces of an autochthonous and legitimating tradition. Perhaps a similar avidity in the rest of Latin America makes Alencar's romances so uncannily familiar to readers of foundational fictions in Spanish. The points of contact, several of which I have been indicating, are no less than remarkable given Brazil's unique history. Some sense of that history, therefore, will help to appreciate how surprisingly well Alencar's romances fit a general Latin American paradigm; it will also suggest how subtle his apparently simple stories really are.

Increasingly during the eighteenth century, Brazilian creoles were becoming politically and commercially dissatisfied with colonial status, much as were the colonists of Spanish America, but not with the same intensity. Portugal had managed to weaken the resistance by softening its grip on the colony. Happily for both, the mother country was either too weak or too pragmatic to be very principled about such things as trade monopolies, Catholic orthodoxy, preference for the European born, or other measures that stifled and offended Spain's colonists.[22] When Napoleon invaded Madrid, Spain's American subjects took advantage of the "outrage" to declare that they were loyal to their own king, owed no allegiance to the French, and that in the absence of a legitimate monarch there was no alternative but to constitute local self-governments. But the Brazilians gained a different advantage from Napoleon's march; they got the legitimate Portuguese king himself, João VI. For the purely strategic reason of controlling a vast empire, there had long been suggestions to move the court from Lisbon to Rio. But the decision was forced on Portugal in 1807, when Napoleon threatened to invade if British ships continued to dock there. By then, João had already packed up his entire court, as had thousands of merchants and artisans packed their households, and they all set sail for Brazil in a flotilla escorted by English warships. Like Ceci's aristocratic father, who was ever loyal to Portugal and left Rio for the fortress rather than be the subject of a usurper, João left Lisbon to another usurper and set out for the colony he considered to be an extension of Portuguese soil.[23]

The prosperity and stability that the move brought to the colony delayed demands for independence. The only serious exception was a military revolt in Pernambuco, a northern coastal region that included Alencar's Ceará. The revolt was joined by some wealthy merchants, Crown judges, priests, tenant farmers, and a few slaveholders who were angry with the king for agreeing to British demands to end the slave trade.[24] Independence became a general issue only after Napoleon left Portugal and João was summoned home. He decided to stay in Brazil, but not for long. In 1822, a Liberal constitutionalist revolution in Portugal forced his return, and Brazilians, refusing to reassume colonial status, demanded independence. As early as 1801 Robert Southey had written, "So heavy a branch cannot long remain upon so rotten a trunk";[25] two decades later the break was imminent. But the predominantly monarchist creoles, terrified at the possibility of popular insurrections like Haiti's, or even like Spanish America's Independence wars, were not spoiling for a fight.

Their solution was to prevail on João's son, Prince Dom Pedro, to stay and to declare an independent monarchy in Brazil. He obliged. And instead of the rupture and disorder associated with a declaration of independence in other countries, Brazil's national history begins with continuity; it begins with Pedro's speech called *O Fico,* the decision to stay. Again, however, the province of Pernambuco had an independent mind, and the revolt of 1824 established a separate state.[26] Whether or not Pedro's Oedipal defiance was staged to flatter Brazil while keeping the country attached to Portugal through family ties, his subjects were soon convinced that the drama was mere theater. Even the troops that João, no doubt under some pressure at home, kept sending to discipline his son caused surprisingly little damage. The private correspondence between Dom João and Dom Pedro suggests that the father anticipated the break and advised his son to ally with the Brazilians to keep both parts of the empire in the hands of the Braganza family, just in case they could be reunited.[27] The Brazilians sensed as much. In any case, they found Pedro I to be too Portuguese and too authoritarian for their constitutionalist taste. In 1831 the creoles forced him to abdicate in favor of his five-year-old son who would become Dom Pedro II.

By 1850, the year Alencar graduated from law school in São Paulo and moved to Rio, Brazil seemed to have come of age along with its young emperor. The three-man regency that governed in the interregnum had within a year put down the mostly urban and nativist rebellions that followed the abdication. The one restorationist rebellion, in Pernambuco again, lasted until 1835. Other revolts were apparently invited by legislation that liberalized political participation, especially in the far north and far south of the country. The struggle in Pará was notable for its large radical population of free blacks, Indians, and *tapuios* (mestizos) who suffered cruel losses.[28] Throughout the disturbances, however, the enormous empire managed to remain unified and relatively prosperous, still without a strong national sense of identity but hopeful that it would follow.[29] Between 1850 and 1870 (Alencar's intensely productive years) major decisions about slavery and commerce, for example, were being made. They were the years when political party lines were continually crossing in government. Conservatives and Liberals participated in a "Conciliation Government" that Roberto Schwarz describes as "an ideological comedy," a black comedy in which the slave economy colored imported Liberal universalism.[30]

By 1853, when conciliation became official policy, Brazilians could congratulate themselves on achieving full political independence and stability. At just about the same moment, almost coincidentally, other Latin American countries were also consolidating new hegemonic governments based on alliances between elite sectors. The coincidence is not entirely fortuitous, however, despite Brazil's unparalleled history. The end of civil warfare that lasted throughout Brazil's sometimes tenuous interregnum, Spanish Americans' desire for cultural as well as political and economic independence, their responses to the commercial opportunities and obstacles England often presented to new nations eager to trade on the world market, all help to account for that shared moment when Brazil and Spanish America came of age and produced national romances. More than ever in Brazil as elsewhere, Americans were receptive to proposals, such as Alencar's, for a cultural independence that would respectfully remove Spain and Portugal into the shadows of a prehistory.

What could be more Brazilian and proclaim independence from the Old World more clearly than casting the nation's protagonists as Indians and as those first Portuguese who, turning their backs to Europe, chose to unite with the natives?

Of course whatever Alencar knew of those unspoiled natives, whom he considered practically extinct by the time he wrote, was mediated by early chroniclers.[31] He preferred to rely on the Huguenot missionary, Jean de Léry (1534–1611) whose accounts had "none of the condescending, fatherly spirit of Anchieta and other Portuguese Jesuits."[32] Although he used them too, their double affiliation was doubly unattractive to the nativist and liberalized public. Alencar's Indians, ideal nativist constructions that they were, made another kind of statement as well. It was the way they spoke Portuguese. "You are the river and Peri is the breeze that blows sweetly, careful not to silence the murmur of the waves; he is the breeze that bends the leaves that say Ce-Ci until they touch the water." Astounded as much by Peri's expression as by his generous intercession, Alvaro wonders, "where has this artless savage learned simple but charming poetry?" (Alencar 1857, 88–89; 208–209). The naked graceful bodies were an emblem of a certain freedom of speech, and they provided ideal personae for a home-grown language.[33] It was part of the romantic reaction to eighteenth-century Arcadianism that valued imitation of Europe above all else. Even if the reaction itself imitated contemporary European romanticism, the fiction of Brazilians now speaking a newly invented language did in fact bring innovative results.[34]

For many, Alencar's greatest contribution was writing in Brazilian: "Generations and generations of Brazilians have recited from memory pages of his prose. This inspiration and nobility of style has, nevertheless, a simplicity and naturalness" that flattered his readers by elevating what might have passed for their speech into a literary language.[35] Alencar consciously made this a mission. "Without doubt," he insisted, "the Portuguese language is being revolutionized here. . . . If Portuguese cannot progress, it must transform itself into Brazilian. Deny that and you deny the future of Brazil."[36] The short sentences that embedded Tupí words in a Portuguese grammar, a flexible grammar that raised pedantic criticism from purists, and the general colloquial departures from contemporary literary norms, these are for some readers Alencar's major accomplishment. In his narrator's voice, as well as in the dialogues, they amount to legitimating "Brazilian" as the language of a country that had finally broken with Portugal and Portuguese.

Of course his innovations would be open to another kind of criticism. Notably there was his young rival Távora who taunted Alencar—much as Twain would taunt Cooper—about his artificial language, neither too high nor too low but simply unheard of.[37] As for his possible debt to Cooper, which readers including Alencar himself cannot but notice, he denied it, repeatedly. Whether for patriotic or for vain(glorious) reasons, Alencar refused to acknowledge how much he may have taken from models. He brushed off Chateaubriand as exoticizing and sterile.[38] And he conveniently exiled Cooper from the scene of American writing by calling him "a poet of the sea." Their work was for Alencar, as it was for that other self-authorized imitator Sarmiento, nothing more than "a copy of the sublime original, that I had read with my heart."[39]

He was also reading Brazilian literature which celebrated the Indian hero before Alencar could consult his heart. Indigenism dates in Brazil from the 1820s, when the Parisian immigrant Ferdinand Denis, steeped in de Staël and Chateaubriand, evoked the innocent natives before the conquest. Denis's legacy of idealized Indians, which more than implied a denunciation of their current misery, lasted through the intensely personal poetry of Gonçalves Dias in the 1840s and probably through what Cândido calls "the persistent exoticism of our self-image even today."[40] But already by 1856, Alencar had to revive the literary Indians. The noble, pure-blooded and heroic variety had apparently been exhausted in Gonçalves de Magalhães's epic poem, *The Confederation of Tamoios*. As the most prestigious writer of the time and a court darling, Magalhães had the poem sumptuously published at Pedro II's expense.[41] The grandiloquent epic kills off its Indian heroes in providential wars that make space for founding Rio de Janeiro. Admirers read it as a celebration of native valor and self-sacrifice. But critics such as Alencar preferred to keep a trace of Indians alive.

His revision of Magalhães's military ideal began with a loosely written manifesto, a series of open letters about the epic. There Alencar observed that praising wartime valor was already anachronistic in a "Conciliation Government." And there was nothing especially Brazilian about the fight between good Indian allies of good whites against bad Indians helping bad whites; that battle between civilization and barbarism, we may call it, was the common history of the Americas.[42] Brazilian society is special, not because of heroic resistance but because of romantic surrender. It was founded, he insisted, when whites and Indians fell into each other's arms and made mestizo babies. Alencar may have been objecting to a certain programmatic affinity between Magalhães and historian Francisco Adolfo de Varnhagen, whose "Memorial Orgânico" (1851) makes the case that a good Indian is a dead one, when not hard at work for a European. And finally, the genre seemed all wrong. Epic poetry, with its necessary marvelous elements and grand style, was simply inappropriate for a historical poem about a modern nation that should be the "truth in verse." It was no use trying to reproduce Homeric cadences, doomed to sound hollow, in an indigenous history that should sound more like melancholic laments.[43]

What was left after Alencar dismissed Magalhães's epic intent at national creationism was, according to Augusto Meyer, a tabula rasa, a cultural emptiness that he was determined to fill.[44] And the sentimental romances that he would soon conjure up from the void were as productively confused in gender as in color. Freyre hears there "voices of men sighing and lamenting until they seem like women's voices . . . less the expression of individual [romantic] rebels than half-breed men who feel, like men of indefinite sexuality, a social and perhaps psychic difference from the purely white race, or from the definitely masculine and dominating sex."[45]

If heroic Independence was no longer the issue, we should add that Indians were quickly becoming a dead letter too, and that after Alencar they hardly survived even in Brazilian literature.[46] Magalhães was not the only one who was killing them off. Indians and mestizos (tapuios) had borne the brunt of horrible repression just after Independence[47] and during the practically exterminationist "Guerra Justa" that lasted until 1845. Racism revived in the anti-"savage" rhetoric that fired the war against Paraguay (1864–1870). The only reason Leslie

Bethell can give for that war is that it probably deflected the guilt at home, a guilt compounded by continuing racial hatred.[48] Why, then, was Tupí still an option for Alencar and his readers?

Because the Indian was precisely that element which gave Brazil its special coloring. If it makes sense to locate Magalhães in Varnhagen's ideological camp,[49] Alencar apparently squared off forces by aligning himself with a different kind of historian, one who identified *mestiçagem* as the matrix of Brazilianness. I am referring to Karl Friedrich Philipp von Martius, the German naturalist whose 1843 essay, "How the History of Brazil Should Be Written," won the 1847 essay contest sponsored by the Instituto Histórico e Geográfico Brasileiro. "Anyone," Martius begins, "who undertakes to write the history of Brazil, a country which promises so much, should never lose sight of the elements which contributed to the development of man there. These diverse elements come from the three races, . . . the present population consists of a novel mixture, whose history therefore has a very particular stamp."[50] Thanks especially to transfusions of Indian blood from the earliest days of the conquest, Brazilians were not only different from the Portuguese, they were also autochthonous and essentially American. Gratefully, but no doubt defensively too, both Martius and Alencar are forced to reason that the Indian element was once noble, generous, poetic, even technically advanced. Otherwise, the degree to which Brazilians were special would have been the degree to which they were inferior to Europeans, a position from which Nabuco would attack Alencar.[51]

Founded in 1838 with the emperor's blessings, the Instituto Histórico received his financial support and increasingly his interventions. No one was more concerned than he to produce a unifying historical project. The nature of that project was presumably wide open until Martius's proposal won, although there is reason to believe that the members of the institute already knew what their position would be. Brazil could have been framed as an outpost of elite European civilization, which was Varnhagen's position and which coordinated quite well with a view of Brazil as a model of continuity, a modern state that avoided the general anarchy of Spanish America. In fact,

Martius's proposed racial union—in which Europeans would improve the "inferior" races to create what Mexico's Vasconcelos would call "la raza cósmica"—was not entirely incompatible with Varnhagen's dream of Indian removal.[52]

I'm not sure Alencar ever referred directly to Martius, but the traces of his winning line are unmistakable in Alencar, as they would be in some of the future historiography that waved the Martius tricolor: "We will never be permitted to doubt that providential will predestined this mixture for Brazil."[53] Both begin with two assumptions. One is that progress and history are synonymous in a young New World, which amounts to assuming that change in America is always a positive advance. The other is that the dynamic element of change and progress is racial (a shorthand here for cultural, linguistic, and political differences), so that history is a record of racial development and improvement through new infusions and of racial decay through stagnation. Martius's "enlightened" racism never doubts which (inferior) races stand to gain the most from Brazil's characteristic crossings. His unflappable logic of racial development and decay begins by observing the desperate condition of contemporary Indians and deducing that they are in a state of decline. It even led him to posit past glories of indigenous civilization and to encourage expeditions that would discover the predictable proof. "Certainly many members of the Institute share with me the desire to support archaeological investigations, especially aiding travelers trying to discover these ruins."[54] The essay has three parts, one for each race. After making a principled and rather imaginative effort to develop what the Indian contribution might be to the Brazilian nation and its history, Martius fills many more pages on the Portuguese contribution, pages full of flattering information about commercial and military initiative, the aristocratic background of the colonists, the avoidance of civil and religious warfare, and the development of very liberal municipal institutions. Where Martius is practically silent, apparently preferring to say nothing when he has nothing good to say, is in the last section about the blacks. "There is no doubt that Brazil would have developed differently without the Negro slaves. The historian will resolve the problem of whether it was for the better or the worse" (Martius, 36).

Despite this limitation, Bradford Burns credits Martius as a "true son of the Enlightenment" who had a "remarkably clear vision of the uniqueness of Brazil" which overcame widely held prejudices and was ahead of its time. Winning positions, it seems, appear precocious and transparent after the fact. Long after, according to Burns. "No one seriously followed his suggested plan until nearly a century later, when Gilberto Freyre took up the theme of racial amalgamation and popularized [it] in his brilliant study *Casa Grande e Senzala*, first published in 1934."[55]

Yet Alencar, hardly a "no one" at all but the lantern that shone on disparate constituents to create a Brazilian effect, had already taken up the suggestion in his novels and in his musings on Brazilian cultural autonomy; his notes for an essay on the subject, in fact, read like an outline of Martius's piece.[56] It is true, however, that Freyre (and others in his generation) would fill in Martius's framework. Freyre's discussion of the blacks' contributions compensates for Martius's barely polite silence by running on into two chapters where one sufficed for the Indians and another for the Portuguese. But in frequently so(m)ber moments amid the enthusiasm, Freyre admits that the conquest was tantamount to genocide for the Indians who refused to mingle with the "civilizing" whites on their "syphilizing" terms, and that African slavery meant more than the healthy opportunities for eugenic miscegenation.[57] It meant humiliation, bodily harm, and despair. He doesn't deny the abuses in a color-coded plantation society, but he is writing principally to legitimate the syncretic and paradoxically democratizing results of forced intimacy.

"Conciliation" and "cordiality" in both racial and party politics, rather than the military convulsions of Spanish America, have become the watchwords in the dominant tradition of Brazilian historiography as well as sociology.[58] The theme so colors the story Brazilians tell about themselves that even the glaring and sometimes exquisite cruelty of conquest and slavery is toned down by the general glow of syncretism. Indians—especially the women—are remembered affectionately for the attention they lavished on the conquerors, for foods they prepared and personal grooming that made them and their mestizo babies so attractive. And black slaves—mostly women again—are remembered for the same reasons, and for the sadism of their jealous white mistresses. To read a classic like Freyre's, Brazil is founded on a history of mutual seduction between white masters and dark women, the one motivated by a lust for self-aggrandizement through self-reproduction, the other allegedly favoring the domestic stability of plantation life over trailing behind nomadic, or semicivilized, men. This is at least the story some Brazilians have been congratulating themselves for, a story that transmutes an abusive past into the fortunate fall that made possible the cultural and racial redemption of a white elite through miscegenation. Here, "racial improvement," so familiar a goal in Latin America for white supremacists who prefer to eliminate others by making love rather than war, is also interpreted as making Europeans fit for the tropics. And despite the consistent evidence of a racially divided society in which blacks continue to be an underclass and the surviving Indians to be threatened with genocide, Brazil's ideal self-image focuses on the blurry spots along the lines of division: primarily in the bedrooms, nurseries, and kitchens of the big house surrounded by barracks.

Perhaps this putative mutuality of affection makes it hard to choose between *O Guaraní* and *Iracema* as *the* national romance; that is, between Indian men loving white women and Indian women loving white men. Alencar does his best to correct what might have become a "black legend" of conquest and to strike a perfect balance in race as well as gender. In his novels, power is not exclusively a white and male prerogative, nor is seductiveness an exclusive trait of dark women. The immediate popularity of his books, of course, makes it possible that the assumption of mutuality and cordiality is to some degree a heritage of his two-faced founding fiction, just as Brazil's mestizo culture owes something to Martius's intervention.

Like Martius and unlike Freyre, Alencar was evasive about blacks in his best-selling books about the racial amalgam that founded Brazilian society. In order to cover over the space where blacks might have made an appearance, Alencar reduced Martius's color scheme from three to two. He makes the fashionable earth-tone cover up the deeper hue, and so helps to paint a lasting picture of Brazil where black is so often taken for brown. "[O]ur romantics have continued to avail themselves of the myth of the good savage," complained Afrânio Peixoto in 1931. "José de Alencar's Peri is a *gentleman*, noble and passionate to the point of amorous mysticism. His Iracema is a divinely lovable creature, one to arouse envy in any Christian and civilized heart. . . . Not wishing and not being able to invoke African fetishes, we have, by falsifying our origins and denying our bloodstream, made ourselves over into the descendants of Indians."[59]

Sensitive as he was, though, to the new cadences of Brazilian speech, Alencar never managed to turn a deaf ear to the Africans he pretended not to see. Probably his clearest, at least his most polemical, linguistic manifesto, published as a postscript to *Iracema,* cannot resist including the voices of people he excluded from the picture. First Alencar adds various Europeans to the mix of Indians and Portuguese. It will not do to forget, he warns the purists, that the New World language is composed of "traditions of indigenous races living in contact with practically all the civilized races" that immigration has brought. But the defense seems to jump ahead of itself when Alencar's sure-footed march through linguistic progress (balanced equally between Indian and European steps) adds a new African beat. "The agents of the transformation of our languages are those representatives of so many races, from the Saxon to the African, who make a single exuberant amalgam of blood, traditions, and languages."[60] Alencar's daring makes him the leader of a linguistic emancipation that would culminate in 1936, with a resolution in the Chamber of Deputies in Rio to call the national language "Brazilian." By then its vocabulary had at least ten thousand "barbarous" words foreign to Portugal, as were the syntax and sound, "softened," as Freyre put it, "in the mouths of African slaves." The resolution was defeated, but the debate still rankles.[61]

Where blacks are protagonists for Alencar, as they are in the plays *Mãe* and *O Demonio Familiar,* they figure as future,

and desired, absences. The black mother of the first play decides to take her life rather than to remain what she senses
is an obstacle to her mulatto son. In the second play, when an
offended master exorcises "the family demon" by sending him
from the house, the manipulating slave becomes the victim of
manumission, interpreted here as just punishment for a typically injurious black. And in Alencar's regionalist novel *Til*
(1872), submissive blacks are the measure of independence for
the Indian hero. "I would not become the slave of a rich man
just because of the crumbs he might throw me, just as he might
to anyone else, or to his Negro."[62] How different are these treat-
ments from *O Guaraní.* There the white master also sends his
slave forth, but he sends him accompanied by his own daughter,
not in order to perish but so they may survive by customizing
Portuguese values for a tropical setting. The aristocrat's suicide
may not be an expression of racial "inferiority," as it is in *Mâe,*
yet it marks him as an obstacle to his own colonizing project.
In *Iracema* one may remark that the dark damsel of the honey
lips dies at the end too, but not before she produced a mestizo
baby, nor before Martim realized that her absence was a loss.
By contrast, the loss of blacks in Alencar's plays is felt like a
relief.

This may surprise readers who imagine that Alencar was
progressive and Liberal, perhaps because they extrapolate from
his defense of a despised race, meaning the practically extinct
Indians of Ceará (in *Iracema*) and the Rio area (in *O Guaraní*),
and from his courageous departures from the classical standards of Portuguese language and literature. But his son, Mário
de Alencar, was convinced that his father was two irreconcilable men: a man of letters and a politician. In Congress the
two men were continually forced apart by colleagues who respected Alencar the jurist and journalist but who made Alencar
the sentimental novelist the butt of their jokes.[63] Nevertheless
the prologue to Casa de las Américas's Spanish translation of
El Guaraní tries to make a pleasing connection between the
Romantic writer and the antimonarchist politician, perhaps as
much to justify the decision to translate him as to justify Alencar. Emir Rodríguez Monegal makes even more of Alencar's
resistance to imperial authority and speculates that it was a dis-

placed and unresolved Oedipal conflict with a father (a priest no less!) who left José illegitimate and slightly paranoid no matter how affectionately society adopted him.[64] The pleasing connections, though, depend on leaving out several details of Alencar's literary and political struggles.

Although it is true that he became an antimonarchist as a result of his conflict with Emperor Pedro II,[65] it should be added that Alencar began as an ardent monarchist and that the conflict was personal, resulting more from Alencar's than from Pedro's authoritarian style. And barely a year after his attacks on the emperor, Alencar reaffirmed his loyalty to the principles of monarchism.[66] The friction apparently began in 1863, when the king dissolved an unmanageable Liberal Congress in which Alencar served. Two years later, a now defiantly Conservative Alencar wrote the *Cartas de Erasmo* criticizing the emperor for governmental instability. But Brito Broca is careful to point out that he criticized a lack of nerve on the king's part and encouraged him to take greater control of government, to be bolder and more decisive. For one thing, Alencar was attacking the Liberal Congress and demanding that the emperor dissolve it again. Far from calling for revolution, he was demanding reaction. Pedro II, of course, was cautious and punctiliously constitutional, perhaps because his father's disastrous personalism was a lesson on how not to govern. The young king was evidently not moved enough by the letters to overstep the rather efficient bureaucracy he oversaw. But he must have been flattered, or at least willing to accept the flattery of the Conservatives in power since July 1868. Soon after, he appointed Alencar as minister of justice. It was an unusual honor for a deputy only thirty-nine years old. It was also the opportunity for Pedro to notice the importance his minister attributed to himself as well as to the emperor. In one telling incident, Alencar lost patience with the imperial practice of minutely inspecting newspaper clippings from the entire country in order to follow and respond to local developments. It was an affront, he wrote the king, "to the constitutional spirit of the sovereign and to the dignity of his Minister of Justice."[67] The same self-importance convinced Alencar that nothing could stop him from being appointed senator for his region, a lifetime appointment far more desirable than a term as deputy or even minister. He was, after all, the most popular politician at home and a member of the ruling Conservative party. He announced his candidacy despite Pedro's lack of support and despite his unmistakable suggestion that Alencar was rather young for the job. But Alencar persisted, rather arrogantly, not imagining that Pedro would dare to slight him, and rather foolishly since senatorial appointments were made by the king. Alencar lost and was bitter about politics until he died. The king, for one, did not mourn him. "Era um homenzinho muito malcriado" [He was a very ill-bred little man] was all Pedro said when he heard the news.

As for Alencar's relationship to slavery, it was that of a master. It is true that Alencar seems to have supported closing the slave trade. Although that decision was made before he came to the Chamber of Deputies, his *Cartas de Erasmo* proudly refer to it as a victory of Conservative leadership.[68] That victory is one symptom of how apparently unpredictable party alliances were during the Conciliation Government. Conservatives and Liberals had split internally over the question. And the division seemed more geographic and economic than ideological. By the middle of the century, the sugar planters of Alencar's northeast region had lost significant political ground to the coffee growers of the central region who were bringing in 40 percent of the country's income. The booming coffee industry needed slaves far more desperately than did the sugar industry, so that the slave trade was clearly favoring one sector over the other. Not surprisingly, northerners like Alencar often allowed themselves to be compelled by Liberal arguments to end the slave trade.

Even more compelling, perhaps, was the pressure England was mounting to end the trade in Brazil and everywhere else. Either because of the principled and numerous abolitionists at home, or because the English Caribbean colonies could not compete for long with the slave-based economies of scale in Cuba and Brazil, England was determined to stop the traffic of human chattel. And she stopped at nothing to do it. When the repeated treaties to end the traffic—in exchange for trading rights and for recognition of the newly independent and very vulnerable Brazil—were repeatedly violated, England stepped up its patrol of the ocean routes. This kind of interference amounted to an abuse of Brazilian sovereignty. And in 1845 the Council actually voted to officially resume the traffic by terminating the anti-slave-trade treaty of 1817.[69] Britain's response was to reinterpret the 1826 treaty, making slave trading tantamount to "piracy," with which her South American Squadron dealt too successfully for Brazil's taste. This mostly diplomatic tug-of-war almost broke out into the real thing when, in June 1850, British ships opened fire on Brazilian ports. But Brazil had no moral or material means to make war. Instead, it made a very wise decision to take matters out of English hands by finally and effectively abolishing the trade. By then, the decision was easier than in 1845, first because of the glut of slaves after years of heavy imports, and then because of the elite's resentment of crass slave traders who had gained far too much power.

All of this was political prehistory for Alencar, although his sympathies may have favored England, if we may infer from Alencar's marriage to the daughter of the (in)famous British admiral who defended Brazil against Portuguese attacks.[70] To his credit, Minister Alencar removed an embarrassing slave market from the center of Rio, which makes his later record seem surprising. When his fellow Conservative, Rio Branco, proposed a Free Birth bill in 1871, Alencar spoke eloquently and passionately against it. "You, the propagandists, the emancipators at all cost, are no more than emissaries of revolution, no more than apostles of anarchy. The retrogrades are you, who imagine progress can be promoted in this country by wounding it in the heart, killing its most important industry, labor."[71] Other northerners were convinced that industry would not suffer from this expanded practice of manumission. Foreign travelers were often struck by the frequency with which Brazilian masters freed their slaves, mistaking it as a liberal (and an economically irrational) habit. In fact, the carrot worked along with the stick to insure control. Besides, with no new imports of workers, masters were concerned about the way "America devours the blacks," as Charles Auguste Taunay wrote in 1839.[72] They were willing to substitute nonrenewable slave labor for the "free" labor of manumitted but still loyal workers, bound by a combination of economic necessity and gratitude.

Alencar's objection to the innovation may have less to do with the unconvincing economic reasons he marshals than with reasons of racial privilege. He wanted, he said, the freedom of slaves as much as anyone; but more gradually, once the Brazilian economy could afford it and once the "brutish masses" of blacks overcame their vice and ignorance. How either development was possible under continued slavery did not occupy Alencar. He was as Brito Broca puts it, a conservative of the repressive variety.[73] By 1875, the bitter old man was spoiling for a fight. He got one in the guise of a duel over how to write the national novel. Joaquim Nabuco's mildly critical review of Alencar's play, *O Jesuita,* and the ensuing polemic owed more to Alencar's political and literary frustrations, according to Valéria De Marco, than to the confrontation between the youth's new-wave realism and the master's romanticism.[74] Alencar's senatorial disappointment was compounded by the silent treatment Liberal literary critics were giving him in payment for his politics. "Alencar-writer would end up at the gallows for the sins of Alencar the politician."[75] The difference between romanticism and realism was political too, with abolitionist Nabuco hailing an emergent society based on patronage, while Alencar defended compensatory idealization in his regionalist novels and in his backward glance at Brazil's interracial roots.[76]

The political lines here may be too clearly drawn, though, when it comes to Alencar's indigenist novels. In his backward glance there was evidently a projection that belied his cantankerous politics, a projection that anticipated the innovation of replacing slavery with clientalism. Setting the clock back allows Alencar to account for the masses of socially restless brown Brazilians through a continuous, nonrevolutionary tradition. Sliding between one racial category and another, substituting Indians for blacks, became, as I said, a convenient move after Alencar.[77] (It was also, quite literally a program of removal in 1850, as Indians were displaced from their traditional lands to replace black slaves after the trade had ended.)[78] The rhetorical move in Alencar doesn't exactly eliminate Africans, but it blurs their genealogy enough to legitimate them as quintessentially Brazilian. The challenge for Alencar's generation after 1850 was, after all, to consolidate a slavocratic country that had just abolished the trade. This meant that labor was now to be supplied internally; it was Brazilian labor. And whether or not it was to be controlled and promoted through "humanitarian" slavery or through patronage, Brazilian labor could not afford to be devoured, as Taunay had complained, by thoughtless abuse.[79]

This is one message of *O Guaraní* that becomes clear from the political climate of the 1850s and 1860s. Interracial war and mutual annihilation of the Portuguese and the Indians at the end of the novel are triggered by Dom Antonio's careless son who kills an Indian girl. Engaging a possible army of workers in battle is simply self-destructive for the whites. This is a warning to the masters. A different warning to the slaves is that absolute equality is illusory. The apparent equality between ruling whites and a subaltern race, between Peri and Ceci, is possible only because Peri chooses to be whitened. As much traitor to his own tribe as Iracema would be, the new Christian survives and gets his girl because he wages war against the bad pagan Indians. And though he benefits from the "liberal" practice of manumission for exemplary slaves, his freedom is guaranteed, paradoxically, by his voluntary submission to every whim of his adored mistress, just as clients should willingly submit themselves to their patrons.

Before we look for any more opportunities for reading contemporary history through a story of the distant past, we should note that Alencar's boldest and most insistent message has nothing at all to do with the political specificity of his own time. It is that Brazilians are a coherent race produced long ago from the mutual love between native nobles and the best Portuguese. This new race is the happy result in both of Alencar's foundational romances. It is also the patent goal of his manifestos on how to produce a specifically Brazilian society, manifestos that are also guides to reading the romances. Alencar obliges us to read them synecdochally; that is, to assume that one character or relationship is a part for a whole race or for a social formation. Peri is all good Indians; Ceci is the willful but fundamentally flexible whites; Dom Antonio is the Old World Portuguese, noble but anachronistic, and so forth.

Among Alencar's ideal readers of this message was Gilberto Freyre, that popularized and Africanized Martius for the twentieth century, who also wrote two pamphlets on Alencar for the Ministry of Education.[80] Certainly since Freyre, genetic and cultural *mestiçagem* has been a standard mark of Brazilian specialness. Ironically, though, it is also the standard of specialness in vast areas of Spanish America where masses of Indians survived and entered national life, notably Mexico and Paraguay (whose official languages are Guaraní and Spanish). And nowhere is Brazilian-style *mestizaje* more evident than all over the Spanish Caribbean where Iberian, Indian, and African peoples are said to have produced an amalgam that is quintessentially "national." Sometimes the emphasis will be on Indians, as in the Dominican Republic, where Galván may have been grateful to Alencar for showing how to account for a dark population without mentioning blacks. Or the focus will be on blacks, as in Cuba's antislavery novels where Indians, if they appear at all, are merely a bloody trace of the same Spanish exploitation associated with the slave trade. Blacks are so central a feature of Cuban culture by now that to call it "Afro-Cuban" may seem redundant or almost schizophrenically defensive of non-African elements. And Puerto Rico likes to imagine itself to be an ideal balance, as in its emblem where a Spanish conqueror is flanked by an equally imposing African and a noble Indian. There, school children are taught that their national character is a combination of European cleverness, African hard work, and Indian docility, perhaps in lessons very similar to the ones taught in Brazil.

In fact Brazil's racial mix is not qualitatively different from the rest of the area, even if there may be a significant difference in degree and in timing. The difference, for example, lured Robert Southey to study Brazil at the beginning of the nineteenth century in order to discover what accounted for the already-proverbial ease of race relations there. He represented many Englishmen who were desperate for leads about how to get on profitably with their Irish subordinates.[81] And Brazil remained a model, if not always for conscious control, then for the productive cohabitation of the races. In Freyre's words, "Although a perfect intercommunication between its cultural extremes has not been achieved in Brazil—extremes that are still antagonistic and at times explosively so, clashing with one another in such intensely dramatic conflicts as that of Canudos— nonetheless we may congratulate ourselves upon an adjustment of traditions and tendencies that is rare."[82]

During and just after World War II when the United States was happy to gird itself with family ties close to home, Brazil was for many Americans a newly discovered and surprisingly mature sibling. The countries could share a romanticized Indian past and a (perhaps equally romanticized) democratic tradition based on the melting-pot effect, a racial improvement sometimes known in Brazil as "Aryanization."[83] This myth of inclusion, which is also a xenophobic exclusion, was taken up in the "literary fascism" of the 1920s in nativist writers such as Graça Aranha.[84] The chief ingredient in that pot is clear from the title of David Miller Driver's 1942 book, *The Indian in Brazilian Literature*. In 1943, the prologue to an edition of *Iracema* published in New York for intermediate students of Portuguese observed that "our belated rediscovery of Brazil" is a result of the "dangers resulting from the totalitarian conflagration."[85] These were also the years when Samuel Putnam was translating Freyre in a variety of ways, through his books and through an introduction to Brazilian literature and culture for an American public. But his *Marvelous Journey,* published a scant three years after the armistice, begins by worrying that North American ardor for Brazil is already cooling off along with the general postwar political chill. A celebration of blacks and whites together was risky enough by then, even without adding red to the mix, by which I mean an element more exotic than the Indians. "Where the culture of the Spanish countries has been, at least until a recent revolutionary epoch, predominantly one created by and for criollos, that of Brazil has been and remains a mestizo culture, the result of racial and cultural fusion. It is no longer the Portuguese with whom we are dealing, but the Brazilian, the Portuguese transplanted to a new land that has become one of the world's greatest melting pots, even more of a melting pot than our own. Only the Soviet Union exceeds it in this respect."[86] But interest revived in the 1960s, with a difference. Wartime enthusiasm for a model democracy typically turned to anger when *mestiçagem* was revealed as the debilitating fiction of racial equality. Eugene Genovese represented a minority position, if not an anachronism in *Roll Jordan Roll* (1974), where he tried to read southern slavery through Freyre's nostalgia for the paternalist institution secured as much by bonds of love as by legal bondage. But even here, the historical shift of interest is apparent, because the focus on Freyre is on his treatment of blacks, not Indians. This was also true of revisionist books written after the civil rights years, like Thomas Skidmore's *Black into White: Race and Nationality in Brazilian Thought* (1974), David Brookshaw's *Race and Color in Brazilian Literature* (1986), or David Haberley's *Three Sad Races* (1983).[87]

Now the very fact that we North Americans can write chapters of our own racial history (slavery, melting pots, civil rights) through the medium of Brazil is another indication—along with the Caribbean "copies" of mestiçagem—that color may not be the country's most special feature. There are surely others, and none so striking as Brazil's peculiar history. From the beginning Portuguese settlers knew their own national, religious, and racial identity to be fragile and in flux. Portugal's recent independence from Spain, its geographic and economic position at the crossroad with Africa, had prepared those settlers to forge something new and open-ended, something that would take advantage of European ingenuity without too much concern for disentangling the African, and then the Native American, influences.[88]

Brazil's history must have seemed like a dream come true for onlookers in the rest of Latin America. From Mexico to Argentina, many leading criollos had resisted the republican rhetoric of independence. The more conservative leaders had Haiti on their minds and were generally worried about the anarchic masses who would surely rush in once colonial institutions were abandoned. So they looked for an appropriate monarch, one who would control the masses, not the creole elite. They looked in several European countries, although none of the

princes there were terribly interested in so limited a constitutional role; and in Argentina they even contemplated—briefly—
exhuming an Incan dynasty to create a legitimating, autochthonous figurehead. With no real alternative, the republicans had
their way, and the decades of war that followed seemed to justify the monarchists. José Mármol, for one, the same Mármol
who went to Brazil during his exile from Rosas's terror, pined
for the possible monarchy that Argentina never had and that
the greatest hero of Independence had fought for and lost.

> Belgrano era más que unitario: era monárquico. Recibió la Repúb-
> lica como un hecho que se escarnecía al empuje de los acon-
> tecimientos . . . pero en sus convicciones de hombre, la monarquía
> constitucional satisfacía los deseos más vivos de su corazón. La
> monarquía, único Gobierno para que nos dejó preparados la
> metrópoli. La Consitución, última expresión de la revolución
> americana.
>
> Muchos otros la querían también. . . . Pero la revolución dege-
> neró, se extravió, y al derrocar el trono ibérico, dio un hachazo
> también sobre la raíz monárquica. (*Amalia*—Mármol 1851, 338)

> [Belgrano was more than a Unitarian; he was a monarchist. He
> accepted the Republic as a necessity of the raging times . . . but in
> his personal convictions, Constitutional Monarchy answered to his
> most ardent desires. Monarchy, the only kind of government that
> the Empire prepared us for. Constitution, the fullest expression of
> America's revolution.
>
> Many others preferred it too. . . . But the revolution degener-
> ated, it strayed too far, and its death blow to the Iberian throne
> severed the roots of monarchy.]

Brazilians, by contrast, managed to have their king and
rule him too. Pedro II, a doubly legitimate monarch because
of Iberian descent and Brazilian birth, was an emperor on
their own constitutional terms. His official title of "Moderating
Power" meant also moderated power. The Brazilians even out-
did the English, whose tutelage Portugal and then Brazil alternately enjoyed and suffered, in developing a modern state
through policies of wise aristocratic flexibility that avoided
major political ruptures. For as long as the Spanish American
civil wars lasted, Brazilians must have been the envy of all but

the most idealistic reformers. With these accomplishments and the admiration they deserved, it seems surprising that popular accounts of Brazil's specialness are hardly ever celebrations of its relatively untraumatic history. Surely João's spectacular arrival in Rio, and then his indecision when Portugal—no longer part of the king's body—was demanding his return while the colony insisted that he stay, surely this is the stuff of unparalleled historical narrative. Even more exciting, perhaps, is Pedro's defiant decision to stay and his success in defending the new empire from his father's troops and from local uprisings.

To venture a guess about why these incomparable stories were not taken up as the popular basis for Brazil's legitimating particularity, one may imagine that it is precisely the apparent uneventfulness of its history, the preference for pragmatism over glory, that made it unappealing if not embarrassing for romantic writers like Alencar. National history may have read to them like a series of nonevents when it was not a series of outright losses. If Alencar was going to celebrate the new Conciliation Government he could hardly do it by reminding his readers that national unity was won at the price of putting down local rebellions, two of which began with conspiracies at his own home.[89] I am not assuming here that Alencar identified with rebellion or with the embattled Pernambucans who preceded him; but I am noting that the frustrated struggles, which neither succeeded nor amounted to full-scale revolutions, may have paled as material for founding fictions next to the colorful Indians. What Brazil lacked in glory it would make up for in love.

And as for the analogy with English political history, which would have fascinated monarchical Argentines were it not for England's support of Rosas, it might have been humiliating for Brazilians. Their general xenophobia was most intense when it came to meddling and bossy England, especially after the British fired on Brazilian ports in 1850. "If there is today a generalized and highly popular idea in the country it is that England is our most treacherous and persistent enemy."[90] So Alencar apparently did what other national romancers did when they found no positive events to develop à la Walter Scott. Like Manzoni, and Gogol, as well as Mitre, Mármol, Isaacs,

Mera, Matto de Turner, and others, he constructed a romance to fill in the void, making it pregnant with future projects. And he colored those projects with the subtle half-tones of racial alliances. If the Brazilian national novel could not be about a possibly uneventful history, at least the melting pot myth could fill in the empty space.

But speculating about why Alencar didn't celebrate events may assume too quickly that setting his stories in the distant past seals his indifference or his humiliation about more recent history. If racial amalgamation is the end—in both senses of the word—of Alencar's writing, reading with only that end in mind will miss whatever historical complexity there is in his romances. Alencar's manifestos would make those romances tell the synecdochal story of conquest when two races made one. But we may already sense that another, allegorical, reading is possible, one that takes character for figures of a different, contemporary, and historically specific narrative. On this reading, Peri may be more than a part for the whole Indian nation, just as Ceci may represent more than the transplanted Europeans. On one possible reading, Peri himself embodies the balance of Conciliation, as did that other autochthonous king known as the Moderating Power; and he embodies the balance quite literally in the scene where the Indian is out on a limb between Alvaro on the right and Loredano on the left as they all look longingly into Ceci's window. And on another reading, Peri is half of the balanced equation with Ceci. She had followed him at first because she was following her father's orders, just as Conservatives were reconciled to Liberals by following Pedro's orders. But by the end it is love that binds her. Are not the racially complementary lovers also the Liberal and Conservative elites who agree to close ranks against England and who learn to cross party lines in the interest of pragmatism and stability?[91] At a level beyond race relations, therefore, *O Guaraní* is an allegory of the Conciliation Government that has resolved its dependence on both Portugal and England and has made Brazil a truly autonomous empire. It may be too much to imagine that the Conservatives are on the verge of kissing the Liberals in the subtext of the finale. But it is surely no wilder an imagining than Alencar's last scene, where the lovers are swept away in a devastating flood presumably to repopulate the world with a new race and thereby to improve on Noah's story.

Loredano is another flat character who gains a dimension from the historical context. On rereading, it is now obvious that the foreign villain is a villain precisely because he is a foreigner, lustful and opportunistic almost by definition. He is England. For good measure, Alencar makes him an ex-Capuchin, reminiscent of the greedy Jesuits with no patriotic allegience in Sue's *Le Juif Errant*. (Italian Capuchin friars actually took over the Jesuit missions during the Indian removal of 1850.)[92] The fortress, then, is plagued not only by the local pressures of rebellious natives, but also by foreign greed and disrespect for the inviolability of Ceci's virginity, and of Brazil's sovereignty. Loredano fails only when the noble Portuguese and equally noble Peri decide to constitute one family.

After that, the romance is hardly transgressive, but like so many other Latin American romances that feature consolidated family ties across apparent social or economic barriers it is intimately incestuous, even more so than Iracema's relationship to Martim. "They were as twin fruits of the Araça shrub, both sprung from the womb of the same flower" (Alencar 1865, 25; 26). It is so exclusively incestuous that Ceci and Peri will call one another "brother" and "sister" to the end.[93] And their father, Dom Antonio in his fortress, is also Joâo VI in Rio, the legitimate Portuguese ruler in his outpost haven who would remove himself from the scene of incipient Brazilianness, refusing either to look on or to get in the way.

The synecdochal and allegorical readings seem quite incompatible, as apparently incompatible as the historical philosophies of Martius and Varnhagen. In one, Brazil is unique because of its racial amalgam; in the other its specialness derives from an enviable history of gentlemanly accords. Alencar the literary critic was determined to make the first reading prevail; but Alencar the politician surely preferred the second. Yet we already suggested a bridge between them. The political intercourse between Conservatives and Liberals in the Conciliation Government may well have been an important event that Alencar allegorizes in the affairs between Indians and whites. Perhaps racial difference was as much a code for resolvable political antagonism as for the promise of an ethnically unique country. Perhaps, after all, a celebratory political history is being told as the story of Europe seduced by the tropics, Varnhagen's aristocratic continuity in the language of Martius's interracial romance.[94]

Alencar's novels slip freely, in fact, from romance to history. *O Guaraní* is not only a projection of the productive matings between European immigrants and autochthonous lords of the land; it is also an allegory of the local prince (Pedro/Peri) who is allowed—even encouraged—to establish an independent realm by a Portuguese master who gives up his own futile efforts to reign and leaves the scene. In one apparently simple and standard plot, then, we can read at least three simultaneous versions of history: the Martius-Freyre interracial affair that will produce the quintessential Brazilian; the love affair between Conservatives and Liberals who are thrown into each other's arms and stay there because of the threat posed by foreigners; and finally an allegory of the relatively smooth transfers of power in Brazil's history.

Less than a decade after this celebration, *Iracema* is already about losses, Iracema's losses of virginity, community, love, and finally her life. But mostly, I think, it is about Martim's loss of cultural moorings, the one loss that transmutes all the others into a gain. First the target of her arrow and then seduced by her charm and her magic, Martim is apparently helpless in the relationship, just as pitifully "helpless" as were whole armies of adventurers before aggressive Indian women. Even though the victims of the Conquest were self-evidently the Indians in a country where they were quickly becoming extinct, and even though sexual exploitation was quite literally a tactic of conquest for "syphilization," chronicles like Father Anchieta worried about the defenseless Portuguese men. "The women go naked and are unable to say no to anyone, but they themselves provoke and importune the men." Freyre spells out the good priest's defensiveness. "No sooner had the European leaped ashore than he found his feet slipping among the naked Indian women, and the very fathers of the Society of Jesus had to take care not to sink into the carnal mire."[95] But Alencar wasn't worried. Being under Iracema's spell, giving in to her uninhibited love, was just what Martim needed to become Brazilian. That and nostalgia for her love.

All the while Martim loved her he also desired home, the home far away where his rightful betrothed lived. On returning there, home now seemed elsewhere again, with Iracema; and Martim turns back again. But loss is inscribed in the very gesture of returning, either to the European colony or to the American hut. Iracema could not survive his restlessness and was dying. By now the ex-adventurer knows that home is always already in the past. Once there is no going back to Iracema, she becomes home too. The Tupí princess, like the Portuguese girlfriend, is the object of his European desire only after she is missing. From one about-face to the other, home (whether Portuguese or native) has changed from a goal to a memory for this interstitial, equivocal, hero. Iracema is less complicated and more admirable; she is where love and desire coincide. She is Alencar's dream of presence, the America that makes an anagram of her name.[96] Martim and his countrymen are tied to her, tragi-paradoxically, only after they have destroyed her. They enjoy her with the kind of masochism that Martim made popular, a poignant longing or *saudade* that is almost a national feeling. "We are still today," writes Sérgio Buarque de Hollanda, "exiles in our own land."[97] It is a country conscious of having borrowed everything—institutions, ideas, models of association—and transplanting them to an often hostile environment.

The Portuguese empire may have felt saudade after dallying with the seductive colony. João resisted the pressure to stay, deferring, like Martim, to those who insisted that home was somewhere else and in the past. But at another and more immediate level, the novel's nostalgia may be for the Conciliation Government, the same conciliation that seemed so promising in the cross-over dream of *O Guaraní*. Soon after, Alencar apparently soured on that government. This change of heart showed signs of restlessness, if not also reasons for disappointment. It was not yet the personal disappointment from losing the senatorial appointment, but very likely some disillusion with the slow pace and the indecision that annoyed him in the rocky marriage that Pedro II had forced between opposing parties. Perhaps the

Conciliation had never really worked, or perhaps it was just a short-lived affair.

And yet the affair had already borne fruit, just as Iracema had with Martim. The political and cultural matches that Pedro made had produced a conflicted but still promising Brazil, as promising as Iracema's baby Moacyr. Even if the political conciliation was only a dream, Alencar seems to be saying, we need not assume that one wakes up empty-handed. Like Borges's dream of the rose that materializes on the dreamer's pillow, Alencar and his readers wake up to Moacyr, to many Moacyrs, Iracemas, and Peris; they are material proof that fiction is not exactly unreal. The pain for which Iracema names her baby, and the saudade that he will surely feel for her, are as quintessentially Brazilian as his mestizo mix of races. Moacyr is a new breed, where an unmistakably Brazilian past blends with an unpredictable future; he is the answer to Brazilianness, both Tupí and not Tupí.

States with date of independence

- Mexico - 1821
- United Provinces of Central America - 1823
- Haiti - 1803
- Gran Colombia - 1819-1830
- Peru - 1821
- Bolivia - 1825
- Brazil - 1822
- Paraguay - 1811
- Uruguay - 1828
- United Provinces of La Plata - 1816
- Chile - 1817

The United Provences of Central America was dissolved by 1839.

Santo Domingo gained its independence from Spain in 1821. Occupied by Haiti in 1822, it finally regained its independence in 1844.

British Guiana was founded in 1831 by uniting Berbice, Demerara and Essequibo.

Mexico
Veracruz
Cuba – Spanish
Belize – British
Jamaica – British
Puerto Rico – Spanish
Trinidad – British
Caracas
Surinam – Dutch
Guiana – French
Bogota
Quito
Lima
Salvador
Argentine Confederacy 1810–1816
Ausuncion
Rio de Janeiro
São Paulo
Santiago
Buenos Aires
Montevideo
Patagonia

Baptism of Camila O'Gorman's Unborn Child, charcoal by Verazzi.

Below: A still from the 1914 film *Amalia,* directed by Enrique Garcia Velloso.

Disembarking in Buenos Aires, 1845, by Mauricio Rugendas.

The abduction of a captive girl, Buenos Aires, 1845, by Mauricio Rugendas.

Enriquillo and Las Casas, illustration by Jose Alloza Villagrasa.

Tabaré and the Monk, illustration by V. Chaco.

"In the monk's cloak deep,
the Charrúa's first tear dropped . . .
For fear of losing his dying race
only his blue eyes could weep."
(my trans.)

Separate worksheet from José de Alencar, *O Guaraní*.

G. G. de Avellaneda

José Francisco by Victor Patricio Landaluze.

María, portrait by Alejandro Dorronsoro in 1880.

Illustration from children's edition of *María*.

La Coqueta by Lic. D. Ignacio Ramírez.

La China by D. José María Rivera.

El Ranchero by D. José María Rivera.

Juárez's Triumphal Entry into Mexico City in 1861.

A still from *Doña Bárbara*, 1943 film by Fernando de Fuentes, script by
Rómulo Gallegos.

La Vorágine (1965) by Ricardo Gómez Campuzano.

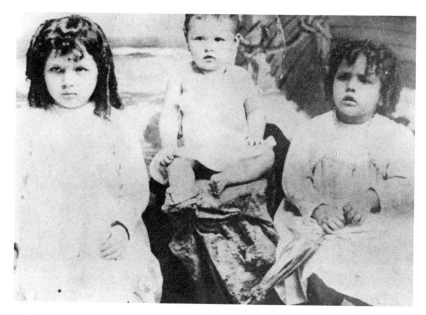

de la Parra's family group.

Teresa de la Parra,
ink drawing by Gastón,
Paris, 1927.

La plaza mayor de Lima, 1843, by Mauricio Rugendas.

6

MARÍA'S DISEASE:
A NATIONAL NOVEL
(CON)FOUNDED[1]

After the lovers make plans to marry, what could possibly go wrong for the title heroine and her beloved cousin in Jorge Isaacs's *María* (1867)? Raised on her uncle's prosperous plantation, after he adopted the orphaned girl, María has loved Efraín since childhood, as he has loved her. And their initially resistant but finally indulgent family requires only that the fiancés wait for each other until Efraín finishes medical school in London. With so much affection and affluence between them, the story is truly distressing when, for some apparently unmotivated reason, María dies of a strange disease before Efraín can rush home.

As Colombia's national romance[2] and probably the most popular nineteenth-century novel in Latin America—more widely read and imitated than any other (to the point of filling the slot for foundational novel in syllabi of countries such as Puerto Rico and Honduras) and also the subject of early and recent films[3]—*María*'s canonical status is surprising, almost perverse. Although the socially engaged novels being written in Colombia and in the rest of Latin America lead up to telling conclusions, this tragedy seems rather gratuitous and unaccountable.[4] National novels tended to project ideal futures for countries that were straining toward development, often after exhausting revolutionary and civil wars. If the future seemed bleak, at least these novels locate the problem that interferes with development. But *María* neither projects futures nor finds any obstacle that it might hope to overcome. Instead, it is inexplicably sad, as sad and reluctant to say why as Latin America's elite readership must have been when it preferred *María*'s lament for lost privilege over the romances that so eagerly embraced and entitled subalterns.

This apparent misfit in the foundational canon remains inexplicable as long as the explanation offered by the book itself is overlooked, drowned and blurred in generations of tear-stained copies as if sadness were easier to bear than the tragedy of insoluble conflict, overlooked along with a curious detail that fits the canon as badly as the novel's ending. I mean the originally Jewish identity of María and her uncle, an exotic identity already announced in Efraín's name. After more than a century of namesakes born to sentimental readers, by now it seems practically indigenous to Latin America; yet I suspect that before 1867 the flamboyantly Hebrew name may have been as foreign as the *converso* father who chose it for his son. These are clues to their collective calamity. I suggest here that their Jewishness is a figure for both sides of the unspeakable racial difference in the plantation society, the difference between black and white. Jewishness, on my reading, is a protean stigma that damns the characters one way or another: as an enfeebled inbreeding "aristocracy" like the planters *and* as a racially different disturbance among the whites. Either María's planter family was too Conservative and white to sustain alliances with abolitionist Liberals and become a hegemonic class, or the family was not conservatively Catholic and white enough. Either the problem is class-wide incest, or it is corrupting miscegenation. However I formulate it, the problem is being "Jewish," a double-bind that becomes Isaacs's vehicle for representing a dead-end for the planter class.

That the book ends tragically is not, as I said, itself necessarily pessimistic, since other novels of the period—among them *Francisco* (Cuba, 1839), *Sab* (Cuba, 1841), *Amalia* (Argentina, 1851), *Iracema* (Brazil, 1865), *Aves sin nido* (Peru, 1889), *Cumandá* (Ecuador, 1879)—use tragedy to fuel some positive program. At the same time as they arouse our sympathies for the love affairs between ideal heroes and heroines, they also locate a social abuse that frustrates the lovers. Therefore they point to an ideal state, in both senses, after the obstacle is overcome. Implicitly, and sometimes openly, these novels demand a possible solution to failed romance (read also national progress and productivity).

These programmatic fictions, however, cannot prepare us for the tragedy in *María*. It has no apparent political or social causality, no racial hatred, no regional conflicts. And unlike the others, where impossible love between historically antagonistic lovers (sectors) underlines the urgency for a national project that would reconcile the antagonisms, the frustration here doesn't point to any solution. Instead, undirected, it festers self-destructively. María simply dies of an illness before her fiancé can return. In fact, the lovers always seem to be missing each other, so that the climax of her death is foretold from the beginning.

The very first line of the novel arches back to the originary loss, when the narrator's father sends the boy into the symbolic world of school and language, effectively exiling him from the prelinguistic, preconscious harmony of the family plantation called "Paradise."

> Era yo niño aun cuando me alejaron de la casa paterna para que diera principio a mis estudios. . . . Me dormí llorando y experimenté como un vago presentimiento de muchos pesares que debía sufrir después. Esos cabellos quitados a una cabeza infantil, aquella precaución del amor contra la muerte delante de tanta vida, hicieron que durante el sueño vagase mi alma por todos los sitios donde había pasado, sin comprenderlo, las horas más felices de mi existencia. (1)[5]

> [I was still a mere boy when sent away from home to study. . . . I fell asleep sorrowful, filled with a vague foreboding of coming trouble. That lock of hair taken from a boy's head; that precaution of love against death, even in the presence of abounding life, caused my thoughts to wander all night about those scenes where I had passed, without knowing it, the happiest hours of my life.] (1)[6]

In the beginning was the deprivation, the necessary violence against happiness that, paradoxically, would make it thinkable and desirable. But happiness, now a word, an abstraction, is always already distanced. In these first lines, Efraín muses on the irony that the signifier becomes speakable only after the referent has slipped away. Before his lock is cut in a symbolic castration, there is no fear of death, and no yearning. Before loss, the boy cannot experience the absence that will require the supplement of writing, an absence that this text has to respect in order to continue writing itself.

Said a bit differently, if this romance had tried to embrace a presence by allowing the lovers to confess their mutual passion and stay together, instead of a lengthy novel we would have an early textual *Liebestod*. The book would simply have little to tell after a "happily ever after." This is at least one, strategic, reason for Efraín's writerly precaution against closing up the distance between himself and María. "One single step would separate us" (16). That very frustration is making the narrative possible. In more conventional novels, where social and political obstacles apparently interfere with the sentimental plot, lovers can try to act on their desire for union, because their efforts at overcoming those problems are sure to fill many pages. Long books like *Amalia, Enriquillo, Cumandá, Iracema, Aves sin nido, Cecilia Valdés* are full of extrapersonal intrigue and struggle. But in *María*, no such thing drives the story on, nor is there a tireless competition for erotic power, as there is in *Martín Rivas* (Chile, 1862).

In addition to the writerly reasons for making sure that Efraín does not overstep his relationship to María, Isaacs includes a narrative restriction. It is her fragile health, her pathologically passionate nature. María, "beautiful and transitory" (35), was already diagnosed as suffering from epilepsy, the disease that had caused her mother's early death. Warned by her doctor that emotional outbursts could be fatal, Efraín holds back the declaration of love that might end her life. "Mine or death's; one step nearer to her would be to lose her" (47; 46). This inherited disease is, as we will see, symptomatic of a social impasse (that single forbidden step) that keeps the lovers apart more surely than does any personal tragedy. For now, however, we should note that the only thing that allows the abnormally emotional heroine and the nonprogrammatic writing to last at all is Efraín's loving restraint.

In fact, his entire relationship with María seems to be a series of restraining orders. Although the cousins are brought up in the same house, they spend most of their youth separated from each other. Even during their brief time together between schools, when the lovers are evidently present for each other and at home, their rapture is heightened by the same kind of future nostalgia or prescience of loss that Efraín remembered on the first page.[7] On reading the tragedy of *Atala* together, for example, Efraín says, "My soul and María's, . . . were overcome with foreboding" (36). Their fears were more than justified. Efraín would soon be departing for England, and María's death in his absence would show how restraint made their love both possible and impossible.

The sense of loss in this novel seems always personal, rather than the regional or national loss felt in other canonical novels of nineteenth-century Latin America. Individual sorrow is something that we readers, too, are obliged to suffer in occasional apostrophes that make sure we are crying along with the narrator. "Those of you who have never wept of joy like this, weep now of despair if your adolescence has passed, because you will never recover love like this again!" (22). The entire novel is framed by just such an apostrophe in a preface "To Efraín's Brothers." "Whatever is missing, you know how to fill it in"; Efraín tells the implied editor. "You can read until the part my tears have erased." "Sweet and sad mission! Read on, then," the editor tells us, "and if you stop reading in order to weep, that will prove I've fulfilled my mission faithfully."

This prolepsis of personal disaster organizes the entire narrative. For one thing, it gives *María* a first-person narrator, the principle sufferer, who tells his story in nostalgic retrospect after María and happiness are already gone. "Cowardly heart," he chides himself in undirected anger, "Where is she now, now that you no longer beat, now that the days and the years pass me by" (47). The narrative strategy is most peculiar for the time and place of writing, since other Latin American novelists were striking omniscient and forward-looking poses. *María* may be the only major novel of its period written backward, from the loss of love and of the stable patriarchal order that this hero yearns for, to the evocation of impossible presence.[8] "Never again shall I admire those songs, drink in those perfumes, or gaze upon those landscapes flooded with light. To-day strangers dwell in my father's house" (132; 155). Other writers would probably have been happy to leave the past buried and to improve on what they might have considered Efraín's semifeudal slavocracy left over from an obscurantist, colonial order. Just to cite a few examples, José Mármol associates that order with Argentina's barbarous past and with Dictator Rosas in *Amalia*; José de Alencar buries a sympathetic but obsolete Portuguese lord so that his heroic slave of *O Guaraní* (Brazil, 1857) can escape with the lord's daughter to found a new society; and Manuel de Jesús Galván's *Enriquillo* (Dominican Republic, 1882) celebrates the freedom that Spain finally grants her runaway Indian slaves.

Yet the retrospective technique and the nostalgic tone, so particular to *María* in midcentury Latin American novels, recalls another strikingly similar work. Like *María*, it too produces an almost masochistic remembering of unattainable pleasure; and it uses a reflexive narrative line that doubles back on the reader like a whip to heighten the sensation of pleasure. I am referring to Chateaubriand's *Atala* (1801), which was evidently an important model for Isaacs (along with Saint-Pierre's *Paul et Virginie*).[9] Like Efraín, the aged Chactas, who survives Atala only to mourn her, asks retrospectively, "Who could have believed that the moment when Atala offered me that first token of her love would be the very one when my hopes would be shattered?" (28).[10] Other Latin American novels that rival *María* for their faithfulness to Chateaubriand's novel (*Iracema*, *Cumandá*, or *Enriquillo*) straighten out his narrative line into progressive chronological time, perhaps correcting the titillating but unproductive eroticism of his and other European romances. Efraín and María read Chateaubriand, just as Bartolomé Mitre's Bolivian heroine in *Soledad* (1847) had read *Julie*, and Alberto Blest, Gana's Chilean hero of *Martín Rivas*, had evidently read *The Red and the Black*. But unlike them, the Colombian lovers don't manage to redeem or to correct the European tragedy. They repeat it and thus prescribe their loss. The fact that *María* straightens nothing out, but instead follows Chateaubriand's narrative full circle, underlines Isaacs's intimacy with the nostalgic mood of the ruined French aristocrat.

After the French Revolution, so unkind to Chateaubriand's titled family, and after a religious conversion that must have come with a sense of guilt for his own complicity with the Revolution, the author of *Atala* and *René* wrote of almost nothing but loss and remorse. These short tragedies were redeemed, nevertheless, as subordinate parts of a more comforting whole, *The Genius of Christianity* (1802). Here, the estheticizing agency of Christianity turned pain back into pleasure in a romantic version of the fortunate fall. Chactas apparently enjoys recounting his tragic romance with Atala, just as the Christian celebrant feels joy in re-presenting Christ's sacrifice. If Efraín experiences a similar paradox, we may ask what loss in Isaacs's life might have compared to Chateaubriand's loss of prerevolutionary France. And what—we may wonder—could have caused his possible remorse. By venturing some answers, I also propose to show how important developments in Colombian history are displaced and appear symptomatically in this apparently nonhistorical novel.

Isaacs's father was a Jamaican-English Jew who came to Colombia looking for gold and stayed to convert to Catholicism and marry the daughter of a Catalan officer. Of their dozen children, Jorge was born in Cali in 1837. That is, just before the ruling sectors definitively split into the Liberals and Conservatives who would engage in apparently endless civil wars.[11] These gave Colombia the unenviable distinction of being practically the only Latin American country that did not achieve some kind of national consolidation in the nineteenth century, which suggests perhaps why its national novel is such an anomaly. Isaacs lived on the comfortable family plantation until he was sent to school in Bogotá, just as Efraín was sent in the semiautobiographical *María*. In the capital, he studied with Liberals when President López's Radical Liberal government responded to a decade of slave uprisings[12] by abolishing slavery in 1851.[13] Fifteen years later Isaacs's nostalgic novel tells us that nothing was gained. Instead of new national projects that might have reconciled Conservatives and Liberals, abolition precipitated a Civil War in Antioquia, Isaacs's Cauca, and other slaveholding southern provinces.[14] After coming home to find his father's health and fortune waning, Isaacs joined the fight to protect his family's privilege. First in 1854, and again in 1860, he enlisted in the government's forces to put down left-wing

Liberal rebellions. In the meantime, Isaacs met and soon married Felisa González, a mere girl whom he describes in the ideal terms he will use for María.[15] By 1863, his patrimony in ruins, Isaacs went to Bogotá to defend himself against creditors and finally accepted a job in 1865 as inspector of the road being built along the jungle of the Pacific Coast. There he started to write *María.*

Still a Conservative in 1866, Isaacs was a congressional deputy for his region and director of a Conservative newspaper when he suddenly announced his new sympathies with the Radical wing of the Liberal Party.[16] Apparently dramatic shifts of allegiance like this one were not terribly surprising, though, especially since the laissez-faire Radicals favored a monoculture for export and tended to ally with Conservative latifundists who could produce the goods and gain from the foreign exchange.[17] Both, however, were opposed to the left, "Draconian" wing of the Liberal party, made up of the artisans, manufacturers, and small farmers who fought for protectionism and against free trade. Isaacs liked to attribute his political change of heart to intellectual progress, as when he quipped to a Conservative critic, "I have come out of the darkness into the light."[18] But given the political alliances of that period between the so-called Radicals and the Conservatives, and given his family ties to English-Jamaican commerce, that early conversion was hardly spectacular. His real break with conservatism and Catholicism (Isaacs became a Free Mason) would come in 1868, one year after *María* was published to immediate acclaim and countless pirated editions that left him as poor as before. By the "Holy War" of 1875, when the church itself recruited armies, the theocratic Conservatives finally split from the Radicals who insisted on the separation of church and state.[19] Isaacs again defended the central government; but this time it was anti-oligarchic and anti-ecclesiastical. By 1880, as the self-declared "President of Antioquia," Isaacs was defending federal rights and free trade against the centralizing and protectionist policies of the Independent Liberal President Núñez.[20]

More than a progression, Isaacs's life seems to be a stalemate between conservative privilege, based on the apparent homogeneity of the ruling class, and enlightened liberalism, which promised equal rights and opportunities to the now-impoverished writer. He also seems poised between repeated and failed attempts to recover the patriarchal order of his child-hood and the struggle to establish himself in a new commercial economy.[21] This undecidability may be a certain kind of position that cannot take sides, because partiality would make little sense after history has apparently passed one by. Yet Isaacs persisted in participating, and Jaime Mejía Duque concludes that it was with a chronic case of bad faith; whatever the failed business venture or the frustrated political campaign at hand, the fault always lay with others. This political and economic (im)posture, claiming to want improvement and continually enjoying the privilege of displacing responsibility, may have spilled over from what Mejía Duque describes as Isaacs's writerly petulance. Although he laments his frustrated potential as a writer de-prived of an original creative spirit, the repeated frustration of that potential is what motivates his novel.[22] It is the same em-powering frustration that kept Efraín one step away from María.

On a first reading of *María* as Isaacs's nostalgic evocation of a semifeudal world, we can hardly consider the novel to be a foundation that hoped to intervene in history. Some readers don't even consider it a historical novel at all.[23] On the contrary and despite the occasional apologist,[24] it appears to be in crisis about history and about the nation-building project. Put differ-ently, it is a national novel that razes foundations and projects an insoluble crisis; it is a representation of failure that founds a particular kind of identity, one based on nostalgia for a co-herent and reproductive, static past.[25] Like *Werther,* which al-legedly caused a rash of suicides and generally spread a gloom of pessimism over young Europeans, *María* has been accused of fostering unproductive defeatism.[26]

But a second and equally plausible reading, an interpretation literally from the margins of plantation life, seems to predict Isaacs's political ambivalence between nostalgic conservatism and New World liberalism.[27] This reading highlights the dy-namic and productive romances that end happily in the back-ground, outside the big house.[28] In other words, beyond the very real tragedy of the first reading, the novel may be pointing to a national renewal based on tenant farmers and independent workers, a "Draconian" renewal that needed to sacrifice the plantocracy (but that in the end would lose to foreign capital). The peripheral romances promised to replace the central tragedy of María and Efraín with relationships more appropriate to the Americas. So instead of a Werther, the hero and narrator of the piece turns out to be an Oblomov singing the swan song of an aristocracy that, in the wake of abolition, is more (in the Russian's case) or less (in the Colombian's) gracefully ceding its hegemony to the middle sectors of society. But *María* has more pathos than irony, more defiance before the inevitable loss and more pessimism than *Oblomov* could muster. As if to highlight Efraín's suffering through an effect of chiaroscuro, the happy marginal romances that should have tempered our experience of loss only make it more acute. We suspect, in fact, that they end happily at the hero's expense.

Efraín's aristocratic class was obviously vulnerable to encroachments, as the reader can surmise from allusions to real estate litigations and from commercial complications for planters.[29] But the vulnerability is more obvious from other sources. In addition to freeing the slaves, histories tell us that the laissez-faire Liberal governments put great emphasis on ending colonial habits of land tenure.[30] Liberal land reforms deprived planters of their traditional rents, as well as expropriating church land for sale.[31] This enfeebled plantocracy was also trapped geographically. Isaacs's fertile Cauca Valley, so productive for the self-sustaining paternalist system, was rather isolated from the external markets that the new commercialism needed.[32] One of the ironies of Isaacs's life was that right after losing his plantations to a shrewder and harder-working American capitalist (who, by the way, made them profitable again),[33] Isaacs would supervise the building of a highway to improve access to markets. Add to the loss of privilege associated with land, and to the economic losses that abolition and isolation brought, the devastating Civil Wars launched by the slavocracy against the Liberal government, and one can form an idea of the inevitable ruin of the planter class.[34]

Efraín confesses to some class-wide blame for social instability and for the resulting ruin by mentioning the abuses of his peers, namely Emigdio's insensitivity to his young slave whose arm was mangled in the sugar mill (58; 58) and the opportunism that Carlos and his father show in wooing María for her dowry (95; 107). However, the true gentleman planter is innocent of the practices that made masters hateful to their slaves and that provoked mass rebellions throughout the area, rebellions that are never hinted at in the novel. That exemplary master is Efraín's father. "It was easy to see that my father, without ceasing to be a master, treated his slaves with kindness. He was anxious for their wives' good conduct [Ogen substitutes this for "domestic happiness"], and he fondled the little ones" (18; 11).[35] Efraín imitates this affable paternalism when, to the horror of Carlos and his father, he obliges the yeoman Braulio to drink the cup of coffee destined for himself (94–95; 106). But egalitarian gestures don't really disrupt, nor do they save, the fundamentally hierarchical order.[36] Without capital, access to markets, slave labor, or simply the energy and respect for work of the new commercial class, Colombia's beautiful plantation society died of choking, as it were, just as María dies in this novel.

How sad that she should die! Certainly in terms of the narrative, the death seems unaccountable. María should have been ideal as Efraín's future wife. Lovely and resourceful, she is also devoted to her adopted family, especially to Efraín. And in addition to the meekness and almost servile devotion that some (notably male) readers seem to enjoy so much, María is also delightfully willful and fearless. This is clear, for example, when she scrambles high onto a treacherous rock to see Efraín coming home (133; 156), or when she proudly rides a barely broken-in horse and boasts—in sturdy colloquial Spanish—that she is braver ("más guapa") than Emma (139; Ogden's tamer term is "skillful," 165). Efraín deserves to be happy too. A dutiful son and enlightened student, he also combines virile heroism (killing the tiger) and the most sensitive, almost "maternal" capacity for affection (274; 294). There is a general (and generic) tendency in this novel for gender crossing between heroes and heroines. The happy neighbors, Braulio and Tránsito are good examples (68; 71), as is Carlos whose "porcelain face" is so attractive (84; 93). In short, Efraín is the typical ideal protagonist for what should have been a more fortunate founding romance. As if to fit the ideal pattern even more perfectly, he and María are cousins, as are the happy Braulio and Tránsito and the heroes of many foundational fictions. At least, the novel seems to be saying, close and equal relations make perfect partners. The legitimate romance between Salomé and Tiburcio, threatened by white Justiniano's interest in the mulatta (210–226; 216–240), makes the point that class and racial crossing is suspect because uneven relationships are likely exploitative, or at the very least unstable. But a new more "hegemonic" possibility, that is nevertheless familiar from other national novels, already announces itself in Emigdio, who is probably a nouveau planter given his charmingly bumpkin and hard-working manner. He dares to marry below himself, as he says, in order to be served by his wife, not to serve her (63; 63).[37]

Perhaps, on straining for some explanation for the central tragedy, we may observe that Efraín and María were too close, more like siblings whose love would have been redundant in the project of founding a national family, than like cousins whose romance could have consolidated that family. But the incest taboo shouldn't really surface here, as it will in *Cecilia Valdés*, *Aves sin nido*, or *Cumandá* where the lovers really are siblings. On the contrary, the family ties between Efraín and María, along with the fact that she has an independent dowry to bring to the marriage, seem to bind them all the more inevitably, as they bind the cousin/lovers who are raised together in *Enriquillo* for example. In fact there seems to be no tension at all in *María*, except for the strain of nostalgia from one perspective and the prescience of loss from the other. Despite a whole range of crises that Colombian politics and economies offered Colombian writers after 1860, none of these difficulties surface in the novel. There is only a beautiful girl who is dying and whose death dooms Efraín to a non-(re)productive afterlife.

What is wrong with this girl that makes her incapable of bearing the children who would perpetuate Efraín's family? Why, in other words, is this romance fated never to conquer the short distance between the lovers? Any reader of the book, or viewer of the film versions, of course knows the answer. And I have been mentioning it all along. The girl is sick, and she dies of the same disease that killed her mother. "It is exactly the same illness her mother suffered from . . . an incurable form of epilepsy" (37; 34), although the diagnosis changes a little later on: "The doctor assures us that María's illness is not the same that Sara suffered" (50; 49). But this just begs the question about why the novel chooses to portray María in crisis rather than someone else. Whether or not María was someone in Isaacs's life[38] matters less in this interpretation than the fact that her infirmity and death seem convincing, irremediable, and that they presage general ruin. It is she who makes the family project fail. Efraín's father warns him that "María can drag you down to disaster, and us along with you . . . since your future and that of your family is at stake. . . . Would you risk everything?" The undaunted lover answers, "Everything, everything" (44; 42).

The question about why *she* causes the ruin of "Paradise" is important, because her illness is the only symptom of crisis in this novel that, on a second reading at least, is about the end of an entire social system. The cause could just as well have been Efraín who might have contracted pneumonia in damp and cold London. Or, more likely, it could have been his father, who was on the verge of physical and financial ruin. Let us consider for a moment the argument for tracing disaster back to the father before we finesse his responsibility the way Isaacs did. Among the double-binds of this novel is the simultaneous yearning for and dread of a paternalistic world; it is leisurely and loving, but it can, unwittingly, cause injustice. The abuse of slaves by the acquisitive and indelicate Emigdio and Carlos have already been mentioned. Regarding Efraín's father, however, the novel recognizes fault only reluctantly. One imagines, though, the excesses of power, similar to the ones our hero suffers at the hands of a benevolent but autocratic father, progressively pushed Isaacs over to the other side in Congress.

It is the father who is responsible for Efraín's first and then the fatal separation from María; yet except for a minor liberty that his mother approves, the son shows only respect and admiration for the father. Everything is under his control. The father even sets the terms for María's engagement to Efraín: that is, delaying the marriage until his graduation from medical school. "'Now tell Efraín,' said my father to her, quite gravely now, 'the conditions upon which you and I make him this promise'" (167; 191). And instead of declaring love for Efraín at that supreme moment, she exclaims, "How good Papa is!" (168; 192). Surely Don Jorge's kindness preempts an Oedipal rebellion. The perfectly socialized Oedipus here wants only to replace the father, to be just like him, a planter and patriarch who stays at home. Unfortunately, a respect for science and the father's ambition for (capitalist?) progress send the son forth. There is no help for it; the residents of "Paradise" need doctors, as María's condition and the father's happier outcome amply prove. Efraín's education away from home already proved to be essential in saving his father from bankruptcy. Yet, by the end of the novel, the filial obedience that should have been rewarded (165; 188) is infinitely delayed, and María complains in her last letter, "If our happiness had not been interrupted, I would have lived for you" (241; 260). Despite his virtues and his plans for progress, or rather because of these virtues and plans, the traditional and well-meaning father becomes the innocent cause of despair.[39]

But the far more innocent María is the vehicle of ruin. This may be the expression of some nonproductive romantic fantasy about the perfect child/woman who must either die or become something else.[40] Isaacs's own romance with Felisa does not seem to have survived the marriage very long, because he evidently preferred travel or being in the capital over being at home with her and their nine children. Alternatively, María's death may represent an unspoken trap of incestuous desire, straining to reestablish an imaginary seamless bond through mother(like) love. I don't deny these possible readings and will in fact return to the incest theme, but I prefer to focus here on another that would account for the novel's singling out of María, specifically her incapacity to marry and procreate, as the only sign of social decomposition in this crisis novel. And the crisis that precipitates decomposition, on this reading as in the histories that offer a backdrop, is largely racial. Either the lovers are racially redundant, as were the white planters who refused to integrate with their recently freed slaves even at the level of a national mythology; or they are a corrupting racial difference, different from each other *and* different from themselves.

True, both lovers are apparently white, if Jews can be legitimately white in a nineteenth-century code that generally equates ethnicity with race, or in any other code for that matter. Their whiteness is, in fact, complicated by an earlier Jewish identity. It is more immediate in María's case and successfully—or at least effectively—suppressed in Efraín's. His father (like Isaacs's) is originally an English Jew from Jamaica who converted in order to marry the daughter of a Spanish captain (22; 16). Don Jorge's cousin, Salomón, would gladly have converted too; and he later begs Jorge to save his child's spiritual and physical life:

> Las cristianas son dulces y buenas, y tu esposa debe ser una santa madre. Si el cristianismo da en las desgracias supremas el alivio que tú me has dado, tal vez yo haría desdichada a mi hija dejándola judía. No lo digas a nuestros parientes; pero cuando llegue a la primera costa donde se halle un sacerdote católico, hazla bautizar y que le cambien el nombre de Ester por el de María. (23)

> [Christian women are sweet and kind, and your wife must be a saintly mother. If Christianity relieves supreme misfortunes, as you have relieved me, perhaps I would cause my daughter's misfortune by allowing her to remain Jewish. Don't tell our relatives, but when she gets to the first shore that has a Catholic priest, have her converted and her name changed from Esther to María.]

It is interesting to note that Justo Sierra Sr., the father of Isaacs's loyal friend, had also given the Virgin Mary's name to his converted Jewish heroine in *La hija del judío* (*The Jew's Daughter*, published serially in 1848–1850).[41] It was Salomón's wife Sara (also the name of Isaacs's grandmother and his sister) who was unrepentingly Jewish and would not hear of conversion (23). Not coincidentally, she was also incurably ill with epilepsy. At least one critic has noticed the possibly diabolical nature of the disease that seems to be neutralized in the free and unprejudiced atmosphere of the New World.[42] Yet the association between Jewishness and racial infirmity will haunt the novel, as it must have haunted Isaacs every time a political adversary, or any anti-Semite, chose to insult him by calling him "the Jew."[43] His back, pushed closer and closer to an economic and social wall, arched in the margins that he sometimes imagined as a gateway out of Colombia, to Argentina for example. Hoping at least to be buried there and to avoid the ignominy at home, Isaacs dedicated to General Roca his long 1881 narrative poem celebrating "Saulo," the Jewish patriarch. And Isaacs continued to launch assertive defenses of the difference that no one forgot. In a poem of June 1882 called "La patria de Shakespeare," he reclaims ties with England, that interfering empire in America: "¡Patria de mis mayores! Noble madre / de Israel desvalido, protectora, / Llevo en el alma numen de tus bardos / mi corazón es templo de tus glorias." [Homeland of my elders! / Noble mother / of helpless Israel the Protectress, / My soul holds the numen of your bards / my heart is the temple of your glories.][44]

While he was writing *María,* though, wounded pride hadn't yet replaced the unspeakable vulnerability that refuses to name the kind of approbation it seeks. Beyond the economic insecurity that the novel does acknowledge through Don Jorge's crisis, some unnamed obstacle seems to disturb the spiritual and physical well-being of the family, making it uncomfortably porous to external pressures. María's and Efraín's romance, which mutual devotion and parental approval should have realized, suffers from a force out of their control. The narrator cannot bring himself to say what he amply demonstrates: that it is the idealized heroine, María herself, who disrupts the family's stability with her inherited disease. She, who fits so perfectly into the languishing world of Catholic planters, is also set apart by her inheritance, as Isaacs may have felt set apart in the militantly Catholic south by his Jewish prehistory. Neither his own devoutly Christian rearing nor his father's apparently uncomplicated conversion ever really buried the difference.[45]

If anyone else might have caused disaster in the novel, it would have been the only other character who was born Jewish; that is, Efraín's father who almost dies of an illness brought on by financial panic. He is also a perennial foreigner who disturbs the social text with reminiscences about his homeland ("In my country . . . " [43; 41]), despite the exemplary status Isaacs tries to give him in the Colombian slavocracy. But the father is saved from economic and physical crises, perhaps because he converted during the Independence struggle when the differences between creole "self" and Spanish "other" apparently overrode internal antagonisms among the new "Colombians," or because his free decision to convert showed no traces of the past, no rupture or displeasure from his parents. María, by contrast, was converted at the age of three, despite the outrage her mother and relatives would have felt. This Esther cannot "come out" and affirm her difference at a moment of her choosing, as did her namesake in the Bible or in Proust's story;[46] her secret is already obscenely public information, unavailable for any liberating or cathartic strategy. In any case, Don Jorge represents a background to this tragic dead-end, which his Jewishness prepares in terms of the racial allegory I am reading here. If we read his "race" as a figure for the slavocracy, the implied obsolescence of the Jewish religion casts a shadow over the planter class. And if we read it as a racial disturbance within that class, Jewishness again shows decay, because the planters could not abide racial or class crossings; the resistance to "new blood" announces the aristocrats' demise in a world of free labor and generally capitalist relationships. That the Isaacs and other "Jewish" families were easily absorbed into the class of latifundists in the Cauca Valley[47] didn't erase their difference from the longer-standing criollos. To assume, as many commentators have, that the neighboring province of Antioquia boasted a happy concentration of Jewish immigrants—that even its name derived from an ancient community in Syria—is to pass over the long and heated polemic about what most residents considered a libelous stigma of Jewishness.[48] And that difference became available to Jorge Isaacs as a sign for the far greater and irreconcilable racial tension that was undermining the planter class.

The Jewish race bears a stain in this novel, a hereditary disease, or at least a special coloring, that this devoutly Christian family tries to blanch out. The 1972 Colombian film version of *María,* directed by Tito Davison, is more successful on that count; it simply eliminates the complication by failing to mention anything about the Jewish background of the family, as if that would have marred the national idyll. Rollo Ogden's English version of the novel, published in 1890, had already mitigated the problem through a partial, elliptical, translation.

Presumably to appeal to an English-language public, he edited out much of Isaacs's effusive sentimentalism. And for some (perhaps imaginable) reason, he also eliminated references to Jews. But in Isaacs's original, less tidy novel, the effort to contain the family's Jewishness seems blocked by his own ambivalence and by the memory of María's unyielding mother. Her curse of mortality plagues the scene, as if she were taking revenge for her child's betrayal of the family's religion.

This reading is not really strained; but it is laconic. And here is where the debate about the relative importance of Isaacs's sources takes on new interest. The empty spaces of the reading can be filled in by the uncanny (and ironic given the religious differences) feeling of déjà vu brought by readers of Isaacs's favorite model, *Atala*.[49] Chateaubriand's tragedy is explicitly caused by the unyielding shade of Atala's mother, an Indian woman who had converted to Catholicism. On her death bed, she forced the girl to swear her preference for death over marriage to a heathen. The constraint extended to all men, just to be sure, since the dying woman reasoned that Atala would probably never meet a Christian youth. Years later, Chactas, who was indeed a heathen, watched his beloved as, "She prayed continually to her mother, whose angered shade she seemed anxious to appease" (43). And the girl is overcome by a paradox that only a Christian *Liebestod* can resolve: "'O mother! Why did you speak thus? O religion, at once my sadness and my joy, my doom and consolation!'" (59). "But your shade, O mother, your shade was ever present, reproaching me with its torments! I kept hearing your moans, I saw you devoured in the flames of hell" (60). Sara's shade does not talk, of course, except through body language; she is felt in the disease she passes on to her daughter. Perhaps this is simply an inevitable and cursed inheritance. But the structural similarities with *Atala* also suggest that this mother must have been tormented to see her daughter not only converted but also in love with a non-Jew.

If Isaacs had given no other sign of ambivalence regarding his Jewish identity, this textual debt to *Atala* would be enough to suggest that he valued it, or at least felt some guilt for "correcting" it. On the one hand, Jewishness is an unredeemable difference that had dared to contaminate an aristocratic order based on clearly marked racial difference. And on the other hand, it is a millennial identity, which can be as proud as any aristocracy. Efraín admires it in María's "light and noble walk [which] revealed all the unsubdued pride of *our* race" (17; 9, my emphasis). From either perspective, Efraín's family of conversos and Christians is doomed. Either María dies because her Jewishness is a stain, or she dies because conversion was a sin.

Some years before Isaacs wrote this novel, Benjamin Disraeli was causing something of a rage with his Orientalist historical romances.[50] In them, the Jewish race became the most ancient and continuous aristocracy, which prepared one biographer to write, "Lord Beaconsfield was of alien, although not obscure extraction,"[51] hardly the social upstart some observers imagined. It is intriguing to wonder if Isaacs's knew of or read Disraeli's *Alroy* (1842), *Coningsby* (1844), *Sybil* (1845), or *Tancred* (1847), all written after a tour of the Orient and a pilgrimage to Jerusalem caused the passionate English assimilationist to glory in Christianity's debt to Judaism.[52] Even if Isaacs had not read them, he must have known a far more standard English model that would have served as well, or better. I am referring to Walter Scott's *Waverly* (1814), which dwells nostalgically on the romance between Fergus and Flora, the ethnically specified cousins/lovers whose death marks the end of Scotland's indigenous nobility of highland chiefs. Like María, these lovers are admirable but anachronistic; and they are sacrificed to modernity by the Jewish writer and the Scot, because modernity promised them assimilation into the ethnically unspecified space of power.[53]

Alongside the sweet good-byes to Jews and to Old World aristocrats there was a danger, however; namely that they would survive. And like nobility, the Jews would produce ever more enfeebled and diseased offspring. So the flip side of Disraeli's strategic self-definition, as an aristocrat who didn't need to compete with English nobility, is the stigma of Jewish aristocratic breeding practices.[54] Whereas incest between cousins is apparently not a taboo in other nineteenth-century Latin American novels, or in *Waverly* for that matter, it amounts to a mark of racial difference in *María* for a Colombian reader such as

López Michelsen, and it gives him an opportunity to project the habit of racial discrimination onto the offended party. "María, one of the chorus of sisters, of Efraín's blood relatives, is logically his ideal wife according to the racist ideas of the chosen people."[55] For most nineteenth-century readers Jews were "aristocrats" only by analogy to the pathologies associated with endogamous, practically incestuous marriages that slowly deteriorated the stock. Being members of the most ancient aristocracy, therefore, may only have meant suffering a greater degree of spiritual and physical decay. Sander Gilman tells us that by the end of the century Jews, like blacks, were often seen as diseased through their "aberrant" sexuality, incest for Jews and lasciviousness for blacks. "The black's sexuality, like that of the Jew, was classed as a disease. In both cases the pathology was one that articulated many of the publicly repressed sexual fantasies of the turn of the century."[56] But María's pathology doesn't manage to distinguish her racially from her "normal" lover. Efraín/Isaacs could not achieve a safe distance from the sick girl despite his training in medicine, because part of his double-bind and ambivalence is that Jews have been credited with curing disease only slightly longer than they have been blamed for spreading it. (One thinks for example of Eugene Sue's incredibly popular *The Wandering Jew* [1844–1845] whose trek through Europe is followed by waves of cholera.)[57]

In fact, Isaacs gives many signs of his ambivalence. At one point Efraín indulgently, or disdainfully, explains his father's superstition as a vestige of his Jewishness. "My father was disturbed by the howling; he was a man who believed in certain kinds of prognostics and auguries" (83; 91). Ogden edits out: "These worries were typical of his race and he had never been able completely to overcome them." But at several other points, the hero and heroine are equally superstitious about a black bird that flies threateningly near. "We saw sitting upon one of the shutters which the wind was shaking, a black bird. . . . It uttered a cry such as I had never heard. It seemed to be dazzled by the light I held, and put it out as it flew over our heads, just as we were running away in fright" (135; 159—see also pp. 35, 38 and 203, 208). Of course the black bird could be Sara's vengeful spirit that is inimical to the light of Catholicism.[58] It may even be the sign of another, more visible and equally black threat of difference in the plantation's world of masters and slaves.

But perhaps Isaacs is most ambivalent in his description of María herself. Rather, he is excessive, describing her as different from either one of her two ideal selves. She is both an admirable Jewess and an ideal Christian maiden. He is fascinated by the inscrutability and depth he associates with "the women of her race" (14; 5) and swoons simultaneously over "the dignity and pride of *our* race" in her gait *and*, in the very same breath, over her "seductive modesty of a Christian virgin" (17; 9).[59] We can also imagine how ultimately troublesome her Christian identity was for planters who, after 1851, defensively distinguished between white self and non-European others. Repeated allusions to María's race, which can spill over from Efraín's pen into "our race," make her and him indelibly different. Jewishness is a fixed biological determinant here, and it signals, among other things, an irrepressible sexuality for many nineteenth-century readers. Jews, blacks, Gypsies—all those dark others (including the hysterics and madmen with whom they often overlapped) were the repositories for much of the "repressed" sexuality so characteristic of bourgeois culture. To illustrate this indifferentiation of the different, Gilman likes to quote Prosper Mérimée's *Carmen* (1845). On seeing her for the first time, the narrator thinks that Carmen "might be Moorish or . . . (I stopped short, not daring to say Jewish)."[60] And although María's English background relaxes these associations, her link to Jamaica (like Jane Eyre's and Cora Munro's) probably strengthens them. Reasonable white Christian men, of course, were not prone to excesses and perversions. Where these developed they were caused by seductive females, often prostitutes (thought to be quintessential women, raw undomesticated femaleness), whose sexual differences from men practically constituted them as a different species and so related them to racially different groups.[61]

María's double marking as both racially and sexually different from the unmarked and powerful planters may have made her affinity with another Virgin of the same name especially problematic. Perhaps the depth of María's devotion to the

Virgin Mary has something to do with her Jewish spirituality, or even with a narcissistic identification with the divinely maternal Jewish maiden whose image she resembles. Tránsito, among others, recognizes "the striking likeness between the face of her future bridesmaid and that of a beautiful Madonna in my mother's oratory" (121; 140). That Virgin Mary must have been visibly Semitic, because Isaacs was quite careful to have his María imagined as a Jewish beauty. He went so far as to suggest to a painter that his portrait of the fictional heroine would have been more perfect if it had a Jewish nose.[62] Her devotion may have had yet another motive related to narcissism; that is to sidestep Christianity and remain Jewish-identified. Paul Roche points out the cunning (converso?) trick of putting a noncanonical book into her hands. Instead of reading the standard *Imitation of Jesus Christ,* María's devotional text is *The Imitation of the Virgin.* While apparently extolling orthodox Christian practice, Isaacs avoids it. The substitution is so strange, Roche adds, that one of Isaacs's most respected critics thinks it is simply a mistake.[63] María, in short, is not only a danger to herself and to Efraín's crypto-Jewish family, she is also a bothersome reminder of Christianity's Jewish origins and therefore of the arbitrary and porous distinction between self and other. There is no point in asking her hero, as the Jewish heroine of Disraeli's *Tancred* asks him, "Pray, are you of those Franks who worship a Jewess, or of those who revile her?" For those Catholic planters compelled to insist on racial distinctions, María confuses the camps; she is an impossible amalgamation of Jewish and Christian identities, an ephemeral combination of the seductress and the innocent. It is as if the contradiction between her excessive (Jewish) sensuality and her heroic (Christian) innocence finally cancels out either term and kills her. The girl literally wrestles herself to death.

Yet thanks to this very excess and the consequent ambiguity regarding absolute values, the book succeeds admirably in making the word *judío,* Jew, available as a term of respect and affection in Spanish. Don Jorge would playfully call María "judía" (which Ogden translates as "little one") to show an intimacy bordering on complicity (128; 149). And his old friend embraces Efraín as the living image of his Jewish father. "'The deuce!'

exclaimed the collector . . . 'If you were not so swarthy, I could swear that you couldn't so much as say good-day in Spanish. . . . But for that sedateness, which I suppose you have inherited from your mother, I could believe that I was with the Jew [Ogden's "your father"]!'" (247; 267). Apparently, the narrator (and Isaacs), is caught between the poles of ethnic identification, unsure whether "Jew" is a religious affiliation that one can convert out of or a race that is biologically and indelibly fixed. In the context of the partisan politics of Isaacs's time, he is caught between an enlightened liberalism that promised to blanch out the stain or merely the difference of being Jewish (through free and individual relationships) and the conservative Catholicism that had redeemed his father but that had kept visible the mark of difference.

Ambivalence about racial identity does not stop at Efraín's family. It also characterizes their industrious and successful neighbors, as if to say that the color lines slavery needed are slippery and can hardly be kept distinct. José, the yeoman patriarch beyond the plantation, deferentially refers to Efraín as "el blanco" (75; Ogden's "this boy," 81). The young man can himself admit a certain deference when he says that during the hunt, José "exercised a paternal authority over me," even if "it disappeared when he entered his house" (68; 71). Besides, they are probably of the same color. Otherwise, Efraín could not have teased Tránsito, the old man's daughter, for refusing to ride a horse to her own wedding. She had objected, "In Antioquia only white people ride horses" (122; 142). Efraín retorts, "Who ever told you that you are not white? And white as few are." She is then forced to spell out what he already knows of course, that class is color-coded: "What I mean is rich people, the great ladies." Yet Efraín's teasing may be something more. It may be an acknowledgement that she is already his equal. Writing a decade and a half after abolition and the rise of small farmers, Isaacs may already have felt a weakening of the traditional class structure in which only planters were white.

This racial ambivalence, nevertheless, must have had its practical limits for Efraín's class. Tránsito and her industrious family are economically and racially mobile; this in itself marks an end to aristocratic exclusiveness. I suggested earlier that her happy romance with Braulio may have been at Efraín's expense. And indeed, on returning home to find María dead and the estate sold, he also finds Tránsito occupying the rose garden where he and María had spent their only happy moments. His practically suicidal grief, " . . . the contempt . . . I had for life" (276), both frightens and offends her. Efraín seems temporarily indifferent to her own joy as a young wife and mother. "After I embraced Braulio, Tránsito laid on my knees a pretty baby, six months old, and kneeling at my feet, smiled in pleasure to see me caress her little boy" (276–277; 298). Her family's encroachment seems friendly, though, a Liberal victory that Isaacs might have half feared and half welcomed; it shows up in the novel as a subtle design of white on white that is obviously not perceived as a dramatic threat of class extinction. That drama is played out in the more colorful difference between indigenous Catholics and exotic Jews.

Now, clearly, part of my reading of the English Jewish versus Spanish Catholic tension has been as a displacement of the far more threatening and destructive racial contrast between black and white. If there were any doubt about the nature of this technique, one could point out that Isaacs himself uses it quite consciously. Displacement, he has the authoritative Dr. Mayn explain, is what caused Efraín's father to suffer a physical fever when the real cause of his illness was emotional. "There are some diseases that spring from the mind, and disguise themselves under the symptoms of others" (148; 176). Some years later, Dr. Freud would join others who were studying this kind of displacement called hysteria; that is, the pathological manifestation of a mental disorder. For example, Don Jorge's spiritual (and economic) crisis manifests itself in the classic symptoms of speechlessness and lack of appetite. When his fortune is restored and Jorge admits the terror he had felt, his hysteria is cured, just as Freud said it would be, once the pain that triggered the symptoms is confronted.[64]

Hysteria was not only a shorthand for displacement but also its own best case. It became a catch-all, almost undefinable, clinical term to label a variety of emotional "disorders."[65] These were often also gender and race specific disturbances (ambitions, advances in public education, riots) in an exclusive social order. Giving the disorder a clinical name helped to control abnormally mobile people. By definition these were people with wandering wombs, that is hysterics, women who resisted male-centered domestication. And by analogy, they were also men whose racial constitution made them unstable, like Jews who forgot their legitimate place in the ghettos. By 1890 Jean Martin Charcot's association of Jews with hysteria (caused by inbreeding and manifested in wandering) became a commonplace in European medicine.[66] Black slaves in the United States, for another example, were repeatedly diagnosed as unstable and mad every time they attempted to escape.[67] And to contain the threat to English hegemony and the legitimacy of colonial rule, the Indian Rebellion of 1857 was deemed an outbreak of hysteria, one of many throughout Europe's empires in the second half of the century.[68]

Jorge's hysterical response to imminent financial disaster and the consequent social ostracism that the Jew must have feared helps to explain María's disease as overdetermined by her being both a woman and a Jew. The predisposition to emotional infirmity underlines her ties with the only other Jew, whose sick body is the symptom either of a tortured spirit or of incestuous breeding. And Freud again (Does it take one to know one?) helps to nail down the relationship when he designates a peculiarly intense manifestation of hysteria as epilepsy. To be precise, he called it "affective" epilepsy to distinguish it from the organic disease and perhaps therefore to deemphasize the hereditary, racial, hypothesis. The difference helped him account for the otherwise inexplicable convulsions of overly sensitive personalities with no clinical history. Freud gives only passing mention to the phenomenon in his early paper on hysteria. But he develops it later in an essay called "Dostoevsky and Parricide" (1928), where Dostoevsky's epileptic fits are attributed to the guilt brought on by a murderous rage against his father. For overly sensitive María too, there is something unspeakable about her apparently loving and docile relationship to Don Jorge; and it may produce the intense self-hatred and punishing masochism that Dr. Mayn diagnosed as epileptic attacks. After all, Jorge had separated her from Efraín more than once. She senses that this separation, meant first to insure his education and only secondarily to prevent her emotional excesses, has cost her life.

She may also have sensed that the prevention prescribed for her was not the only possible treatment; and her anger may be an allusion to the alternative cure for hysterical women. Although the causes and the cures seem undefinably contradictory in nineteenth-century medical literature, they generally break down into two versions. One located the problem in a primitive, female sexuality, so that the cure was to control it; whereas the other version understood female pathology to be the lack of normal sexuality, so that the cure was to supplement the lack that made her female and crazy. The doctor and father here evidently favor the restrictive hypothesis, as did many contemporary experts in Europe. In England, Dr. Edward Tilt was advising mothers to delay their daughters' sexual maturation by having them take cold showers, avoid featherbeds and novels, and always wear drawers. "But without doubt," Nancy Armstrong writes, "the most ghoulish effort to regulate women's minds by regulating their bodies was Dr. Isaac Brown's surgical practice of clitoridectomy. Brown believed that by eliminating masturbation, removal of the clitoris could halt a disease that began with hysteria and progressed to spinal irritation, idiocy, mania, and death."[69] The England of Drs. Tilt and Brown, where domestic management of female sexuality is furiously being taught and where the medical establishment is busy criminalizing female-centered folk cures, is precisely where Efraín's father sent him to study medicine.

But for a while Efraín refuses to go. At the same time he plans to administer the alternative and slightly more modern cure to María. As I said, it was to give the hysterical woman what she lacked, a penis. Domestic management could therefore mean early and happy marriage. This became a commonplace of medical jokes, such as the one Charcot told about being consulted in a case of hysteria. The doctor who called him in concludes, "The sole prescription for such a malady is familiar enough to us but we cannot order it. It runs: Rx. Penis normalis/ dosim/ repetatur!"[70] As lover, Efraín could have supplied what the medical student could not. This is one aspect of the double-bind that strangles him. María's body (like Colombia's body politic) is being debated between the thesis of preventive repression (Conservative Dr. Mayn) and the thesis of domestic satisfaction (Efraín, the Liberal lover). Both want to domesticate her, the question is how: as a girl or as a woman?

It is on the horns of this debate that Efraín's Oedipal struggle can be read in larger, national dimensions. While his Jewish father and Dr. Mayn (whose profession and surname practically give him away as Jewish and therefore a double for the father) direct Efraín both to the old country and to the conservative cure, María and the lusciously maternal Cauca Valley she evokes tempt him to rebel and to stay with her in "Paradise." America, after all, is where desire doesn't need to be controlled because it can be satisfied. This suggests that the more American cure for the mass "hysteria" of the black uprisings was not the conservative control that kept the races apart as long as possible but the sociosexual satisfaction that eliminated desire for change by filling in the lack. Efraín finally resists this solution because he is so dutiful a son and so diligent a student. And his caution or cowardice has everything to do with Colombia's national frustrations. The question for Isaacs's class was whether to satisfy the blacks' and the liberal whites' desire for change, or to control those desires and forestall a racially mixed, possibly monstrous progeny. Like Efraín, the planters hesitated to break colonial habits, and they discovered that postponements through Civil Wars could be disastrous. By the time they stopped fighting there was little left to protect, neither plantations nor María. Efraín's choice of filial loyalty over conjugal duty is the same as choosing between one cure and another. As a result, María loses her life. In other words, her advanced hysteria may have been the effect rather than the cause of the chastity forced on her by the doctor and the Don, just as Colombia's black rebellions are the effect rather than the cause of the planters' control. María is the first to understand this metaleptic inversion between cure and disease, as we saw in her letter. The longer passage reads: "Come, come quickly, or I shall die without seeing you. . . . For a year that disease of which happiness was curing me has been killing me. If our happiness had not been interrupted, I would have lived for you" (241; 260). Small wonder if her epileptic attacks were brought on by what Freud calls a guilt-ridden desire for parricide.

Would it be, however, too adventurous to suggest that in her case the possibly parricidal fantasies may themselves be a displacement for a repressed desire for spiritual "matricide," if, that is, the shade of María's mother continues to interfere in the girl's affairs? In other words, Sara may be the cause of her daughter's suffering whether or not the epilepsy was inherited. As María is unable, or too guilt ridden, to "talk out" or even to name her pain, she must be its victim. But perhaps she was doomed in any case, since her combined Jewishness and femaleness determine her destiny. The nagging problem about blaming Efraín and his father for the wrong choice of cure is that María may not have survived anyway. Perhaps that is why the book remains undecided about whether the epilepsy is organic or affective, and about which cure to favor.[71] Even if she had survived, María's congenital Jewishness is the double-bind that would make her unfit to bear Efraín's children, either because she was racially identical to him or because she was racially different. Compared to ideal heroines of the Latin American canon, José Mármol's Amalia, for example, or Blest Gana's Leonor, María lacked "manly" dignity and self-control. Therefore the very liberties she took with feminine propriety, liberties that seemed to ally her with other romantic heroines, slip dangerously on a closer reading into the "barbarity" of uncontrolled femaleness. Unlike the others, she wept too easily, spoke her mind, initiated flirtations, went outside barefoot, and literally trembled with passion. In short, she revealed her inferior undomesticated gender, as well as her origins in an inferior race. Had Efraín married María, the couple would have had an imbalance of femaleness, that is Jewishness.

Efraín and Isaacs evidently prefer to show María's tragic death than to tell us how it was overdetermined, because that would have amounted to admitting that María's infirmity was both a matter of aristocratic exclusiveness *and* of racial inferiority. If it were clear that she (and they) represented the undomesticated blacks as well as the dying plantocracy, how could generations of readers—nostalgic for a colonial world buried by hegemonic projects and novels—sigh for María? Rather than spell the connection out, Isaacs practices his own kind of writerly "hysteria," by finding a substitute for the racial antagonism he will not record. In other words, *María* used something of a narrative defense mechanism that Freud would call "displacement" as such. By displacement Freud meant a substituting function of memory in the obsessional neurotic. When a particular experience is too painful to remember and too intense to forget, memory replaces that event for a related but inoffensive element.[72] The process is metonymic, a sliding from the essential part of that experience to the "inessential elements . . . something in the neighborhood." The memory of that obsession therefore seems trivial.[73] No doubt slavery and racial rebellions were as traumatic for Efraín (and for Isaacs) as were the more narrowly personal obsessions for Freud's patients. One sign is the narrator's silence on the rebellions; another is the novel's general tragedy brought on by María's disease, a disease unmotivated by the narrative except as a displaced symptom, as I said, of either too little or too much sexual adventurousness. In the author's idealizing recollections of plantation life, her illness offers a way of leaving out the obsession with the threat of racial adventure while at the same time responding to its affective power. She is the safer, historically trivial "neighbor" of an unmentionable memory. As an "aristocratic" inbreeding Jewess, María is also the better figure for Colombia's exclusive plantocracy; either way both must die, whether through disease-provoking endogamy or through racially corrupting miscegenation.

Isaacs's defense mechanism almost breaks down, though, when despite the "neurotic" symptom formation that displaces race riots for María's epilepsy the metonymy between blacks and Jews borders on metaphor. He apparently cannot resist interpolating the long and tragic romance of Nay and Sinar, the African lovers who are tragically separated by slavery. The tale, scrupulously omitted from Ogden's English translation, is the only extended treatment of blacks in the novel; and it draws some telling parallels with the central romance,[74] as if Isaacs were purposefully pointing our symptomatic reading back to the obsessive experience he cannot mention. Like Esther who was converted to become María without abandoning a certain racial pride, Nay remained very conscious of her African nobility after taking the Christian name Feliciana with her new religion. And like the main romance, doomed at least in this interpretation because of insurmountable racial differences that seemed irrelevant to the father's generation, the interpolated romance seems at first to overcome ethnic/tribal antagonisms (between the fathers of Nay and Sinar) but then succumbs to war and racial exploitation. If Don Jorge saves María from an orphan's pain and from Jewish superstition, he also saves Feliciana from the humiliation of slavery (186). The parallels between Nay and María become undeniable when Efraín is touched to see María, "humbling herself like a slave to pick up those flowers" (33; 30), and especially when he imagines her funeral: "Woe is me, as humble and silent as Nay's!" (273).

Efraín, too, with his unabashedly Hebrew name, is implicated in the identification with Nay. Like her (178), and like Atala, one of his parents had converted to Christianity. And like them, the conversion had not saved the child from tragedy. In general the double resonance here of Chateaubriand's story, both in the main romance and in this interpolated tale, suggests how many points of contact there are between María's story and Nay's. Even in terms of narrative strategy, Nay's tale is as true to Chateaubriand's retrospective technique as is Efraín's. Her story may even have been his model, since Efraín grew up hearing its "rustic and touching language" (169). Just to underline the rhetorical connection between Jews and blacks here, slipping toward the commonplace identification between pathologically passionate Jews and sentimental blacks that Gilman traces, I would add that *María* is one of the only national novels of the period where blacks, along with mulattoes, are described as beautiful. (See p. 79; 86, where Efraín refers to Juan Angel as "good-looking—one might almost say, handsome," and p. 108 where he praises Estéfana for "her sweet nature and beauty," although Ogden omits this admiration.) The only other classic that comes to mind is *Francisco* by the Cuban Anselmo Suárez y Romero.

As in Galván's *Enriquillo* and Alencar's *O Guaraní*, the real racial threat of blacks in a plantation society becomes unspeakable to Isaacs. In their cases, the unreconcilable differences between blacks and whites cede ground to the more easily idealized relations between whites and Indians. In one stroke, the working masses of the Dominican Republic and Brazil are lightened and customized for a constructive national program. But what program could have been convincing in the national novel of Colombia, probably the only Latin American country that remained fragmented throughout the nineteenth century? Isaacs evidently did not choose to project an Indian nation, although his ethnographic studies show that he knew Indians far better than did most novelists,[75] perhaps because Colombian Indians continued to defend militarily their territorial rights. In any case, Isaacs was not displacing one fearsome race for another more promising one in the interest of constructing a national myth. On the contrary; he seems to be saying that no myth of amalgamation is possible, because the partriarchal world he yearns for will not have it. Any mestizaje will necessarily be counterproductive, as counterproductive as racial exclusivity, for the ex-masters who rose in devastating civil wars rather than share power with their ex-slaves. Instead of Indians, he displaced the inassimilable black masses and the anachronistic planters onto his innocent but flawed Jewish heroine. And by extension he displaced them onto part of himself. María is admirable in every way, and her desire for love and family is only natural and justified, as justified as the blacks' desire for abolition or the planters' desire for survival. But María is genetically inappropriate for marriage to the hero either way one interprets her. So Isaacs kills her off, as if the death were determined by the disease she inherits from her mother whether Jewishness is racial redundancy or racial difference. Just as plausibly, the death is determined by Efraín's scrupulous distance from María. The very restraint that enabled their love makes sure it will not be consummated.

In another single stroke, this historical romance kills off any possibility of racial amalgamation between the Colombian aristocracy and its recently freed slaves. Blacks and whites may love each other, but only from a distance. Isaacs also kills himself off in a symbolic suicide, both as a planter who can no longer be productive and as a Jew, in other words, a difference that corrupts the earlier partriarchal coherence that his father, iron- ically, represented. This demise of Isaacs's aristocratic order, and the possibility of his complicity as a corrupting racial differ- ence, may help to explain why he could evoke so poignantly Chateaubriand's kind of masochistic nostalgia.

7

SOMETHING TO CELEBRATE: NATIONAL NUPTIALS IN CHILE AND MEXICO

Everything ends well in the main plot of *Martín Rivas* (1862), by Alberto Blest Gana, just as everything could be construed as coming out all right for Chile's ruling elite in the political struggles of the preceding decade. In my general remarks in chapter 1, about how national romances staged a mutual grounding for public projects and private desires by adjusting European models, I already let on that Chile's national love affair across class and regional barriers ends blissfully in marriage and that it "corrects" Stendhal's tragic-heroic ending in *The Red and the Black*. In this bourgeois revision, personal heroism is reasonable, not sacrificial; it is also practically indistinguishable from public virtue. Young Rivas embodies this (intra)personal virtue as soon as he arrives in Santiago in 1850 to study law. His recently deceased father was an unlucky mining speculator, in the northern town of Copiapó, who had ceded his only rich mine to Dámaso Encina, a usurer in Santiago. Dámaso takes Martín in, although his gorgeous but domineering daughter Leonor seems to disdain the provincial's evident attentions. Nevertheless, his industriousness ("God will reward my constancy and my work" [14; 11])[1] and Dámaso's intense ambition to disengage from business and become a senator (either party would do) combine to make Martín the usurer's secretary. Many pages later, pages full of erotically charged power struggles reminiscent of Julien's affair with Matilde (esp. chap. 17), and after much philosophical dialogue about love with direct references to Stendhal's treatise *De l'amour* (e.g., 111, 122, and 269; 308), Martín and Leonor are finally brought to a happy and practical union.

The tangle of politics and passions straightens out just as neatly in Mexico's *El Zarco* (1888) by Ignacio Altamirano, when the Indian hero (as pure blooded as President Benito Juárez) completes the racially redemptive domestication of Scott's *Ivanhoe* by choosing the dark heroine over the light one. Like Scott's England some decades before, both Chile and Mexico had something to celebrate by the 1860s, something that was rhetorically akin to a marriage made in heaven. It was a national history that already boasted political accomplishments, while so many sister republics were still projecting them. The national romances of Chile and Mexico are less the imaginings of sectoral or racial consolidation, like the ones written in Argentina, Colombia, Cuba, or Ecuador, than they are commemorations of consolidating events.

To compare these novels with the fantasies or frustrating romances written elsewhere in America, is also to recall the contrast Lukács established between Walter Scott and his contemporaries, between the historically specific and celebratory model of what historical novels should be, in Lukács's doctrinaire opinion, and the disappointingly ahistorical projections of lesser writings. Lukács himself was, of course, sensitive enough to the differences between English and, say, German or Italian history to admit that the comparison was unfair. The kind of celebrations Scott could provide for successive moments of interclass alliances and national consolidation in England were simply unavailable to writers like Goethe or Manzoni, however talented they were and however passionate about their respective country's delayed development. They might well have agreed with Lukács that English history was more pleasing than the humiliating chronology of petty regional warfare and foreign interference which couldn't amount to a national record; patriots logically preferred to leave it behind for conciliatory projections.

The Latin American novelists, all heirs to Scott after the 1840s,[2] could have found little offense in Lukács's bias in favor of winners. Many were at least equally programmatic and just as disposed to identify esthetic value with political convenience.[3] It is no wonder, then, that Chile's and Mexico's most respected writers should take the opportunity to dwell on the recent and enviable chapters of a history in progress. In the decade before Blest Gana published his novel, Chile had already become a worldwide banking center, had built the first major railroad in South America, and was exploiting coal and copper mines for domestic industries as well as for export.[4] The country had also managed to constrain the disintegration of an elite consensus to make Chile a model of stability and productivity since the 1820s. And in the Mexico that the Indian patriot Altamirano fought for and won on the battlefield and in print, the overwhelmingly mestizo and indigenous population had managed to inaugurate an Indian president in 1861 and to return him to power six years later, despite political and military interference from European(izing) monarchists.[5] By the time Chile's and Mexico's national novelists recorded these triumphs, the glory seemed tarnished to be sure; and much of their motive for writing was surely to renew the luster obscured under layers of compromising developments. Blest Gana was crafty enough not to mention either the popular-based eruptions that followed the radical bourgeoisie's confrontation with conservatives or the erosion of elite consensus that would ensue, just as Altamirano wisely preferred to stop his story with Juárez's resolve to end banditry. What positive purpose could be served by exposing the new vows taken in Chile as a sign of crisis in the elite marriage contract, or by mentioning that Juárez's recklessly conciliatory policies weakened Mexico to the point of allowing the French occupation under Emperor Maximillian, an international humiliation that made Porfirio Díaz's despotic style seem preferable to pardon?

In each case, a particular event was salvageable from contemporary history, a political milestone that gave Chileans and Mexicans reason for national self-congratulations and—if the novelists succeeded—for self-confidence about future political gains. Blest Gana was as clear and prescriptive as was Altamirano about the utility required from American novels. They were to invest economic and political gains with social meaning, to give the kind of cultural currency to progress that progressive statesmen could bank on. "Above all else," Blest Gana exhorted at his 1861 investment as the first professor of Chilean literature in the University of Santiago,

Debemos establecer con satisfacción el hecho de que Chile puede tener una literatura propia, que corresponda a los progresos en cuya vía se encuentra lanzado y que contribuiría poderosamente a impulsarle en esa senda de lisonjeros adelantos. . . . Las letras deben, por consiguiente, llenar con escrupulosidad su tarea civilizadora y esmerarse por revestir de sus galas seductoras a las verdades que puedan fructificar con provecho de la humanidad. (460–461)[6]

[We must establish with certainty the fact that Chile can have its own literature, a literature that would correspond to the progress upon which the country has embarked and that would contribute powerfully to promote this direction of welcome advances. . . . Writing should, therefore, scrupulously fulfill its civilizing mission and make every effort to embellish productive truths with seductive charms.]

The chaired appointment was itself proof that Blest Gana was in very good company as he (self-)promoted national novels, because it followed directly on José Victorino Lastarria's and Miguel Luis Amunátegui's choice of his *La aritmética en el amor* as the best Chilean novel. They were judges in the contest meant to encourage national novelists and sponsored by the University of Chile, founded in 1842 under the rectorship of Andrés Bello (that master of conciliation) as the state's training center for a modern citizenry.[7] Blest's audience was therefore probably happy to hear his formula, specifically his rationale for novels of manners. The speech begins, as we saw, by demanding that literature be socially responsible, much as Lastarria had done a decade before as he fomented the cultural climate for progressive politics.[8] Then Blest narrows down the genres to the most useful and worthy of developing (460). Poetry, he objected, has always attracted the best Chilean writers, a fatal attraction according to Blest Gana. For one thing, lyrics tend to lament to little purpose; and for another, very few people read poems, whereas everyone seems to be reading novels (465).[9] And if Chileans don't write edifying novels, the avid public will have only the morally dubious European imports, abundantly available in the literary supplements of newspapers and in domestic reprints. Like Mitre's prologue to *Soledad* (1847), which had circulated widely in Chile,[10] and even more like Altamirano's "La literatura nacional" written seven years after Blest's essay, "Literatura chilena" takes no offense at the novel's broad-based appeal. On the contrary, Blest apparently finds more reason for offense in the vestigial literary snobbism that ignores the novel's potential as a vehicle for general social improvement. Evidently, the educational and democratic promise of novels had to begin with defending the genre itself. "The novel has a special charm for all levels of intelligence . . . it speaks everyone's language, . . . and brings civilization to the least educated classes of society. . . . Its popularity can therefore be immense, and its utility unquestionable" (465).

His bias against poetry sounds almost like an early Mikhail Bakhtin, moralizing against its fetishized individualism. Poetry's small public is not only a function of uneven educational development, but also of an esthetic and social narrowness that resembles narcissism (463). Blest's preference for prose, he explains, comes from observing that every reader recognizes him/herself in the novels' varied characters and the range of language uses. Therefore, the best kind of novel for Chile is the one in which the broadest range of people are portrayed: the novel of manners.[11] At the same time, he defends a simple style of writing for the widest possible appeal, which may also be a convenient justification for his notably prosaic writing.

Manners made sense as the focus for Chile's novels, thanks to the country's admirable stability and prosperity. Its novels did not have to project an ideal state but merely had to represent it in a way that would acknowledge and consolidate the gains. Blest Gana understood this to be a mandate for writers during the "transitional" midcentury period, when cultural vestiges of colonial life were inhibiting Chile's material and political strides. Moreover, the peculiar juxtapositions between old and new provided wonderful opportunities for producing lively and quintessentially Chilean novels (468). The *novelas de costumbres* would focus attention on who Chileans already were, not on what they could become. Presumably, the nostalgic fantasies, sometimes called historical novels, were written elsewhere, where a collective national identity needed to be fictionalized for the past and projected to cover over a factious present. Nevertheless, Blest Gana did write a historical novel late in life,

Durante la Reconquista (1897), and the rage for serialized historical best-sellers from 1860 to 1900 is a hint that he was polemicizing in this speech for what he must have considered alternative, mature manners of reading.[12] In 1862, Chile's present seemed a project fulfilled. This historical advantage—and the stylistic corollary of "Balzacian realism" that critics make much of, and which *Martín Rivas* did in fact introduce into a continent still in love with Chateaubriand's fantasies and Scott's large-scale historical romance—might make Blest Gana seem eccentric among Latin American contemporaries.[13] It is true that he learned from Balzac, including his commitment to writing a long series of novels (in contrast to the single novel of some other American nation-builders), his attention to money, local details, and a love of intrigue.[14] But it is also true that he "improved" on Balzac in ways worthy of Latin American colleagues, just as he also "corrected" Stendhal. Perhaps the most significant way was to marry money to morality, partners who seem irreparably estranged for Balzac. Martín, who understands money's value as social mediator, is the novel's double but uncontradictory agent. He negotiates love affairs as the go-between *and* mediates in brilliant business deals, sometimes making one arrangement work for the other. Leonor's affected but adorable brother gets the moral of this story right when he quips: "The French . . . say *L'amour fait rage et l'argent fait mariage*; but here love makes both, *rage et mariage*" (249; 282–283).

This wonderfully synthetic inspiration is one sign of Blest Gana's politico-esthetic success one year after his inaugural pronouncements. He had followed up with published proof that his practice was fully caught up with his theory. *Martín Rivas* was modern (even precociously realist), seductively melodramatic, and yet managed to be relentlessly moralizing as well. Even when things end badly in the subplots of this novel, the infallible justice meted out produces a kind of readerly happiness derived from our satisfaction with the book's, and the country's, narrative logic. Punishments fit crimes in practically all the amorous and financial intrigues. These include developments that follow visits by Martín and his law-school friend Rafael San Luis to the *medio pelo* ("popular" or lower-middle-class) Molina sisters. Martín's friendship with Edelmira Molina causes Leonor's unfounded jealousy. But Rafael's affair with Adelaida is less innocent; and it will ruin any chance of happiness with his real love, aristocratic Matilde Elías whose father had initially objected to the match on economic grounds. Martín tries to help Rafael win back Matilde, although he admits that Adelaida's family is right to be outraged and to demand that he marry the mother of his child (234; 265). Martín also tries to protect Leonor's brother Agustín from blackmail for attempted seduction of the same girl. But these conflicts dissolve during a political intrigue of Liberals against Conservatives, a confrontation in which lovesick Martín, convinced of Leonor's indifference, risks his life and ends up in jail. Far more desperate Rafael takes a suicidal vanguard position (as did other Liberals in 1851) and dies in battle.

Rafael is obviously a casualty of the broad-based uprising against the newly appointed Conservative President, Manuel Montt, a pivotal event in Chile's history. But the political circumstances of the death come into play here almost as retribution for sins against love. Edelmira's frustrated passion for Martín is a less dramatic casualty, but a necessary one for the poetic and political justice of the novel. Her error was to imagine that she could realize the fantasies she was reading in (probably European) novels (153; 172, and 167; 188), fantasies that were bound to be disappointed when their object became Martín, a paragon of constancy no matter how indifferent Leonor seemed. The main (elite) plot's success depends on Edelmira's (popular) assent, because only she can dispel Leonor's jealousy. But she does even more. By marrying her peer (a police officer whom she detests) she smuggles Martín out of jail after the rebellion, out of jail and into Leonor's arms. In Chile's surrender to love, one possible consort for Martín's Liberal bourgeoisie gives up more than the pride of power and control that Leonor would forfeit: Edelmira surrenders her dream man to a more privileged woman.

This kind of happy ending should be no surprise in the national novel that became required reading in Chile's secondary schools.[15] Its institutionalization had something to do, no doubt, with its celebration of what historians call the Liberals' political victory that followed repeated military defeats.[16] The "victory" was an alliance with Conservatives which seems natural, almost inevitable, in the novel because the union is cast as a mutual passion that overcomes regional and class differences. Perhaps the Liberal-Conservative conciliation and the consequent political continuity were indeed inevitable. In one view, nothing effectively challenged the stability of a compact elite in a manageably small territory, not even the civil wars of 1851 and 1859 in which the provinces rebelled against the capital.[17] And although interregional harmony had to be achieved, there seems to have been no need for a racial romance that would project national harmony. In Chile, a white elite managed the harmony internally.[18] Years before *Martín Rivas* was published, the country already enjoyed stability as a "democracy of the oligarchy."[19] Popular and factional struggles had been contained through O'Higgens's authoritarian government and through the Liberals' democratizing experiments in the 1820s to give Chile, by the 1830s, the enviable reputation as the only stable democracy in all of Latin America (and most of Europe). In 1852 Juan Bautista Alberdi spoke for all the Argentine refugees from Rosas's government when he proposed a toast to this haven from anarchy, "the honorable exception in South America."[20]

But this practically seamless retrospective reading of Chile's history should be suspect as a version of the victorious. The vanquished might tell the story differently. The fact that Chile's "Conservative" democracy survived the repeated assaults does not necessarily mean that the continuity was always predictable. Surely some Liberals who fought and died in the civil wars must have objected to conservatism. They could not all have been romantic suicides like Rafael San Luis. Through the 1840s, in fact, the anticlerical Liberals were opposing Catholic Conservatives, not wooing them.[21] And by 1850, after almost twenty years of liberalism's political eclipse, its intellectual leader in Parliament and the founder in 1842 of the *Sociedad Literaria*, José Victorino Lastarria, had gained a strong following for secular reform (perhaps the most explosive issue of the 1870s).[22] At the same time, socialist agitators who joined the notorious Francisco Bilbao, author of *Sociabilidad Chilena* (1844), and who were encouraged by the French Revolution of 1848 (like Edelmira who acquired unrealizable fantasies from her novels?) were mobilizing Santiago's artisans in the *Sociedad de Igualdad*.[23] In the long run, the church's power waned; by 1865 de facto religious toleration was formally granted, and by 1875 the church's special privileges (*fueros*) ended. But before those defeats, Catholic Conservatives hoped to defend their ideas and practices by choosing Manuel Montt as president in 1851. Montt's election was immediately challenged during three months of full-scale civil war. It was not only the Liberals, competing for state resources, who wanted to be rid of him, but also, and more seriously, the southern provinces where masses of peasants were being displaced by oligarchic landowners who were stepping up their expropriations of small holdings. The varying degrees of resistance would make a political difference later, once the revolutionary demands of the agrarian sector produced an insoluble contradiction with developing capitalism and predicted an elite conciliation: business needed masses of workers (for the "Liberal" bourgeoisie's industrial development), workers who could be freed up by the rural encroachments of "Conservative" agrobusinessmen.[24] But before the contradiction between peasants and industrialists could unravel their alliance, Montt's heavy and even-handed National Guard (25,000 men as compared to 3,000 of Chile's standing army) put an end to the 1851 rebellion.

Six years later, Montt's authoritarian style had alienated most Conservatives and pushed them into the Liberals' arms, although some Radical or "red" Liberals refused to call that 1857 embrace a love affair. Before the general amnesty of 1862, the Radicals saw Chile's history as a series of repressions, not as a democratic continuity. The amnesty was primarily for militants in the 1859 civil war that challenged what was left of Montt's base, now known as the National party. This time, the war was based in the northern mining region, the home territory of Martín Rivas and of the new Radical party. The novel, then, collapses two wars into a single romantically resolved confrontation: the 1851 rebellion, which was originally led by Santiago Liberals but soon got out of their control as fighting continued among the popular classes and to the south, and the 1859 uprising in the north. In this way, the book fuses the capital's Liberal bourgeoisie with dissident miners who were fast becoming Chile's most productive sector. That fusion, in the person of Martín, conquers "aristocratic" Leonor and her father, all with the self-denying support of out-classed Edelmira.

There have been at least two ways of reading Blest Gana's most popular novel; and in some ways they reproduce the historical debate about the 1851 uprising. Either it was merely a ripple that underscored the elite's tenacity or it was a horrific challenge to the capital's authoritarian elite. *Martín Rivas* has been read as representing either a political conflict that hints at a radical potential or a seamless history that is free to focus on social detail. The hyphenated adjective of his subtitle (*Novela de costumbres político-sociales*), nicely suggests the dialectical inflection of the terms and the imprudence of choosing between the readings. On the one hand, social manners—which in this book focus on correct conduct for erotic liaisons—are a political matter; and on the other hand, political comportment has everything to do with the ethics of (inter)personal manners.

Nevertheless, some readers seem convinced that national politics hardly matters in *Martín Rivas,* since the overwhelming concern here appears to be the mores of courtship. A contemporary novel of manners (*costumbres*) hardly promised Chile's readers the political intrigues they associated with the "historical novels" inspired by Scott, Dumas, and Sue, novels such as *La novia del hereje o la Inquisición en Lima* (1845–1850 in serial form) by Vicente Fidel López and *El inquisidor mayor* (first published in Lima, 1852) by Manuel Bilbao.[25] Instead of arguing for particular public programs, this novel was condemning illicit relationships, especially those in which privileged young men abuse girls of a lower class. It was censuring parents for imposing marriages of convenience on their children, and was rewarding middle-class virtue. For Hernán Díaz Arrieta, the novel prudently avoids political theses. "Martín Rivas lives, not because of this idea or that one, but because he won Leonor's love. . . . And also because their intimate affair . . . is laced through with exciting scenes and with very local accents of Santiago."[26] And Raúl Silva Castro goes so far as to say that the novel could have little political interest, because it portrays class-related antagonisms that were already history in Chile.[27] Although Guillermo Araya disagrees, pointing out that the social classes in *Martín Rivas* maintain a rigid and archaic parallel structure that makes no room for lasting points of contact, he further observes that this impasse doesn't trouble the novel. Politics is an afterthought, a filler for heroes who become engaged in history because they cannot become engaged to their girls; that is, the heroes court politics out of escapism rather than conviction.[28]

There need be no escapism, however, in the slippage between politics and love, neither here nor in other national romances. A very early example, which Blest might have known, is the Mexican novel *El criollo* (1835) by J. R. Pacheco, in which the local hero cannot marry his beloved because she is Spanish; instead he joins Hidalgo's revolution against the caste system that kept the lovers apart.[29] And another example that Blest could not have known is Paraguay's *Aurora* (1920) by Juan Stefanich, a historical novel about the contemporary revolts in Asunción. After the title heroine disappoints the student hero at love, he dedicates himself to "the new Aurora," the future of Paraguay.[30] When Rafael San Luis replaces one "lover" for another, announcing to Martín that, "My new love . . . is politics" (307; 353), he is not switching codes but rather revealing that love and politics already inhabit each other, as Blest Gana's subtitle had announced.

Clearly, when the love problems get solved so do the political conflicts. And it is perfectly possible that love and politics are not alternatives for the heroes but that they rather intentionally conjure each other up. Certainly the "codes" of love and politics, if we consider them independently, make similar demands of constancy, discretion, and heroism on the protagonists. If one of the "social" customs being criticized here is the elite youths' habit of declaring love to girls of the underclass in order to seduce them,[31] there may well be a simultaneous critique of the elite's "political" abuse of the popular classes. A more virtuous example is Martín's friendship for Edelmira. And his recompense in her decision to marry a peer who is useful to the hero is probably more than a model of chivalric behavior between the sexes. Their mutual respect and willingness to serve each other also shows an ideal relationship between an honest bourgeoisie and its enlightened, reasonably modest subordinates.

It therefore seems to miss the generic point of this national romance to criticize Martín for abandoning the political struggle once he has won Leonor. Winning her (aristocratic class) was precisely what his (middle-class) struggle was about.[32] And while it is true that the popular classes do not enter the marriage and instead sacrifice their illusions as obstacles to a greater happiness, their blessings make marriage possible. In this romance, a genre that often reveals enemies to be potential allies, the assent is generalized even to the Molina sisters' lazy brother Amador, who has been blackmailing Leonor's brother and planning the same for Rafael. Finally, he too recognizes that Martín is worthy of support. Critics are right to point out that Blest Gana evades the more revolutionary potential of 1851, especially since his representation is limited to the urban uprising and cuts short the nationwide repercussions. But his celebration of a newly porous and flexible, if still "oligarchic," democracy is an undeniable if not satisfying "Liberal" gesture.

Social and political considerations are not easily separable in *Martín Rivas*. But we have seen that some readers are seduced into luxuriating in the purely domestic and rather banal affair at the center, because the book's action is circumscribed almost entirely to a cozy private sphere. Besides a general suspicion about the wisdom of divorcing politics from domesticity in Latin America's "historical novels," the particular case of Chile makes the separation especially suspect. Here more than anywhere, drawing rooms and bedrooms can provide the scene for putting political heads together. By the early 1860s Santiago had been the hub of a centralized government for thirty years. What challenges there were to its control hardly shook the government, despite the loss of lives and property. That is, the state had "domesticated" the country by subordinating its regions and interests early on into a modern hierarchical bureaucracy. From another perspective, though, it was also a place where all Chileans were at home, where legal and juridical principles insured private property but also equality before the law, freedom of movement, of contract, trade, press, and assembly.[33] Domestic dramas, therefore, could not but resonate with the class and regional struggles outside.

Other readers do not doubt the political sincerity of *Martín Rivas,* nor even its efficacy. It was, they can observe, dedicated in the 1875 Paris edition to Manuel Antonio Matta, cofounder of the Radical party, which developed from the resistance to the Conservative-Liberal alliance of 1857. Jaime Concha finds this ignominious moment to be the most significant in Chilean history for Blest Gana, as opposed to 1851, or to the Revolution of 1859 on which the novelist is silent.[34] On Concha's reading, Blest Gana is a principled, though generally moderate, Liberal, who treats that opportunist alliance with disdain and hilarity in, for example, an earlier novel that bears the calculated title of *La aritmética en el amor* (1860). Two years later, with *Martín Rivas,* his irony and defeatism seem to have changed "Radically," thanks to the general amnesty and the hope associated with the new party. If this reading is right, the book did more than represent these progressive tendencies; it helped to promote radicalism.[35] But the fact that this possibly promotional text took its historical anecdote from events of more than a decade before suggests that in order to write a constructive romance, moderate Blest Gana could not bring his stories up to the 1857 disgrace. His later novels would keep going backward in time, in search of positive foundational events. (José de Alencar dealt with his reluctant pessimism in the same way, regressing in time through his novels in order to offer a progressive, promising vision of Brazilian history.)[36] But on a different reading, the amnesty itself, along with developments in the new party, may have been the founding moment of Chile's new democracy for this peace-loving writer.

Concha is surely correct to emphasize that beyond the personal obstacles to the lovers in *Martín Rivas,* more general social barriers—and barricades—are assaulted. This is why he concludes that despite the multiple love affairs that make up the book's plot, it is not simply "a love story."[37] Of course it is not. But it *is* a love story just the same, and its historico-political dimension is not simply incidental to the generic form. Even Lastarria wrote romances—notably Manichean and politico-philosophically correct—in his attempts to write a progressive novel.[38] By framing the alliance between bourgeois heroes and the popular classes as a supreme moment of sentimental realignment that was sure to affect its readers, no matter what their political positions, Blest Gana assures for himself the broadest possible sympathy.

In many ways, *Martín Rivas* is paradigmatic for Latin American national romances. For one thing, its often unexpected turns away from binary categories of class and gender seem particularly refreshing, but they are rather typical in the context of romance's generic assault on static paradigms. Blest Gana shares with contemporary national novelists a penchant for disturbing or violating the ideally gendered types that might be associated with heroic narrative. Even physical descriptions cross categories, in Rafael, for example, whose "features [are] so chiseled as to be almost feminine" (41; 42). But the most striking cross is Blest's consistent habit of portraying docile or benighted men alongside active and enlightened women. Except for the two heroes, his male characters range from the ineffectual to the contemptible. Dámaso is indecisive, lazy, and married "more for advantage than for love" (9; 6). Matilde's father Fidel Elías ruins her happiness when he rejects impoverished Rafael. And despite their class differences, Agustín Encina and Amador Molina are equally foppish and unproductive. Even admirable Rafael is censured for sentimental inconstancy. Blest's women, by contrast, are more often than not both principled and daring: Leonor rules her house and plots Martín's escape from prison (for contrast we have her silly and submissive mother); Edelmira insures Martín's happiness and accepts her loyal policeman; Adelaida is right to hate richboy seducers; her mother, Bernarda Molina is grotesquely portrayed, but she will not be bought off after her daughter's disgrace, unlike Amador (and the Liberals of 1857?). "Even a poor girl has her honour" (255; 290); Francisca Elías is a feminist who reads George Sand and thereby incurs some sarcastic comments from the narrator. But he gives her distinct moral superiority over her husband who calculates Matilde's affairs instead of feeling them as a woman would.[39] Only Martín himself exhibits all the laudable characteristics, some associated with men (e.g. his financial good sense) and others with women (his unbreachable loyalty and his sensibility). "Thus he wept for a long time"; at Rafael's death, "his eyes were scalded with tears; then came to his remembrance the man, the stoic resignation of his courage." (349; 404). As a result, in the fictional company he keeps, Martín's androgynous virtuosity seems unbelievably ideal.

These flexible or transgressive gender-related attributes are, as I observed, probably common to romance throughout Latin America; but they constitute an unorthodox convention for Blest Gana and his readers. Part of the novel's work is precisely to replace the conventional (oligarchic) habits of command with modern and more flexible (bourgeois) relationships. The romantic heroes in *Martín Rivas* are not surprised by the transgressions, but frivolous Agustín, for example, is shocked by them. "Caramba," he exclaims, "she [Leonor] got all the energy that should belong to me as a male and the eldest!" (345; 399). The coexistence here between transgressive genders and a conventional hierarchy of male over female may therefore make us wonder about what form the marriage between Martín and Leonor will take. Will it be a new kind of "democratic" relationship, one that would approximate a nonhierarchical love based on mutual respect for the other's power and desire? "Where love is concerned, social hierarchies shouldn't matter at all" (221; 249),[40] says Martín in one of their erotico-philosophical discussions. Or, will the romance work only at the expense of this freedom from stereotypes, after a traditional inequality replaces the negotiations between equals. In that case, one (female) partner would cede all authority to the (male) other. These alternatives also bear on how we read the interclass solidarity during the rebellion of 1851. One ending would suggest that unity can be based on a coalition of autonomous popular and bourgeois politics; the other would show that oneness is won only at the expense of one (traditionally subordinate) class that is spoken for by another.

Before we reach the end, though, the strength of character shown by women, especially by Leonor and Edelmira, allows us to entertain the democratic alternative. Yet by the last pages, no question and hardly a trace remain of the possibility for an unconventional relationship-coalition. Edelmira had made her "realistic" choice, and domineering Leonor has become "a treasure of sweetness and submission" (373; 431). Her declaration of love amounts to surrender: "Only you have been able to conquer my will . . . your will is now stronger than mine, . . . your desires will be commands for me" (369; 427).

This romantic resolution resonates politically in two simultaneous directions, because Leonor's place in the allegory is a slippery one, causing something like a double exposure. She is Martín's oligarchic conquest, of course; and this establishes a modern and democratizing new hegemony of the productive bourgeoisie. But she is also a woman who exercises extra ordinary dominion over her own family, just as the traditionally submissive masses were making demands on the bourgeois elite. The narrator puts her (and them) back into place, once middle-class virtue declares its productive love for the naturally submissive partner. "Her vigorous moral organization yielded to the law of passion because she was a woman before being the spoilt child of her parents and of Society" (311; 358). With her new husband, Leonor's strong moral sense, as well as the *medio pelo's* demands, become superfluous. This nervous recuperation of female and popular strength under a middle-class hegemony surely limits the political promise some readers are encouraged to entertain in the novel, and perhaps also in the events of 1851.

Before this "happy" ending, the narrator seemed to complain that the populace lacked independent motivation; they lacked "arms and leaders, without whom nothing can be done in taking the initiative by the masses, who always require to be led by the Caballeros, who—notwithstanding the propaganda of equality—they always look upon as their natural superiors" (332; 383). But this alleged lack of self-determination may well have been Blest's rationalization for imposing bourgeois leadership, just as assuming women's naturally submissive nature justified male dominance. In any case, by the time he wrote *Martín Rivas*, the popular classes had shown him far too much initiative, and Blest Gana knew that his complaint was unjustified. He purposefully cut the history of the rebellion short and left it off in the capital where, in its first stages, it was indeed led by the Liberal bourgeoisie. But the revolt would soon spread to the suburbs and to the countryside; and once it became truly popular it was out of the Liberals' control. To have included that development would have posed yet another alternative to Blest's writing: could he have continued to celebrate the rebellion even though it exceeded the norms of a hierarchical historical romance; or would he have been forced to disapprove of the 1851 uprising because it transgressed legitimate paternalistic leadership? Blest Gana took the elegant way out of the dilemma. He simply decided not to address it, stopping the narrative short before romance burst its own seams, or before it revealed the lover as a boss. Blest Gana's romantic version of the 1851 conflict undoubtedly helps to blur the difference and, thereby, to embroider Chile's alleged historical continuity.

Except for the very special case of Brazil, to which the Portuguese monarchs transferred their court in 1808 and which became an independent monarchy in 1822, Mexico is the only Latin American country where monarchism didn't die a natural death from loss of prospects or loss of interest by the end of the wars of Independence. Instead, the republican and egalitarian ground swell led by Father Hidalgo and José María Morelos lost to a more conservative approach. After a decade of social and racial wars, Independence came to Mexico in 1821 with the revolt of a royalist brigadier, Agustín Iturbide, who by the next year had himself proclaimed emperor. Those who resisted him were not only republicans (prominent journalists, lawyers, and progressive clergy) but also traditional monarchists whom the self-declared "emperor" had offended. The offense was mutual, since an established Mexican nobility looked with disdain on upstart Iturbide, the son of a merchant. They yearned for a European prince who would acknowledge the superiority of breeding over brutality and were seconded by the Spanish-born *hacendados* and traders who hoped that a real prince would cancel the loans and other fiscal burdens forced on them.[41] From then on, and throughout the nineteenth century, the conflicts between Liberals and Conservatives were played out in large part at the level of republicans against monarchists. At another level the battles were between supporters of the Indian and mestizo masses and those of the Creole elite.

The conflicts included the 1831 execution by the Conservatives Bustamante and Alamán of Vicente Guerrero, the mestizo hero who had fought under Morelos and then became Mexico's second president. Conservatives hoped to consolidate power by establishing a monarchy, and the project was thwarted only by the war with the United States (1846–1848). Conflicts continued with the secessionist Civil Wars in the Yucatán (1847–1850), precipitated by Mayan Indian rebels, the Revolution of Ayutla (1853–1855) against Santa Anna's pretensions to perpetual dictatorship and in which Juárez became a national figure, the Wars of Reform (a dozen years of Liberal revolution, principally against the church), and the French occupation under the Emperor Maximillian (1864–1867), followed by the restoration of Indian President Benito Juárez's republican government.

It may be predictable from even these spotty allusions to a political history colored by racial antagonisms that Mexico's patriotic ideology in the wake of French rule would exalt indigenous and mestizo virtue against the white imperialists and their local supporters. Among Creole nationalists even before Independence there had been a tradition that celebrated Mexico's racial past, but existing Indians seemed out of place in the national project until the encouragement for assimilation and mestizaje during the nineteenth century. The elegant pomp of monarchy and by extension the white "aristocracy" at home, admired by so many Mexicans, must have seemed treacherously attractive to intellectuals like Ignacio Altamirano, himself an Indian, who were bred on European refinement that disdained brown people.[42] We will see that Altamirano tried to loosen this double-bind (his "white" training and his patriotic-indigenous pride) by, among other things, touching up Europe's favorite literary genre so that it would highlight dark heroes and overexpose fair villains. He may have acquired this kind of "practical" palette rather than more subtle shadings from his experience as a soldier who was obliged, after all, to draw differences. But Altamirano is best remembered for his personal generosity and his conciliatory, constructive cultural politics after the fighting ended.[43] In retrospect, his mood and that of younger writers whom he promoted through periodicals like *El Renacimiento* (1867–1887), and through his teacherly encouragement of everyone including women writers during Juárez's restored government,[44] must have felt like a rehearsal for another "cultural revolution." It was the conciliatory nativism that would follow the decade of social upheavals starting in 1911, upheavals that brought these early novelists back to the attention of a somewhat jaded Mexican intelligentsia.[45]

But the dates show that the Mexican revolutionary performance suffered costly and complicated delays beyond the Reforma rehearsal. After Maximillian had been defeated and executed, Juárez returned in 1867 with the support of a broad patriotic front, including an enthusiastic Porfirio Díaz. But Díaz rebelled later and is now remembered for consolidating a morally empty power ("Nothing of politics, and a lot of administration")[46] with the approval of elite Mexicans who were not quite ready to submit to a principled Liberal and Indian president like Juárez. Díaz was an Indian, too, as well as a military hero, which gave him a relatively wide base of support; but he became increasingly happy to win favors with the privileged and to quell opponents with a policy of *pan o palo* (bread or beatings). In other words, he took advantage of the reluctance among Conservative white Mexicans to suffer humiliation by a president who identified with Indian masses after their French Prince Charming proved a disaster.[47]

Mexico's racial romance had to wait. Whites were not about to embrace victorious Indians, even though the "dictator" Díaz had other, Liberal, supporters, a detail that may by now be easy to forget. Mexico's interregional romance waited too. Centralists could not easily persuade enclaves of Federalists to give up local privileges for the national good. The province of Texas, which had resisted Santa Anna's move toward centralism in 1835, rebelled under the protection of the United States. And Texas's success encouraged the Creoles of Yucatán, including Justo Sierra Senior,[48] to secede as well. They finally declared independence in 1841, although the regular army forced them back into Mexico. After the war with the United States, which cost Mexico a devastating half of its former size, the Yucatán

Creoles were still disaffected from the central government and, during the race war of 1847, they offered their province to Great Britain, the United States, or any other country willing to protect them.[49]

Altamirano survived all these struggles. He fought in the Revolution of Ayutla, the Wars of Reform, and against the French Intervention.[50] He also survived the promising moment of Juárez's return. Altamirano must surely have identified personally with the indigenous president, since both came from equally humble backgrounds and learned Spanish at the rather advanced ages of fourteen and twelve respectively.[51] They worked closely to promote Liberal reforms, despite their noisy differences in Congress over the question of amnesty for Conservatives, once the Liberals gained power in 1861.[52] While moderates like Juárez and Conservatives were advocating amnesty, hardliners like Altamirano spoke forcefully against misplaced generosity. One result of the amnesty was to encourage the Conservative General Márquez to continue his scourge of the State of Mexico, prolonging the civil war after the exhausted country had declared an official peace. Another result was to promote the misfired strategy of recruiting bandits into the regular army in order to fight Márquez and other Conservative generals. And final consequences were Mexico's total bankruptcy and her precarious military control, weaknesses that ushered in the French invaders. Not until Márquez's army reached the very suburbs of Mexico City did Porfirio Díaz's troops finally defeat him, showing Liberal Mexicans the folly of self-defeating sympathy for their enemies.[53] The disciplined and selective sympathy in Altamirano's novels keeps that lesson alive.

Juárez died of a heart attack in 1872, after twice defeating Díaz in presidential elections. The future dictator now won by default and, in retrospect, Mexico's national romance seems to have suffered a long postponement. But at the time, Altamirano and other *puros,* or radical Liberals, were hardly discouraged. In fact, they preferred Díaz, although some biographers purposefully overlook Altamirano's early sympathies, fearing to taint him with later developments.[54] At first, Díaz's decisiveness and the unparalleled prosperity of his early years seemed to be proof that Mexico was now a sovereign, modern, and promising nation. So Altamirano continued to work as the government's representative, although he preferred to do so from a comfortable distance in Europe, once his honeymoon with Díaz's "positivist" regime ended.[55] Increasingly, he dedicated himself to teaching and encouraging young writers in order to promote a national culture beyond factional differences. The national romance, in other words, may have seemed imminent to Altamirano, in need only of some galvanizing articulation that would underscore what Juárez's presidency had meant—autochthonous democracy—and that would enflame the country's desire to embrace a now corrected and strengthened ideal of a Liberal indigenous republic. *El Zarco (Episodes of Mexican Life in 1861–63)*, finished in 1888 and published posthumously in 1901, is Altamirano's most highly respected novel and probably his best effort to project that realizable desire. If the effort came late in Mexico, it is probably because, despite Altamirano's optimism, national consolidation kept getting postponed.[56]

The historical event that prepares the romantic complications in this novel is the hasty marriage-of-convenience between Liberals and local bandits in order to resist General Márquez's rampage in 1861. Juárez had just assumed the presidency and had granted general amnesty to the enemies of the Liberal party. Later, the regular army tried to discipline the monster-outlaws it had promoted, not least of all because they were sabotaging the federal project to build a railway between Veracruz and Mexico City, the emblem of liberal progress and also the subject of Manuel Payno's popular novel, *Los bandidos del Río Frío* (1888).[57] But the bandits kept escaping, both because their capture did not lead to prosecution and because the government now had a more urgent, international, front. "Everything was different now. The federal government found that it was too involved in the war against the hosts of Márquez, Zuloaga, Mejía and the other pro-Church leaders . . . ; the foreign intervention was a threat that was beginning to translate itself into deeds" (55).[58]

This general information and some specific data about the war against banditry became the backdrop of the sentimental plot. On the first page, that plot is located in the town of Yautepec, Morelos. At the time, however, Morelos was still part of the central state, known synecdochally as Mexico.[59] "Up close, Yautepec presents an uncommon and picturesque sight. It is a half-European, half-American town" (3). That impression comes from its variety of vegetation that combines orange and lemon trees growing alongside tropical banana and mamey plants, although the European oranges and lemons dominate by their numbers. In case this allegory doesn't bear immediate fruit, Altamirano explains it in specifically racial terms on the next page, after he tells us that the town rose from being administratively dependent on Cuernavaca to heading up the district. Yautepec is entirely Spanish speaking, "it is inhabited by people of mixed race. Pure Indians have disappeared there completely" (4).

It is probably redundant to observe that the town is a central(izing) haven where regional and racial conflicts have been resolved by establishing European norms embellished by local flora and people. This utopian beginning suggests that Altamirano has let the projected effect of his novel slip metaleptically before the cause, representing reconciliation before we read about the conflict. Perhaps he does this to condition our desire and channel it in a productive direction, since sentimental choices will have to be made in what follows. In any case, after reading that pure races had disappeared, it is a bit surprising to find that the hero of the piece is an Indian named Nicolás and that he is in love with a haughty white beauty named Manuela. The right girl for him is Pilar, a humble mestiza who is capable of forgiveness and determined to save/get her man. The predictable happy ending for Nicolás and Pilar, nevertheless, has some interesting twists that indicate how elusive, and how fragile, a prize national solidarity would be.

For one thing, the hero is indifferent to the heroine's love for too long, and he courts the wrong woman until his dignity should have felt the affront. (Is he the Mexican masses who continued to defer to ecclesiastical and economic elites?) All this time, he was encouraged by Manuela's mother who wants him as a son-in-law. This reverses the generational tension of novels such as *Soledad, Martín Rivas, Enriquillo, Cumandá,* and *Sab,* among others, where young people are heroic to the extent that they overcome their elders' binary thinking and strive for a loving synthesis. In this belated novel there is evidence of political backsliding, as the white mother (liberal intellectuals?) encourages her daughter to marry the Indian. "I have taught you to love decency, not good looks or money" (10). But the white girl despises the "horrible Indian" who evidently repells her (9). Like "a disguised aristocrat . . . Martha or Nancy who would escape from court to have a rendezvous with her lover" (6), she prefers to run away with the title character, a blue-eyed blond who is leader of a gang of silver-clad bandits known as *plateados*. (Is Manuela symbolic of the monarchist Creoles who pine after a European prince when they have an Indian prince for president?) Later, too late, after her curiosity about adventure has turned to disgust and her virgin body has become common spoil, she repents having scorned the industrious and affectionate home-boy. Like Enrique Otway, the antihero of *Sab*, el Zarco's color announces him as dangerously attractive, a foreign (U.S. or French?), colorless body that threatens Mexico's warm tones. "He was young, and not at all bad-looking. His pale skin, the color of his light blue eyes which the common people call 'zarco,' his blond hair, and his wiry body" made him dangerously attractive (25).

The blame for the country's "prostitution" to foreign exploiters seems to fall wholly on Manuela/monarchist Mexico whose self-defeating opportunism mistakes dazzle for elegance. But in fact, Nicolás is subject to the same kind of criticism. He desired her for the same superficial reasons that made her desire the bandit; and he ignored the correct object of desire, just as Manuela ignored him. Paradoxically, it is thanks to her injustice, first to the Indian and then to her heartbroken, dying mother, that Nicolás finally discovers his error and Pilar's love. (Is their love Mexico's united front against the French?) Pilar had always adored him and now she (Mexico's new mestizo ideal?) saves him both from sentimental despair and from the corrupt regular army that would rather kill him than risk its own safety by following his lead against the bandits. The redeemed Nicolás then admits that what he had felt for Manuela was "a whim in which my pride was at play, but not my happiness" (51).

Although this novel celebrates heroism in the "real men," meaning Nicolás and the mulatto Martín Chagollán (a hero against banditry in Mexican history)[60] who successfully argues with President Juárez that the captured bandits deserve no pardon, *El Zarco* very much belongs to the domesticizing norm of foundational novels. The two patriotic heroes fight only in order to live at home, whereas the villains live to fight in an obscene and parodic afterlife of legitimate mobilizations against the Conservatives. Nicolás, fearless before the bandits, is a characteristic combination of heroism and sentimentality. "Altogether, he loved tenderly, submissively, but with honor, passionately perhaps, but with dignity" (49). Altamirano apparently finds the balance hard to manage in this quote, hastening to add masculinizing and elite qualifiers after each feminine trait. It is a gesture he will repeat several pages later: "Nicolás leaned over that death bed, and there, the man of iron, who would not be subdued by misfortunes or dangers, began to cry bitterly" (53). A less obvious combination, perhaps, is Pilar's gender-crossed identity; her intrepid valor combines with an ideally sweet and submissive nature. It is she who organizes the popular resistance to the army that has imprisoned her man, mobilizing political and then paramilitary support. Like Leonor of *Martín Rivas* and perhaps in the tradition of Scott's Rebecca or even Chateaubriand's Atala, Pilar is an ideal romantic heroine *because* she is resourceful and fearless.

But Manuela and el Zarco are equally gender-crossed in a parody of romantic lovers: she because her love of adventure conquers her feminine delicacy, and he because cowardice plagues his machismo. This uncomfortable doubling of heroes and antiheroes underlines another contextual doubling. It is the bandits' parody of militarism that comes embarrassingly close to and contaminates the real thing, just as Nicolás's original love was contaminated by the racist and unproductive longings of Mexican society. Bandits are related to soldiers not only analogically, because both used the same tactics (56), but also by metonymy, since the legitimate army had recruited criminal gangs when monarchists seemed to be the worse threat. Now, in 1863 (and perhaps also at the end of the 1880s while Altamirano was writing under the increasingly authoritarian Díaz regime) internal freedom was urgent. The solution was to recognize the enemy, as well as the ways in which enemies deformed decent citizens by association, and then to eliminate the evil by eliminating the bandits, not by risking their reform.

Altamirano's militancy, in this otherwise conciliatory novel, is probably carried over from his legislative resistance to amnesty for the Conservative "bandits" who would do anything to regain power, including selling their country to the French.[61] It seems important for Altamirano to make his point unequivocally, not stopping to be distracted by contextual subtleties. He never hints, for example, that Maximillian would horrify his Conservative supporters by courting the opposition and passing Liberal legislation, nor that the popular legend of El Zarco identified him as Salomé Placencia, a valiant and admirable Robin-Hood-like character, nor even that the most brilliant hero against Márquez was Porfirio Díaz, who would ultimately replace Juárez's democratic ideals with inglorious maneuvering.[62] Altamirano was evidently more concerned with writing an uncomplicated, programmatic, national allegory (the kind that embarrassed later Mexican novelists including Azuela) than with offering narrative richness or even respecting historical data.[63]

Perhaps more revealing of the man than the novel's traces of his legislative campaign against Juárez's miscalculated benevolence are the suggestions of personal experiences and fantasies that spill over into the romantic plot. Altamirano evidently craves the poetic justice of Manuela coming to desire the lover she once despised and who had become indifferent to her. This wish-fulfillment of a spiritually superior but physically unattractive Indian lover who finally wins over the white object of his desire is repeated obsessively throughout Altamirano's novels, pointing perhaps to a deeply personal yearning.[64] But the individual fantasy of a passion that would cross racial categories is rather hard to distinguish from Altamirano's patriotic longings for a unified and indigenous republic. His own theorizing about the novel made the connection between desire and democracy clear when he offered a recipe for mixing personal erotics with political campaigns. And it would be difficult, if not pointless, to determine which passion was the more authentic in this exemplary nation-builder.

No one has had to guess at Altamirano's intentions in writing the novel. Twenty years earlier and just after Juárez had come back, Altamirano published a manifesto for producing a "National Literature" (1868) in which nation and novel were already engaged in a way that predicts his own fiction. Like Mitre's manifesto of 1847, Blest Gana's academic exhortations, and Martí's later incitations to literary nation-building, Altamirano's essay celebrates his country's opportunities for writing excellent historical novels:

> ¿Pues acaso Fenimore Cooper tuvo más ricos elementos para crear la novela americana y rivalizar con Walter Scott en originalidad y en fuerza de imaginación? . . . Nuestras guerras de independencia son fecundas en grandes hechos y terribles dramas. Nuestras guerras civiles son ricas de episodios . . . no han sido todavía recogidas por la historia ni por la leyenda . . . ¿Y el último Imperio? ¿Pues se quiere además de las guerras de nuestra independencia un asunto mejor para la epopeya? ¡El vástago de una familia de Césares, apoyado por los primeros ejércitos del mundo, esclavizando a este pueblo! ¡Este pueblo mísero y despreciado, levantándose poderoso y enérgico, sin auxilio . . . !

> [Did Fenimore Cooper perhaps have richer material from which to create the American novel and to rival Walter Scott in originality and power of imagination? Our wars of independence are full of great deeds and terrible dramas. Our civil wars are rich in glorious episodes . . . that still have not been recorded in either history or legends. And the last Empire? Could anyone wish for a better theme for an epic? The scion of a family of Caesars defended by the greatest armies of the world enslaving our people! Our poor and disdained people, raising themselves mightily without aid . . . !] (12)[65]

Like the other apologists for novels, Altamirano underlines the urgency to write them. The task, for him, was not only to fill a historical gap, but also to replace foreign, pernicious versions of Mexican history with authentic and constructive ones (10–11). Some of the more popular versions, nevertheless, were

Spanish romantic novels that probably challenged Altamirano's national pride more than his writerly program.[66] After the last war, Mexico's fascination with Europe was reversed. It was now Europe, so avid for Mexico's wealth and so stunned by her moral and military valor, that wanted to know about "her history, political organization, her intimate life" and therefore devoured everything written about the country. If Mexicans leave that writing to exoticizing and impressionistic foreigners, Altamirano warns, "We run the risk of confirming their image of us" (15).

The most promising medium for writing that cultural self-defense and also for raising consciousness at home was the novel. First, as Altamirano observed along with Blest Gana, because it was the most popular genre and was becoming more popular all the time. And second, because it lent itself to the patriotic work he assigned to literature. Intellectuals (Voltaire and Rousseau among them) had already made good use of the novel, filtering though it doctrines and ideas that otherwise never would have reached the masses (17). His formula starts with rejecting popular French models, "whose form is inadaptable to our customs and mode of behavior," in order to follow the lead of South America's best novelists, most notably José Mármol to whom he would later add Jorge Isaacs (33).[67] It is not that Altamirano was blind to their European borrowings, but rather that he recognized their creation of something beyond "servile imitation." Given Mexico's recent history of glorious struggle against a European empire, literature's "patriotic mission today" could hardly be served by slavishly copying the enemy's model (13–14).

In considering the type of novel that would most likely become Mexico's "new Bible" or her "daring revolutionary program" (Altamirano evidently wanted to cover a range of readerly bases), he first distinguishes among the available subgenres. Historical novels, rooted in the classic epics come first in importance for the engaged modern writer, although one wonders why "costumbrismo" or the novel of manners that Blest Gana would favor isn't preferred, since Altamirano was one of its masters. But for his grand purposes, he is taking risks with literary legitimacy even with historical fiction; it was just barely defensible for moral and political appeals, if Clementina Díaz de Ovando is right to say that a contemporary "historicist" prejudice led readers to resist any mixing of fact with imagination.[68] Altamirano's justification for what was already popular in Mexico was to insist that there was an authentic historical truth in local traditions and myths (recalling Andrés Bello's preference for personal over "scientific" narrative). It would be positively unpatriotic to disregard them in favor of a European vogue.

Love stories come last in Altamirano's review, derived as they are from the bawdy works of Apuleius and Petronius, even though an occasional Greek romance is more chaste. Romances, Altamirano writes disapprovingly, generally incite young readers to the least productive fantasies and curiosity. "*Werther* . . . misled many souls; and more than one pure heart has owed its misfortune to a novel by George Sand" (38). But his lengthy moralizing begins to sound like a polite or strategic acknowledgment of outdated concerns among conservative readers, when the argument takes, perhaps, an unexpected turn. It becomes the only theoretical articulation in Latin America known to me which formally and programmatically marries eros to politics. If one of the dangers of romantic novels is an unconstrained imagination, Altamirano reasons, why not take advantage of this rampant liberty to combine enchantment with morality? Affairs of the heart need not be corrupt to be consuming. "In love stories, the Imagination is free to do what it wants; and since it can do anything, why not join captivation to morality?" (38). Scott's novels are some examples of the combination, and Cooper's are others (32). But Mexican fiction had already put romance and nationalism together. The "historical novels" that J. Lloyd Read treats in his 1939 book are (except for Lizardi's picaresque *Periquillo* and Manuel Payno's episodic *El fistol del diablo* [1845]) almost always stories about lovers who confront social obstacles such as the Inquisition, colonial constraints on criollos, and lascivious priests.[69] In *El Zarco*, Altamirano takes his own synthetic, conciliatory advice and joins a tradition of marriages between politics and passion.[70]

Neither *El Zarco* nor Altamirano's other novels invented a new form;[71] instead, like Brockden Brown, Hawthorne, Melville, and other great romancers of New England, he treated a given genre self-consciously and programmatically.[72] It is Altamirano, rather than his predecessors or his perhaps more talented contemporary Manuel Payno, who became a patriotic institution in Mexican literature. Payno's still popular *Los bandidos del Río Frío* is more complicated and less zealously critical than is Altamirano's *El Zarco*; and his judicious ambivalence makes Payno both appealing and subversive, so that Altamirano's didactic clarity is far safer as a literary institution.[73] It is he who is remembered by his countrymen with affection and respect as *maestro* Altamirano.[74]

8

STARTING FROM SCRATCH: LATE BEGINNINGS AND EARLY (T)RACES IN *ENRIQUILLO, CUMANDÁ,* AND *TABARÉ*

Enriquillo (1882) begins with an abrupt ending, a full stop in the shape of a bloody smudge on the first page of American history. "The conquest, leaving a horrible erasure [*borrón*] as a period at the end of Jaragua's poetic existence, surrounded that name with a kind of sinister aura the color of blood and fire" (Galván, 7; 3).[1] Queen Anacaona's earthly paradise ends when our history as Americans begins, in this version by Manuel de Jesús Galván (1834–1910). Otherwise there would perhaps be no room to write it. Conquest here is quite literally a scratching-out, a necessary violence that clears enough space to reinitiate writing. By the time Galván wrote, he knew that the space of Dominican history had been densely overwritten, by those who continued to exterminate Indians, by inquisitorial orthodoxy, and by "devastation" and depopulation, black slavery, territorial losses to France, fear of Haiti, racial warfare, reannexation to Spain, and tenuous independence. Cunningly, Galván stops the vertigo with a new start, with the irresistible seductiveness of first beginnings for a country that struggled longer than most to establish some national identity. Galván pushes that identity so far back, back to the earliest voyages of Columbus and to the first European settlements in the New World, that only one initial and horrible erasure seems to mar it. But starting from the "beginning," of course, supposed a whole series of opportune erasures that lightened the (t)races of intervening history.

Cunning too is the delicacy of this initial record of violence, a delicacy that refuses to say what Galván begins to act out and will continue to demonstrate for many long pages. After the proverbial *borrón* comes the *cuenta nueva* (new reckoning), Galván's calculated account of a providential history. As paradoxically Christian as the fortunate fall itself, the terrible emptiness left by Jaragua is also the ethically charged room to recount losses and gains. Galván's prosaic, linear writing is a kind of *midrash* on the earliest chronicles of Bartolomé de Las Casas and Gonzalo Fernández de Oviedo. It is as fanciful and purposeful as the midrashic supplements to the Bible by belated rabbis or church fathers, and as inimical to the poetic, circular orality that was so seductively innocent and so pagan.

> El nombre de Jaragua brilla en las primeras páginas de la historia de América con el mismo prestigio que en las edades antiguas y en las narraciones mitológicas tuvieron la inocente Arcadia, la dorada Hesperia, el bellísimo valle de Tempé, y algunas otras comarcas privilegiadas del globo, dotadas por la naturaleza con todos los encantos que pueden seducir la imaginación y poblarla de quimeras deslumbradoras.

> [The Indian kingdom of Jaragua, in the island of Hispaniola, shines out from the early annals of the New World with much the same glamour as illumined Arcady, the island of the Hesperides, or the lovely valley of Tempe, in the legends of the Old; these were favoured places, endowed by Nature with delights to seduce the crassest imagination.] (Galván, 7; 3)

If there was a contest at all between the lethargic haven of pagan poetry and the dynamic heaven of redemptive prose—instead of a merely constitutive fiction of (feminine) barbarousness that Christians should exorcise—the contest is won along with the telling.[2] The very act of telling violently displaces the past as it writes it. The alternative, as round and inclusive as the Indians' ritual Areíto dances, perishes along with the timeless American "Arcadia" when the circle of song is forced into a straight line with a beginning and an end. Galván's classical epithets for Jaragua reduce it to that beginning, a mythical and unredeemable past already blurred by the blood and flames that baptized the land and renamed it. The first violation recorded in the novel, and repeated like a leitmotif, is a masculine pen that scratches out the virgin prehistory of America. And Galván's reflection on writing—occasioned by the reddish glare around Jaragua—makes him acknowledge the inevitability of violation for a productive history. Jaragua is a past glory, a matter of pity, but also an absence that relieves European writer's block. If Galván seems as guilt-ridden as his favorite model, Bartolomé de Las Casas, he is as celebratory too, because of the way providence is apparently writing through him.

"Enriquillo" was Las Casas's invention before he was Galván's. The novelist could candidly point to the model in frequent footnotes, as if he were modestly developing the pious work, when in fact Galván was learning more than models from Las Casas. He was learning a strategy for producing simple truth by subtracting complications. The holy chronicler showed Galván how to subtract in the case of Enriquillo, as we will see; and Galván made the same calculation with Las Casas, now simplified into a sentimental saint who no longer has an adventurer's past nor a record of advocating black slavery as a solution to the genocidal labor exacted from frail Indians, and whose general "lobbying" for Indian rights seems more personal than emblematic of the political rifts that shaped the colony.[3]

Galván's Enriquillo, born Guarocuya, is the direct heir of Queen Anacaona and the legitimate chief of surviving Indians. Christened Enrique by the Franciscans who raised him, guided by Padre Las Casas, and pampered by the vice-regal court of Diego Colón, he was known to all by the affectionate (or condescending) diminutive, Enriquillo. After Jaragua is wiped out, Enriquillo joins Anacaona's daughter Higuemota (also called Doña Ana since her marriage to don Hernando de Guevara) and her child Mencía. Orphaned and widowed, the princess soon dies, begging cousin Enriquillo on her deathbed to eventually marry Mencía so they may console each other for so many losses.

The rest of the romance is about the efforts to reunite the royal American family, a family with significantly mixed loyalties because of Mencía's Spanish father and Enriquillo's Padre Las Casas. A cross between guardian angel and matchmaker, Las Casas presides over the story of conquest and foundation that Galván turns into a story about love. Lovers and their allies personify the good, while interlopers are evil, like arch-villain Pedro de Mojica, Galván's only pure fiction on whom blame can fall without compromising the historical Spaniards. The years of waiting for marriageable age, the interference from Mojica, the support from Diego Colón, concessions granted through Las Casas, are all predictable in this plot to redeem indigenous society by joining Enriquillo with his legitimate bride.

Despite Las Casas's efforts, Enriquillo was allotted like any other Indian to a Spanish master. And having grown up with enlightened Catholic ideals, Enriquillo was concerned when the master appropriated his personal possessions. The concern escalated to outrage and rebellion, however, only after villain Mojica incited the master to seduce Mencía. She resisted, but her worried husband complained to a local court, then to a higher court. When the law did not punish Enriquillo outright, it was powerless to help, whereas the lecher had renewed opportunitites for offense. So the Christianized Indian felt forced to defend civilization against the civilized. He and his tribesmen fled to the mountains and established a saner community. It was not the massacre at Jaragua, or the delayed and cold-blooded hanging of Anacaona, or less still the daily humiliation of enslaved kinsmen, but the threat to conjugal virtue that sent the valorous chief and his Indians into the heroic independence that lasted for about fourteen years. Repeated failure of the authorities to subdue the rebels forced Charles V to concede liberty and land to his valiant indigenous vassals.

Before considering what this happy ending scratches out (and why), and as a way of suggesting the links between *Enriquillo* and other belated beginnings in Ecuador's and Uruguay's national fictions, I should admit of course that Galván's novel is hardly unique for starting with an enabling violence. We already saw in *Amalia*, for example, that however lamentable the Mazorca's attack, it gets the writing to flow. If anything is to happen there, Belgrano can no more remain on Calle Belgrano striking stubbornly aristocratic poses than Anacaona can continue to entertain Spaniards with her seductively monotonous ways. Perhaps we should remember too that practically all the books considered here begin with an ink-letting violence: *María* starts with that tender violation of a small boy's lock of hair on the eve of his forced departure for school; *Martín Rivas* comes to the capital only because his father has died, along with the rest of Chile's independent mining bourgeoisie; Mexico's farms and freedom are violated by the *plateados* in the first pages of *El Zarco*; and Martim is greeted by Iracema, against whose tribe he has been fighting, with an arrow shot straight to the face. Writing, of course, always assumes some kind of initiating violence. But my point about *Enriquillo* is that Galván calls attention to his hand gripping the eraser on the overwritten text, killing off the Indian world in a condensation of multiple erasures before he can deliver it to the reader. Nowhere, at least in this canon of national novels, is textual violation so self-reflexively dramatic.

Nowhere, that is, except for the equally late indigenism of *Cumandá* (1879) by Ecuador's Juan León Mera (1832–1894). In an introductory chapter that sets the scene of the novel he subtitled *A Drama Among Savages,* Mera offers a geographic tour that would become his hallmark along with the anothropological detail that came from studying Quichua poetry and lore.[4] Then his story begins with a drastic double-cross. Civilization itself had crossed out its own best work with one pen-stroke on expelling the Jesuits in 1767 and destroying their missions. "A sudden frightening thunderbolt, in the form of a *Pragmatic Decree*, wiped out in one blow the gigantic project which had for so long claimed untold self-denials and such painful sacrifices" (Mera, 49).[5] The unbelievable violence of setting pen to paper makes Mera insist on the image. "The politics of the Spanish Court eliminated, by a mere stroke of the pen, half a million souls in only this part of its colonies. How devastating are the pen-strokes of kings!" (Mera, 49).

In some ways, Mera's work is quite different from Galván's. For one thing, *Cumandá* begins in relatively recent history, the promising year of 1808 when Independence begins; for another, it is not Indians who disappear in the national novel of Ecuador, where Indians notoriously still live, but their Jesuit missionaries. Still another difference is that unlike Galván's straightforward narrative line, Mera's far more tragic reflexivity will bring his own text full circle, reducing his characters to

traces of an already dense and enduring history written by
generations of civilizers in Ecuador.

Progress in that country was erratic. It had been part of Gran
Colombia until 1826, when Ecuador, Colombia, and Venezuela
divided along contested borders. And Ecuador's classic cultural
and ideological standoff between the Conservatives of the interior highlands (*sierra*) and the Liberals of the racially mixed
coast helped to prolong destabilizing and empoverishing civil
wars until the end of the century. Although Mera was from
the highlands, where Indians dominated demographically but
never politically, he began in the provincial city of Ambato as
a Liberal along with his childhood friend Juan Montalvo.
Among his Liberal friends and fans was Miguel Riofrío who
would publish *La emancipada* (1863), an arguably feminist adventure that is now forgotten, probably overshadowed by the
disciple's novel.[6] Mera's background, and his outrage at García Moreno's military takeover in 1861, made him resist the
dictator; but enthusiasm for the man's nerve and for his results soon converted Mera. He virtually gave up writing poetry
for writing polemics, often against Montalvo and other ex-allies.
It was the dictator, not they, who was imposing peace, building roads, granting universal manhood suffrage, and making
primary education obligatory even for Indians, reforms that
generally exceeded Liberal programs.[7] García Moreno was also
handing public education over to the experienced Jesuits, whom
he brought back in 1862. The Liberals had expelled them
in 1851, only a year after Jesuits returned from a century's
exile.[8] Mera was a loyal supporter during García Moreno's term
of 1861–1865, to the point of conspiring in the 1869 revolution
that returned him to power; and Mera was an eloquent mourner
when the Catholic president was assassinated by "pagan" Liberals in 1875. Two years later, after failed attempts to make
matches among divisive Conservatives, and after they unkindly
accused him of treason for trying to reconcile with the Liberals who won that year's election,[9] Mera was making sure that
García Moreno's mark would not fade. He began to write the
work that traces the indelible progress of civilization from
exiled Jesuits, through political martyrs like García Moreno, to
his own novel.[10] Unlike the illegible stain on Galván's first page,

Catholic good works survive in the (intriguingly generative) results of writing. "The blood of martyrdom often stained the silent rivers of those regions. . . . But that blood and those holy relics, blessed by God as testimonies of His truth and His love for man, could not have been sterile. They reproduced in the thousands of souls won for heaven and in the numerous populations gained for civilized life" (Mera, 49).

Among those unforgettable martyrs, Mera and his readers will include Cumandá, the unusually fair and curiously Christian savage in love with Carlos, her white admirer. Cumandá's village along the river (coast) of the tropical forest is at some distance from Carlos's home in the sierra, where his father is a Dominican missionary.[11] Once an abusive landowner who lost his wife and small children in an Indian uprising (based on the historical revolt of 1790), the father repented the evils he had admittedly brought on himself.[12] The courtship between the youths who call one another "brother" and "sister," under enormous palms evidently transplanted from *Paul et Virginie*, is cut short (along with the loyal trees) when her white-hating father and brothers determine to kill Carlos and manage to marry the girl off to an ancient chief. But virtuous and virile Cumandá, who rhymes with Atala in more ways than one, saves soft Carlos from every element, from water, fire, arrows in the air, and poison from the land. She saves him only to lose him again in what reads today like a tragicomedy of errors, as he returns to his father and then sets out to look for her while she arrives at the mission. Cumandá had escaped the hut where her venerable husband died before the wedding night.

In the chase scene that follows her abduction by Indians who demand the ritual death for widows, distracted Carlos joins his father and some Christianized Indians to free Cumandá. But on the way, they meet her dying father, who is none other than the very Indian whom the missionary had abused and offended long ago. When still a youth, Tubón watched the Spaniard torture his parents, and he complained to the same kind of court that never worked for Enriquillo (Mera, 75). More furious than discouraged, Tubón organized the uprising in which the missionary's family died. The now aged Indian's wife admits that she saved one of the children, Julia, and raised her as Cumandá.

What a choice the good Christian father has to make! To run to his own daughter who might yet be rescued, but who would in any case die a Christian, or to stay with the expiring Indian who still despises Christians and try to convert him through love. Evidently the best bet for the church is to stay. And the pagan from the "coast," stunned by the solicitude and sacrifice of the "sierra" man, cannot resist the first and last rites. The sacrifice was Cumandá, the woman over whose dead body Spanish and Indian fathers can love each other. Carlos wept, but he was too weak to pursue her alone or to survive her for very long. Carlos might have gained a sister, but not a wife. The "surprise" identities revealed so late are rather clumsily clear from the beginning, so clear that Carlos must continually defend his spiritual love for Cumandá against his father's base assumption that the two should marry and have children (Mera, 83 and 147). The only surviver is the missionary padre, and the only productivity has been one more soul for a Christian afterlife. Unless, of course, the conversion leaves an inky trace of love and conciliation on Ecuador's national purpose.

The differences between *Enriquillo* and *Cumandá*, between Dominican Galván and Ecuadorian Mera, make their commonality quite striking. They have in common a self-consciousness of the latecomer to historical writing who must first acknowledge erasures; a common conviction that Spanish Catholic humanism, as opposed to imperial convenience, should be the motor of history; and a common taste for classical prose that delighted in the local exoticism of late indigenism, which pleased Spanish as much as American readers.

The very same commonalities coincide uncannily, I think, with Uruguay's Juan Zorrilla de San Martín (1855–1931), author of *Tabaré* (1888). It is a long poem that he alternately subtitled epic and "novel in verse," after Juan Valera used those labels in his letter of praise for the poem. This is some justification for focusing on Zorrilla when a more orthodox identification of national novel might have been a work by Eduardo Acevedo Díaz (1851–1921),[13] but the more compelling reason is the degree to which Uruguayan readers embraced *Tabaré* as a collective prehistory. Valera, Spain's literary arbiter, had also praised Mera in 1886 as the "Fenimore Cooper of the

South."[14] Like Mera, Zorrilla was honored by the Real Academia Española with a special foreign membership; and both men understood their Spanish American identity to be, precisely, a dual allegiance. Ricardo Palma agreed with Valera's characterization of Zorrilla in the same terms that Mera used for himself: "very American, which doesn't stop him from being very Spanish too."[15] Even later to history (along with Uruguay itself) than Galván or Mera, Zorrilla de San Martín managed to extend a "second," rarefied romanticism until the very eve of modernism's triumph.[16] Fervently Hispanophile and militantly Catholic, all three founded Catholic newspapers, which both Mera and Zorrilla dreamt would develop into Catholic political parties.[17] And if the others practiced indigenous exoticism, Zorrilla tried to perfect it. At a time when Spain was in the midst of an Orientalist, Moorish craze,[18] the bard of the Banda Oriental was playing to an international audience. After the book came the opera *Tabaré* set to music by Tomás Bretón, which opened in Madrid and in Buenos Aires during 1913.[19]

To read these three authors together, along with José Enrique Rodó's *Ariel* (1900), is to get an idea of the revival of Catholic humanism and the revalorization of Spain which flattered and inspired several countries by the end of the century. A Catholic opposition was developing during long years of manipulation and interference by other powers, years of unstable secular governments that typically disenfranchised the church only to concentrate wealth elsewhere, years of failing to resist Liberal self-interest or of making a virtue of greed. If the state had to be authoritarian to rule effectively, at least the authority should be incontestable. These writers agreed that recuperating a Catholic humanist past would be the surest and shortest way to a humane and stable future. That is why, among other reasons, Galván revives Las Casas, and why Mera (along with García Moreno) reinscribes the Jesuits in Ecuadorian history after the royal pen had crossed them out. The spiritual revival, so crucial for Catholics in the Dominican Republic and in Ecuador, must have seemed even more urgent in Uruguay, where Catholic children like Juan Zorrilla were sent to Argentina or Chile to study with Jesuits, and where patriotism required nothing less than a leap of faith.

Believing in Uruguay as an independent and sovereign country was almost a tragic joke until 1879, when Zorrilla de San Martín started converting skeptics into believers. That was the year he feverishly wrote *La Leyenda Patria* in a few nights so that he could recite it at the inauguration of the Independence monument in Montevideo. The enthusiastic crowd listened for hours to the epic poem that rehabilitated José Gervasio Artigas into the national hero. Artigas had been America's first hero in 1811, when he gave Spain its first real defeat. But from the time he broke away from the United Provinces of the River Plate in 1814, practically until the 1879 inauguration, most Uruguayans called Artigas a rebel. That's what he was for Argentina, the country that would surely annex—or reunite with—its Banda Oriental.[20] From Artigas's time to Zorrilla's, Uruguay was conquered, shared, fought over, or threatened on both sides by Brazil and Argentina. But Zorrilla, for one, had that "robust faith" that cynics credited to patriots.[21] First in the poem and then in a multivolume history called *Epopeya de Artigas* (1910), commissioned by the government, Zorrilla recuperated the hero as a kind of proto-populist who distributed land to his troops of gauchos, blacks, and Indians, and then preferred to defend the land reform policy over making deals with Argentina.[22]

Argentina, after all, had done nothing to protect its Banda Oriental in 1811, when the Portuguese sent in a "pacifying force." It intervened only to subdue Artigas, after the British got Portuguese troops to leave and the coast was clear in 1814. But within a year Argentines left too, so busy with other fights that they left Artigas in charge. In 1816 the Portuguese returned, supported this time by Uruguayans who didn't like the agrarian reform; and by 1821 the Banda Oriental was incorporated into Brazil as the Cisplatine Province, which joined the independent empire in 1824. A year later the area was claimed by the United Provinces, and the war thus declared with Brazil annoyed Britain so much, both for blocking trade and for raiding its trading vessels for sailors, that it pressed both sides for mediation.[23] In 1828 Uruguay was declared an independent buffer zone, a rather ignominious beginning compared to the Artigas episode.

But freedom resembled nothing so much as anarchy. With no central power, rival caudillos did whatever they could to stay in power, including making alliances with Brazil, Argentina, or even France. Rivalry escalated into the Guerra Grande between *blancos* (mostly from the countryside) and *colorados* (mostly in the capital), which became an international war by 1838. Peace finally came in 1851, but it cost Uruguayans a very unfavorable deal with Brazil. They were, in fact, in danger of losing their independence again, since Brazil was a kind of informal metropolis for Uruguay throughout the decade.[24] During the renewed caudillista conflicts, and the short truce or *fusión* that got production going before overproduction itself caused a new crisis, and during the multiple misreadings of territorial designs that dragged Uruguay into the Triple Alliance against Paraguay, the porous buffer zone kept trying to balance one empire against the other when it was not merely betting on a winner. General Latorre's coup in 1876 brought a tight-fisted nonpartisan order that pleased Zorrilla, but Máximo Santos soon made a costly spectacle of national government, until the opposition (including Zorrilla) forced him into a "ministry of conciliation," a passing parody of Brazil's stability. Not until the 1880s, when both Argentina and Brazil were too busy at home to bother with the interstitial territory, did Uruguay consolidate its national identity.[25]

The strident and heroic *Leyenda Patria* might have been enough to consecrate Zorrilla de San Martín as Uruguay's national poet. But a different kind of originary poem, more melancholy and eroticized, occupied him from 1876, when he wrote the first, theatrical version of *Tabaré*. Zorrilla never produced the play, written while he studied law at the Catholic University in Santiago de Chile. There, one of his professors pointed out the surprisingly light eyes and hair of some Araucano Indians whose ancestors had obviously taken some white women captive. The Artigas story added a heroic beginning to Uruguayan history; but by the time Zorrilla wrote it, the country needed to establish itself by subtraction.[26] It had been reborn, reclaimed, and renamed so many times that any lasting regeneration would have to choose among competing pedigrees. Rebirth would mean purification, or amputation of some of Uruguay's overwritten cultural body. Like Galván, Zorrilla pushed his story back far enough to reduce complications, back before Portuguese, or Brazilian, or Argentine claims could blur Uruguayan identity. So much cutting left only the first Spaniards and the practically forgotten Charrúa Indians, the expendable bodies that condense several purifying sacrifices into one missing identity in this not quite nostalgic poem. Although Indians and especially mestizos surely populated Zorrilla's Uruguay, his exclusive focus on the lost Charrúas suggests that all Indians had been exterminated. Only the Catholic bard could revive them for a while, long enough to produce the catharsis that comes with renewed and alleviating loss. Long after Alencar briefly revived literary Indians in a country where Indians were becoming extinct, Zorrilla would exhume the figure from a terrain that he assumed to be Indian-*rein*. *Tabaré* literally begins with an excavation at the forgotten grave site:

> Levantaré la losa de una tumba;
> E, internándome en ella,
> Encenderé en el fondo el pensamiento,
> Que alumbrará la soledad inmensa. (Zorrilla, 1–4)[27]

> [I will lift the slab of a grave;
> and lowering myself into the pit,
> Ignite the recesses of thought,
> To light the immense loneliness.]

The shade he conjures, a mestizo named Tabaré from the Guaraní words that allegedly mean "stranger to community," was born to a Spanish captive of a Charrúa chief. The blue-eyed savage is as much an outsider among the whites as among the Indians. Tortured by his mixed, "impossible," and sick duality, alternately crying like the most sentimental Spaniard and remaining as stoicly mute as any brave, he expects an early end. Tabaré is also love sick, for Blanca, the very image of his dead mother and the little sister of the new commanding Spanish officer. Despite her name, Blanca is a dark-skinned Andalusian with the straight black hair one expects from an Indian, a perfect complement for the racially confused lover. Although her brother mistrusts the mestizo after soldiers find him pining under Blanca's window (in a parody of Peri's vigil), the girl reciprocates his interest; and it pays off when she is stolen by another chief and trembles, arms around knees, before a fate worse than death. Tabaré saves Blanca and delivers her to the brother who, blinded by fury and worry, dashes toward the hapless halfbreed with a murderous lance.

The simple story is not Zorrilla's most admirable achievement, according to some critics; they prefer the exalted simplicity of his American Spanish, inflected by indigenous words and local scenes, and recited from memory by generations of Uruguayan school children.[28] But one wonders if apologizing for the plot may not also have to do with a cultural uneasiness about this frustrated romance. Instead of Alencar's casting of Iberian racial hygienists as the prehistoric and now absent causes of a new mestizo nation, Zorrilla's latter-day indigenism gave that vanishing role to Indians. And his mestizos were hardly a racial improvement but rather a self-destructing, sterile hybrid, rather like sentimental donkeys. Tabaré is half Indian and half "human" (Zorrilla, 1259), as Zorrilla writes in a candidly racist moment that survived four corrected editions. If I am right to read the schizoid figure as the hopelessly divided spirit of Uruguay, so torn between the expansionist designs of Argentina and Brazil that it was practically bicultural, not to say culturally divided, only the "human" Spaniards can survive to weep over him.

Reading *Tabaré* must have been a collective exorcism of internal dualities in Uruguay, a curative bloodletting of Indians (and indigenist Brazilians) in order that lovely but racially equivocal Spanish creatures like Blanca could be safe from the recurring temptation of allying with the enemy. In Brazil, literary *mestiçagem* was an active writing project that promised a coherent and unique national type; but in Zorrilla's defensively Hispanic Uruguay, it is an unwelcome, erasable supplement that could confuse Spain's character to the point of defenselessness. Like Frankenstein's unnatural mix of man and monster, Tabaré wants nothing so much as release from the impossible mix that Zorrilla sends forth: "Breathe and start walking, / Impossible form of the dead race!" (Zorrilla, 183–184).

Zorrilla's pure Indians are less lovable than Tabaré, but they have the decency to be simple and to die cleanly without traces. They are among the noble, and therefore unaccommodating, heroes of past struggles. And like those unmeltable Europeans of Alencar's romances, the anachronistic Indians offer readers the double pleasure of relief at their absence and pride in the unyielding nature that can be claimed as a national heritage. Also, readers love the poet who reforms the senseless cadavers at will. Why not make them the first unwavering and undivided heroes of the nation, and at the same time make himself their immortal(izing) bard? Only a Christian could weep over the decently silent Indians, as if their pagan pain were the fortunate chance to write, the opportunity for a prayer that would redeem them all. "But something you are. The Christian bard / Throws, tear moistened, / a sprig of laurels into your grave . . . / In case you were martyred to our country!" (Zorrilla, 1059–1062). And the redemptive tears that the hero sheds on Friar Esteban's shoulder flow only because Tabaré is the living death of his Indian identity. "Only that blue eye could cry, / for the expiring race!" (Zorrilla, 2443–2446).

Uruguayan identity is classically tragic in this conservative mode of telling it, as tragic and cathartic as Magalhães's epic poem that would have done with Brazilian Indians once and for all. Contending armies of natives and conquerors are equal, if not in strength at least in posture. And neither is more blameworthy than the other, since providence brought them together. It is the same irreproachable providence that established new strongholds for Spanish Christendom, a robust body for decadent Europe's surviving head (Zorrilla, 807–825). Galván's grafting of Spanish identity onto an American body required an equally violent first operation. What else could Galván or Zorrilla have hoped to do with the exhumed literary Indian except to (guiltily) celebrate the liberated space over the grave, or to incite outrage in oppositional readers? And Mera's drama among savages turns out to have dispensed with Indians just as surely; it is hardly about them at all but about whites who write their circular, incestuous, apparently self-defeating but divinely sanctioned histories on a pagan backdrop. How different is this exoticizing indigenism from the "realist" kind Clorinda Matto de Turner practiced in Peru's *Aves sin nido*

(1889). Even if she failed to show Indians in their own society, she was at least experimenting with contemporary "photographs" of overwhelming vice and frustrated virtue among the whites who affected Indians.[29]

This rather stark reading of American exoticism can invite, as I said, either relieved resignation or outraged resistance. But popular readings are seldom so stark that they miss the productive excesses of these chaste books. Mera, it is true, defended Spanish civilization, but he also celebrated American barbarism. Yes, Cumandá is appealing because she is really Spanish; but readers surely remember that much of her appeal for Carlos comes from her being raised by savages. "Your mixture of youthful tenderness and savage pride is so enchanting to me; . . . The refinements of civilization have robbed Spanish women of charms that Nature safeguards only for the innocent daughters of the desert" (Mera, 59). And Tabaré's double-bind makes him more sentimental, more sensitive, and more admirably romantic than any simple Spaniard could be. Culturally complicated Uruguayans can love themselves because they love tortured Tabaré. But of the three self-servingly Americanist fictions considered here, it is *Enriquillo* that continues to give the most consistent service as the popular handbook of national history. Perhaps this is because the author galvanizes America's conflictive history into the pleasing form of requited romance. He makes the type of fit between passion and progress that late and cautiously Catholic Mera and Zorrilla would have associated with earlier Liberal projects.

Galván, for example, practically reduces Las Casas's passionate defense of Indians to his work as their go-between, the supportive agent of amorous laissez-faire, since social progress in this novel is based on love. The "apostle" succeeds for the Indian lovers, but not for the tragic Spaniards María de Cuéllar and Juan de Grijalva whose romance takes up far more space in the book. Our frustrated investment in their affair makes us feel how retrograde "feudal" paternal authority can be when it sacrifices love for economically convenient marriage. The unfeeling authority that allows María's father to deny nature also blinds him to love's role as the motor of history. Galván makes sure we get this point, in a characteristically long-winded aside, mercifully cut short in Robert Graves's version:[30] "I cannot but deplore the exaggeration of the principle of authority and its vain attempts to turn back the hands of the clock by presenting the Crown as an authoritative rallying point against the forces of demagoguery, and thus delaying the triumphant march of civilization and human freedom" (Galván, 78; 86). The domestic tyrant dooms all concerned: María, her boyish beloved, her heroic husband and, not least of all, her disconsolate father. The fainting heroine was married to Diego Velázquez and died six days later. The marriage and death are in the chronicles; the rest is midrash, the moral of which (as in Enriquillo's happier story) is that love can save. It can save lives; it can save the faith (thanks to ecclesiastical go-betweens); and it can save the nation, as when Charles V acknowledged his love for Indian vassals. Diego Colón's only failing was to prefer Velázquez's expedition to conquer Cuba over María de Cuéllar's romance (Galván, 148; 175). Galván was not so much evading history here, as Concha Meléndez assumes,[31] as establishing a continuity between domestic harmony and political prudence. This indiscriminately laudable loving contrasts boldly with *Cumandá*, which is excruciatingly selective about what kind of love could last, selective to the point of sacrificing procreativity to purity and of sacrificing Cumandá herself in Mera's care to distinguish between eros and agape. For Zorrilla too, desire leads straight to the grave, where it survives as a disembodied spirit of love, thanks to Christianity's paradoxical passions and to Zorrilla's occasionally irresistible poetry.

> . . . Y amó a aquel hombre
> Como las tumbas aman;
> Como se aman dos fuegos de un sepulcro,
> Al confundirse en una sola llama;
>
> Como, de dos deseos imposibles,
> Se unen las esperanzas;
> Cual se ama, desde el borde del abismo,
> El vértigo que vive en sus entrañas. (Zorrilla, 4163–4170)
>
> [. . . And she loved that man
> As tombs love;
> As fires love each other in a grave,
> When they become a single flame;

When, from two impossible desires,
two hopes unite;
Love at the edge of the abyss,
And vertigo in the heart.]

Galván's religion was far more catholic, more inclusive, and less evidently defensive than Mera's or Zorrilla's. By the 1880s the Dominican Republic was finally about to modernize with the money brought in by phenomenal productions of sugar.[32] It was a time when an encompassing atmosphere of cooperation would truly pay off. Before then, exports to Europe of barely renewable hardwoods and of small-scale tobacco crops kept the country economically and politically precarious. But sugar promised to be a major industry for what seemed an insatiable North American market that had been consuming Cuban sugar. The Ten Years' War (1868–1878) in Cuba had sent a good number of planters to cultivate the climatically ideal neighboring island. Galván knew that if the Dominican Republic could establish a similarly ideal political climate, sugar could really boom there. The challenge was not merely how to avoid the wars with Spain and the slave rebellions that were interfering with Cuban production. It was how to stop similar wars at home. From the conquest through the 1870s, the Dominican Republic had one of the most spectacularly unstable histories in all of Spanish America. And Galván's stabilizing solution, as I mentioned, was to coax his readers into forgetting all the unfavorable messiness of the Dominican past, to start again from scratch.

This meant remembering only the glory of being Europe's first American colony, and forgetting that "Hispaniola" was also the first colony to suffer virtual neglect after the conquerors had all but eradicated the Taino and Arawak people and then gone off to plunder the more opulent mainland. Very early on, the island became a port of call for Spain, not a destination. Forgotten too were the 1605 Devastations, when the authorities set uncontrollable fires to Northern Coast towns to burn away contraband traffic with Protestants who could have revived the colony. The depopulated island was now open to French incursions and the eventual shameful—and therefore unmentionable—establishment of Saint-Dominique in 1672. A generation after that colony evicted France, took on the indigenous name of Haití, and initiated Latin America's independence movement, Dominicans declared their freedom from Spain in 1822. Unspeakable for Galván, the event was greeted by a Haitian occupation that first abolished slavery and then competed with the ex-masters for land tenure. Haiti stayed until 1844, through Galván's childhood, although the peace treaty was signed only in 1874. The delay had to do with a succession of racial rebellions, often incited by Haiti. As Núñez de Cáceres, the first hero of Dominican Independence, knew but Galván silenced, "the majority of the Dominican population was colored and favored annexation to Haiti."[33] Instead of siding with either the merchant Rojo party or the landholding Azul party, both of which tried to enlist Dominican workers in the interelite civil wars after 1844, many Dominicans chose to side with "African" Haiti.

In 1861, a desperate move of class-wide self-protection made Azul President Pedro Santana ask Spain to reannex its oldest colony. He left the negotiations to his secretary, Manuel de Jesús Galván, who preferred not to mention the treason years later. If Dominican whites were to be colonial subjects again, at least they could choose a "civilized" master over the "barbarous" one whose name was taboo. The temptation to beg the mother country for help may not have been unique (it was after all General Flores's only strategy for staying in Ecuador after 1845),[34] but giving in makes the Dominicans a special case. In fact, very few were in favor of turning colonial history backward, and with renewed patriotism far more Dominicans spent the next four years fighting off Spain and the party that invited it back. Their successful War of Restoration (1861–1865) meant that Galván needed another job. He found one in Puerto Rico where he continued to work for the Spanish Crown. In exile, the man whom Dominicans can still despise for having written that patriots were "faithless and senseless traitors . . . Spain's domination is the salutory anchor for all social principles, against the deleterious elements that threaten,"[35] apparently composed himself sufficiently to learn when to keep silent. His new subtlety amounted to learning how to forgive and forget, just as Galván would show his novel's Spanish authorities learning amnesiac subtlety after their frustrations with Enriquillo. Where pursuit of the rebel, and reannexation centuries later, failed to preserve Spain's supremacy, her magnanimous incorporation of non-Spanish subjects was more efficient. In the 1882 dedication of *Enriquillo,* Galván says that his immediate inspiration for the book came in 1873, while watching Spain's governor proclaim the emancipation of Puerto Rican slaves after years of unmanageable rebellions. "Loud and enthusiastic shouts of 'Long live Spain!' crowned that sublime scene."

Perhaps Enriquillo could be the Dominican condensation for that dark crowd, so gratefully loyal to white masters. The inspiration must have taken on a clear narrative shape when Galván remembered that the happy scene of Enriquillo's capitulation to the king was incontestable, one of the few agreements between Las Casas's *History* and that of his nemesis, the royal chronicler Oviedo.[36] "Enriquillo placed the Emperor's letter upon his head as a sign of obeisance, embraced the gallant emissary, and instructed all his caciques to do the same" (Galván, 285–286; 350). Galván's condensation was wonderfully convenient for projecting the kind of conciliatory and culturally coherent nationalism that the Dominican elite needed. First, it reduced disorganized and multiply-threatening black masses to strictly hierarchical leaders with whom deals could be struck, as it were, among gentlemen. Galván's Enriquillo practically passes for a white one. "He dressed gracefully in the best contemporary style which was a modification of Castilian severity by the new Italian fashions. . . . In a word, Enriquillo with his fine regular features, tasteful dress, easy and courteous bearing was at first sight indistinguishable from many scions of rich and noble houses in Hispaniola" (Galván, 168; 203).[37]

But even more convenient than the hierarchy is the surprisingly lighter color of the condensed crowd. By pushing his story so far back that blacks seem not to figure in Dominican origins, by squinting at the Dominican crowd to create an optical illusion of racial simplicity, Galván manages to write a national identity by erasing. Thanks to Galván, "in Santo Domingo there are no blacks. When a dark-skinned man fills out his official identity card, in the space for color he writes, Indian."[38] But the omission is glaring even for the Santo Domingo of 1503–1533.

Guilt-ridden Las Casas (promoter of African slavery) was laconic about the blacks, but Oviedo was candid about their great number, "because of these sugar plantations, which makes this land look like the very copy or image of Ethiopia itself."[39] The unproductive history of those first plantations and the endless rebellions begun by those first blacks (who slip into the novel as murderous Africans and whom Diego Colón punishes to everyone's relief) were hardly promising foundations for the modern sugar industry. Galván chose simply to forget them, offering instead an alternative to the racial hatred and the exclusivity that Oviedo remembered. By shifting the historical emphasis from the mass of black slaves to Enriquillo's remnant of a tribe, he offered a conciliating fiction that such distinguished readers as José Martí and Pedro Henríquez Ureña enthusiastically claimed as a model of American writing.[40] From the time Galván published *Enriquillo,* almost immediately institutionalized as required reading in Dominican schools,[41] Dominicans are Indians or mestizos, descendants of Enriquillo's valiant tribesmen and of the Spaniards to whom they were bound by love and respect, whereas blacks are considered foreigners, Haitians.

Mencía is the model mestiza, the doubly noble daughter of an Indian princess and a Spanish gentleman. Although she stays singly unprocreative in this founding fiction, Dominicans somehow manage to claim her as the nation's mother. They are not exactly wrong, but the filiation is spiritual or literary rather than literal. Like their racial mix, mother Mencía's mestizaje is pure fiction, a genealogical invention that lightens Dominican identity. Among Galván's erasures was Mencía's native color. Las Casas—who Hispanicizes her name to Lucía—leaves her Indian identity alone; but Galván whitens her skin and gives her blond hair (Galván, 81; 90). He probably modeled his heroine after half-European and all-Christian Atala, though meek Mencía is a rather pale copy. Galván perhaps took more than one lead from Chateaubriand, whose books include *The Martyrs,* a reconstruction of French national roots in the period when Druids met Christians.

Galván was good at taking leads, literary leads from Las Casas, Chateaubriand, probably Cooper, and perhaps Alencar, and also political leads from those who happened to be in power. After his artless denial of family ties with Haiti helped to bring Spain back for a disastrous second reign, Galván learned political flexibility along with laconic subtlety. Opportunism seems so unkind a word, especially since he did have some consistent principles. One was to avoid reverting to Haitian "barbarism." And since military resistance hadn't worked, another principle was to promote civilization through prosperity, a stable prosperity grounded in fairness. If Dominican masters had been fair, Indians and blacks would probably not have rebelled or supported Haiti. Oviedo knew long ago that Spaniards were causing their own problems on the island. Certainly no Indian-lover like Las Casas, Oviedo knew just how far a parasite could drain its host before the host took revenge. If Enriquillo had been satisfied in court, Oviedo assured, he would not have cost the Crown fourteen years of expensive military defeat.[42] And Galván knew that the elite's self-defeating abuse of subordinates was a structural problem that could not be entirely eliminated by scapegoating a fictional Mojica. Even the priests sent on a commission to reform the labor laws after Enriquillo's rebellion, even they caught gold fever in the colony. It is an occasion for Galván to moralize, at length again, about how the spirit of gain can degenerate into greed (Galván, 206, 250).

With these principles, Galván returned to the Dominican Republic in 1876, once the government was rid of the Rojos who had competed with Galván's Azules, mostly by insisting that the country be annexed to the United States rather than to Spain. He returned to become minister of foreign relations, a post he resumed in 1887 and 1893 under the black president Ulises "Lilís" Hereaux, whose suspiciously Haitian name and unmistakable color might have distanced a younger Galván. Late in life he also served as president of the Supreme Court (1883–1889) and professor of law in the Instituto Profesional (1896–1902).[43] Galván is sometimes misunderstood as an irrational conservative Hispanophile, opposed both to the imagined continuous threat of Haiti and to the encroachments of the United States.[44] But the checkered political career that enrages some observers shows a man willing to listen to reason. When

Lilís began to win support (meaning loans) abroad, after having bought off or killed off troublemakers at home, he needed someone to negotiate the rental of Samaná Bay to the U.S. armed forces.[45] And no one was more appropriate for the secret mission to Washington than Galván, that ex-Azul who had once drawn up the reannexation treaty with Spain and had called the Rojos traitors for trying to do the same with the United States.

Galván was surely learning flexibility from a tradition of humanitarian colonialism that spanned Las Casas to the Puerto Rican governor, but he had an indigenous teacher too. Enriquillo himself may have been Galván's model as much as his creation. It was Enriquillo, after all, who knew when to fight and when to cooperate, when to escape and when to return. He also knew when to strike the deals that a naive or idealizing observer might condemn as compromising. I said above that Enriquillo's peaceful capitulation was recorded by both Las Casas and Oviedo, but where the imperial agent is expansive, the apostle skimps on embarrassing details.

Las Casas's version of the conquest in general is purposeful to the point of making some readers furious. One was Ramón Menéndez Pidal who lost his accustomed academic patience when he called the self-styled historian a paranoid and pathological liar.[46] Perhaps the exaggerations and the exclusions owe to the forty years that intervened between event and writing; but Las Casas's ardor for the Indians surely intervened too. He could not be as candid as Oviedo, because the Dominican's double objective was to prove the improbable assumptions that Indians were practically naive Christians and that good Spaniards could help them assimilate into the civilized family of Mother Church and Father Capital. The Erasmist recommendations that he brought to the New World included colonizing with industrious Spanish farmers and with priests who would convert Indians into more farmers. The friar's own attempts at peaceful conquest and gentle assimilation failed dismally. But the very fact that the Crown allowed him to experiment, as well as to liberalize Indian laws, shows how persuasive he was at court.[47] To paraphrase Menéndez Pidal, Las Casas was sometimes given to redeeming history with pious lies, as for example in his account of Enriquillo's capitulation. His chief is the most

Christian of knights, pardoning even the life of his former rapist master and submitting gratefully to royal authority.

Centuries later, the story seemed absurd to a Spanish Capuchin historian. Fray Cipriano de Utrera explained why to an assembly of Dominican dignitaries in "Trujillo City" during 1946. He documented Enriquillo's revolt, like that of other Indian bands, as a rash of raids and killings in Spanish towns. The incident of the chief's pardon, however, is not pure invention according to Utrera; it is merely bungled data. Oviedo had recorded a remarkably similar pardon, not by Enriquillo, but by his fierce rival Tamayo. When Utrera asks himself which of the accounts is more plausible, he easily sides with Oviedo, first because Oviedo wrote on site and second because his hostility to Indians kept him from inventing good reports about them. Oviedo's bad reports were questionably passionate, not the good ones.[48] As for the rape or attempted rape as the cause of revolt, Utrera finds it ridiculous; the Indians rebelled after repeated Spanish raids on Indian towns to capture slaves.[49] Just as unbelievable is Enriquillo's peaceful return—with some prodding from Las Casas who takes too much credit—when Emperor Charles V offered him a title, freedom, and land. A skeptical reader like Utrera asks why, after a generation of annihilation by Spaniards and fourteen years of successful resistance, Enriquillo would accept the offer. And why did the Crown make it, if the freed Indians were no longer bound to serve the king?

Oviedo and contemporary documents give Utrera some answers. First, the Spanish army was learning a more effective style of roving combat that endangered Enriquillo's violent livelihood and made an opportune settlement attractive. Like Galván, Enriquillo conceded to unequal forces, preferring to maintain a degree of constructive unity over glorious defeat. Second, the Spaniards were eager to pacify Enriquillo because of the special service he could render, a service that Las Casas erases from his story and that Oviedo celebrates. For the price of their personal freedom, Enriquillo and his Indians were obliged to hunt down and sell back to white masters escaped Indian and black slaves "who had once fought together with his Indians, believing that their fate was thus bound together."[50]

Of course Utrera could have taken issue with any one of Las Casas's improbable stories. The fact that he chose this one shows Galván's hand. It was the novel that made Enriquillo the national hero of the Dominican Republic, the ideological shelter against the imputation of African (that is Haitian) identity in a country of dark people. The reaction to Utrera was immediate and impassioned. Trujillo's ideologues and the mulatto dictator himself (who could massacre 20,000 Haitians on the border just to defend Dominicans' racial purity)[51] depended on the Enriquillo myth as much as did earlier oligarchs. Years later, after most Dominicans repudiated Trujillo, they held on to Enriquillo right or wrong. Utrera's *Polémica de Enriquillo* was published posthumously, in 1973, with an uncomfortably short preface by his disciple Emilio Rodríguez Demorizi. Utrera had addressed himself to Las Casas, as if Galván's novel were unworthy of his meticulous empirical critique. But neither the editor nor other offended Dominicans made any distinction between history and fiction where national identity was at stake.

Galván learned from Las Casas how to erase; and his erasures became indelible for Dominican "Indians." Any attempt to restore the missing details was not only infuriating, Rodríguez Demorizi was sure that the real Enriquillo was literally beside any empirical point. "At the margin of a historical Enriquillo, whatever stature he may have, the legendary Enriquillo, Galván's Enriquillo, will remain undamaged for us. And we will continue to venerate him as the symbol of the beloved aboriginal race, our race."[52]

9

LOVE *OF* COUNTRY: POPULISM'S REVISED ROMANCE IN *LA VORÁGINE* AND *DOÑA BÁRBARA*

—Mulata, le dije: ¿Cuál es tu tierra?
—Esta onde me hayo.
—¿Eres colombiana de nacimiento?
—Yo soy únicamente yanera, del lao de Manare. . . . ¡Pa qué más patria si son tan beyas y dilatáas!
—¿Quién es tu padre? le pregunté a Antonio.
—Mi mama sabrá.
—Hijo, ¡lo importante es que hayas nacío! (49)[1]

["*Mulata*," I asked her, "what region do you come from?"
"The one I'm in now."
"Are you a Colombian by birth?"
"I'm only a plainswoman, from the Manare side. . . . Why any more country, when these pampas are so beautiful and so large?"
"And who's your father?" I asked Antonio.
"My ma must know."
"Son," the old woman said sharply, "the important thing is that you were born."] (65)[2]

In this stunning juxtaposition of apparently nonsequential questions, and of those questions with the repeated refusal to answer, there is an ideological standoff. From either side, the failed conversation from *La vorágine* (1924), by José Eustacio Rivera (1889–1928), shows a gap in a rhetorical cluster adapted from earlier founding fictions for a more proprietary and less conciliatory kind of patriotism. That the question of fatherhood follows directly on that of fatherland is neither a coincidence nor a pun, but a familiar metonymy in a tradition of populist discourse.[3] For that tradition, legitimate fathers are—by extension—consorts of an entire Land, husbands who struggle against foreign or barbarous usurpers to establish proper dominion. She, by contrast, is not an extended figure but a displaced one, the result of a metaphoric move that has substituted mother for an ideal terrain—as extensive as man can cover— for his reproduction. Whereas man's agency swells metonymically to national dimensions, woman's work is canceled by metaphoric evaporation. As the inanimate motherland, woman's very identity depends on him, because the feminine *patria* literally means belonging to the father. He is dependent too; the father needs the female land to bear his name, to give him national dimensions and the status of father. But if metonymy hints at an absence or a loss (because the trope begs for completion by extension), the implied measure of the imagined patriarchal figure is notably grand. And if he is unable entirely to overcome the *patria,* or to replace the illegitimate rival who would father bastards on her body, the husband's striving to conquer her and him remains heroic. Any feelings of insufficiency, in this patriotic scheme, surely come from the father's expecting so much significance for himself.

This rhetorical adaptation of national romance is an understandable response to a series of economic and political disappointments. By 1924 and virtually until the Boom, the conciliatory Liberal embrace of the foundational fictions was generally constrained by defensive, binary, anti-imperialism. One of the most serious disappointments was the Monroe Doctrine. Throughout the nineteenth century, several Latin American countries appealed to the United States to intervene against European aggression, even though they admitted that the doctrine gave them the kind of protection that a cat gives a mouse when other cats are around.[4] There was very little active protection; instead there was a war against Mexico (1846–1848) that took half its national territory without causing too much worry in countries that felt safely distant from the predator. But in 1895, Secretary of State Richard Olney responded to a dispute between Britain and Venezuela by predicting far more intervention than Latin Americans could have wanted from the Doctrine. The United States, he pronounced, "was sovereign on this continent, and its fiat is law upon the subjects to which it confines its interposition."[5] After "Olney's fiat," there was Roosevelt's corollary to Monroe, then the Spanish American War for Cuba and Puerto Rico, followed by a staging of Panama's rebellion against Colombia in 1903, and multiple manipulations in Central America and the Caribbean, all of which added up by the advent of World War I to sixty interventions in fifty years.[6]

Writer-statesmen, including Colombian Rivera and Venezuelan Rómulo Gallegos, responded to this, and to abusive racial and economic privilege at home, with a new wave of socially grounded fiction, often referred to as "novels of the soil."[7] It may be helpful here to add the characterization of populist to many of the writers who made up what Pedro Henríquez Ureña called the "new" politically engaged generation; many in fact had ties to populist parties.[8] In Colombia and Venezuela, as elsewhere, populists usually associated oppressive regimes with an industrial center (increasingly the United States) that first exploited local materials and labor and then flooded whatever local market existed with foreign goods. A national elite, understandably resistant to change, was the beneficiary of what we now call economic and political dependency. But foreign draining of Colombia's rubber sap and Venezuela's personalist dictatorship had squeezed the elite to the point where it rallied behind a militant patriotism that was not content to "let the others rule."[9] While rubber still promised to offset the waning price of coffee in Colombia, and during the Venezuelan oil boom of 1927, through the 1930s and 1940s there and elsewhere, at least some elite sectors had decided that they could do better. Depending on their particular resources, this is a period of land reform and of import substitution industrialization (ISI), while in politics it is a time when charismatic leaders moved the masses with appeals to national glory and sovereignty, appeals that echo the rhetoric of Independence struggles before romantic conciliations.

Whereas nineteenth-century national novelists generally welcomed foreign enterprise to help inscribe civilization on the blank space of America, Rivera's contemporaries had learned the political and social costs of free competition. Along with leaving one's country open for foreign investments and loans, thereby inviting intervention every time an "interest" was threatened or a payment delayed, the spirit of gain was making national governments virtually indifferent to large sectors of the population. This lack of concern may be what Rivera intended to show in the interchange I quoted above, because the mulatta, Sebastiana, returns the government's indifference. Another cost was the freedom of thousands of Colombian workers in the rubber plantations owned mostly by foreigners. The government's silence amounted to practical complicity for critics like Rivera. Political projects in this context logically abandoned the optimistic and open language of classic liberalism, a language now associated with slave-driving bandits: "*Viva* the progressive Señor Barrera! *Viva* our enterprising contractor!" (118; 153); "*Viva* Colonel Funes! Down with taxes! *Viva* free trade!" (230; 286). Instead, the militant and defensive language of populism insisted on establishing clear boundaries around the beloved land and on establishing national economic rights to her, the legitimate husband's conjugal rights.

Now, obviously, old Sebastiana doesn't need either the father of her children or of the land to legitimate herself and her son. She stops the conversation short at two related points, because she refuses to assimilate the centralizing and hierarchical terms that seem so natural for the inquisitive white man from Bogotá. Sure that his paternalist questions are purposeless, she dismisses in advance the patriotic points of his future writing. But Arturo Cova is quite as sure that she *should* answer his interrogation and submit to its legitimating power. The white man doesn't pursue his line of questioning, though. Instead, he lets the woman brush him off. And one doubts if Cova really expected so much significance from himself. Rivera seems intent on revealing the pretense and the posturing of Cova's quest for an illusory manhood and an equally illusory patria. Perhaps the greatest virtue of *La vorágine* for a post-Boom reader is that it allows the contradictions, or aporias, in the above dialogue to exist without forcing them into some totalizing, omniscient discourse about personal identity and national mission. Rivera lets the woman have a convincingly skeptical word, whereas other

Latin American novelists of the period were insisting more on correct, programmatic, answers.

Cova, the aimless narrator-"hero" of this fractured romance, is more lady-killer than lover, more violent than valiant, an adventure-addict who needs new thrills to keep writing his decadent poetry. He has therefore fled to the plains with Alicia, a recent conquest who refused to stay and marry her parents' choice of husband. At the time he tries to talk with Sebastiana, Cova is enjoying the hospitality of rancher Fidel Franco and of his companion, "la niña" Griselda. Franco has already tired of her, and the way is clear for Cova to enjoy Griselda too, along with pregnant Alicia. But the women leave him for Barrera, a dashing dealer in slaves bound for the Amazonian rubber plantations. In retaliation, Cova goads Franco with puerile jealousy to follow the fugitives southward, not so much to win back the women as to conquer the man. The farther they get from civilized Bogotá and from the quintessentially Colombian *llanos* ("We too want to return to our plains; we too have mothers" [222; 277]), the deeper they get into the rubber jungle where the borders with Brazil and Venezuela and Peru blur under the oozing rubber trees. There Cova finds raw material for new writing: rubber magnates greedy for money and sex, like Turkish Zoraida Ayram; their desperate enslaved workers; the menacing forest itself; and also the guide who can free them all from the morass because he can tell one country from another. He is Clemente Silva, and his very name is a softened, domesticated, and lyricized version of the *selva* or jungle. The pathfinder is also the model father and patriot who risks everything to repatriate the bones of a son who died for Zoraida, the killer-lady of unchartered forests.

All this gives Cova two projects. One is to document the horrors in a set of denunciatory documents spurred by new patriotic purpose—like the papers Mármol included in *Amalia* but that we see here only in the fragments that frame the text. The other writing project seems purposeless, a progressively delirious symptom of the sick and sickening jungle to which this esthete of decay submits in order to produce a few striking pages.[10] Those contradictory pages, where the poseur continu-

ally catches himself striking ridiculous poses in a theater that
won't resonate with his words, are the pages that (de)compose
this narrative.[11] But in this infamously untidy text, the act of
delaying or displacing the documentation, continually referring
to its contents, is itself a way of documenting allegedly extra-
textual inscriptions. Rivera insisted on that civic function of the
novel when, for example, he published a spirited reply to an
unresponsive reader, the same reader who, as consul in Manaos
(Brazil's rubber boomtown), failed to respond to Rivera's denunciations.[12] "How could you have missed the patriotic and
humanitarian purpose that drives this novel? And why didn't
you join your voice to mine in defense of so many people enslaved in their own country? . . . God knows that as I wrote my
book I had no other motive than to save the unhappy souls
whose jail is the jungle."[13]

Rivera's sincerity is never at issue for another reader, Eduardo
Neale-Silva, who traces the novel's documentary and autobiographical accuracy from the firsthand reports of the llano to
the informed analysis of the jungle.[14] Anyone who doubts that
Rivera continually spills over into Cova might keep in mind that
the portrait of Cova, published in the first edition, was Rivera's
own photo,[15] showing a carefully coiffed, meticulously mous-
tached and starched dandy. The mechanical resemblance has
mislead readers into celebrating Cova the man, seeing only an
optical illusion of coherence that misses the fragmented, self-
inculpating voice of the narrator.[16] His love-hate sort of narcissism makes him imagine, for example, that "had it not been for
me" (133; 169) Franco might not have been lured in the mire
of jealousy and revenge. Guiltily, he arrogates to himself the
power to set examples. But the celebrant readers don't see the
twist of ethical judgment into arrogance; they prefer to follow
the single-minded pathfinder Silva, who advises us not to look
at the trees, because they make signs, nor to listen to the mur-
murs, because they say things, and above all not to make any
noise, because the trees mock our voices (193; 243).[17]

Rivera's own odyssey began in 1922 when as a young lawyer,
statesman, and poet he was appointed secretary to Swiss en-
gineers and local representatives in a commission to settle a
boundary dispute between Colombia and Venezuela by map-

ping the rubber-rich Amazon area. The multiple contests over that area, including Brazil and Peru, may have been a competition over an economically dead body, because rubber production had declined significantly by World War I, when the Germans developed a synthetic substitute and British transplants of Brazilian rubber had matured in Ceylon, Malaysia, and India.[18] The vague fiscal rationality of the mapping venture was probably unequal to the patriotic intention, and certainly unequal to the obstacles. Amazonia's rivers, swamps, and forests so resisted the possessive contours that patriots adore, that Rivera's entire physically and emotionally exhausted team resigned before the job was finished.[19] The jungle was a tropical analogue to Sarmiento's hermetic desert, an unredeemed feminine space that infuriated men with its flirtatious proliferation of identities, a gushing, overwhelming womb that refused patronymic interventions. Besides his firsthand experience of the jungle, Rivera's novel includes some historically verifiable characters, notably the bandits he denounces. Barrera really existed, as did the Peruvian Julio César Arana—whose imperial name matched the "civilizing" domination that flattered his compatriots and outraged the Colombians.[20] Historical sources also corroborate the courageous denunciations of Benjamín Saldaña Roca, another Peruvian. But the model Colombian patriot and father is Rivera's sentimental invention.[21] Clemente Silva is a necessary imagining, much like the redemptive fiction of imagined communities. This dream of a man, the pathfinder, also finds and names Cova's lost party: "'You are Colombians!' he exclaimed. 'You are Colombians!' . . . He embraced us as if we were lost sons of his" (141; 179). And his metonymic greeting of word and gesture will make Silva the populist measure of fathers for a fatherland. (Old Sebastiana could never have measured up, of course, and she would probably not have been im-pressed by him.)

Rhetorically, the boundaries that populism erects begin with a pronominal opposition between mine and yours, which suggests an ethical opposition between good and bad. And territorially clear limits were precisely the objective of Rivera's mapping mission. From the time Colombia lost Panama to the United States—a loss that gained a spirit of militant cohesion for the fragmented country—throughout Brazil's, Peru's, and Venezuela's unneighborly incursions into Colombia's rubber-rich Amazonia, plain lines were being drawn between countries and people. Citizens were either patriots or traitors, generous or devouring, heroic or cowardly; and these oppositions were based on the fundamental difference between self and other, husband and usurper, active males and passive females. The space that Rivera pries or simply leaves open in this populist patriarchal discourse allows for intimations that any or all of these oppositions are not eternal but are constructs that have come to seem natural.[22] The earlier mutual relationship between love *and* country is naturalized in populism by collapsing the alliance into love *of* country; it is a significant grammatical slip, from a dialectical connective to a metaphorical genitive. And the possessive assumptions that the slip generates may have seemed evident to Sebastiana, the woman whom Cova addressed generically as *mulatta*. When she refuses to be possessed, his populist and paternalist discourse is unhinged. And it stays indefensibly open throughout Cova's unpromising apprenticeship as an ideal man, but especially through Alicia's resolve to make her own way through the jungle. Going their own ways was a competitive, not an indifferent, move. In a strangely perverse way, it recuperates the "democratizing" tensions of the founding fictions. I mean the tensions either between the lovers or between them and the world, before the romances' final hegemonic resolutions. If we can manage to resist tautological readings of those books, we may notice the hundreds of pages on which Leonor, or Amalia, or Ceci, or Cumandá, and Alicia, too, are equally independent and often more valiant than are their lovers.

Read in this company, Rivera's destabilized rhetoric is uncannily familiar. Like the canonical novels it evokes, *La vorágine* makes no neat figural distinction between metonymic men and metaphorized women. These novels fit as uncomfortably as his into the tidy gender-coding of passive land and active people. Romantic love was an opportunity for alliance, not for metaphoric evaporation. If Amalia is Tucumán, Eduardo is Buenos Aires, and together they are Argentina, just as northern mining falls in love with Santiago's banking in order to renew Chile.

Alencar, for his part, figures Brazil in an indigenous hero and an indigenous heroine alternately. And to mention just one more example, Carlota may carelessly be confused with Cuba but, to be more accurate, she is the legitimate name of Cuba whose "re-creation" depends on Sab's expert gardening. She's not the space he gardens but the beneficiary. In short, found ing fictions of the last century tend to be about daring political deals that would construct a national territory. By contrast, populism is about a rigid fortification of those now feminized constructions.

Rivera doesn't refuse populism's rhetorical and grammatical moves as much as he records the effort of fitting, forcing, and helplessly exceeding their static terms. His is the Archimedean paradox, familiar by now to feminist and poststructuralist scholars, whereby one acknowledges one's place inside the object of criticism.[23] To be outside the organizing populist and patriarchal rhetoric of the symbolic order, the order of the Father and his land, would be to sacrifice communication, adherents, admirers. Rivera's seductions must begin there. And in some ways, *La vorágine* seems to fit the nation-building mold: its journey through jungle in order to wrest Colombianness from indistinguishable frontiers; the romance between the llano, Cova's birthplace, and the city through Alicia; and the obstacles, including parental disapproval (as in *Martín Rivas*) and a lecherous usurper (as in *Amalia, Enriquillo,* or *O Guaraní*). Cova is also capable of a militant populist style that Ernesto Porras Collantes (for whom Alicia equals la Patria and Cova her People) wants to consider authoritative.[24] Revenge on a mercenary, for example, is summed up by the hero like this: "Thus died that foreigner, that invader, who at the borders of my native land scored the jungles, killed the Indians, enslaved my countrymen" (255; 315).

On this reading, Cova resembles populist protagonists by assuming that the enemy is the other, foreign interests, the indomitable Jungle that develops man's most inhuman instincts; "cruelty pricks like a thorn, invades souls; covetousness burns like a fever" (139; 177). Or the Jungle is an aggressive woman like Zoraida—who is ironically but also idolatrously called *la Madona,* "the insatiable she-wolf [who] has burned up my virility with her breath. She wastes me like a [sperm] candle that burns upside down" (234; 290). Her unproductive eroticism is unnatural, immoral, unpatriotic. Because her power competes with that of fathers like Silva, the seductress has to be subordinated, or eliminated along with the bandits, local caudillos, and other anarchisms. The interdiction here goes for any mix of Old World habits and the new acquisitiveness, because they threaten reasonable, productive love. As dangerous as the Turkish spider woman is Barrera, a brutish boss, macho rather than manly, lustful rather than loving. If masculinity and machismo are hard to distinguish here, it is because the fixed gender assignments of populism valorize virility as a male attribute by definition. Yet in earlier versions, when romance reconciled equally legitimate members of the nation-family, the heroes were remarkably feminized. Their brand of productive heroism, in fact, depended on it. Militant machismo had become a sterile trap, outliving its purpose in the heroic past. But populism's revised romance wants to recover that past for a heroic future.

In Rivera's revised revision, however, the obstacles that define populism's purpose lose their Manichean simplicity. Is the obstacle to national integration Barrera's and Zoraida's greedy sensuality? Or is it Cova's jealousy, inconstancy, his flair for launching reckless projects that may promise only the thrill of defeat? Cova's enemy here often turns out to be his less-than-admirable self. When he helps Alicia to run away from the arranged marriage, no passion or truth drives him forward; ennui had driven him out. Alicia herself has no illusions, either about Cova's love or about the prospects for reconciliation with her parents. Although she can demand that Cova marry her, she chooses to demand nothing. This willful vindication of her namesake in Cooper's romances shows that Alice doesn't mean transparent naturalized truth that man can build on. As for Barrera's interference, it would have been impossible had Cova been either faithful to Alicia or indifferent to that sensuous rival.[25] And the slave-driver Zoraida Ayram—whose initials already indicate the inversion of an arbitrary order—could never have ensnared or simply overcome Cova, were it not for his unbounded and unfounded sexual self-esteem. He and Alicia are more dynamic than the lovers in romance. Their passion wanes and waxes; they learn that love is an option, not an inevitability. And perhaps most important, Cova may have learned after so many failed attempts that to be a man is precisely not to deny those aspects of himself that spill over beyond ideal masculinity.

In this alternative to the populist reading, the most daunting obstacle to heroic patriotism is Cova himself, that narcissistic and self-aggrandizing part of himself that has lost its charismatic appeal after the civilizing liberalism of founding fathers lost its ethical charm. Cova gives the lie to those early projects—"it is civilized man who is the champion of destruction"—but adds immediately in his perverse penchant for estheticizing horror: "There is something magnificent in the story of these pirates who enslave their peons, exploit the environment, and struggle with the jungle" (183; 231–232). Along with this tortured admiration for a monstrously ideal manhood comes, as we saw, a new quasi-identification with those whom heroes exploit, the workers and perhaps the women. I am aware that this may be a strong misreading and that Cova's empathy may just as easily be a requirement for good theater. Certainly the women here are morally problematized. Especially in the ample shape of Zoraida, they are as insatiable as the jungle or as capitalism; all consume men to produce monsters. Yet the entire book resonates with a parable told by a veteran of the jungle about one such woman who upsets the terms of exploiter and exploited. It is a story of *la indiecita Mapiripana*, the fecund but malignant spirit of the forest who had been raped by the very missionary who planned to burn her as a witch. She ensnared him and seduced him only to bear two monstrous, parricidal children (123–124; 159–160). Again and again, women and the jungle respond with lethal defensiveness to men's greed and desire for power.

Writing against populism's instrumentalist grain, Rivera makes even the patriarch Silva explain that, "The jungle defends itself against its murderers" (139; 176); "[A]ny of these trees would seem tame, friendly, even smiling in a park, along a road, on a plain, where nobody would bleed it or persecute it; yet here they are all perverse, or aggressive, or hypnotizing" (181; 229). Could this suggest a vindication of Zoraida, the

woman who uselessly warned Silva's boy not to possess her?
That was just before his unwanted embrace put pressure on the
trigger of her self-defensive pistol, firing from her breast to
his. Forty years of experience with men and money may have
warned Zoraida, in Artemio Cruz's rude vocabulary, that *chin-
gar* is the only defense against being *chingada*.

As early as a jealous dream that Cova has about Barrera, a
man whom Alicia had yet to meet, the book associates offended
women with the lacerated, uncontrollably oozing trees whose
revenge on male interested sexuality is an exorbitant female
sexuality, a prophylactic mire of rubber sap that makes sure
nothing can come of man's desire. Cova's nightmare includes
a vision of Griselda, dressed in gold and standing on a rock that
flowed at the base with a stream of whitish rubber sap (36; 48).
But in its own slippery *jouissance*, the text disaggregates the
equation of woman and nature as it makes it. In the dream,
Alicia seems to be part of exploitable nature, just as one tree
seems to be like another, but her dying complaint about Cova's
careless metaphorizing betrays her as a parasite of the desired
tree. She is a figure for the abused and vengeful *indiecita Mapiripana*, associated with the same parasitical flower; therefore she
is *also* abusive to the trees, like the men are.

> Llevaba yo en la mano una hachuela corta, y colgado del cinto, un
> recipiente de metal. Me detuve ante una araucaria de morados
> corimbos, parecida al árbol del caucho, y empecé a picarle la corteza
> para que se escurriera la goma. "¿Por qué me desangras?," suspiró
> una voz desfalleciente. "Yo soy tu Alicia y me he convertido en una
> parásita. (36)

> [In my hand I carried a hatchet, and, hanging from my belt, one
> of the tin cans used to collect latex. I stopped before a tall pine,
> festooned with purple corymbs, rising like a rubber tree, and began
> hacking at the bark to see the precious liquid flow. "Why do you
> bleed me?" moaned a dying voice. "I am your Alicia, now but a
> parasite!"] (48–49)

The dreamer may not get the destabilizing point, missing it
the way he misses Sebastiana's point about the unnecessary pos-
sessiveness of fathers and fatherlands. By refusing his terms,
Sebastiana puts into motion, and into question, an entire social

map of national, sexual, and racial identities.[26] He may not get it, because Cova continues to find insubordinate women, like Zoraida, to be un-Natural. "What a singular woman she was, how ambitious, how masculine!" (207; 259). Until the end, he cannot imagine that Alicia and Griselda could be agents of their own fate and assumes they were forced into the jungle by Barrera like so much sexual merchandise. But the reader can hardly miss the message from the time these women become inseparable allies, despite the jealousy Cova thinks he can provoke between them. Then we find out that Alicia is the one who cut Barrera's face and Griselda the one who killed her abductor (243; 301). As for their reason for being in the jungle, Griselda explains as any man might, "We came alone where we could; to seek a living in the Vichada!" (249; 307).

I have obviously opted for a utopian reading of this book, one that chooses to notice the no-man's-land, the no-place of unmapped Amazonia, in which constraining patriarchal borders and meanings are only imperfectly produced. Why not pick a promising interpretive option, when its best readers admit that this is a supremely contradictory work?[27] Sylvia Molloy, for example, reads the text as infected by the social decomposition it reports, an aggressively impotent answer to the positivist pretense of narrators who diagnose pollution without admitting to their own contamination.[28] Why not valorize this textual infirmity as an exorbitant proliferation of voices and styles, an uncontainable oozing of meaning that makes the illness strangely analogous to the jungle's female disease? Feeling the jungle also initiates Cova into an alternatively gendered autochthonous lore, like that of Guahíba Indian husbands who writhe with their wives' birthing pains (108; 141). Even though Cova's titillating pain comes from inadequately reproducing (either the populist clichés of propriety or the modernist clichés that would make decomposition waft in the air like perfume), the pain may have some therapeutic purpose, if only as a gadfly to demands for patriarchal or estheticizing closure. Pain is the effect of histrionic failures to become his own oxymoronic stereotype of a precious hero. As the poet's controlled verses turn into uncontrollable prose, it may dawn on him and on his readers that the ideal image is itself his major problem. Chimera of passion and power over women and nature, competition, love of violence, only mock the jungle's victimizing victim. A utopian vision sees Cova become a man, not by conquering and possessing Alicia in a grand patriarchal gesture, nor by achieving some transcendental coherence at the end of a spiritual quest,[29] and still less by defending the privileges of white masculinity that understandably outrage some feminist readers.[30] Instead, this option locates Cova's paradoxical achievement of manhood at the points where he stops insisting on what he should be. That is, when he glimpses woman as subject and as his counterpart. Feeling the jungle may also mean that he recognizes himself in the female "devourer," Zoraida, as a projection of his aggressivity and guilt.

My own text at this point may be contaminated by Cova's love of contradiction because, after having pleaded for a non-tautological reading of founding romances, I find myself reading Cova's story from their promising resolutions, forcing the apparently self-defeating text into a *Bildungsroman*. But of course there are no resolutions in this novel. Its reconstitution of a social remnant at the end is notably equivocal. Cova finally escapes to a clearing and finds Alicia, Griselda, Franco, Heli, and his prematurely born son. But, after killing Barrera, Cova dismisses a boatfull of diseased compatriots who might contaminate his newfound family, and he turns the group back to the jungle. Has he learned to be a productive and possessive patriarch, to defend *his* woman and *his* son whose gestation period is the same period the novel covers? (259; 319). Was his lesson that fathering could be more manly than fighting—that if fathering a country is a metonymic construct, it begins at home? Was it the same lesson nineteenth-century heroes were learning from novels? This variation on national romances might be called ecological with feminist overtones. Or has paternity literally steered him away from his patriotic duty to the drifting Colombians who endanger his private family? Has he learned enough to acknowledge Alicia as his legitimate counterpart? Is it absurd to imagine that he loves her, not only because of triangulated desire through Barrera, nor only through the narcissism of reproducing himself through her baby, but also because he becomes a father and her ally? Or is he bossy and suicidal enough to believe that certain death in the jungle is preferable to losing command of his party? The suspended answers at this extreme of the novel recall Sebastiana's refusal to answer related questions at the beginning. They leave the novel inconclusive, just as they leave its heroes debating between the demands of fathering and of fatherlands in an unmapped, contested, and contestatory space. Cova's possible *Bildung* may therefore amount to nothing more or less than a liberating disintegration of "patria-rchy."

The novel's undecidability is something that distinguishes it from the foundational as well as populist romances. In its practice of setting up equivalences in order to see how they fail to add up, *La vorágine* is closer to de Manian allegory than to the dialectical bravado of founders. In their romances, limited registers of language remain distinct, character bound, and generally unambiguous; but here one character's discourse bleeds confusingly into another's, and style can transform in midparagraph. Virtue has a double private-political meaning in romance; but here the doubling of codes makes sexual and civic virtue continually compete with each other.

Some readers, especially the first ones, have been impatient with Rivera's rambling form and overt contradictions. He has been criticized for all of these slips as if they were literary failings, a want of organization and control to be censured or excused. Rereading now, I have chosen to dally at these slips as moments of freedom from oppositional thinking. There is no need to assume a liberating intention here; Rivera's own protest to the ex-consul suggests that he intended to be perfectly clear about who the enemies and the victims really were. His novel, however, is a porous text in which speech events seem less intended to happen than simply allowed to happen. It may appear that I have made too much of the short interchange between Cova and Sebastiana quoted at the beginning. After all, I am claiming that it provides a space for appreciating the difference between conciliatory romances and the populist, patriarchal stranglehold on many novels of the first half of the twentieth century. And I am even suggesting that it encourages a rethinking of gender and race as variable social constructions. Perhaps, though, I am not suggesting enough, because this unruly novel persists at picking away those constructive and constraining fictions. It continually transgresses the norms of gender; it deconstructs notions of heroism and ownership; and it disorganizes the traditional straight line of narrative until we feel as lost as the protagonist.

But debilitating convention and constraining borders are not the only ruins here; and my utopian reading turns quixotic as it detours from feelings of giddy relief to lamentable loss. It is the loss of meaning, in the most unexamined and passionately referential sense of the term. This was a sorry loss for the lawyer and statesman who kept pointing his finger at an enemy whom others could claim not to see. Readers who choose to identify with Sebastiana, Alicia, Griselda, and even with Zoraida may feel liberated by seeing through Cova's imperfectly constructed fictions. But rubber bosses who read Rivera were also freed by his literary laissez-faire, simply by pointing out that Cova, after all, wrote fictions. Writing a de Manian, self-mocking allegory opened up so much space for skeptical readings that Rivera would bemoan the evaporation of his patriotic spleen through the porous text he produced. Above, I quoted his insistence that no reader could miss his outcry for justice. But the passage continues, arching back with the kind of guilty reflexiveness that his readers are used to: "Nevertheless, far from achieving justice, I aggravated the situation, because I managed only to turn real suffering into unbelievable myths. 'Stories from *The Vortex*,' is what the magnates can now call reports on the horrors that rubber workers actually live through."

And what was even more frustrating, and no doubt more guilt-provoking too, was that Rivera's literary writing project so contaminated even his documentary work that the purposelessness of one canceled the purpose of the other. "And no one believes me, although I am in possession of and make public the documents that prove the most iniquitous bestiality, the most outrageous national indifference."[31]

Rivera's most celebrated fan, one whose practical kind of admiration borders on plagiarism for some Colombians, was not about to risk this kind of missed reading.[32] I am referring to Rómulo Gallegos who became Venezuela's first freely elected president as the culmination of his career as educator and novelist. Before much direct involvement in politics, Gallegos published his best-known novel, *Doña Bárbara* (1929) during a trip to Spain, almost as if he were smuggling the book out.[33] It responded to a series of events that led up to the 1928 riots, incited by some of Gallegos's best students, against Juan Vicente Gómez.[34] The dictator tried to silence the students with a paternal warning; continued demonstrations would bring harsher measures. His patriarchal authoritarian style of address had generally secured a proper reception, counting on a paradoxical combination of traditional respect for caudillos—who dared to subdue regional interests to national cohesiveness—and the modern military-communications technology that guaranteed obedience. For an elite class that would have preferred to share his power, this became especially irritating in 1927 while foreign companies were extracting oil from Lake Maracaibo. Venezuelans might finally have looked forward to the enormous sums of money needed to develop their own industries, as well as to build schools, provide good housing, create jobs. But very little money went to local businessmen or to reform, an oversight that lead Gallegos's students to make public accusations and demands.

What began as a week of benign university celebrations (cosponsored by the Rotary Club and showing more than a glimmer of carnival) escalated into a month of passionate denunciations that sparked strikes in the nation's nascent working class. Students had taken up the long-silenced practice in Venezuela of collectively renewing Bolívar's unfinished struggle for liberty.[35] Their persistence enraged Gómez, after his initial pardon, so he sent some leaders to jail and others into hiding or exile. The "Generation of 1928" came out and came home in 1935, when the dictator finally died. Before then, inevitable pressure on Gallegos himself forced a choice between retreating from his principles or from his home. He would certainly have preferred to avoid confrontation, as is evident from his stay in Venezuela until 1931. But when Gómez insisted that Gallegos finally take sides by appointing him as senator for the State of Apure, the gentle but ethical man saw no way but out. He followed his students into exile, returning in 1936 as the father of that new generation. Led by Rómulo Betancourt, who would share power with the army in an interim government (1945–1948), become president (1959–1964), and under whom OPEC would be founded (1959), the students returned from exile with models for establishing broad-based, populist politics.

Although Venezuelan populists were inspired by marxism, they objected to their "dogmatic" communist competitors who insisted on proletarian leadership, despite the alleged impracticality of Venezuela's small and inexperienced working class. Instead, Betancourt invoked Lenin's judgment that, where foreign capital dominated, a "national bourgeois" government must first promote native industrialization before a socialist revolution was possible.[36] That meant providing an elite leadership and protecting it from, among other things, communist efforts to organize workers' strikes. It also meant that when the communists in Venezuela, as elsewhere, made alliances with unpopular national governments during World War II—in order to resist fascism and to support the allies—the populists preferred to put "Venezuela first" rather than become embroiled in the war's "interimperialist" rivalry.[37] By 1948 their appeal to the masses was warmly reciprocated when Betancourt's three-year provisional government ended in free presidential elections, and his beloved teacher won on the populist Acción Democrática ticket. Through *Doña Bárbara*, President Gallegos had also been a great popularizer of populist programs in Venezuela.[38]

Long before they came home, the exiled intellectuals took up the novel as the narrative projection of their future victory.[39] And after the 1943 film version, produced in Mexico with a script by Gallegos himself, *Doña Bárbara* reached a very broad, variously educated constituency in the crucial decade before the national elections. Since then, there have also been several "telenovelas" based on the novel. It has become, arguably, Venezuela's national novel, barely having to compete for that honor with nineteenth-century books, the way, for example, *La vorágine* might be said to compete with *María*. Likely Venezuelan contenders might be *Peonía* (1890), an evocation of Isaac's *María*, by Manuel Romero García (1861–1917), or *Zárate* (1882) by Eduardo Blanco (1838–1912). But neither Romero's idyll about a young engineer who visits his uncle's ranch, falls in love with his cousin, and plans to save both from the uncle's barbarity, nor Blanco's adventure that reads like a cross between *El Zarco* and *Tabaré* about an honorable bandit who is hastily killed by the man he has saved, can compare today with *Doña Bárbara's* status.[40] Venezuelan critics had generally been disheartened with the level of commitment or ardor in the earlier works. For them, Venezuelan romanticism was either irresponsibly apolitical or too politically incontinent to produce mature writing.[41] Its novels seemed disappointingly derivative, and too often fixed on Europe. To its credit, *Los mártires* (1878) (to cite another possible classic) by Fermín Toro (1807–1865) is a denunciation of monstrous class inequality, but its target is inequality in England, not at home.

A certain impatience with early novels may be as much the effect as the cause of the national literary celebration surrounding Gallegos and his generation, an effect similar to the Boom's denial of literary value in Latin America's narrative tradition.[42] Venezuela could finally boast of a novelist who was read in the rest of America and in Europe.[43] His disciplined research into local lore, his flair for recording popular speech, the patriotic purpose evident from the portrait of aimless dilettantism in *Reinaldo Solar* (1920), the legitimating family conciliations of *La trepadora* (1925), and the modernizing mission of *Doña Bárbara*, all these gave Gallegos's first readers the same kind of satisfaction that made one skeptical character of *Doña Bárbara* finally exclaim about its hero: "We've got a man" (40; 59).[44]

Published after his disciples had already left Venezuela, at the nadir of oppositional activity, *Doña Bárbara* is Gallegos's fantasy of return and repair. It proposes a double emancipation, from an internal tyrant and her external ally; that is, from the local boss, Bárbara (Gómez), and her North American accomplice, Mr. Danger (oil industry). The failure of any internal resistance during the Gómez years must have made anything short of emancipation seem wholly impractical to Gallegos. There could be no romantic project of hegemonic alliances if the enemy refused to negotiate. Nor could Rivera's hallucinations have seemed to the point, blurring the instrumental oppositions between heroes and villains, or between a metaphorized land and the metonymized husband who might repossess her. Gallegos reinscribes those oppositions with a vengeance in *Doña Bárbara.* Neither love across enemy lines nor a self-critical respect for unconquerable terrain were terribly promising for a man who had just lost his country to a usurping "barbarian." The question of whether or not the country should be controlled might have seemed irresponsible to the exiles who raged against the control of Gómez and foreign interests. Instead they asked how best to repossess the national patrimony.

Gallegos stages that reconquest as a tale of triumphant civilization, in the person of aptly named Santos Luzardo, who has come home to the llano after graduating from law school in Caracas. His first intention was merely to sell the family ranch and to spend the earnings in Europe. But the llano makes claims on its rightful master, and Santos stays to put his ranch in order. In the process he must subdue the barbarous woman who has been rustling his cattle and seizing his land. Her very identity as a domineering woman is a signal for censure, a rhetorical trespassing of populism's gendered code. Gallegos makes her the "personification" (21; 29) of the seductive land and of lawless usurpations, an oxymoronic obstacle to Santos's demand for legally binding terms. She justifies her territorial trespassing with a partial reading of the law; but Santos, in his drive for progress, insists on turning the page and winning his claim (107–108; 176–177). Meanwhile, his newly fenced-in property adds newly diversified dairy products to the original meat and hides, and production develops with factory efficiency. Borders, fences, frontiers are civilization's first requirements, the kind of writing that refuses to risk barbarous misreadings (86; 137). Undecidability was precisely the semiotic transgression that gave seductive charm to the llano—with its hallucinatory circle of receding mirages—and to Bárbara's exorbitant sexuality, her "imposing appearance of Amazon [*marimacho*] put . . . the stamp of originality on her beauty: there was something about her at once wild, beautiful, and terrible" (31; 45–46).

With his land, Santos also reins in Bárbara's wild daughter, Marisela. Abandoned at birth by her mother, Marisela had been living in a swampy no-man's-land between Bárbara's treacherously expansive *Miedo* (Fear) and Santos's reconstructive *Altamira* (Highview). She lived there with her father, Lorenzo Barquero, Luzardo's feuding cousin. This drunken ruin of a man, since Bárbara despoiled and abandoned him, had been Santos's childhood idol. Santos hopes to save him from that liminal space, as he saves Marisela from Mr. Danger, Bárbara's lascivious associate. But Barquero is finally lost to drink, and to the despair of his own empty eloquence. Marisela, though, has by now acquired the civilized contours of the perfect wife.

To acquire the necessary shape and tone, Marisela had first to learn how to groom herself, and especially how to speak standard Spanish, like a city girl. Her regional, traditional language, that which distinguishes her as a llanera, is corrected in this cultural improvement or whitening. It is an ironic, perhaps self-defeating victory for the hero who learned to love his country because he learned to love his particular region (20; 26). But to follow his elite, hegemonic lead means that Marisela must learn an elite and self-consciously regulated code, to banish the undisciplined grunts and cries that amount to a linguistic pathology. And Santos's teacherly promises of improvement are his most effective seductions, as if educator Gallegos were pointing to his own political seductiveness.

—¿Hasta cuándo va a estar ahí pues?—gruñó Marisela—¿Por qué no se acaba de dir?
—Eso mismo te pregunto yo ¿hasta cuándo vas a estar ahí? Ya es tiempo de que regreses a tu casa. ¿No te da miedo andar sola por estos lugares desiertos?
—¡Guá! ¿Y por qué voy a tener miedo, pues? ¿Me van a comer los bichos del monte? ¿Y a usté qué le importa que yo ande sola por donde me dé gana? ¿Es acaso, mi taita, pues, para que venga a regañarme?
—¡Qué maneras tan bruscas, muchacha! ¿Es que ni siquiera te han enseñado a hablar con la gente?
—¿Por qué no me enseña usté, pues?—y otra vez la risa sacudiéndole el cuerpo, echado de bruces la tierra.
—Sí, te enseñaré—díjole Santos, cuya compasión empezaba a transformarse en simpatía—. Pero tienes que pagarme por adelantado las lecciones, mostrándome esa cara que tanto te empeñas en ocultar. (78–79)

["How long are you going to stay there, eh?" Marisela grumbled. "Why don't you get going?"

"What I want to know is, how long are you going to stay there? It's time for you to go home. Aren't you afraid of being alone in this deserted place?"

"*Guá!* and why should I be? Are the wild animals going to eat me, maybe? And what's it to you if I go alone wherever I want to? Are you my daddy, maybe, to come around scolding me?"

"Don't be so rude, child. Haven't you even been taught how to answer people?"

"Well, why don't you teach me?" And once more the prone body shook with mirth.

"I *will* teach you," said Santos, whose pity was beginning to change to liking. "But you've got to pay me in advance for the lessons by showing me that face you're so bent on hiding."] (125)

For good reason, this novel has been read as a fairy tale, the story of Prince Charming who searches out the princess (land) that he is destined to husband and arouses her with his irresistible touch. One unmistakable reason is Gallegos's title for part I, chapter 11, in which Santos meets Marisela; he calls it "Sleeping Beauty." But the story could just as well be read as a morality play. Civilization conquers barbarism. The holy light (Santos Luzardo) of modern Reason banishes the archaic darkness of barbarous black magic, one source of his antagonist's power. The naturally public sphere of man replaces the obscenely personalized dominion of woman, returning her— through her daughter—to a more modest and procreative domestic space. An elite intelligentsia puts Venezuelan productivity first, instead of preferring alliances with local tradition or with foreign allies. However one reads it, *Doña Bárbara* respects a far more binary code than that of most nineteenth-century national novels. The Hermes-like heroism of Daniel Bello would, for example, be mere travesty here, as would Leonor's powerfully seductive privilege.

By the time Gallegos published his founding fiction, Venezuela was certainly a different place from the newly established nations, and some reformers were cautious about particular kinds of liberty. It had generations of experience and disappointment with the kind of liberal participation in the world market that some earlier writers were hoping to achieve. With Independence in 1810, the cocoa it had been exporting to other Spanish colonies began to bring foreign exchange. But decades of civil war devastated many of the groves, while the North Atlantic market began to prefer coffee. So coffee is what Venezuela produced, for a market whose ups and downs sent political tremors through the country. Venezuela also had a century's worth of political experience behind her. An Independence movement, led by her own Simón Bolívar, was followed, as in many new Latin American nations, by civil wars between centralists and advocates for a loose federation.[45] The wars ended, as they did in Argentina, only when a provincial caudillo took over the capital in 1830 and began a long and relatively stable dictatorship.[46] The problem in Venezuela (and elsewhere) was that conflict did not end there; caudillos, usually from the llano, continued to raise personal armies and to destabilize the government. Well into Gallegos's youth, Venezuelan history showed a pattern of implacable dictatorships alternating with impractical and short-term regimes.

In 1909 the intellectuals of Gallegos's generation saw hope for a change when a young military man named Juan Vicente Gómez replaced the conservative president Castro. To celebrate the apparent dawning, several writers inaugurated a journal called *Aurora,* in which Gallegos published one article after another on such issues as political principles, the need for parties, respect for law. The optimism was of course unfounded. Gómez turned out to be as ruthless a dictator as Venezuela had known, but more effective. And the populist response echoed the emancipatory demands of early nineteenth-century revolutionary Independence movements. But by now, after the experience of long civil wars following the wars of Independence, it was clear that freedom without stability leads back to (neocolonial) bondage.

So the new nationalists often dealt in a mixed rhetorical economy, circulating terms coined during the emancipation struggle in combination with others from the period of national consolidation. The emancipatory oppositions between patriotic self and foreign other gave currency to populism, together with the Sarmentine oppositions between an ideal, modernized self

and the backward vestiges of a local culture that had compromised the nation's sovereignty. That the abstract and binary
terms of civilization versus barbarism in Gallegos's novel are inherited from Sarmiento's *Facundo* (1845) shows that Gallegos
faced challenges much like those of Argentines almost a century
earlier; at least it shows that he understood them to be similar.
This binarism is at the core of the general principles in the
novel, principles that were later adapted in the platform of
Acción Democrática; they are: respect for law as opposed to
personalism; education as the foundation for democratic sovereignty as opposed to servile ignorance; and national industrial
modernization to replace traditional methods and to supplant
foreign industry.

A curious anomaly suggests itself when we consider how
important *Doña Bárbara* has been for this modernizing platform
in Venezuela, where economic and political renewal are practically oil by-products, namely the novel's distance from the oil
controversy. Although the crisis over getting and spending new
petroleum revenues no doubt helped to motivate Gallegos's
writing, as it did the pronouncements of his students, this novel
is not about oil but about cattle. Now cattle or hide was no
longer an important export commodity, so that the project of
modernizing Venezuela's ranches would have apparently little
effect either on her revenues or on her sovereignty. A novel of
course can displace an immediate crisis to dwell on a related
one; and in this case the choice seems most appropriate. Gallegos tells us that he was inspired to write during a visit to one
of Gómez's ranches, and more generally that he chose to set the
story on the llano because that was where local caudillos (Gómez
and minor versions of him) dominated vast and largely empty
spaces.[47] It was also where besides raising cattle they raised personal armies that would periodically threaten civilization in the
capital. The untamed llano, then, takes on a woman's name
as Gallegos's protagonist, just as the wild pampa took on the
identity of an indomitable virgin for Sarmiento. A reader like
Borges would know that her vast emptiness could be as sure a
labyrinthine trap as Rivera's swampy jungle; if it enchanted
men into beasts, so did the uncharted plain. And man's possessive gaze blurred just as surely in the vacant expanse as in

the prolific vortex. Land as the stubborn virgin and land as the voracious whore: it is probably less an ethical difference, since neither has the decency to submit to a husband, than a practical one. The reluctant virgin may yet become the productive wife, a man-ipulation for which Sarmiento wrote the handbook. "The really necessary thing," muses Santos Luzardo, practically quoting Sarmiento (and Alberdi), "is to change the circumstances that lead to these evils, to populate the country" (21; 28). Like Sarmiento, Gallegos was convinced that physical environment, more than race, determined human behavior and produced, to give one example from the novel, the difference between bellicose llano Indians and communitarian Guajiro Indians of the coast. On the endless plains one's sense of freedom goes wild and assaults social convention. The only solution was to eliminate barbarism by filling in the empty space, by populating. In the conjugal instrumentalism of populist romance, civilization was to penetrate the barren land and to make her a mother.

The fact that *Facundo* gave an early formulation to the opposition has earned Sarmiento the vanguardist title of "prepositivist"; but by Gallegos's time, positivism had a long and often conservative if not reactionary history in Latin America. Much of his writing, in fact, brings him uncomfortably close to the positivist ideologues who admired Gómez as the necessary strongman and father for a barbarous childlike country like Venezuela.[48] One wonders if Gallegos admired him too; he certainly admits fascination for the dictator's incarnation into "the appealing body of a woman" (literally her "appetizing flesh").[49] Gómez is said to have reciprocated by approving enthusiastically of *Doña Bárbara,* which, he said, "Venezuelan writers should imitate instead of getting involved in those goddamn revolutions."[50] Gallegos and his critics also acknowledge that Santos, the civilizing "city-zen," has something to learn about self-defense and necessary violence (I would add passion) from Bárbara before he can replace her. This is certainly a plausible reading; and it easily resolves the apparently bad fit between the year of the novel and its economic focus. As a critic of Gómez, Gallegos was exposing him as a barbarous caudillo, a formidable but vincible obstacle to prosperity and reform.

But the novelist's enchantment by the Venezuelan vamp exceeds the references to Gómez, even when we admit the writer's barely veiled admiration for the tyrant. Perhaps even more admirable than Rivera's Zoraida, aging Bárbara is as dangerously and aggressively sexy; but she is also grand enough to be the novel's solution as well as its problem. At the end, after losing legal and erotic struggles to Santos, she prepares to win anyway; when feminine wiles don't work, she can use her phallic option and place Santos at gunpoint. But seeing him in Marisela's arms brings back the memory of her own language teacher and of herself as the avid disciple. The gun drops and Bárbara leaves the llano to the promising lovers.

I cannot help thinking that Gallegos's own passion for the llano, both the worst and the best of Venezuela, surfaces here as one of the reasons for displacing oil for cattle. Along with his "scientific" conviction that the open plains breed violence and superstition, the romantic in Gallegos seems to feel that this space is admirable and capable of arousing conflicting passions. Unfortunately, civilization has room for neither. In his essays, Gallegos tried to make room for both by projecting the fundamental populist strategy of harnessing raw (childlike or female) American vitality for a hegemonic project; that is, enlisting popular forces under an elite leadership.[51]

But in the novel, a tension persists between the controlled, "classic," narrative style and the potentially disruptive colloquialisms that it contains (in both senses). The omniscient Venezuelan voice necessarily needs to harmonize a regional vocabulary with more standard dictionary entries. But the extravagances are purely lexical, never grammatical, never a challenge to the language's controlling structure. And whereas the regional archaisms that survive in Marisela's speech suggest a venerable alternative to Santos's modern(izing) Spanish, the kind of regionalisms included in the third-person narrative are nouns and adjectives referring to flora and fauna, the New World's embellishments and additions to an inviolable standard language.[52] Even so, smuggling those words in is a reminder of what remains categorically out, namely the popular alternatives to Gallegos's control. In programmatic terms, the tension is repeated between his need to rationalize, to fill up the llano, achieving the stability and prosperity that will safeguard Venezuela's sovereignty, and, in contrast, a nostalgic love for the tradition that has been most typically Venezuelan, the very tradition that modernization will make extinct. More paradoxical or tragic than programmatically contradictory, this kind of tension is endemic to populism in general. In order for "developing" countries to secure a sovereign and solvent condition in the world, populists tend to advocate further development; but since what is being protected is a certain national difference that resists becoming an extension or a clone of the industrial powers, populists also tend to celebrate local traditions. Populism's Janus-face, to quote Lenin,[53] can hardly balance itself. Tradition may be a source of national pride, but it is also associated with economic and political backwardness. So the backward-looking face of Janus necessarily withers under populism, and tradition is mummified into folklore. Perhaps I have already exceeded any reasonable speculation about guilt or self-implication in Gallegos's novel, but I cannot resist the thought that it extends to Venezuela's broader (con)text. Rómulo Gallegos was always a peaceful man, advocating change by degrees in the interest of avoiding violence. But he probably knew or felt that his politics would inevitably do violence, not quite the physical kind, but the necessary violence of a writer-statesman who displaces words and projects from existing contexts, as, for example, Venezuelan populism was displacing indigenous tradition with an efficient and metropolitan culture.

This double-dealing helps to account not only for Bárbara's seductiveness but also for another possible anomaly: the fact that in so deliberately schematic and didactic a novel, Bárbara's evil is sometimes hard to distinguish from just revenge, and Santos's enlightened goodness seems tarnished with a burden of guilt. It is to Gallegos's credit that his "archetypes"[54] are less, or more, than ideal. Bárbara, herself the child of a submissive Indian mother and a white adventurer, began to tyrannize men after she had suffered a gang rape as a teenager. To compound the offense, her assailants first killed Asdrúbal, the youth she is learning to love. She is also, literally, learning because he had been teaching her to read and write, just as Santos would teach/ seduce Marisela (23; 32). What the girl conceives from the violation (of her productive capacity, of her rights to education) is a hatred for men and a need to revenge herself on them. For some reason Gallegos decided to explain her motivation. Is it possible that, instead of a geographical explanation for the barbarity of the llano, and beyond the social reform messages about the need for education and for legitimate (national) production, Gallegos is suggesting a historical interpretation? Is the history of original and consecutive rapes and expropriations of an indigenous population somehow responsible for the confusion between rights and revenge? One hint of an answer is his return in *Canaima* (1935) to brood over the guilt in terms and terrain evocative of *La vorágine*; another is his compulsion to absolve the guilty through the redemptive agency of the offended mestiza in *Sobre la misma tierra* (1943). And even in this novel, Gallegos further confuses the issue of moral right by introducing Santos with a flashback to childhood on the llano, when the violence of an argument at home ended with his father killing his brother and then starving himself to death. At that point, in a kind of inverted Parzifal plot, his mother moved him to Caracas so that the boy could grow up civilized. It is possible that the hero knows he cannot be entirely spared his family history of violence, understood by extension as Venezuela's civil wars. No side is free from blame in an internecine conflict; even winners mourn the other side's loss. It might be that Santos perceives his struggle with Bárbara as another round in the wars between modernizing centralists and fiercely independent regionalists. In that case he may feel ethical qualms about the fight, even though he feels justified. In fact, Santos suffers a moral crisis after shooting one of Bárbara's men. Unless his historical conscience is at work, it is not clear why Santos should feel so guilty for a shot delivered in self-defense.

It is even possible that the historical guilt goes deeper and further back than the civil wars. Perhaps it extends to the beginnings of Venezuelan history, when white men started the process of modernizing or Europeanizing the colony. That meant first violating or exterminating the Indians, just as half-Indian Bárbara had been raped by others and was being removed by Santos. My speculation about Santos's unspoken guilt, or his uneasiness about the possibility that he and his forebears are implicated in the chain of usurpations on the llano, shares some ground with Roberto González Echevarría's reading of the novel's dilemma. He points out that the litigation over land with Doña Bárbara is not only an occasion for censuring her lack of respect for the law; it is also an occasion for doubting the very legitimacy of law, if, that is, legitimacy is grounded in natural, genealogical rights. This is the vexed moral issue of Santos's legal victory, his lawyerly maneuvering through fine print. In order to win, he is forced to contemplate all the guilt-provoking issues raised above, by contemplating the judicial history of his entitlement. It began with the indefensible conquest of the land from the indigenous, natural masters, by his "centaur" of a grandfather Evaristo Luzardo. If genealogical rights were the grounding for legal rights, then Santos has no more right to the land than does Bárbara, perhaps less, since the mestiza can claim an immemorial genealogical grounding on her mother's side. But, as González Echevarría points out, the incommensurability between Evaristo's initial violence and the later law doesn't stop Santos from pressing his claim; this produces a moral and semantic undecidability that makes this novel precociously modern.[55] Too self-interested to confess the contradiction between moral right and legal rights, Santos is not the persona for Gallegos on this analysis. Instead it is Lorenzo Barquero, the once-brilliant law student who dropped out of everything once he saw through the fiction of all language; one cannot use it without lying, and one cannot be human without using it.[56]

Yet I think we may read beyond this endlessly reflexive dead-end, fascinating as the de Manian musing on meaning may be. We may, simply because Gallegos writes beyond it, just as he wrote beyond the 1920 novel about Reinaldo Solar's self-defeating self-consciousness. A possible figure for Barquero, Solar leaves all of his projects—agricultural improvements, a new religion, literature, love—as soon as he realizes that his ardor was the cause, not the effect, of his inflamed will. The ardor abates and the will lags when he realizes that all these projects are his willful projections, fictions that have no (truth) value. Solar finally commands a guerrilla troop and is murdered by his own men when they learn of his collective suicide plan.

He might be seen, of course, as an existential hero, but some contemporary Venezuelans saw an irresponsible dilettante.[57] Solar's irresoluteness was hardly heroic to them, because any one of his fictional projects might have taken on real density had he developed the discipline and pragmatism so uncharacteristic of his privileged class. Surely the teachers in *Doña Bárbara*, Gallegos himself, Asdrúbal, and Santos, must have been as aware as Solar and Barquero that social, legal, religious, linguistic systems are all arbitrarily constructed. But none of this paralyzes them. Sensitive to the semantic bleeding between words like *right* and *wrong, civilization* and *barbarism, national* and *foreign, male* and *female,* Gallegos insists (where Rivera desists) on damming up the leaky system of oppositions, because he is convinced that a system (of grammar, phonetics, law) is superior to systemic anarchy. However fictitious and arbitrary, rules are codifiable, generalizable, and therefore generally binding in a way that produces a society. "Although the law does not provide for fines or penalties or arrests," Santos retorts to Bárbara's refusal to comply, "it is binding *per se.* It obliges everyone to fulfill it, purely and simply" (107–108; 176–177).

Gallegos calls attention to the social practice of binding in several related scenes. One is the chapter devoted to branding cattle (II; iv), where he virtually performs the arbitrary gesture of stamping "meaning" on the animals and, by extension, on the land and the people bound to it. People are explicitly included, for example, through old Melesio, who is delighted to see Santos again, as delighted as a forgotten calf might be on the master's return: "I was born a *Luzardero* and I'll die one. You know what they say about the Sandovals, that we've all got the Altamira brand on our backsides" (36; 53–54). To stamp meaning in this context gives a rather literal kind of currency, less a matter of substantive nouns than of possessive adjectives. The referents for cattle, land, and people remain apparently the same: a cow is a cow before and after the sign of Altamira is emblazoned on her hide. But now she has a specific belonging, a dependent meaning like that of the patria. In the aggressively proprietary code of the novel, this is also the kind of meaning that Santos teaches Marisela in his recurring language lessons. There is no question here of distinguishing what she

means to say in her archaic and regional Spanish; Santos understands it very well and never bothers to correct it in peons. The
problem is not one of referents but of propriety, a meaning that
distinguishes mine from yours, correct from incorrect, an elite
intelligentsia from the redeemable masses. Humiliated and frustrated, Marisela sometimes has enough of the lessons: "Let me
go back to my woods again." But Santos insists on finishing with
her (just as Carmelito—on the same page—insists that the wild
mare destined for Marisela accept and enjoy his mastery). "All
right, go. But I'll come after you with: 'Don't say "seen" but
"saw" or "met"; don't say "looka" but "look" or "see"'" (110;
182).

Gallegos is surely reinscribing the excess and dissemination,
putting his finger on the wound of language from which meaning continues to ooze every time he tries to stem the flow, every
time he stages the binding and suturing of meaning against
the vagaries of roaming cattle, people, and popular speech. But
he nonetheless continues to act out/on his control, staging it
to some—perhaps—temporary effect. The lessons, the branding, and the whole system of arbitrary proprietary oppositions
so nervously repeated throughout the novel all resonate, of
course, with the scene of assigning ultimate possessive meaning, the morally equivocal legal arbitration of the land. And
read in the context of the shock waves and insistent sutures this
confrontation sends through the book, the scene is the occasion
for settling moral ambiguity by fiat. When Santos forces the
issue, the authority in town settles the question of property with
a legal-speech act: "the laws must be fulfilled just because,
otherwise they wouldn't be laws, that is, orders from the Government" (107; 177–178). Thanks to this kind of tautological
voluntarism, Santos accepts that his entitlement is merely legal
fiction; yet he accepts it all the same as constitutive of a modern
order. And he is willing to consider the fiction foundational
because, in this self-serving tautology, it promises to found
something. If law is merely a simulacrum for the right to possess, it nevertheless can stabilize the irrational dissemination
that Bárbara puts into motion (her androgynous eroticism, her
scattered cattle and boundless borders). The simulacrum can
become a horizon for future representations; it can domesticate

the llano's mirages by fencing in the land, by writing clearly. Truth, in other words, need not be the immutable given that Barquero demanded; it can be a procreative assumption. Although Santos may have no real genealogical claims, the legal fiction allows him to make generative claims, like the ones made in romantic founding novels. And like the language of love and politics in those dialectical romances, Santos's legal language has no a priori grounding; instead it lays the ground for productive relationships.

The analogy is hardly fortuitous. Marriage, after all, is a fiction, a contract that can be read as an allegory of the Law of the Llano. It makes no genealogical claims to legitimacy, since marriage partners need hardly be blood relatives; but it does make a promise of productivity. And Santos's projected marriage to Marisela both repeats and makes possible, in a familiarly dialectical way, the legal fiction aimed at populating the desert. To read *Doña Bárbara* as a national romance is to read a series of defensively populist sutures where all of *La vorágine*'s loose ends are anxiously bound up and where any bleeding between categories, such as male and female, is felt like a hemorrhage.

Still, the apparently ideal man who controls barbarism has a paradoxical lesson to learn from the feminized heroes and heroic heroines of nineteenth-century romance. Santos has to become as passionate as a woman in order to maintain control. "[W]hen one hasn't a simple soul, like Marisela's, or a too complicated one, which Luzardo's was not, solutions always have to be positive ones. If they are not, it happens as it happened to him—he lost control of his emotions, and became the plaything of contradictory impulses" (164; 277). The dialectical lesson that the teacher learns from his student is that the fiction of elite control needs another fictional grounding: falling in love and getting married to the object of control. This hegemonic romance was precisely the kind of banal domestic fiction that neither Bárbara nor Gómez cared to make up.[58] After Santos learns to love Marisela, and to love staying home with her, Gallegos can leave the rest to nature. In the fine print of this self-legitimating marriage contract, though, Gallegos can still be seen busily covering over his guilt-ridden writing, supplying the kind of excessive legitimation that doubts its own sufficiency. Marisela need not have been Santos's blood relative to have made a legal wife, yet her genealogical claims to him and to the land help to bind her contract. And his offer of legal and loving status to the disenfranchised mestiza shows Gallegos trying to patch up the problem of establishing a legitimate, centralized nation on a history of usurpation and civil war.

But this is to dwell on the difficulty of establishing historical legitimacy, the very problem the future-looking contract can displace. Legitimation here is not retrospective but proleptic, through the resourceful management and the procreative marriage that the legal fictions project. By contrast, Bárbara's equally fictional claim on the land promises to found very little. Maternity for her was an infuriating victory of men who reproduce themselves on women; and management was left to traditional terror (28; 40). Santos plans to populate the llano with legitimate children; Bárbara doesn't. This practical difference allows us to sense a shift from the moral to the legal questions this novel raises, from personal claims to patriotic duty, from genealogical rights to the generative responsibility of fathering the fatherland. It is a responsibility that Gallegos and Santos can translate imperfectly but pragmatically into the transparently constructed but nonetheless effective difference between better or worse for civilization, for or against the necessary fictions that will ground productivity and prosperity.

In one revealing aporia, Santos cannot answer his loyal peon's objections to the plans for fencing in the land, a proprietary measure sure to offend the landsmen: "The Plainsman won't have fences. He likes to have his land open the way God gave it to him. . . . If you took that pleasure away from him he'd die of grief." Santos has no defensible response to this morally messy objection, so he remains silent but not stumped. The dialogue ends because Santos is busy contemplating his mandate to translate this kind of unproductive moral standoff into neat legal demarcations: "Luzardo nevertheless kept thinking of the necessity of implanting the custom of fencing. Through that the civilizing of the Plain would begin. The fence would be a bulwark against the omnipotence of force, the necessary limitation" (86; 137).

10

"IT'S WRONG TO BE RIGHT": *MAMÁ BLANCA* ON FATHERLY FOUNDATIONS

Fortunately, the mother of six little girls in *Las memorias de Mamá Blanca* (1929), by Teresa de la Parra (1889–1936), was wrong most of the time, wrong especially about the names she chose for her daughters. More demiurge than New World Adam, this mistress of a controlled plantation paradise finished her own creations with names that just wouldn't fit, as if to laugh at the pretense of forcing bonds between a system of arbitrary signs and her flesh-and-blood, delightfully unpredictable, referents. "Poetic" and impractical, this mother took advantage of the whimsical opportunities for finishing touches: she "scorned reality and systematically endeavored to rule it by pleasant and arbitrary laws" (27; 15).[1] In the very first paragraph of Mamá Blanca's memoirs, a series of vignettes and evocations that never really add up to a coherent story about Venezuelan plantation life at the turn of the century,[2] the eccentric old lady recalls how absurd—almost perverse—her mother's choice of names seemed to the girl of five:

> Blanca Nieves, la tercera de las niñitas por orden de edad y de tamaño, tenía entonces cinco años, el cutis muy trigueño, los ojos oscuros, el pelo muy negro, las piernas quemadísimas del sol, los brazos más quemados aún, y tengo que confesarlo humildemente, sin merecer en absoluto semejante nombre, Blanca Nieves era yo. (27)

> [Blanca Nieves [Snow White], the third of the girls in order of age and size, was five years old at the time, dark of skin, dark-eyed, black-haired, legs tanned to the color of saddle leather by the sun, arms darker still. I must blushingly confess that, wholly undeserving of such a name, Blanca Nieves was I.] (15)

By referring to herself in the third person, which inexplicably coincides with the first, Blanca begins by dramatizing the liberating distance between the child referred to and the linguistic referent that cannot, or should not, catch up to her. The mother dictated absurd connections, not because that would change reality ("reality never submitted") but because reality didn't matter. So, far from fostering the kind of nominalism that would challenge unexamined facts on higher epistemological ground, this linguistically irresponsible mother knew that her prodigious hand was simply "sowing a profusion of errors that had the double property of being irremediable and absolutely charming" (27; 15). Throughout this surprising little book, the distance between the child and her name, a distance repeated already in the dis-encounter between the narrator's third-person voice and her autobiographical subject, and in the unstable difference between error and charm, will provide a space and a mandate for the conciliatory work of time-honoring tolerance and of love.

The narrator and her name, that inseparable companion, were one mismatched couple, "a walking absurdity." And if that was a joke at her expense, she puts it into a mitigating context on the same first page of the memoirs, comparing it to an even better (or worse) joke: an older tomboy of a sister named (what else?) Violeta. "She and the modest little flower, were two opposite poles" (56; 37). Violeta was so rough and ready, she was more like a brother in disguise than a sister (56; 37). And of the six little girls who saw themselves at the center of the universe, a plantation called Piedra Azul, this was the only one who almost satisfied their father's insistent desire for a son. "I believe that Violeta's body lodged the spirit of Juan Manuel the Desired, and this was the reason he had never been born: for six years he had walked the earth disguised as Violeta. The disguise was so transparent that everyone recognized him. Papa first of all" (56; 37). The jumble of sexual identities and gender roles, where the terms are not so much mismatched as available for mix-and-match permutations, is not only a recollection of the old lady's dynamically "disordered and pantheistic soul" (17; 7); it is also the entire plantation's acknowledgement of normally missed encounters between one system of signification and another. Everyone in Piedra Azul could see that a person's gender did not necessarily coincide with his or her sex. The father's second daughter was also his son. And this liberating mistake is, as we will see, part of a general phenomenon here in which the sign doesn't quite manage to describe its referent but rather leaves a space for interpretation; that is, for empowering play.

Before we follow many more playful moves, we should put this sort of irreverent linguistic freedom into a different context from that of Violeta, this time more stark than extenuating. *Las memorias de Mamá Blanca* was written in the same country and in the same year as Rómulo Gallegos's *Doña Bárbara*. And, focusing for the moment on Violeta, both novels are about women who are also men. For Gallegos, of course, this jumbled identity is literally a mess, a monstrous transgression of neat social constructions of nature, a threat and obstacle to the oppositional logic that positive progress depends on.[3] He measured Bárbara's hatred for men and the fear she engendered by a criterion of inviolable nature in which those feelings amount to depravity, even though he must have been aware of the arbitrarily—almost legalistically—drawn distinctions between legitimate and illegitimate sentiments.[4] But here, by conspicuous contrast, virile Violeta is loved by everyone: her admiring sisters, her amused mother, and not least of all by her gender-lonely father. And if Mamá Blanca could have met Doña Bárbara, it is possible that she would have loved her too. At the very least, she would have perceived Bárbara's uncontrollable energy and a certain pride in womanly independence as evocations of her beloved Violeta. As for Mother Nature, she loses all authority to real mothers in this book, because her work is sometimes unfeeling and almost always unfinished. A fatherly text, like Gallegos's may take nature to be a sacred ground; but mothers seem to take her as a challenge to their own creative authority. Blanca Nieves here is more amused than disappointed about her mother's nominal mistake, an innocent joke that brought laughter but never malice from other people. But she is furious with that false mother, Nature, for giving her straight hair, a cruel joke that had to be corrected each day at her own and her mother's expense. Nature was merely a "cruel, heartless stepmother. But as Mamá was a mother, she defied her in a struggle without quarter, and the stepmother was defeated and thwarted" (43; 27).

Juxtaposing the novels by Gallegos and de la Parra is hardly arbitrary. A comparison practically forces itself on the reader who notices the coincidence of time and place, as well as the thematic similarity between two books about women who occupy the center of their rural worlds until they are deposed by men who dispute property and propriety.[5] Through these disputes, and the changes they announce, both novels comment on the process of social modernization. By every other comparison, though, the books could hardly be more different. The one Gallegos wrote continually forces itself into a straight line—with possibly compromising flashbacks about Santos and about Bárbara clearly marked off as prehistory—aimed at positive, economically rational change. Proper language and legitimate propriety are two sides of the same civilizing coin whose purchase is never at issue. If the relationship between language and legitimacy is admittedly allegorical here, it is not attributed to metaphoric leaps from one system of representation to another, the kind of moves that predictably fall short of a close fit. Instead, we saw that the allegory here is generated metonymically and dialectically (perhaps tautologically), from the legal implications of authoritative language and from the authority conferred by a linguistic construction called law. By contrast, so much of Teresa de la Parra's novel seems to take place in one single moment, a single and sonorous moment that exchanges time for space and gives room to the most diverse and equally legitimate codes in a world that is doomed by positive and rational change. The mother's aristocratic disdain for referential language, the father's incontestable but also inconsequential pronouncements, the English-speaking governess' absurdly ungrammatical insistence on being proper, Vicente Cochocho's popular archaisms, Cousin Juancho's pleasing and pointless monologues, cowherd Daniel's precisely modulated calls to each of his bovine wards. Finally, there are the little girls whose indiscriminate imitations produce a democratizing effect among these codes and whose permutations construct flights beyond the linguistic pluralism. It is something like a playfully

postmodern instability, inspired perhaps by the mother's genteel disregard for "reality," far more inclusive than hers and as
irreverent about the signifier as about the signified.

This kind of contrast between the novels' narrative trajec-
tories and their linguistic strategies, even their ideological implications, probably has some relevance for what may broadly
be called literary criticism. But I am moved to leave that ground
for a moment when I imagine the two books in terms of a possible confrontation between the "personifications" of barbarous
dissemination in one book and of playful permutations in the
other. My own feminist longings and readerly desire for poetic
justice make me unable to resist a temptation to shift the discursive ground from criticism to intervention. Instead of ana-
lytical categories, the two female protagonists begin to loom
independent from their texts, like participants in a very intimate, unscheduled but unavoidable, consciousness-raising ses-
sion. Deposed and displaced, Bárbara would surely have found
an empathetic interlocutor in Mamá Blanca, the exile from
paradise where she had learned how to listen to everyone. Their
hypothetical conversation, as I choose to imagine it, would manage to get beyond the inevitable racial and class differences,
although Bárbara's resentment toward the sheltered aristocratic
breeding of the white woman—white to her very name—would
surely make her wary of sharing indiscreet confidences. But
Blanca's unaffected tone, the nostalgia for Violeta that this
exorbitant guest would evoke, and especially the discreet but
knowing questions with which Blanca would make room for
Bárbara, would soon generate a friendly dialogue. They would
tell each other about their respective stories, stories already
written and, perhaps, those they might still write. Bárbara's resistance to this sort of intimacy would necessarily falter as she
considered the self-legitimating possibilities of the narrative
strategies developed by the author of her own memoirs. Incredulous, she would ask how Blanca managed to organize
her chapters so unsystematically, or how she could side with
Vicente and Daniel over her father, the legitimate authority of
the place. "What, you? A five-year-old authority? Don't make
me laugh. . . . You're right; why not laugh?"

If my mind wanders from time to time along the conciliatory

and syncretic narrative paths where Doña Bárbara could meet up with Mamá Blanca, it is probably because Blanca taught me to meander there. And if I needed any justification for imagining the meeting, I could quote her own (un)reason, not so much a lack of reason as an awareness that there was no need to be reasonable. The only excuse she gives for letting herself combine, distort, and reframe the stories her mother told her is, "Nobody told me I couldn't" (51; 33). Guided by her intertextual lead, I can hardly be expected to keep the stories about Bárbara and Blanca straight. And even if that were possible on my reading, I am convinced that she would have experimented with a dialogic (con)fusion between the two, had she heard the tale of the nostalgic old lady and the one about the despoiled cattle-boss. I am persuaded that the same five-year-old girl would have imagined them as I do: sitting together in the garden, sipping coffee, chatting and remembering a Venezuela "tan relejos," long, long ago (15; 5). The girl's own habit of blending and twisting her mother's stories is so contagious that it becomes useless for me to refrain from the narrative mixes that she herself prepares. How else can we listen to these compatriot and contemporary books after Blanca Nieves shows us the charm of listening actively?

Now the scene of her deceptively passive activity hardly seems promising. She is sitting in front of the big mirror in her mother's bedroom, this and every morning, getting her hair curled. Like a penitent for the sin of having straight hair, or like a convict for esthetic crimes with an insistent parole officer, Blanca Nieves suffers the daily humiliation of being only temporarily improved. But the Hegelian intuition of the ward hints to her about the power she exercises over the warden. If curls were the mandate, since curls are beautiful and "a woman's first duty is to be beautiful" (42–43; 27), Blanca's black head of hair would have to remain absolutely still in front of that disciplinary mirror; any lack of cooperation would frustrate the process. So her captive captor was forced to concede to a coterminous demand: to captivate the girl with stories as long as the curling process lasted. And just as the result of the curling would produce a pleasing excess, so the telling would be excessive, because Blanca Nieves sometimes insisted that the stories be repeated with unprecedented borrowings from other stories, with tragic endings required by some caprice and comic endings by another. The girl dictated, unpredictably, and the mother dutifully narrated. While her mother curled her straight hair, adjusting stepmother Nature to higher esthetic standards, the daughter was also stamping her creative will on the stories that she demanded for entertainment. Like her hair, those stories were mere raw material, the pretexts for supplements that never achieved stable or definitive shapes. In front of the great mirror that conspired in the daily ritual, mother and daughter supplemented all they wanted. This is certainly not the mirror that some female autobiographers complain can only frame them in the male gaze; nor is it Luce Irigaray's penetrating speculum, an instrument that promises to reflect on feminine interiority.[6] It is a screen for aimless projections, a compensatory diversion, a forced freedom to recount without being held accountable to models, or to nature.

We may also want to read this scene of manipulation as a figure for the primal scene of Hispano-American creativity, akin to Sarmiento's self-arrogation of authority every time he saw a hint of himself in an imperfect model. Contemplating themselves in the mirror of European and North American art, Latin Americans create specular distortions that return very different images or "identities" from that of putative models. The difference is not always parody but quite often represents a "correction" or an improvement of the adoptive parent culture, as we have seen in Latin American rewritings of Rousseau, Chateaubriand, Scott, Stendhal, Cooper, Balzac. Along with the acknowledgment of foreign authority comes the greater measure of local authority that can respect models and supersede them at the same time. Blanca's straight hair is evidently acknowledged in the curling process, but the rectilinear matter is returned with pleasing twists every time Blanca's mother wins her battle against nature. And the European stories come back from the mirror equally transformed, domesticated and perfected in various and contradictory ways. Far from being content with the foreign stuff, or from repeating it in servile imitations, the childish narrator was learning from her mother how to tangle, tie, and adjust the malleable matter in ways that kept giving it new life. There was no reason why established plots always had to coincide with their traditional developments, as little reason as there was to make names identify with their subjects or to make genders coincide with sexes.

Frustrated, bored, or offended by the ending of Bernardin de St. Pierre's *Paul et Virginie,* for example, where the chaste girl prefers to die in the storm at sea rather than expose her limbs enough to swim safely to her lover, Blanca Nieves sometimes demands a happy reunion. Although at other times she makes all the characters die together in a final cataclysm. On hearing "Beauty and the Beast," to mention another example, she decides that the metamorphosis at the end is an extraneous concession to those who cannot truly love. So, she has it omitted, charging that it is an offense to the noble Beast, and to her dog, Marquesa, whom she identified with the hero. "How wonderful!" Bárbara would interrupt, slapping her thigh and throwing her head back to laugh outloud. "You cast the bitch as hero!" "Of course," Blanca would giggle, "it was the only thing I never changed in that story."

> —Pero ya sabes, Mamá, que la Fiera se quede Fiera con su rabo, su pelo negro, sus orejotas y todo y que asimismo se case con la Bella. ¡Que no se vuelva Príncipe nunca! ¿Ya lo sabes?
> Mamá tomaba nota.
> Es inútil decir que Pablo y Virginia acababan a veces muy bien. Virginia salvada milagrosamente de las aguas caudalosas se casaba a menudo con Pablo y eran muy felices. Si dadas las circunstancias mi alma sentía un vago, voluptuoso deseo de bañarse en la tristeza, dejaba entonces que las cosas siguieran su curso normal:
> —Mamá, que llueva muchísimo, que crezca el río, que se ahogue la niñita y que se muera después todo el mundo.
> Mamá desencadenaba los elementos y la escena quedaba cubierta de crespones y cadáveres. (54)

["You remember, Mama, the Beast is to remain Beast, with his tail, his black hair, his ears and everything, and he is to marry the Beauty like that. He is never to become a Prince. You won't forget?"
Mama took due notice.
Naturally, *Paul and Virginia* at times had a happy ending. Virginia, miraculously saved from the flood waters, married Paul and they lived happily ever after. But if it so happened that my soul

felt a vague, voluptuous desire to immerse itself in grief, then I let things take their course.

"Mama, let it rain terribly hard, and the river rise, and the little girl drown, and then everybody die."

Mama unleashed the elements, and the scene was covered with crepe and corpses.] (35–36)

Little Snow White is infectiously willful, with her requirements for stories to fit her childish moods, and with the liberating lack of discrimination that lets her daydream about her mother's wedding on hearing *El Cantar de Mío Cid* (96–97; 65–66).

Reading her extravagant or extraneous demands, and watching them take pleasing shapes in the makeup mirror, goads me to reflect back on another possible narrative twist and to wonder what Bárbara and Mamá Blanca might have said to each other with their first introductions. "Good afternoon, I am Bárbara. I mean, I am called Bárbara and that's been a problem." "Oh, names are so absurd," Blanca would say with soothing levity, "it took me all these years and all these white hairs to fade into mine." Doña Bárbara, trained to recognize the indelible mark of barbarity in (or as) her calling, would be surprised to learn that, in Piedra Azul, names didn't announce characters with some supposed allegorical immediacy; instead, they alluded indirectly, almost against the grain, in the same way that the stories Blanca Nieves demanded were hardly self-identical but rather capricious misrepresentations. As for the visual language of faces and physical features (so expressive of Santos's superiority, Marisela's unwashed nobility, and Bárbara's unnatural appeal), it was no more reliable a code than other words in Piedra Azul. Marquesa was one incongruous example, another was the gentle peon nicknamed for a stinging bug: "Vicente Cochocho, who was a giant in kindness of soul, could hardly have been smaller in physical stature" (101; 69). These representational disencounters, multiplied throughout the memoirs, are instances of a general (and merciful) crisis of authority here. So, perhaps it will suffice to mention only one more emblematic failure to find transparent correspondence between expression and experience: the evident authority that the father wields is hardly a controlling force, since Vicente Cochocho and cowherd Daniel can both lord it over the master's "absolute power" (114; 78). Like Blanca Nieves under her mother's beautifying authority, the master's underlings understand his dependence on them. Daniel leaves graciously when Don Juan Manuel fires him for his scandalously personal treatment of the cows, because the employee knows long before the soon-desperate employer that he will be called back. And the patriarchal outrage caused by Vicente's multiple marriages or his occasional leadership of regional revolutions do little more than humiliate him and the master who is caught between principled pronouncements and his inability to let Cochocho go. By contrast, we saw Gallegos forcing the hierarchy, and the supporting verbal correspondences, into a tidy construction. That Santos is meant to rule, Altamira to command an encompassing vision, Bárbara to be banished, and El Miedo along with her, are all announced by their names. Hardly insensitive to verbal and narrative waywardness, *Doña Bárbara* is determined to erect a tight allegorical defense against surprises.

But in Piedra Azul, the end of verbal surprises is quite literally a discursive dead-end, death itself. As if to underline the paradoxical reasonableness of irrational and anti-allegorical naming—and of the generally liberating gap through which referents can escape, finally unnamed and unmanageable in any allegorical system—Blanca Nieves tells what happened once, by "mistake." It was the only time that her mother forgot her disdainful precaution against reality while naming her little girls. Tragically, she named one Aurora, the one who would die just as her life was beginning.

> El geniecillo exquisito y mal documentado que aproximando su boca al oído de Mamá le dictaba atolondrado nuestros nombres, acertó una vez. Su acierto fue funesto. No hay que tener razón. Para segar dichas no es indispensable sembrar verdades. Tú lo supiste, pobre Mamá, tú lo llevaste tatuado en lo más sensible de tu corazón. El haber acertado por casualidad una vez, debía costarte raudales de lágrimas. . . . Aurora fue la aurora. (157)

> [The charming, whimsical genie that carelessly whispered our names into Mamá's ear happened to be right in one instance. His accuracy proved fatal. It's wrong to be right. To reap happiness it

is not necessary to sow truth. Poor Mamá, you knew it, you bore it tattooed on the tenderest fibers of your heart. This having been accidentally right once was to cost you floods of tears. Aurora was the dawn.] (114)[7]

The self-identical sign, like a simple-minded equation too redundant to repeat, closes up all the space between the girl and the controlling symbolic order. By reaching its goal so directly, her name fixes her as an immobile sign; and she suffers the same fatality that dooms Bárbara. "Poor Aurora," Bárbara would agree, "and poor Mamá," because by now she will have caught on that, thanks to the fissured nature of language, and to the desire that language cannot (and perhaps refuses to) satisfy, words usually fail to name adequately. Luckily, the effort to name can become a continual game of hide and seek, frustrating for a "positivistic soul" such as the Governess Evelyn (55; 36), but hilarious in the disordered and aimless affections of Mamá and Mamá Blanca. If, by a paradoxical disfunction, the symbolic order occasionally functions the way it pretends to, it can produce a glimpse of what Lacan called imaginary harmony—a postulated, prelinguistic, immediacy between child and mother before spoken interventions by the father teach a rhythm of cleavages. That preconceptual, even prehuman, harmony is the rapport that some fathers imagine the mothers to foster; but mothers may choose to evade this dubious and debilitating honor, preferring to play in the gaps that the "order of the father" (of Gallegos, for example) dreams of closing up.[8]

Hardly discursive obstacles, the linguistic failures and maladjustments between desire and experience describe a playing field where Blanca Nieves and her mother enjoy re-creation. It was also the space enjoyed by María Eugenia, the young lady who wrote a diary out of boredom in Teresa de la Parra's first novel and who was sacrificed to convention like the Ifigenia of her title.[9] Certainly in this second novel, those disencounters constitute no communication crisis between mother and daughter, presumably exiled into a linguistic diaspora from which there is no going home. They no doubt understand each other very well, precisely because of their shared disappointments with a symbolic order in which, for example, hair should mean curls although it cannot always mean that. The current and future mothers make themselves accomplices in covering over the difference between reality and desired ends. But the process of curling, shaping, and deceiving becomes more than a compensatory process; it becomes a series of willful, creative impositions that inevitably reinscribe the gap. If, in Lacan's terms, that order belongs to "Poor Papa, . . . [who] took on in our eyes the thankless role of God" (31; 18), it may be because he demands that it work. He yearns to reconquer the supposed originary harmony by insisting that desire be satisfied, that signifiers *mean* their signifieds, without stopping to take creative advantage of the disappointments. He yearns, for instance, to reproduce himself perfectly in a male child who could carry on the legitimating name of the father. Each year, his renewed insistence would send his wife off, heavy with child, to Caracas where she would deliver another daughter. The mother, evidently, was taking her own sort of control of the paternal order, enjoying the annual and irremediable slips between intention and issue, the intention to introduce a son and the consecutive debuts of six little girls, an excessive production that nevertheless could not satisfy the father's unmovable desire. "The truth of the matter is that we never disobeyed him but once in our life. But that single time sufficed to disunite us without scenes of violence for many years. This great disobedience took place at the hour of our birth" (33; 20). Being born female was the original sin that had them expelled, not from maternal harmony but from the divine order of paternal paradise; yet thanks to the exile, these little women were also let loose in a fully humanized world where the constitutive distance between desire and realization, language and experience, gave them room to play. If they had been born male and fully legitimate for the father, perhaps their unauthorized games would have taken longer to develop.

A study in contrast is Primo Juancho, the girls' aging uncle who demonstrates better than anyone the mechanisms of verbal misfirings. But he seems stubbornly to delay any acknowledgment of a systemic difficulty. The impoverished old gentleman shows all the intellectual disorder these memoirs associate with great spirits, but he resists calling it that, because he worships positive programs even if they don't work. When one scientific scheme fails him, another quickly takes its place; the value of scientific thinking is never at issue. Juancho's verbal aim was as far off the mark as Mother's, but not by a choice that would make the best of an impossible system. He wanted to *make* a difference, not just to play with it. He would dream, for example, of being appointed to powerful government positions, but he "could not govern or direct anything, not for lack of ability, but because of too much thinking. His learning was his ruin" (73; 48). This is one unmistakable hint that at the end of the novel, after the plantation is sold to appease the father's family, the successful modernization of the new owner (let's call him Santos) is accomplished thanks, precisely, to the modernizer's limited knowledge. To organize anything rationally one has to make choices, to exclude, to resolve debates in favor of one speaker, in favor of one code of conduct, just as "Santos" would do in Piedra Azul and in Altamira. It was a narrowness that could not contain Juancho. (Dis)ordered arbitrarily, like an unbound dictionary (74–75; 50), which includes everything in scattered juxtapositions and metonymical relationships that need no hierarchy, and composed also like this almost static novel that recognizes Juancho's particular brand of purposeless heroism, and like Mamá Blanca herself, with her noisy failures in every practical venture (19; 8), cousin Juancho's exorbitant humanity gets in the way of his own positive projects.[10] In equal measure, his un-self-conscious flair for traitorous language manages to articulate, not the desired projects, but rather his loyalty to "the idealistic soul of our race" (86; 58). English-speaking Evelyn, for example, was brought by his insistence so that the girls would learn her "sane mentality and indispensable language." What happened instead was that Evelyn learned creolized Castilian, and spoke it badly, without definite articles. So the diametrically opposed result of Juancho's efforts to "Europeanize" the plantation was to instill there a love for indolent tolerance and for "Mamá's dulcet, affected, lilting Spanish" (85; 58).

Juancho would even trip himself up quite literally when his ideal code (alternately and conflictively positivist and chivalric) might fail at the moment of the communication he yearned for.

This happened, for instance, when he slipped on a fruit peel and fell on top of the very lady to whom he was preparing to bow on the street. The indignant woman made an inappropriately insulting remark, because she could never have understood this "master of etiquette" (77; 52). If we understand Juancho, and love him, perhaps it is because by now Blanca Nieves has taught us how admirable linguistic (verbal and gestural) misfires can be, especially when they attempt to respect a disinterested code of behavior out of date and dear to the same degree. Juancho lives from one disaster to the next without admitting that a quixotic pattern trails behind, a weave of idealized notions repeatedly surprised in their encounter with reality. And reality here is, by contrast, nothing more than a discourse that refuses to be surprised, exiling whatever is unpredictable as, by definition, unrealistic. It is a fatal discourse for Cousin Juancho whose ingenuousness amounts to an ethical posture. As if to insure our empathy, or at least to dramatize his almost helpless sense of wonder, these memoirs continually confront us as readers with the impossibility to predict anything, or to hold on to the stereotypes that might make our reading less hazardous, and perhaps less rigorously ethical.

It should not come as a surprise, therefore, that the young woman and friend who "edits" Mamá Blanca's posthumous memoirs criticizes herself for organizing, clarifying, and polishing what the old lady called, aware of how writing distances what it brings into focus, the "portrait of my memory" (23; 12). The young professional writer might have defended herself, nevertheless, by noting how Blanca Nieves loved to put her mother's stories in order, giving "unity to the whole" (51; 33). But the editor surely recognized a difference in the two procedures. Blanca Nieves would weave her stories together and take them apart, without worrying about achieving a final form or about the reception by an anonymous public. Her future friend deviated by submitting Blanca's loose pages to the kind of logical *Nachträglichkeit* that the vogue for biography imposes on diffuse material. The difference comes into relief against the background of continuity between these characters, since the old writer's pains to cultivate the young one suggest a transfer of mantle. Their contiguous relationship (literally at the piano or at the table) accounts, in fact, for much of the charm of their friendship. But the editor could not have forgotten that her indiscriminate transfer of text to a faceless public violates the old woman's confidence.

—Ya sabes, esto es para ti. Dedicado a mis hijos y nietos, presiento que de heredarlo sonreirían con ternura diciendo: "¡Cosas de Mamá Blanca!," y ni siquiera lo hojearían. Escrito, pues, para ellos, te lo legaré a ti. Léelo si quieres, pero no lo enseñes a nadie.... Este es el retrato de mi memoria ...

Siendo indiscreción tan en boga la de publicar Memorias y Biografías cortando aquí, añadiendo allá, según el capricho de biógrafos y editores, no he podido resistir más tiempo la correinte de mi época y he emprendido la tarea fácil y destructora de ordenar las primeras cien páginas ... a fin de darlas a la publicidad.... Mientras las disponía, he sentido la mirada del público lector, fija continuamente sobre mí como el ojo del Señor sobre Caín. (23)

[Now you know, this is for you. It is dedicated to my children and grandchildren, but I know that if it came into their hands they would smile tenderly and say: "One of Mamá Blanca's whims," and they wouldn't even bother to read it. It was written for them, but I am leaving it to you. You read it if you want to, but don't show it to anybody.... This is the portrait of my memory ...

Since the publication of Memoirs and Biographies has become one of the more fashionable indiscretions, cutting here, padding there, according to the taste of biographers and publishers, I have been unable to resist the trend of the times, and so I have undertaken the easy destructive task of arranging the first hundred pages ... to bring them to the public.... While I have been arranging them I have felt the eye of the reader fixed upon me like that of the Lord on Cain.] (12)

We readers, titillated by the illusion of conspiracy, read on; but this rather conventional ploy of arousing voyeuristic interest is more than that here. It is also a staging of the forced displacement narrated in the following pages, a proleptic loss of privacy with the sale of the plantation and the move to Caracas, which also amounts to the loss of a pointless freedom to make and unmake texts. By extending the continuity from Mamá Blanca, through the editor, to a general readership that can identify with the story, the introduction frames the impersonal process of modernization that will end Blanca Nieves's private haven and her narrative. And after her irresistible decision to bring the memoirs out, the modernizing agent reinscribes her fatal, Cain-like, guilt every time she transcribes (or invents) Mamá Blanca's own objections to fixing words in writing. "As many times as I have attempted to explain to you how Vicente talked and how Mamá talked, those two opposite poles, one the essence of rusticity and the other of refinement or preciosity, one in which the rhythm predominated, the other the melody, I have sadly realized the uselessness of my endeavor. The written word, I repeat, is a corpse" (111; 75). For the price of that guilt, however, the editor gains the purchase of a conflicted—modern—freedom. It allows her to resist a traditional and maternal authority by submitting to the contemporary sway of market and fame. It is as if she had learned from Mamá Blanca herself how to perform inside the contradiction between codes. Writing is a death that, paradoxically, assures the memory of what it has killed, not the death of "meaning" that might concern a more rigorously deconstructive reading so much as of musicality and gesture, always an impoverished, but also a repeatable, representation.

Far less tortured or coyly self-deprecating, the narrator of *Doña Bárbara* sees things differently. For this modernizer, the flatness and public visibility of writing are great advantages, not lamentable losses. They are the preconditions for distinguishing written and generally binding law from oral tradition, which amounts to distinguishing civilization from barbarism. This mandate to draw neatly demarcated terms of opposition would have been dangerously impatient with the plurivalent heteroglossia that survived in Piedra Azul. Blanca Nieves would find out that, after a while, Bárbara was left with no space between signifier and signified in which the feminine subject could enjoy re-creation. On the contrary, that space for enchantments, interpretations, and seductions was the measure of Bárbara's abnormality. The same kind of verbal and gestural freedom that made the naughty little girls of Piedra Azul charming, made Bárbara the target of a linguistic cleanup campaign. Her independence and power were interpreted as the wages of hatred, perversions of her female nature. By wedging a space between the word woman and her aggressive, virile persona, Bárbara had dared to untie the bond between virility and virtue, father and fatherland, and had sent the entire rationally demarcated system into motion. Obviously she had to be eliminated.

In Piedra Azul, by contrast, nothing is eliminated; all the rational and irrational discourses cohabit in common-law polygamy if not altogether legally, like Vicente and his two wives. Ancient and noble traditions, together with popular practices, eccentric superstition, races, generations, all occupy the same inclusive and static space. Everything coexists and each element enriches Piedra Azul, although the adults don't see it that way.

> Ni Evelyn (en su intransigencia inglesa y puritana), ni Mamá, ni Papá, ni nadie eran tampoco capaces de apreciar el buen sabor a español noble y añejo del vocabulario que empleaba Vicente. Nosotros sí, y porque lo apreciábamos lo copiábamos. Evelyn nos corregía asegurando severa que hablábamos vulgarmente; también Mamá nos corregía, pero ellas no tenían razón: la razón o supremo gusto estaba de parte de Vicente y de parte nuestra. Sólo muchos años después pude comprenderlo bien. Fue leyendo a López de Gómara, Cieza de León, Bernal Díaz del Castillo . . .
>
> Vicente decía, como en el magnífico siglo XVI, *ansina,* en lugar de así, *truje,* en lugar de traje; *aguaitar,* en lugar de mirar; *mesmo,* por mismo; *endilgar,* por encaminar; decía *esguazar,* decía *agora,* decía *cuasi,* decía *naide,* . . . (107–108)

[Neither Evelyn (with her British and Protestant intolerance) nor Mama nor Papa nor anyone could appreciate the flavor of the noble, vintage Spanish that comprised Vicente's vocabulary. We could and because we appreciated it we copied it. Evelyn corrected us, assuring us that we were talking vulgarly; Mama corrected us too, but they were both wrong. Right, or supreme good taste, was on the side of Vicente and us. Only many years later did I realize this. It was when I came to read López de Gómara, Cieza de León, Bernal Díaz del Castillo and other authors of the period who came to America and generously bequeathed us the Spanish which Vicente used, just as one uses a strong, solid, comfortable piece of old furniture inherited from one's ancestors. Vicente's Spanish was that of the Golden Age.] (72–73)

These very archaisms, which Harriet de Onís wisely decided not to translate and which are preserved by Teresa de la Parra as a precious inheritance of the original "American" language, were being presented at the same time in *Doña Bárbara*. And just consider the difference in presentation. Coming from Marisela, they really do seem to be the vulgarities that Evelyn and the girls' parents thought they heard in Piedra Azul. For Santos Luzardo, a man obsessed by the ideal of a centralizing and efficient language, variations are disturbances, or they are reduced to the opposition between correct and incorrect usage, and always, ultimately, between civilization and barbarism. By contrast to Sarmiento's pampa and to Gallegos's llano, Piedra Azul knows no barbarism. The narrator doesn't perceive it because her memoirs don't represent a fight to the death between two cultural-linguistic systems where the "other" is almost by etymological definition barbarous, or foreign. Bárbara is, of course, the "other," the one who competes with the Father.

It is possible that while she listens to Doña Bárbara's story, Mamá Blanca may come to the same conclusion about "other" being unfairly coded as evil, because there is abundant reason for thinking that the apparently ethical difference between civilization and barbarism is, as I have said, also a proprietary difference between mine and yours. In my imagined epilogue for their books, the two women would certainly develop a profound friendship based on their common and rending experience that made them "ex-centric." They are already absent from their ideal contexts, an absence that both allows for and obliges them to write. In one case, it is in order to supplement the emptiness that nostalgia leaves; in the other, writing is the caricature of another writer that banishes Bárbara and makes her absent. Long before she sat down to write her memoirs, Mamá Blanca evidently knew the value of distances, between names and people, between experience and the "portrait" of a life that she was writing. Her editor is no less sensitive to the calculus of loss and gain when she describes "my hands touching the places where now absent hands had lingered" (13; 3).[11] By extension, she is also describing how our hands caress the same pages and occupy an analogous position to hers in the chain of absences that paradoxically make our association possible. But Bárbara would only begin to conceive of absence as an opportunity now that she was far from the llano and planning to write her own story. Her version might take advantage of Mamá Blanca's appreciation for what was missing, her flair for narrative mismatches and contempt for absolutely binding signification, because in the other version, his version, Bárbara's history seems so terribly present. It pretends to be as coherent as if a person could signify anything so categorical as evil.

Gallegos declares the immediacy of his writing in the very first words, "Who goes with us?," where present tense and first-person plural interpellate the reader as participant. He writes as if interpretation and slips of meaning were entirely conquerable. And when he appeals to literary subtexts, as in the case of "Sleeping Beauty," it is not to remark on a literary continuity that may be affecting his own production. It is rather to enlist an apparently transparent allegory for didactic purposes, where Beauty is a figure for Marisela or Venezuela. But now that Gallegos has put us on the track of the allegorical possibilities of using fairy tales, Bárbara, or Blanca, or we, may continue to experiment where he stopped. Minds that lack the necessary discipline may wander beyond Gallegos's demarcations. We may think, for one obvious example in this epilogue, about the fairy tale of Snow White while we reread his Sleeping Beauty. And perhaps by this path of associative reading, as well as through the writerly leads given by Parra's heroine, we can imagine a feminist rereading of *Doña Bárbara* through Snow White. In the fairy-tale version, the heroine is a good little girl, good fundamentally because she is a little girl. That is, she is innocent because, at her prepubescent age, she lacks the maternal power to reproduce herself in daughters. The mother (stepmother here, in order to underscore their discontinuity) is necessarily evil, basically because she exercises power that challenges the father. Sandra Gilbert and Susan Gubar offer these provocative observations and add that the supposed real mother in the story had died shortly after giving birth, as if that very demonstration of maternal power somehow annulled her validity as mother.[12] This apparent absurdity, and the radical separation of mother and daughter (Bárbara and Marisela) in this story so basic to our Western narrative habits, represents a kind of Oedipal struggle between parent and child in which father is the prize. It is a construct of familial relationships that has by now been shaken by tools in feminist psychoanalysis that describe female development as a process of continuity and extension with the mother and by a feminist literature that disarticulates inherited models.[13] There is probably no better example of the literary assaults on the Oedipal model than *Las memorias de Mamá Blanca,* where the spatial figures of extension and metonymy become the very principles of narrative organization. Here the bedroom mirror is no magic mirror on the wall to judge competing women's worth, no determining voice of the absent and desired father as in the fairy tale, but the projection screen for a mother's hands entwined in her daughter's hair while they become accomplices in creative daydreaming.

If Bárbara had the chance to write her own story, inspired as much by the "evil" (enterprising) Queen as by that other Snow White, the naughty, oxymoronically dark one, perhaps she could have extended her entrepreneurial plotting to include literary plot-making in the demonic reflections of her own witch's conjuring table. There she would surely have enjoyed the twists she could give to some of the neat lines of the patriotic "epic" named for her. The heroic genre, always told with the suffocating self-respect of the victor, was no place for a woman's willful tangles. Perhaps, in the untidy novelized result that her literary conjuring might produce, there would have been more room for mothers to be accompanied by their daughters.[14] In Gallegos's version, mother and daughter get together too, but as antagonists, when Marisela barges into Bárbara's bedroom to confront the "witch" who is casting a spell on Santos. The women fight (over him) and Santos overturns Bárbara's advantage by breaking in to save the girl.[15]

It is entirely possible that my rereading against the grain of *Doña Bárbara* may seem a bit perverse, and short of perverse it may be at least anachronistic or irresponsible.[16] No one should forget the importance that Rómulo Gallegos had as figurehead for the Generation of 1928 that opposed dictator Juan Vicente Gómez. And of course it is true that his 1929 novel did much to build bases for the victorious populism of Acción Democrática. The educator, author, and president was, without a doubt, "progressive," advocating as he did a binding legal system as well as economic development that would promote general prosperity and welfare. To a great degree, modernization did, in fact, equal social improvement. And there is no question that it was preferable to Gómez's outmoded authoritarianism that organized the state as if it were his personal estate. Perhaps the one, halting worry that I would like to voice in the dialogic pause that Bárbara would give to Gallegos's epic flow is an observation about a certain rhetorical and emotive continuity between populism and personalism. Both kinds of political culture tend to be centralizing under the leadership of a practically cultlike figure. And although the centralizing project in a populist novel like *Doña Bárbara* grounds itself in a legal and apparently impersonal system, the victorious result seems suspiciously like the problem it has conquered. With even more clarity than the novel, the movie script that Gallegos later prepared, dramatizes the coincidence. The problem that Santos has come to resolve is the absolute power that Bárbara wields on the llano. And the solution celebrated at the end of the movie is the almost equally absolute power that Santos has wrested from her. By then his cousin and possible rival for real estate has conveniently died, Marisela has learned to speak correct Spanish, and Bárbara has taken the lady's way out, disappearing into the background. First she and then he are in control. Between them is what might be called a metaphoric relationship; a semantic substitution that, however radical, does not destabilize the verbal organization. The invariable is the protagonist's position as leader. This simple observation suggests the possibility that some authoritarian habits might survive in a populist project that, say, could not satisfy the popular demands it helped to formulate.

It seems hardly promising, by contrast, that Teresa de la Parra was never really concerned about progressive or popular demands. Even her feminism was, in her own words, quite moderate and never went so far as suffrage.[17] For many readers she tended to be rather conservative, even reactionary in the strictest sense of the term, given her pride in illustrious forebears, the charm and refinement that distinguished her in elegant society, and her alleged nostalgia for colonial life.[18] Born in Paris and raised on the family's sugar plantation outside of Caracas until she was ten, when her father died and the family moved to Spain, Parra's short life of shuttling back and forth between Spain and France—with short stays in Venezuela and visits to Cuba and Colombia—was given to the re-creation of a lost world. More poignantly absent from Venezuela (and from her truncated childhood) than la Avellaneda was from Cuba, Teresa de la Parra knew just as well how to turn distance to literary advantage. One might call her compensatory writing project reactionary, in terms of literary as well as political history, because it reverts to the episodic, loosely articulated, "costumbrista" literature that produced static "portraits" of rural life, the same word Mamá Blanca used for her memoirs. This characterization, though, is excessively simple; it comes from the kind of political imagination that reduces everything to left and right, to good and bad, to a binarism as proper and constraining as Santos Luzardo's language. Instead of forcing her into one pole or another, one might place her more commodiously on an anarchic tangent. If her persona Mamá Blanca is conservative, it is because she wants to conserve everything, from the most archaic practices to the most unpredictable variations on the modern, like the special brand of Spanish without articles that Evelyn perfected. Blanca refuses to thoughtlessly equate new with improved and thus leaves room for those whom history, and even her adored mother as well as her "all-powerful" father, would marginalize and finally erase. What is more, she orchestrates a rhythmic and melodious polyphony from the equal linguistic marginality of each inhabitant of Piedra Azul, a concerted simultaneity of sound supported by the contiguous and metonymic mapping of the place, where it would be impossible to substitute anyone (metaphorically) without sacrificing the general effect.

With an analogous and imitative gesture, I might find a tangent from which to preserve the politically promising aspects of this novel: its tolerance, flexibility, and the merciful "incoherence" of its multiple voices.[19] If one cared to extract a moral from all this, it could be suggested, perhaps, that marches of progress might take note where and on whom they step;

otherwise, progress may turn into something else, as it did for some critics of Acción Democrática when it "progressively" silenced internal voices that challenged party leadership. To step (or sidestep) gingerly might be preferable, and not necessarily utopian. The Nicaraguans, for example, were learning this lesson in the wake of trespassing on too many Misquito settlements. After the surprisingly effective resistance of the Indians, whose refusal to submit to Nicaraguan centralism had identified them merely as obstacles for some time, the state questioned the political virtues of insisting on a centralized, Spanish-language culure. A linguistically and culturally diverse polity no longer seemed an impossibly complex alternative to unattainable uniformity. One real concession was that the constitution ratified in 1987 made provisions for locally legislated education in which a Spanish-speaking teacher could no longer take the place of one who speaks Misquito, or English, or Rama. The polity was beginning to understand itself by metonymic accretion rather than by metaphoric substitution.

Teresa de la Parra's reluctance to assign definitive meanings to words, and her framing of what might be called a feminine lineage by an introduction that stages a transfer of text between two women, makes my mind wander in another direction from where Bárbara meets Blanca. Besides the literary confrontation with foundational fathers like Gallegos, Parra's book invites us—and her three lectures on "The Influence of Women in Forging the American Soul" direct us—on a trail of continuity with other women writers. In these talks, which she was invited to deliver about her life and work in Cuba and Caracas, Parra prefers to put herself in good company rather than to make a tokenized spectacle of her female self. She mentions Delmira Agustini and Gabriela Mistral as admirable contemporaries and then arches back to America's beginnings, with Queen Isabel's humanizing influence and Doña Marina's multilingual agility, to linger on the accomplishments of Sor Juana Inés de la Cruz, quote whole poems by the pseudonymous "Amarylis" ("How many Amarylises have lived since then behind our latticed cities watching life go by!"),[20] and remember her own grandmothers and aunts to whom the nation is indebted. This catalogue of

foremothers arouses a speculation on the possibility that finding and pausing at imperfect meanings may be a common feature among the most interesting women writers of Spanish
America. I cannot help thinking that it is because their keen
sense of irony comes from being over- (or under-) whelmed
before a verbal system that cannot correspond to their lived
experience. By dramatizing the incommensurability between
experience and expression, they keep pointing to a gap between available words and the world, a valuable pointer for
rereading male Latin American writers as well. Perhaps the
women's obsessive discourse of disencounters derives, in part,
from a certain feminine distancing, either reticence about public scrutiny or playfulness, from a language of stable authority.[21]
In that case, being a woman and therefore marginalized may
be, how ironic, a real esthetic advantage, somewhat like Eve's
fall and expulsion from paradise (followed by Adam), a transgression that makes women creatively compensatory. This is the
way Blanca Nieves, at least, understands her humble superiority
over her "brother" Violeta.

> Yo admiraba a Violeta en las mismas proporciones en que Violeta
> me desdeñaba a mí. Era natural. Yo podía apreciar la puntería de
> sus pedradas y la elegancia de sus maromas, mientras que a ella
> no le era dado contemplar aquellos brillantes cortejos de príncipes
> y hadas que tras de mi boca abierta asistían con magnificencia a
> las bodas de Pablo y Virginia. Era yo respecto a ella lo que es en
> nuestros días cualquier poeta respecto a cualquier campeón de
> football, de la natación o del boxeo: es decir, nada. Pero mi humilde
> superioridad aplastada y oscura tenía su encanto. Mis ensueños
> limpios de todo aplauso, asaeteados por Violeta y desbaratados por
> Evelyn, al igual de un arbusto después de una poda, reflorecían a
> escondidas con más abundancia y mayor intensidad. (57)

> [My admiration for Violeta was in inverse ratio to her contempt
> for me. It was only natural. I could appreciate the accuracy of her
> stone throwing and the elegance of her acrobatics, whereas she
> could not see those brilliant corteges of princes and fairies which,
> behind my gaping lips and ecstatic eyes, attended the marriage of
> Paul and Virginia. In her eyes my status was that of a poet as
> compared to a football, swimming, or boxing champion; that is to
> say, negligible. But my poor trampled, cowed superiority had its

charms. My hidden dreams, transfixed by Violeta's arrows, rudely
shattered by Evelyn, like a pruned tree, only flowered with greater
lushness and intensity.] (37–38)

If women, more consistently than men, are exiled from the
athletic paradise where signifiers reach their signifieds, it is possible that their conscious frustration may become an incitation
to play with possible miscombinations. In other words, thanks
to our disobedience and our deterritorialization, we already
remark on the arbitrariness of authority.[22]

It may easily, and correctly, be objected that this kind of
distancing or defamiliarization is constitutive of all writing, and
that language, by its allegorical nature, necessarily dramatizes
the absence that it hopelessly strives to fill in. Nevertheless,
differences matter among the many possible ways to manage
that tension between desired but unattainable presence (of
truth, of authority, nature, etc.) and the absence left in the short
fall of words that don't reach their referents. Indifference to
the variations would be strangely to lose sight of the same deconstructive terms that bring the absences into focus. Gallegos,
for one, may be as keenly aware as Parra that his language can
be treacherous; but his punitive policy for traitors is quite unlike
her amused benignity. Faced with the restlessness that makes
writing run away with lived experience, she manages, not by
consigning them both to closer quarters, but by acknowledging
the futility of authorial discipline.

This is not the first time we have noticed a woman's bemuse-
ment or complaint about an uncooperative language. We saw
it in Gertrudis Gómez de Avellaneda's *Sab*, where an entire
glossary of racially identified color categories was unequal to the
description of Cuba's most typical resident. Signification was an
indirect process in which, for example, black, white, and yellow
couldn't quite describe Sab and yet suggested him by a double-
play of composite and default. Signification was as indirect as
Sab's letter writing to Teresa, while Carlota was the ideal but
unreachable destination. Like Mamá Blanca's memoirs, written
for her sons and yet delivered to an adoptive daughter, Sab's
authoritative letter was handed over to a sympathetic accom-

plice. On the same tangent of women's circuitous communications, I am tempted to add that soon after Avellaneda's novel, three Argentine women took advantage of the political indeterminacy following Rosas's defeat to clear some discursive space for themselves in the journal they published, anonymously, a journal called *La Camelia* and dedicated to "Liberty, not license: equality between both sexes [secsos]" (April 11, 1852).[23] One strategy was to introduce themselves, indirectly of course, in their anonymity, with analogously (in)appropriate signs to those Avellaneda used for Sab: "Without being pretty little girls, we are neither old nor ugly." In that same generation, writers like Rosa Guerra, Juana Manuela Gorriti, Mercedes Rosas de Rivera, and Juana Manso were taking issue with their Unitarian fathers and husbands over the unitary and limiting language that was sure to reproduce some of the same abuses they opposed in Rosas. In its stead, the women cultivated a heterogeneous national discourse, in which Indian languages, Italian, Gallician, English, and gaucho dialects made a heteroglossic mix with standard Spanish.[24] At the same time, they staged complaints about specious associations that particular words force, associations like family and fatherland, or feminine and frivolous. If home was the site for establishing civilized social relations, as the male Generation of 1837 never tired of saying, then the women demanded consistent and balanced foundations for the new national family. Wives had to assume equal responsibility and equal rights; otherwise the celebration of an unexamined domesticity would backfire and mire the country in feudal, barbarous habits.

From this tangent, it is easy to note the unmistakable difference between their straining for consistency and Parra's straying. Her almost aggressive defense of incoherence is the other side of their demand for fits between family and state. Where they and perhaps Avellaneda may feel their marginality to authoritative language as an exclusion, she feels it as a liberation. This constitutive distancing from absolutes may be common to all literature, but it is not always as self-reflexive or as promising as in Parra, and to other degrees in Avellaneda and her Argentine contemporaries. It doesn't always provide, as it does for them, a negotiating point from which to wrest a furlough from the prison-house of language, or at least an account for redecoration.

From her particular cell, disobedient Sister Juana Inés de la Cruz (1648–1695), the model for generations of naughty novice writers including Teresa de la Parra, had time to reflect on her own relationship to language. The prospect of strategically manipulating the impossibility of language obviously appealed to her, and never so much as when she was preparing her famous response to Sor Filotea. The superior had just instructed her ward to desist from debating with church authorities and also from pursuing secular studies of literature and science. These were unauthorized activities for a woman who had joined a religious order. But the feminized signature on the strident reprimand reveals some reserve, because Sor Juana's superior and confessor was a man, the bishop of Puebla. Signing as "Sister Friend of God," he was probably attempting to cover over his requirements by casting them as appeals to the nun's sense of common decency. Earlier, the bishop had encouraged his spiritual charge to be more daring, when he urged her to dust off a forty-year-old provocation by the Portuguese Jesuit Vieyra about the nature of Christ's virtues and then had her criticism published and circulated. Sor Juana's brilliant casuistry—in the critique the bishop published and called "Carta Atenagórica" (after the goddess of wisdom)—was more proof of women's ability than he would later want. As candidate for archbishop of Mexico, competing with a Spanish Jesuit who was Vieyra's personal friend, and also as a man whose ecclesiastical career boasted special attention to the education of women, it had been important for the confessor to demonstrate his special contribution to Mexican society through women's accomplishments. But once he lost the competition to the Spaniard, an incorrigible misogynist, the Mexican bishop chose to make amends by making Sor Juana repent of her presumption to argue with men.[25] She was, however, hardly the pious pawn to be moved forward and backward as he pleased. Sor Juana's response to his reprimand is to heap one self-legitimating argument on another, to overdetermine her right to write.

Many readers remember the scant autobiographical details

about her irrepressible, God-given intelligence (anthologized time and again): how she would steal off behind an older sister to learn to read and write; how she would punish herself with unwanted haircuts and dessert deprivation for not learning fast enough; how she dazzled the doctors at court with her wit and erudition; and how she entered the convent as a sanctuary for learning, free from the responsibilities of marriage and children. Other readers are beginning to value the impressive tradition of foremothers Sor Juana constructs (mixing and matching Catholic saints with pagan and heretical victims of the church) in order to license herself in their company.[26] This kind of self-celebration through other notable women evidently appealed to Parra, who repeated the scheme in her talks. But I would like to call attention, in the present context, to her literary critical arguments (hardly ever acknowledged as far as I know) about the instability and the infinite interpretability of any text, including those called sacred texts. When her confessor suggested that she dedicate herself to the exegesis of sacred scripture, he seemed to have forgotten that the terrain would be as slippery as that of the profane letters in which she dabbled. The effort, she feared, would distance her more than ever from the authoritative doctrine of the church. If Virgil, Homer and all the great poets and orators are subject to (mis)interpretation, Holy Scripture is no less so, according to her. It is fraught with grammatical difficulties, such as using plurals for singulars, switching from second to third persons, giving adjectives a genitive rather than an accusative case, and replacing feminine for masculine genders.[27]

This last category calls special attention to itself by its boldness and baldness; it is the only one that appears without examples. Certainly not because examples of gender slippage don't exist in the Bible; Sor Juana must have known some to conceive of the category at all.[28] Instead, it is likely that she omitted the target examples because her target here was the confessor himself, the male authority, disguised in the epistolary crossdressing of Sor Filotea, who was hoping to simulate an identification with the (in)subordinate nun and to gain her confidence. Sor Juana, of course, has no choice but to let him have it, his way. At the same time, though, she takes advantage of the transparent fiction to dramatize how unstable and flexible attributions of gender can be. And so, excusing herself, with a wagging tongue barely contained in her cheek, she ends her response by reminding her confessor that if she has been transgressive of gender proprieties, it is because he taught her how it is done. She begs "forgiveness of the homely familiarity, and the less than seemly respect in which by treating you as a nun, one of my sisters, I have lost sight of the remoteness of your most illustrious person; which, had I seen you without your veil, would never have occurred."[29] To be sure, it would have been less strategic for the bishop to have attempted a more naked intervention, because it would have insured his absence from the convent. In order to feign his presence there, he absents himself as a man by covering over the difference. It's not that his game fails to convince his ideal reader, but that the bishop himself is reluctant to play it to the logical end. Sor Juana, by comparison, has no hesitations and forces him into the next move. The confessor may have been criticizing her for presuming the kind of ecclesiastical authority reserved for men, but what he acts out is his equal flexibility as a gendered sign. To enter into debate with her, he had to "(a)veil" himself of a female identity, neither superior nor inferior to his opponent.

I will not insist on many more examples, primarily because this chapter might become far too long and also because it may not be necessary. Nevertheless, Sor Juana's inspiration, the catalogue of matriarchs that she and then Parra prepared in their self-presentations, lead me by an irresistible mimetic desire for remembering good company to mention some works that dramatize what might be called a feminist distancing in language. One favorite is *Balún Canán* (1957) by Rosario Castellanos, a novel narrated by a seven-year-old girl who can't seem to make the racial and sexual codes in conflict around and through her coincide with the scenes she puts together. Her initial ingenuous confusion never clears up; it becomes fixed, repeating the fragmentation of a Mexico that never manages to congeal into a society and repeating also the national language that excludes, more than it includes, Indian territory. By way of the discursive clashes in the book, between Indians and whites, women and men, workers and landowners, Castellanos writes an anti-*Bildungsroman,* a personal history without development or goal. Another favorite writer is Clarice Lispector (1926–1977), that ingenious narrator of the domestic uncanny, who makes perfectly quotidian situations gnawingly grotesque by the same kind of static focusing and disturbing repetitions that can make women's lives unbearbly familiar. With her, I also remember Luisa Valenzuela, whose best stories in *Cambio de armas* (1982), defamiliarize a politico-linguistic system that doesn't correspond with her logic of loving.

But perhaps the most dramatic example of what I would like to call an esthetic tradition of feminine estrangement is the testimony given by Rigoberta Menchú, the young Quiché woman of Guatemala who learned Spanish in order to organize a multi-ethnic resistance to government expropriations and violence. She, even more than the childish narrators or the social pariahs, is a newcomer to the system of language in which she must defend herself. Her special treatment of Spanish is often a reminder of her social marginality, not a marginality to one particular ideological code from a sense of belonging to another, but a repeated posture of the linguistic bricoleuse who combines native traditions of the Popol Vuh with Catholicism, ethnic exclusivity with national struggles and with marxism, because she has learned that no one code fits or contains her. The lack of fit is also the mark of her advantage as a new speaker, one who maintains her distance from and in language, who translates unheard-of expressions to express unheard-of experiences. Not all those experiences are meant for a Spanish-speaking readership, though. And Rigoberta's most telling reminder of her difference is a cautious reluctance to get everything right, as cautious as Mamá's deceptively irresponsible habit of naming little girls. It is surprising, I think, to come continually upon passages in the testimonial where Rigoberta purposely withholds information. Of course the audible protests of silence may well be responses to anthropologist Elizabeth Burgos—Debray's line of questioning. If she were not asking particular questions, the informant would logically have no reason to refuse answers. But what is noteworthy here is the way Rigoberta's refusal to tell secrets remains on the page after the editing is done. Either the informant, the scribe, or both were determined to keep a series of admonitions in the published text. From the beginning, the narrator tells us ever so clearly that she is not going to tell: "Indians have been very careful not to disclose any details of their communities."[30] By some editorial or collective decision, the very last words of the testimonial are, "I'm still keeping secret what I think no-one should know. Not even anthropologists or intellectuals, no matter how many books they have, can find out all our secrets."[31] Yet the almost 400-page book is full of information: about Rigoberta herself, her community, traditional practices, the armed struggle, strategic decisions. A reader may therefore wonder what she means by referring to secrets that "cannot be known," and why so much attention is being called to our insufficiency as readers? Is she saying that we are *incapable* of knowing or that we as subjects of a centralized and centralizing culture *ought* not to know (just as Mamá *ought* not to have announced Aurora's name), for reasons of ethnic safety?

Paradoxically, perhaps, the writer who most cleverly keeps us (and herself) at a safe distance from a hegemonic Hispanic culture was the one who seems to have fit in most effortlessly. I am referring again to Teresa de la Parra, writing though a childish narrator who knows, without bragging, that she and her sisters were at "the center of this Cosmos" (30; 17). That's why she explains, defamiliarizing the familiar form of address, everyone referred to them in the royal second-person singular: "Thou" (110; 75). Defamiliarization here doesn't suppose a lack of familiarity with the modern world, as in Rigoberta's case, or a grotesque decomposition as in Lispector's. It assumes a virtually divine sense of security that turns everything into raw material available for manipulation, an absolute security that recognizes with more humor than horror the space between, say, regal and familial appeals for attention. It is also a security that authorizes simultaneous linguistic differences, holding them together with the loose bonds of indulgent love, since, as Avellaneda, Castellanos, Menchú, and many others would discover too, no one code is entirely adequate to the narrative.

Those horizontal bonds, dramatized by the *Memorias'* episodic organization, by the scene of writing and rewriting in the proliferating mirror, and finally by the narrator's caution against confusing change with progress, may remind us of one of the promises that, according to Benedict Anderson, novels made to their first Latin American readers. It was to open their imaginations to the idea of an inclusive national community by including them all, horizontally, in one flexible and secular concept of calendrical time. If the foundational fictions of the nineteenth century and the populist romances that revised them for anti-imperialist projects tended to take the inclusions for granted and to strain forward rather than laterally, pulling time into straight, rational lines that go from barbarism to civilization, and if the recurrent pattern of Boom novels can be visualized as a vicious circle that reaches the end of patriotic history to find out that end no longer means goal, this feminist novel stops the dynamic or the dizzying movement. Instead of a straight line or a circle, the shape of *Las Memorias de Mamá Blanca* is fanlike. It unfolds a bit wider with every page to make room for the next speaker, only hinting that the central fulcrum is being manipulated by one who was born in the center. But the design she produces is hardly the hegemonic or pyramidal structure of founding fictions. It is an acknowledgement of the mutual dependence of every fold on the others.[32] Anything less would fail to capture the polyphonic airs of a society so admirable for its complexity.

Notes

1. PART I: IRRESISTIBLE ROMANCE

1. See Carlos Fuentes, *La nueva novela latinoamericana* (Mexico: Joaquín Mortiz, 1969), and his admirer José Donoso's charming self-indulgence: "the monumental omnipresence of the mighty [literary] grandfathers engendered . . . fathers weakened by their preoccupation with their brief tradition." The next generation was "fatherless, but, because of that missing link, without a tradition which might enslave us." José Donoso, *The Boom in Spanish American Literature: A Personal History*, trans. Gregory Kovakos (New York: The Center for Inter-American Relations, 1977): 12.

Cortázar, at least, modestly admitted the continuity in his interview "Un gran escritor y su soledad: Julio Cortázar," *Life en Español* 33, 7 (Mexico, April 1969): 43–55. Also translated in Rita Guibert's *Seven Voices* (New York: Vintage, 1973).

2. Julio Cortázar "Approach to Lezama Lima," from *Vuelta al día en ochenta mundos* (Mexico: Siglo XXI, 1967), trans. Naomi Lindstrom, in *The Review for Contemporary Literature* 3, 3 (Fall, 1983): 22–26.

3. Joyce, Faulkner, and Kafka are the most often cited masters. As for debts to the nineteenth century, Vargas Llosa for example dedicated an entire book to his multiple rereadings of Flaubert, in which he never mentions the titillation he surely experienced in *María* or other standard school classics. See *The Perpetual Orgy: Flaubert and Madame Bovary* (New York: Farrar, Straus, Giroux, 1986).

4. See Severo Sarduy, "El barroco y el neobarroco," in *América Latina en su literatura*, ed. César Fernández Moreno (Mexico: Siglo XXI, 1972): 167–184.

5. In *La nueva novela latinoamericana*, Fuentes accounts for circularity, or for the novels' collapse of eternity into one moment, through the "mythic" quality of new narrative which, he says, makes it universal, p. 64.

6. The novelty is evident from Alejo Carpentier's preface-manifesto to *The Kingdom of This World* (1949), where he complained that "magic realism" was everywhere in Latin American history except for its literature. See his "De lo real maravilloso americano," in *Literatura*

y conciencia política en América Latina (Madrid: Alberto Corazón, 1969): 116–117.

7. See Doris Sommer and George Yúdice, "The Boom in Spanish American Literature: A General Introduction," in *Postmodern Fiction: A Bio-Bibliographical Guide,* ed. Larry McCaffery (Westfield: Greenwood Press, 1986): 189–214; and Fredric Jameson, "On Magic Realism in Film," *Critical Inquiry* 12, 2 (Chicago, Winter 1986): 301–325, where he measures the "enfeebled" postmodern history of glossy nostalgia films in America against the historically dense Latin American cinema he calls "magic realist."

8. See "The Boom Twenty Years Later: An Interview with Mario Vargas Llosa," *Latin American Literary Review* 15, 29 (January–June 1987): 201–206. "When I wrote my first novels, I wanted very much to be modern. I wanted to differentiate myself from previous Latin American writers. The other Latin American writers and I were in a kind of war against what was Latin American narrative at the time, which was very conventional, and written by writers who didn't pay much attention to formal problems. I wanted to be different. Many Latin American writers still want to carry out a formal revolution. And this has become in some cases a kind of new tradition—the tradition of experimentation and of being modern," p. 202.

Emir Rodríguez Monegal comes to the same observation in "Tradition and Renewal," in *Latin America in Its Literature,* ed. César Fernández Moreno and Julio Ortega, trans. Mary G. Berg (New York: Holmes & Meier, 1980): 87–114.

9. Percy B. Shelley, "Poets are the unacknowledged legislators of the world." "A Defence of Poetry" (1821).

10. Pedro Henríquez Ureña, *Literary Currents in Hispanic America,* "The Charles Eliot Norton Lectures, 1940–1941" (Cambridge: Harvard University Press, 1945): 243.

11. Henríquez Ureña, p. 185.

12. Henríquez Ureña, p. 187.

13. See Richard Chase, *The American Novel and Its Tradition* (Baltimore: The Johns Hopkins University Press, 1983; originally Anchor Books, 1957): 13.

14. This is Leslie Fiedler's first point in *Love and Death in the American Novel* (New York: Stein and Day, rev. ed. 1966): 23.

15. Benedict Anderson, *Imagined Communities: Reflections on the Origin and Spread of Nationalism* (London: Verso, 1983): 30.

16. See the beginning of Gramsci's *Notes on Italian History.* See also Chantal Mouffe, ed., *Gramsci and Marxist Theory* (London: Routledge & Kegan Paul, 1979): 181. "[A] hegemonic class has been able to ar-

ticulate the interests of the other social groups to its own by means of ideological struggle. This, according to Gramsci, is only possible if this class renounces a strictly corporatist conception, . . . and presupposes a certain equilibrium, that is to say that the hegemonic groups will make some sacrifices of a corporate nature."

17. Neil Larsen writes that the problem, inverted from the one Gramsci studied in Italy, was that with Independence the Latin American bourgeoisie took over a state to which citizens felt little belonging. *Modernism and Hegemony: A Materialist Critique of Aesthetic Agencies* (Minneapolis: University of Minnesota Press, 1990), chap. 4.

18. A recent, typically unexamined version is Samuel A. Arango's *Origen y evolución de la novela hispanoamericana* (Bogotá: Tercer Mundo, 1988).

19. Djelal Kadir, *Questing Fictions: Latin America's Family Romance* (Minneapolis: University of Minnesota Press, 1986): 4.

20. Before the "modernist disencounters" by the last quarter of the century, literature *was* politics, as Julio Ramos boldly puts it. Literature provided the civilizing "code" that would conquer barbarism as surely as the civil codes being promulgated by the same writers. Julio Ramos, *Desencuentros de la modernidad en América Latina: Literatura y Política en el siglo XIX* (Mexico: Fondo de Cultura Económica, 1989): 62–63.

21. Jean-François Lyotard, *The Postmodern Condition: A Report on Knowledge,* trans. Geoff Bennington and Brian Massumi, foreword by Fredric Jameson (Minneapolis: University of Minnesota Press, 1984).

22. Paul Veyne, *Writing History,* trans. Mina Moore-Rinvolucri (Middletown: Wesleyan University Press, 1984). In one chapter called "History Does Not Exist," Veyne makes a point similar to Bello's but makes it more generally: "Science is de jure incomplete; history alone can be allowed de facto to have gaps—because it is not a fabric, it has no weave," p. 18.

23. Andrés Bello, "Autonomía cultural de América" (1848), in *Conciencia intelectual de América,* ed. Carlos Ripoll (New York: Eliseo Torres, 1966): 48–49. An editor's note informs that the present title "has been used in various Anthologies to present this piece."

24. The grammar represented one side of the debate with romantic youths who preferred autonomous variations of Spanish. A fine review of the not-so-oppositional argument, mostly with Domingo Faustino Sarmiento, is by Julio Ramos, *Desencuentros* . . . , chap. 2. See also Allan Woll, *A Functional Past: The Uses of History in Nineteenth Century Chile* (Baton Rouge: Louisiana State University Press, 1982). In his Prólogo to the *Gramática de la lengua castellana, dedicada al*

uso de los americanos (Santiago, 1847), reproduced in *Obra literaria,* ed. Pedro Grases (Caracas: Biblioteca Ayacucho, 1979): 553–558, Bello argues for grammatical contours flexible enough to allow Spanish its vitality in America and yet sturdy enough to safeguard communication and continuity. The balance would avoid both the brittle pedantry of Latin (which broke down along national boundaries in Europe) and the consequent proliferation of mutually incomprehensible languages. For a sense of Bello's vast foundational work, see the volumes published in honor of the bicentennial of his birth, *Bello y Chile, Bello y Londres,* and *Bello y América Latina* (Caracas: Fundación La Casa de Bello, 1981–1982).

25. Bernardo Subercaseaux's informative "Filosofía de la Historia Novela y Sistema Expresivo en la Obra de J. V. Lastarria (1840–1848)," *Ideologies and Literature* 3, 11 (Nov.–Dec. 1979): 56–83, draws the polemical lines clearly by suggesting, perhaps correctly, that Bello's preference for narrative amounts to empiricism.

26. As if heeding this advice, whether he knew it or not, the Spanish ambassador to Chile would write a biography/history of Valdivia and call it a novel. José M. Doussinague, *Pedro de Valdivia: O la novela de Chile* (Madrid: Espasa Calpe, 1963).

27. Bartolomé Mitre, "Prólogo" to *Soledad* (Buenos Aires: Editorial Tor, Lecturas Selectas, n.d.): 9.

28. For a useful collection of these manifestoes, see *Los novelistas como críticos,* ed. Norma Klahn and Wilfrido H. Corral (forthcoming in coedition by Fondo de Cultura Económica of México and Ediciones del Norte, Hanover, N.H.).

29. José Martí, *Obras completas* (Havana: Editorial Ciencias Sociales, 1975), 23: 290.

30. Martí to Galván, 19 September 1884, as preface to *Enriquillo* (Mexico: Editorial Porrúa, 1976): 5.

31. Martí, *Obras completas,* 6: 227.

32. A variation of this literary intervention, for the case of Greece, organizes Vassilis Lambropoulos's *Literature as National Institution: Studies in the Politics of Modern Greek Criticism* (Princeton: Princeton University Press, 1988). He assumes that criticism that treats works of fiction instrumentally, as possible purveyors of "Greekness," produces the national tradition. Although this is true to some extent for Latin America, as Beatriz González Stephan argues in *La historiografía literaria del liberalismo hispanoamericano del siglo XIX* (Havana: Casa de las Américas, 1987), it is also true that the main national propagandists were propagating through libidinally charged fiction.

33. For a brilliant study of the way gaps and absences partly con-

stitute even apparently programmatic literature, see Roberto González Echevarría, *The Voice of the Masters: Writing and Authority in Modern Latin American Literature* (Austin: University of Texas Press, 1985).

34. D. A. Miller makes a parallel point for Victorian novels in England, for their disciplinary history and lingering effects in other media. As for the destabilizing potential that modern readings prefer to focus on, Miller argues that the function of "scandal" is to inscribe the norm by contrast. See *The Novel and the Police* (Berkeley, Los Angeles, London: University of California Press, 1988).

35. Luis Alberto Sánchez, in *Proceso y contenido de la novela hispanoamericana* (Madrid: Gredos, 1953): 70–73, argues against Henríquez Ureña's allegation that the colony was fiction-starved (p. 71). See also Nancy Vogeley, "Defining the 'Colonial Reader': *El Periquillo Sarniento*," PMLA 102, 5 (October 1987): 784–800; 785.

36. See Beatriz González S., "Narrativa de la 'estabilización' colonial: *Peregrinación de Bartolomé Lorenzo* (1586) de José de Acosta, *Infortunios de Alonso Ramírez* (1690) de Carlos de Sigüenza y Góngora," *Ideologies and Literature*, new series, 2, 1 (Spring, 1987): 7–52. In n. 2 she cites Pedro Henríquez Ureña as the lone voice among critics who in 1927 challenged the assumption that there was no fiction in the colony.

These early books prepared what Roberto González Echevarría calls Latin America's three master narratives: legal, travel, anthropological. See his "Redescubrimiento del mundo perdido: El *Facundo* de Sarmiento," in *Revista Iberoamericana* 143 (April–June 1988): 385–406. With national consolidation, I want to argue, a fourth and immensely popular erotic master code developed.

37. Vogeley, p. 787, where the quote appears from Eco's *Postscript to The Name of the Rose* (New York: Harcourt, 1983): 50. Mexico was an exceptionally prosperous colony. By contrast, Adolfo Prieto chastens us about assuming that even a newspaper public was either stable or sizable in Argentina or Chile. "Sarmiento: La forja del lector" (MS.).

38. See Jorge B. Rivera, *El Folletín y la novela popular* (Buenos Aires: Centro Editor de América Latina, 1968). Technological advances in printing and a gradual incorporation of "marginalized sectors," especially women readers of serialized novels, accounted for a dramatic rise in Europe's newspaper consumption during the 1820s and 1830s (p. 15). "The English and French *folletines* spread almost immediately through Europe and reach America rapidly, where they are consumed with identical enthusiasm and quickly become the

preferred genre" (p. 13, my trans.). See also Elizabeth Garrels, "El *Facundo* como folletín," *Revista Iberoamericana* 143 (April–June 1988): 419–447; 436–437. While Sarmiento serialized his own *Facundo* (10 Nov. 1824–4 Oct. 1845) in Santiago's *El Progreso*, ten titles by Alexander Dumas appeared. Another popular *feuilletoniste* was Eugene Sue, whose *Los misterios de París* Sarmiento sampled in a few issues of March 1844 and was published entirely by *El Mercurio* of Valparaíso for subscribers in 1845.

39. Romance, writes Fredric Jameson, solves the dilemma of difference by "something like a semic evaporation" (p. 118), an "imaginary resolution of a real contradiction" that Lévi-Strauss found to be the general effect of individual narrative, in his essay "The Structural Study of Myth" (1963), in *The Political Unconscious: Narrative as a Socially Symbolic Act* (Ithaca: Cornell University Press, 1981): 77.

40. Leslie Fiedler, *Love and Death in the American Novel* (New York: Stein and Day, rev. ed., 1966): 23.

41. David Bushnell and Neill Macaulay, *The Emergence of Latin America in the Nineteenth Century* (Oxford and New York: Oxford University Press, 1988): 7.

42. Bushnell and Macaulay, pp. 12, 53.

43. Susan Kirkpatrick, "The Ideology of Costumbrismo," *Ideologies and Literature* 2, no. 7 (1978): 28–44; 37. The Spanish bourgeoisie's cultivation of the genre in newspapers of the 1830s developed and catered to a reading public that wanted to consume new images of itself.

44. Ludmilla Jordanova, ed., *Languages of Nature: Critical Essays on Science and Literature*, foreword by Raymond Williams (London: Free Association Books, 1986), especially the discussion of de Sade and Laclos in A. E. Pilington, "'Nature' as Ethical Norm in the Enlightenment," pp. 51–85, and Jordanova's "Naturalizing the Family: Literature and Bio-Medical Science in the Late Eighteenth Century," pp. 86–116.

45. Michael Mitterauer and Reinhard Sieder, *The European Family: Patriarchy to Partnership from the Middle Ages to the Present*, trans. Karla Oosterveen and Manfred Horzinger (Chicago: The University of Chicago Press, 1983).

46. Jacques Lacan coined this usage in *Ecrits: A Selection*, trans. Alan Sheridan (New York: Norton, 1977): 1–29. Fascinated by its image, the human child stops at the mirror to play hide and seek with itself. This is love at first sight, and the dyad of self-identification can be repeated between child and mother, a closed and reciprocal system that Lacan calls the edenic Imaginary realm.

47. See Miriam Williford, *Jeremy Bentham on Spanish America: An Account of His Letters and Proposals to the New World* (Baton Rouge: Louisiana State University Press, 1980).

48. Juan Bautista Alberdi, "Las Bases y Puntos de Partida para la Organización Política de la República Argentina" (1852). See Tulio Halperín Donghi, *Proyecto y construcción de una nación* (Argentina, 1846–1880) (Caracas: Biblioteca Ayacucho, 1980): 84–111; 92 (my emphasis).

49. Alberdi, 107.

50. In other countries, militarism had a longer afterlife (or a less interrupted cultural history) and continued to present a political value in the novels. Even when the civil marriage and domesticated, feminized heroism represented one novelist's ideal, another may have opposed it with a celebration of aggressive masculinity. See for example, Covarrubias in Mexico, Acevedo Díaz and Javier de Viana in Uruguay, Picón Febres in Venezuela, Leguizamón in Argentina, among other novelists.

51. See Asunción Lavrín, ed., *Latin American Women: Historical Perspectives* (Westport, Conn.: Greenwood, 1978), for pioneering essays on women's active participation. And K. Lynn Stoner has collected a twelve-page bibliography of recent histories, many of them about the nineteenth century. See "Directions in Latin American Women's History, 1977–1985," *Latin American Research Review* 22, 2 (1987): 101–134.

52. Jean Franco, *Plotting Women: Gender and Representation in Mexico* (New York: Columbia University Press, 1989), describes a "virilization" of literature, as one compensatory response to Latin America's lowly place in the world system, so that women were struck by the triviality of their own preoccupations (p. 94). But during the heyday of Liberal victory in Mexico, the distinction blurred at least in Ignacio Altamirano's supremely patriotic love stories.

53. Domingo F. Sarmiento, *Facundo: Civilización y barbarie* (Buenos Aires: Espasa-Calpe Argentina, 8th ed., 1970): 12–13.

54. See Tony Tanner, "La Maison Paternelle," in *Adultery in the Novel: Contract and Transgression* (Baltimore: Johns Hopkins University Press, 1979): 120–132.

55. Jameson, *The Political Unconscious,* chap. 3, "Realism and Desire: Balzac and the Problem of the Subject": 151–184. In the "allegorical" structure of the comic narrative of *La Vieille Fille,* sex is a figure for the longing after a landed retreat as well as after the resolution of social and historical contradiction (p. 158). The story is set in 1816 but written in 1836, after the failure of Restoration with the overthrow

of the Bourbons in 1830 by Liberal middle-class forces. The return of Comte de Troisville seems briefly like a "solution" (aristocratic and military) to her problems; but he's already married. He's the horizon figure in the narrative who blocks out a place of genuine Restoration.

56. The title heroine is saved here much as Soledad is saved, by a childhood guardian with whom she escapes, from an abusive husband and an opportunist lover, to a remote island where justice reigns. As for the conventional love stories, see the ones Paul de Man mentions in contrast to *Julie*. See *Allegories of Reading: Figural Language in Rousseau, Rilke, Nietzsche and Proust* (New Haven: Yale University Press, 1979): 215.

57. René Girard, *Deceit, Desire, and the Novel: Self and Other in Literary Structure*, trans. Yvonne Freccero (Baltimore: Johns Hopkins University Press, 1965): 108.

58. Julio Cortázar, *We Love Glenda So Much and A Change of Light*, trans. Gregory Rabassa (New York: Aventura [Vintage], 1984): 249–263. The Spanish original, "Manuscrito hallado en un bolsillo," appeared in *Octaedro* (Madrid: Alianza, 1974): 49–66.

59. From Robert Darnton, "What Was Revolutionary About the French Revolution?" *New York Review of Books* 35, 21 & 22 (January 19, 1989): 4.

60. Girard, p. 108.

61. Nor should we lose perspective on the delays nation-builders faced amidst the ruins of the colony and exhausting wars. See Tulio Halperín Donghi on this point and in general. "Una larga espera," in *Historia contemporanea de América Latina* (Madrid: Alianza Editorial, 7th ed., 1977): 134–206.

62. Diana Balmori, Stuart F. Voss, and Miles Wortman, *Notable Family Networks in Latin America* (Chicago: University of Chicago Press, 1984); also Diana Balmori and Robert Oppenheimer, "Family Clusters: Generational Nucleation in Nineteenth-Century Argentina and Chile," *Society for Comparative Study of Society and History* (1979): 231–261.

63. Balmori, Voss, and Wortman, p. 4.

64. Commerce was one role open to creoles in the late colonial period when a Bourbon reform put Spanish-born *intendentes* in general charge—economic, bureaucratic, and military—of provincial governments that had largely been ignored in the earlier and looser structure. See John Lynch, *Spanish Colonial Administration, 1782–1810* (London: University of London, 1958).

65. For the discussion of women as risk capital, see Voss, "The

Gente Decente in the Latin American Foundational Fiction and Historical Reality: Some Observations," paper presented at LASA Convention, Dec. 1989.

66. Balmori, Voss, and Wortman, p. 19.

67. Jean Elshtain, ed., *The Family in Political Thought* (Amherst: University of Massachusetts, 1982), "Introduction": 1–30.

68. Clorinda Matto de Turner's *Aves sin nido* (1889). For informed and engaging readings of this novel see Antonio Cornejo Polar *La novela indigenista* (Lima: Editorial Lasontay, 1980) and *La novela peruana: Siete estudios* (Lima: Editorial Horizonte, 1977). He points out that Matto de Turner's project is to civilize, to educate, the Indians, not to safeguard their culture, which has allegedly been corrupted beyond repair.

69. In the open letter to Ramiro de Maeztu, which appears as the prologue to the edition of *Matalaché* prepared by Juan Mejía Baca and P. L. Villanueva (Lima: Ediciones Populares, n.d.), López Albújar pronounces: "Above the distances imposed by title, fortune and the color of one's skin . . . is the attraction between the sexes, the irresistible power of human nature. . . . Love conquers all obstacles," pp. 10–11.

70. Fuentes bid a premature farewell to populist narrative in *La nueva novela latinoamericana* (Mexico: Joaquín Mortiz, 1969). One good indication is a Cuban revival of *Doña Bárbara*; *La última mujer y el próximo combate* by Manuel Cofiño López. I translate it, *Good-bye to Women and Hello to War*. Originally published in Cuba in 1971, this novel had already gone through fourteen editions in ten years, winning acclaim in Latin America and in the Soviet Union.

71. The Argentine exiles in Chile, though, did try to keep them apart in their pronouncements. Vicente Fidel López wrote that "any worship of the past, similar to Chateaubriand's paean to the Middle Ages in *Génie du christianisme* (1802), could only be unfavorable to Chile's future development." See Allen Woll, *A Functional Past: The Uses of History in Nineteenth-Century Chile* (Baton Rouge: Louisiana State University Press, 1982): 17, where he refers to López's "Clacisismo y romanticismo," *Revista de Valparaíso*, no. 4 (May 1842).

72. George Lukács, *The Historical Novel*, trans. Hannah and Stanley Mitchell (Boston: Beacon Press, 1963): 70, Lukács's emphasis. Other page references will be made in the text. J. M. Bernstein, *The Philosophy of the Novel: Lukács, Marxism and the Dialectics of Form* (Minneapolis: University of Minnesota Press, 1984) argues persuasively for the Hegelian continuity between *The Theory of the Novel* and *The Historical Novel*.

73. Georg Lukács, *The Theory of the Novel,* trans. Anna Bostock (Cambridge: MIT Press, 1971): 60.

74. Walter Scott, "Essay on Romance," in *Essays on Chivalry, Romance and the Drama* (London: Frederick Warne, 1887): 65–108.

75. In his preface to *The House of Seven Gables* (1851), Hawthorne says that, "When a writer calls his work a Romance, it need hardly be observed that he wishes to claim a certain latitude, both as to its fashion and material, which he would not have felt himself entitled to assume, had he professed to be writing a Novel." Undoubtedly, Hawthorne was hereby distinguishing his ambitious and broadly social projects from those sentimental novels of the "female scribblers." And Perry Miller was convinced in retrospect that American romances were precisely not novels because they were not love stories. "[T]he true burden of Romance in America, . . . was not at all the love story. What all of them were basically concerned with was the continent, the heritage of America, the wilderness." Perry Miller, *Nature's Nation* (Cambridge, Mass.: Belknap Press, 1958): 252.

76. Miller, p. 250. And Scott, in his late musings, seemed not to care about the gen(d)eric differences. In 1829 when he reissued the *Waverley* novels under his proper name, Scott made little if any distinction between romance and novel in his "Advertisement," "General Preface," or his "Preface to the Third Edition." The terms seem interchangeable. Scott, in fact, helped to domesticate romance, to bring the adventurous hero back to earth and back home. And home was Rowena, not Rebecca; it was the legitimate, pre-scribed family.

77. Several years before he wrote his great romances, Cooper was training himself as a writer by imitating, not the manly historical romancer Walter Scott, but that English gentlewoman and mistress of the domestic psychological novel, Ms. Jane Austen. Cooper's earliest novel, titled like one of hers, *Persuasion* (1820), was no parody but a serious attempt to study the problem of marriage; and this "first maker of America's myths" continued to impersonate a female with the pseudonym of Jane Morgan until 1823. See Leslie A. Fiedler, *Love and Death in the American Novel* (New York: Stein and Day, rev. ed. 1966): 186, 190. In general Fiedler shows how the genres bleed into one another even in their own nineteenth-century terms. The idealizing "new-comic" plot of the historical romance (boy gets, loses, and regains girl) is evidently a love story; while the sentimental tales of seduction, repentance, and female triumph are in America quite as allegorical and morally ideal as the patriotic romances.

78. Meyra Jehlen argues that the core of America's stable and transcendent ethics is the bourgeois family, which has "inspired the

strident masculinity, even the celibacy of its heroes." The domestication, or "bourgeoisification," of romance in the Americas either assumes that the hero is a lover turned husband or that he should be. Whether we fix on a notion of romance as an erotic quest for stable love or as the quest for freedom that apparently gives up stability, the North American examples finally bring their heroes home or watch them self-destruct. "New World Epics: The Novel and the Middle-Class in America," in *Salmagundi*, a Quarterly of the Humanities and Social Sciences, no. 36 (Winter, 1977): 49–68.

79. Georgi Dimitroff, probably the main cultural theorist for the Third International of the Communist Party in 1935, defended a similar popular front position. He announced that it was a mistake for Communists to abandon national heroes and traditions to the manipulations of fascists; it became legitimate and desirable to address the masses in a familiar rhetoric of soil and blood (nation and family) despite the political ambiguity in the party's desperate appeal for mass support. Georgi Dimitroff, *The United Front* (San Francisco: Proletarian Publishers, 1975): 78.

80. Anderson, p. 49. About the American states he writes, "For not only were they historically the first such states to emerge, and therefore inevitably provided the first real models of what such states should 'look like,' but their numbers and contemporary births offer fruitful ground for comparative enquiry."

81. Richard Chase considers this difference in register to be fundamental in singling out English literature: American writers, he says, are either "high-brow" or "low-brow," as opposed to the "middle-brow" quality of English literature, "the only one, it may be, in history." See Chase, p. 10.

82. Northrop Frye, *The Secular Scripture: A Study of the Structure of Romance* (Cambridge: Harvard University Press, 1976): 15.

83. His more recent *Una familia lejana* (1980) tries to recompose the bourgeois family, transnationally. "This invocation of the family acts as a tourniquet to national disintegration in both cultural and historical dimensions." See James V. Romano, "Authorial Identity and National Disintegration," *Ideologies and Literature* 4, 1 (Spring, 1989).

84. Carlos Fuentes, *La muerte de Artemio Cruz* (Mexico: Fondo de Cultura Económica, 1962): 82.

85. Carlos Fuentes, *The Death of Artemio Cruz*, trans. Sam Hileman (New York: Farrar, Straus and Giroux, 1985; originally 1964): 76.

86. The ruling party of Mexico since the end of the Revolution has been called the Partido Revolucionario Institucional (PRI).

1. PART II: LOVE AND COUNTRY:
AN ALLEGORICAL SPECULATION

1. Franklin J. Franco tells us that *Enriquillo* was "elevated since
the past century to the level of required reading in the public school
system." *Trujillismo: Génesis y rehabilitación* (Santo Domingo: Editora
Cultural Dominicana, 1971): 67. But other national novels became
required reading later, after governments had resources for massive
publication of anything but textbooks (often of natural law, philosophy, literature, through selections of Latin classics, and later history).
As in the United States, American literature didn't have immediate
academic legitimacy. The first documented "Programa de literatura
española y de los estados hispano-americanos" in Argentina is the
1884 course by Prof. Calixto Oyuela for the fourth year at the Colegio
Nacional de la Capital (Buenos Aires: Imprenta Biedma, 1884). On
p. 16, *Amalia* figures along with *La Cautiva* and gauchesca poetry. But
literature as part of patriotic education was still being argued for by
Ricardo Rojas in *La restauración nacionalista* (Buenos Aires: Librería
de la Facultad, 1922; originally 1909). In Mexico the first university
courses in literature were instituted in 1912, with the beginning of
the (antipositivist) Revolution. See Alfonso Reyes, "Pasado inmediato"
(1939), *Obras completas* (Mexico: Fondo de Cultura Económica, 1960),
12: 214. By 1933, required readings had for some time included
Altamirano along with Fernández Lizardi, Payno, Sierra, and others.
See *Programas detallados para las escuelas secundarias* (Mexico: Secretaría
de Educación Pública, 1933): 54.

The example of Chile has a documented analog in teaching national history. It is the delayed cult of Arturo Prat, the 1879 hero of
the War of the Pacific. Iván Jaksic speculated for me that *Martín Rivas*
was probably required by the same nationalist leaders and educators
who responded to civic demands during the Depression—and in the
face of "alien" ideologies—by institutionalizing Prat's heroism, turning it into a model of hard work and national reconciliation. See William F. Sater, *The Heroic Image in Chile: Arturo Prat, Secular Saint*
(Berkeley and Los Angeles: University of California Press, 1973).

2. See Beatriz González Stephan, *La historiografía literaria del liberalismo hispanoamericano del siglo XIX* (Havana: Casa de las Américas,
1987), esp. 193 and 159. Most of the literary historians had rigorous
religious training, and some studied to be priests. They borrowed
esthetic criteria from Aristotle, Boileau, and Luzán, and worked in
party politics as lawyers, university professors, or deans; most were
senators, deputies, ministers, and diplomats. Often the project was

more a desideratum than a record, since new countries, so resistant to their colonial past, had little literature to report on, Brazil being an exception.

3. Also excluded from first literary histories were indigenous literatures, oral hispanic literature, many chronicles, and various hybrid forms. González Stephan, pp. 191–192.

4. In anticipation of such a sociology of literature, one way to read the history of institutionalization is symptomatically, from the record of publications. I am grateful to Antonio Cornejo Polar for this suggestion, and to Ludwig Lauerhaus of the library at UCLA for assenting. That record is often thin until the 1920s or 1930s, when large editions would follow one another almost yearly. In the admittedly spotty entries of *The National Union Catalog Pre-1956 Imprints,* several editions of *Amalia* appear before the 1930s (more in Europe than in Buenos Aires, and two editions for American students, with notes and exercises). But from 1930, Sopena—first in Barcelona then in Buenos Aires—begins to repeat printings every two or three years even in this incomplete list. Simultaneous publishers of *Amalia* are Espasa-Calpe in Madrid and Buenos Aires, and Estrada. Altamirano's *El Zarco* (another favorite of American Spanish teachers, as indeed were almost all of these national novels) appeared in 1901 and shows three printings in this list until 1940. In the following decade, Espasa-Calpe of Buenos Aires and Mexico reissued it four times, joined by Mexico's Editora Nacional in 1951. *Tabaré,* by Zorrilla de San Martín, to give just one last example from the *Catalog,* has had a remarkable number of printings and editions over time, especially since the 1920s (two full pages of the catalog for this one work). And Blest Gana's *Martín Rivas* seems to have been standard reading early (for Chileans as well as for American students through the D. C. Heath edition). Jorge Román-Lagunas's "Bibliografía anotada de y sobre Alberto Blest Gana," *Revista Iberoamericana,* nos. 112–113 (July–December 1980): 605–647, informs that during the last century the novel had five printings; in this one, by 1980, it has already had thirty.

5. This is John Breuilly's general definition in *Nationalism and the State* (Chicago: University of Chicago Press, 1985).

6. See Breuilly, p. 342. "The demand for a nation-state with many of the features of other nation-states seems hard to reconcile with the justification that a unique nation needs its own special form of independence."

7. Beatriz González Stephan repeatedly notes (e.g., p. 184) that this was one of the contradictions faced by elite nation-builders in the nineteenth century. Because they were elite they imitated Europe; and

because they were American nation-builders they celebrated their premodern surroundings.

8. Benedict Anderson, *Imagined Communities: Reflections on the Origin and Spread of Nationalism* (London: Verso, 1983). Subsequent page references will appear parenthetically.

9. Michel Foucault, *The History of Sexuality: An Introduction*, trans. Robert Hurley (New York: Vintage Books, 1980): 78. Subsequent page references will appear in the text.

10. See Anita Levy, "Blood, Kinship, and Gender," *Genders*, no. 5 (Summer, 1989): 70–85; 75.

11. Patriotic passion evidently has a long history, which Ernst H. Kantorowicz masterfully traced as a progressive reconquest of classical patriotism in "*Pro Patria Mori* in Medieval Political Thought," *Selected Studies* (Locust Valley, N.Y.: J. J. Augustin Publisher, 1965): 308–324. Very schematically one can summarize the progression as follows: the early Middle Ages denied an earthly patria; then made it (France is his prime example) parallel to Jerusalem; shifted the mystical body of the church to the corporate body of the state; understood corporation as the nation's body with the king at its head; and finally left the king behind. But in this return, the ancient *patria* (city, polis) is substituted by the idea of inclusive nation as it developed during the Middle Ages.

12. Nancy Armstrong, *Desire and Domestic Fiction: A Political History of the Novel* (New York: Oxford University Press, 1987): 9.

13. Regarding timing, Foucault prefers to highlight the Victorian age rather than the seventeenth century, which would coincide with—and be explained by—the rise of capital.

14. A recent example of the consensus is Henry Abelove, "Towards a History of 'Sexual Intercourse' During the 'Long Eighteenth Century' in England," *Genders* 6 (November 1989): 125–130, where he argues that a cult of bourgeois productivity coincided with an increased taste for reproductive love that redefined other sexual practices as mere foreplay.

15. D. A. Miller notes that "perhaps the most notable reticence in Foucault's work concerns precisely the reading of literary texts and literary institutions," as if they couldn't amount to objects of analysis. See *The Novel and the Police* (Berkeley: University of California Press, 1988): viii, n. 1.

16. Michael Davitt Bell, *The Development of American Romance: The Sacrifice of Relation* (Chicago: University of Chicago Press, 1980): xii.

17. Ignacio M. Altamirano, "La literatura nacional" (1868), *La literatura nacional*, ed. and prologue by José Luis Martínez (México Edit. Porrúa, Col. de Escritores Mexicanos, no. 52, 1949): 9–40; 17.

18. George L. Mosse also takes the position that sexuality is repressed or deformed, not constructed, by the state. *Nationalism and Sexuality: Middle-Class Morality and Sexual Norms in Modern Europe* (Madison: University of Wisconsin Press, 1985).

19. Mary Louise Pratt offers some cautionary remarks on Anderson's assumption of community through national languages; they can be exclusionary and caste-coding in an internal map of dialectical differences. See her "Linguistic Utopias," in *The Linguistics of Writing: Arguments Between Language and Literature*, ed. Nigel Fabb, Derek Attridge, Alan Durant, and Colin MacCabe (New York: Methuen, 1987): 48–66.

20. In a recent paper, Benedict Anderson comes to a similar observation for Southeast Asia: "The official nationalist model was drawn from Europe. But I am now increasingly convinced that the colonial state was more significant." It may have been violently *anti*nationalist, but below the rhetoric is a "grammar," a mapping grid, of territorial specificity that nationalists inherited. "Census, Map, Museum: Notes on the Origins of Official Nationalism in Southeast Asia," draft of January 1989.

21. "Messianic" as against "homogeneous, empty time" (on which Anderson suggests "every essential modern conception is based," p. 30) are concepts borrowed from Benjamin's "Theses on the Philosophy of History," *Illuminations,* ed. Hannah Arendt (New York: Schocken, 1969): 253–264. Homi K. Bhabha argues that Anderson's utopian misreading of homogeneous time misses Benjamin's warnings about our incommensurate differences in experiencing time. "Introduction," *Nation and Narration* (London: Routledge, 1990).

22. I develop this in "Allegory and Dialectics: A Match Made in Romance" (forthcoming, in *Boundary* 2, 18, no. 1 (January 1991).

23. Fredric Jameson, "Third-World Literature in the Era of Multinational Capitalism," *Social Text* 15 (Fall, 1986): 65–88; 69. "Third-world texts, even those which are seemingly private and invested with a properly libidinal dynamic—necessarily project a political dimension in the form of national allegory: *the story of the private individual destiny is always an allegory of the embattled situation of the public third-world culture and society.* Need I add that it is precisely this very different ratio of the political to the personal which makes such texts alien to us at first approach, and consequently, resistant to our conventional western habits of reading?" Following page references to this essay will appear parenthetically.

24. See Stephen Melville, "Notes on the Reemergence of Allegory, the Forgetting of Modernism, the Necessity of Rhetoric, and the Conditions of Publicity in Art and Criticism," *October* 19 (Winter, 1981):

55–92. This is a "response to a series of essays recently published in *October*." They include: Douglas Crimp, "Pictures," *October* 8 (Spring, 1979): 75–88; "On the Museum's Ruins," *October* 13 (Summer, 1980): 41–57; Joel Fineman, "The Structure of Allegorical Desire," *October* 12 (Spring, 1980): 47–66; Craig Owens, *"Einstein on the Beach*: The Primacy of Metaphor," *October* 4 (Fall, 1977): 21–32; and "The Allegorical Impulse: Toward a Theory of Postmodernism," *October* 12 (Spring, 1980): 67–86, and pt. 2, no. 13 (Summer, 1980): 61–80.

25. This is what Aijaz Ahmad does in his otherwise apt response, "Jameson's Rhetoric of Otherness and the 'National Allegory,'" *Social Text* 17: 3–25.

26. Published originally as *Ursprung des deutschen Trauerspiels*. I will refer to the English translation by John Osborne (London: NLB, 1977) in parenthetical page references in the text.

27. Walter Benjamin, "Central Park," trans. Lloyd Spencer, *New German Critique*, no. 34 (Winter, 1985): 32–58; 47–48. "The correspondence between antiquity and the modern is the only constructive conception of history to be found in Baudelaire. It excluded a dialectical conception rather than contained it." Despite Baudelaire's rage against the system of commodity production, his allegory is a record of decay as strangely alienated from process as the (other) commodities produced around him.

28. Jonathan Arac notes a "powerful pattern of omission" in de Man's adaption of Foucault and Benjamin for "The Rhetoric of Temporality," the omission of genealogy or periodization that had "placed" Foucault's Mallarmé in the postclassical episteme and Benjamin's Baudelaire at a formal and contextual distance from baroque allegorists. Jonathan Arac, "Afterword: Lyric Poetry and the Bonds of New Criticism," *Lyric Poetry: Beyond New Criticism*, ed. Chaviva Hošek and Patricia Parker (Ithaca, N.Y.: Cornell University Press, 1985): 345–355; 351.

29. Other readers, of course, can and have interpreted this intervention as de Man's elucidation of the impossibility that Benjamin prepares. They may be entirely justified; but from my interested position something has been lost. It is the promise that Benjamin's unorthodox matchmaking will contribute to a critical vocabulary for describing a commonplace and canonical but little understood genre. One such reader is Geoffrey Hartman who applauds de Man's reading of allegory as freeing the term from Benjamin's tragic overtones (which are erroneously cast here as independent of history). "Looking Back on Paul de Man," *Reading De Man Reading*, ed. Lindsay Waters and Wlad Godzich (Minneapolis: University of Minnesota

Press, 1989): 3–24, esp. 8–9. In the same volume, Kevin Newmark explains in "Paul de Man's History," 121–135, that de Man's apparent impatience with history was with "organic," nonlinguistic and empirical history. An alternative, one that began from tropological relationships and from reading history through, not as, metaphors, was far more promising to him.

And Lindsay Waters offers a sustained comparative reading in his introductory essay, "Paul de Man: Life and Works," for the volume *Paul de Man, Critical Writings 1953–1978* (Minneapolis: University of Minnesota Press, 1989): ix–lxxiv. His periodization places "The Rhetoric of Temporality" at the turning point to his last and most rigorous stage of academic writing; it augurs a deliberate emphasis on rhetoric and language.

Lloyd Spencer, the translator and commentator of "Central Park," apparently reads Benjamin back from the use de Man would make of him. P. 63: "Allegories, even those which proclaim the stability and fullness of meaning in the (hierarchized) universe can thus be seen as deconstructing themselves, as revealing the opposite of that which they seek to imply." And Stephen Melville's "Notes on the Reemergence of Allegory" explicitly begins with a reference to de Man as the most important figure for the reemergence in literary criticism. See n. 24.

In another effort to redeem allegory, Wai-chee Dimock's *Empire For Liberty: Melville and the Poetics of Individualism* (Princeton: Princeton University Press, 1989): 22–25, makes it a functional development of personification. She begins from de Man's reduction of time to an effect of allegorical rhetoric, assuming that Benjamin's backward view over time's ruins amounts to the same, and concludes that the "timeless order of allegory" is the space that governs both Melville's self-governing narratives and the social governance in antebellum America.

30. Originally published in *Interpretation: Theory and Practice*, ed. Charles S. Singleton (Baltimore: Johns Hopkins University Press, 1969): 173–210, and then in de Man's *Blindness and Insight: Essays in the Rhetoric of Contemporary Criticism* (New York: Oxford University Press, 1971).

31. See Michael W. Jennings, *Dialectical Images: Walter Benjamin's Theory of Literary Criticism* (Ithaca: Cornell University Press, 1987). He is careful to point out the ambivalent use Benjamin makes of allegory. It was not simply the record of self-alienation, the ruinous result of totalizing efforts, but also a frame for "living images," once historical projects are read back from the ruins. (Pp. 172–173.)

32. Paul de Man, "Pascal's Allegory of Persuasion," in Stephen J. Greenblatt, ed., *Allegory and Representation* (Baltimore: Johns Hopkins University Press, 1981): 1–25; 23.

33. Thanks to Richard Rorty, I can call these moves pragmatic and "postphilosophical" (having given up the stable ground of human nature) rather than sloppy. "If we come to see the novel rather than the theological or scientific or philosophical treatise as the paradigmatic repository of wisdom we shall not be inclined to say . . . that 'philosophy and democracy were born in the same time and in the same place.' We shall be more inclined to say that *fiction* and democracy are connate." See his "Comments on Castoriadis's 'The End of Philosophy,'" *Salmagundi*, no. 82–83 (Spring–Summer, 1989): 24–30; 28.

34. de Man, "Pascal's Allegory of Persuasion," p. 17.

35. From the Second Preface to *Julie*, quoted by Paul de Man, *Allegories of Reading: Figural Language in Rousseau, Rilke, Nietzsche and Proust* (New Haven: Yale University Press, 1979): 198. Page references to *Allegories* will appear parenthetically.

36. Alberto Blest Gana, *Martín Rivas (Novela de costumbres político-sociales)*, Prólogo, Notas, y Cronología de Jaime Concha (Caracas: Biblioteca Ayacucho, 1977): 249.

37. Kenneth Burke, *The Rhetoric of Religion: Studies in Logology* (Boston: Beacon Press, 1961): 51.

38. Joel Fineman, "The Structure of Allegorical Desire," in Stephen J. Greenblatt, ed., *Allegory and Representation* (Baltimore: Johns Hopkins University Press, 1981): 26–60; 46.

39. See Leo Bersani, "Representation and Its Discontents" in Greenblatt, pp. 145–162. He describes the "Sadean view of sexual excitement as a shared commotion . . . we do not have sex with others *because* they excite us; excitement is the consequence of sex rather than its motive. . . . Sexual excitement must be represented before it can be felt; or, more exactly, it *is* the representation of an alienated commotion": 145.

40. I owe this provocative comment to Jean Bethke Elshtain.

41. Catherine Gallagher, *Industrial Transformations in the English Novel* (Chicago: University of Chicago Press, 1985), develops a similar double reading. I am grateful to Marshall Brown for pointing the book out to me.

42. See Roberto Schwarz, "Misplaced Ideas: Literature and Society in Late Nineteenth-Century Brazil," *Comparative Civilizations Review* 5 (1979): 33–51.

43. Northrop Frye, *The Secular Scripture: A Study of the Structure of Romance* (Cambridge: Harvard University Press, 1976): 15, 38.

44. Northrop Frye, *Anatomy of Criticism* (New York: Atheneum, 1968): 193–195.

45. Fineman, p. 32. After a review of the scholarship, he concludes that allegory works in two possible ways: perpendicularly, in which case metaphor organizes it (like the great chain of being and other visual, hardly narrative models), and horizontally, organized by metonymy that produces narrative. Jakobson, he says, sees metaphor, however, as central in either case: "It is always the structure of metaphor that is projected onto the sequence of metonymy, not the other way around, which is why allegory is always a hierarchicizing mode, indicative of timeless order, however subversively intended its contents might be . . . an *inherently political and therefore religious* trope, not because it flatters tactfully, but because in deferring to structure it insinuates the power of structure, giving off what we can call the structural effect" (my emphasis).

From my vantage point, this seems to be arguing tautologically. Why does the political level necessarily look sacred?

46. In the 1873 Prologue, Hostos emphasized the book's combative intention against Spain's continuing despotism in the Antilles. To insure an allegorical reading, Hostos introduces the letters of this epistolary novel with a *clave*, or key. It explains that the protagonists Bayoán, Marién, and Guarionex are also Puerto Rico, Cuba (his beloved), and Hispaniola (her father). See Eugenio María de Hostos, *La peregrinación de Bayoán* (Río Piedras: Ediciones Edil, 1970): 37. On p. 251 the protagonist repeats his characteristic lament: "Glory and love! . . . The former conquered by the latter!" I thank Julio Ramos and Rubén Ríos for their suggestions about Hostos's special case. See also Ramos's *Desencuentros*: 52–57.

2. PLAGIARIZED AUTHENTICITY: SARMIENTO'S COOPER AND OTHERS

1. Jorge Luis Borges, "Pierre Menard, Author of the Quixote," *Labyrinths*, ed. Donald A. Yates and James E. Irby (New York: New Directions, 1964): 42.

2. Jorge Luis Borges, "Pierre Menard, autor del Quijote," *Ficciones* (Buenos Aires: Alianza Emecé, 1982): 59.

3. Borges, *Labyrinths*: 44.

4. These opportunities for misreadings, even in so didactic and

heavy-handed a novel as Cooper's, are perhaps the only point at which I depart from Jane Tompkins, *Sensational Designs: The Cultural Work of American Fiction, 1790–1860* (New York and Oxford: Oxford University Press, 1985). Her generally convincing defense of best-sellers as indicators and arbiters of our political culture tends, nonetheless, to underestimate the likelihood that messages may be processed differently even when that message is passionately put forth. See her p. xviii.

5. Martin Green, *The Great American Adventure* (Boston: Beacon Press, 1984): 23.

6. Walt Whitman, "Song of Myself": 47. *The Portable Walt Whitman,* selected and with notes by Mark Van Doren, rev. Malcolm Cowley (New York: Penguin Books, 1981): 92.

7. James Fenimore Cooper, *The Last of the Mohicans* (New York: Signet Classic, New American Library, 1980): 35. Subsequent page references appear in the text.

8. Domingo F. Sarmiento, *Facundo: Civilización y barbarie* (Buenos Aires: Espasa-Calpe Argentina, 8th ed., 1970). Domingo Faustino Sarmiento, *Life in the Argentine Republic in the Days of the Tyrants; or Civilization and Barbarism,* trans. Mrs. Horace Mann (New York: Hurd and Houghton, 1868). Subsequent page references will appear in the text, citing first the Spanish then the English versions.

Juan Bautista Alberdi would accuse Sarmiento of having his book published in the United States with the underwriting of a translator who would necessarily be confused with her illustrious husband for Spanish readers. See Alberdi's *Proceso a Sarmiento,* prologue by León Pomer (Buenos Aires: Ediciones Caldén, 1967): 13.

9. Nina Baym, "The Women of Cooper's Leatherstocking Tales," *American Quarterly* 23 (1971): 696–709. Baym observes (698) that women are the "chief signs, the language of social communication between males"; and thus the basis for male civilization. To develop this we might say that the ideal basis for Cooper's civilization was the transparent, unmarked language that Alice represented, rather than the polyvalent traces that Cora bore.

10. Annette Kolodny explores the land-as-woman metaphor and Americans' self-defeating relationships to it. See her, *The Lay of the Land* (Chapel Hill: North Carolina University Press, 1975). She points out an inevitable slippage from our pastoral desire to regress to a pre-Oedipal and "passive" love for the land as Mother, through the fear of castration and enclosure, to an aggressive post-Oedipal desire to dominate her, a desire I identify with romance. Despite this repeated

move (farther and farther West), Kolodny continues to plea for a pastoral America. The scene at Glenn's Falls shows the extended company of heroes and helpers hiding in Nature's caverns, which open conveniently from the front and the back *(Mohicans*: 63–66, 96–97). See also Cecilia Tichi, *New World, New Earth: Environmental Reform in American Literature from the Puritans to Whitman* (New Haven: Yale University Press, 1979): 173.

11. The assumption of female stability that "grounds" male activity is provocatively developed by Luce Irigaray in *Speculum of the Other Woman*, trans. Gillian C. Gill (Ithaca: Cornell University Press, 1985). See especially the essay "Any Theory of the 'Subject' Has Always Been Appropriated by the 'Masculine'": 133–146. "Subjectivity denied to woman: indisputably this provides the financial backing for every irreducible constitution as an object: of representation, of discourse, of desire. Once imagine that woman imagines and the object loses its fixed, obsessional character. As a bench mark that is ultimately more crucial than the subject, for he can sustain himself only by bouncing back off some objectiveness, some objective. If there is no more 'earth' to press down/repress, to work, to represent, but also and always to desire (for one's own), no opaque matter which in theory does not know herself, then what pedestal remains for the exsistence of the 'subject.' If the earth turned and more especially turned upon herself, the erection of the subject might thereby be disconcerted and risk losing its elevation and penetration": 133.

12. "Taxinomia" is how Foucault spells this. Michel Foucault, *The Order of Things: An Archaeology of the Human Sciences* (New York: Vintage Books, 1973).

13. Tompkins, in *Sensational Designs*, is at least one recent North American reader who might agree with Sarmiento's brutally lucid reading of Cooper. On p. 94, she notes that Charles Brockden Brown's *Arthur Mervyn* is about cross-cultural marriage as resolution to social tension; the hero marries a Portuguese-Jewish widow. This is the kind of mix that doesn't happen in *The Last of the Mohicans*. She claims that most critics try to apologize for Cooper's plots and characters, but Tompkins wisely attends to the obvious and conventional racism in Cooper. The subject of *The Last of the Mohicans* is cultural miscegenation (114). And the lesson, especially at Fort William Henry, is that when social controls start to break down the ultimate consequence is a bloodbath (117).

14. See Leslie A. Fiedler, *Love and Death in the American Novel* (New York: Stein and Day, rev. ed. 1966), and his reading of *The Wept* as

"the first anti-miscegenation novel in our literature." He continues that "*The Last of the Mohicans* must be re-read in its light," and refers to Cooper's contemporaries who lamented Cora's death. Fiedler: 204.

15. Her father confesses to Heyward that in the West Indies, "[I]t was my lot to form a connection with one who in time became my wife, and the mother of Cora. She was the daughter of a gentleman of those isles, by a lady whose misfortune it was, if you will, . . . to be descended, remotely from that unfortunate class who are so basely enslaved to administer to the wants of a luxurious people. Aye, sir, that is a curse entailed on Scotland by her unnatural union with a foreign and trading people" (187–188).

Jane Tompkins's chapter, "No Apologies for the Iriquois," makes too simple a case for Cora's whiteness (*Sensational Designs:* 119). The danger of her confrontation with Magua is compounded, I think, by the fact that she is already a corrupt category, porous to his darkening effect. Wayne Franklin even surmises that she feels an erotic attraction to Magua. See his *The New World of James Fenimore Cooper* (Chicago: University of Chicago Press, 1982): 224.

16. Annette Kolodny shows that Cooper's relationship to the organizing metaphor of American pastoral offers a good case for reading both the self-defeating dimension of land-as-woman and the reifying dimension of woman-as-land. Like many of the authors Kolodny studies, Cooper has his share of ecological guilt that predicts either barrenness or nature's revenge by entrapping the despoilers in her womb: 90–97.

17. Typically, this is an image that Mrs. Mann judiciously substitutes for dead metaphors in English: "penetrates its very heart." See, Sarmiento, "El mal que aqueja a la República Argentina es la extensión: el desierto la rodea por todas partes, se le insinúa en las entrañas; la soledad, el despoblado sin una habitación humana."

18. Roberto González Echevarría reminds us of Sarmiento's secondhand nativism and develops an argument about the travelogue nature of *Facundo,* which, like other books of its genre, takes care to produce an identification with civilized readers at home by distancing the narrator from the strange or wonderful scenes beheld. See his "Redescubrimento del mundo perdido: El *Facundo* de Sarmiento," *Revista Iberoamericana,* no. 143 (April–June 1988): 385–406.

19. See Leopoldo Zea's classic work, *The Latin American Mind* (Norman, Okla.: University of Oklahoma Press, 1963), and his Prologue to the anthology he edited, *Pensamiento positivista latinoamericano* (Caracas: Biblioteca Ayacucho, 1979).

20. See Sylvia Molloy's excellent "Sarmiento, lector de sí mismo

en *Recuerdos de Provincia*," *Revista Iberoamericana* 54, 143 (April–June 1988): 407–418, esp. 415 and 417.

21. For the most passionate and playful guide to hearing that multiplicity and the conflict with the gaucho genre of poetry which also constitute *Facundo*, see Josefina Ludmer, *El género gauchesco: Un tratado sobre la patria* (Buenos Aires: Editorial Sudamericana, 1988): 24.

Elizabeth Garrels notes that Sarmiento chose to publish *Facundo* during 1845 in the new section for serialized novels, in *El Progreso*, the newspaper he edited in Santiago between 1842 and 1845. By contrast, he published his perhaps comparable biography of Aldao in the "Sección Correspondencia." See "El *Facundo* como folletín," *Revista Iberoamericana*, no. 143 (April–June 1988): 419–447; 426.

22. For this powerful observation, I am indebted to Carlos Alonso's paper, "Reading Sarmiento: One More Time, with Passion," delivered at the 1988 MLA meeting. See also Julio Ramos, *Desencuentros . . .* , chap. 1, "Saber del otro: Escritura y oralidad en el *Facundo* de D. F. Sarmiento": 19–34.

23. Ludmer makes a similar point: "Barbarism doesn't only dramatize the confrontation with "civilization" but another internal confrontation with itself. . . . The double tension, outward and inward, is the best definition of *Facundo*, Sarmiento's text": 26.

24. Alberdi, *Proceso a Sarmiento:* 16. "*Facundo* is a Janus-faced book: one face is Civilization; the other is Barbarism. . . . It has two consciences, two moralities. It is for and against the same questions about its country."

25. Sarmiento mentions this as early as p. 6; but he's explicit on p. 217. "The Unitarian ideal is realized; only the tyrant is an addition; the day that a good government is established, it will find local resistance overcome and everything ready for a Union."

26. Alberdi, *Proceso a Sarmiento*: 30. " . . . since the ideal and interests that motivated Facundo as Rosas's agent are the same that motivate Facundo's biographer."

27. More than from Cooper, Sarmiento probably learned about the "American" sublime from François-René de Chateaubriand's chapter, "To America," in his *Memoirs,* trans. Robert Baldick (New York: Alfred Knopf, 1961): 114–161. About Niagara Falls, for example, he writes, "I was unable to express the thoughts which stirred me at the sight of such sublime disorder": 150.

28. While it is true that Cooper lamented the "corruption" of place names in his 1826 Preface, he also laments Cora's death, the Mohicans' demise, and the general disturbance of paradise. Yet, the narrative

shows him willing, for the time, to pay the price in order to establish his American family. Later, the more circumspect and less optimistic Cooper of *The Deerslayer* (1841) attempts to foreswear the violence of naming, even as he writes about Glimmerglass, or Otsego Lake: "'I'm glad it has no name,' resumed Deerslayer, 'or, at least, no paleface name; for their christenings always foretell waste and destruction."

29. Octavio Paz, *El laberinto de la soledad* (Mexico: Fondo de Cultura Económica, 1980; originally 1959): 40. "Ninguneo is the operation of making Someone into No one. . . . It would be a mistake to think that others impede one's existence. They simply make believe he doesn't exist, they act as if he didn't. They nullify him, annul him, *ningunean.*"

30. It is one thing for Sarmiento to say it, and quite another for the Englishman Walter Scott who shows reluctant admiration: "'The vast plains of Buenos Ayres,' he says, 'are inhabited only by Christian savages known as Guachos' (gauchos, he should have said), 'whose furniture is chiefly composed of horses' skulls, whose food is raw beef and water, and whose favorite pastime is running horses to death. Unfortunately,' adds the good foreigner, 'they prefer their national independence to our cottons and muslins.' It would be well to ask England to say at a venture how many yards of linen and pieces of muslin she would give to own these plains of Buenos Ayres": 16; 12.

31. Peter Hulme, "Versions of Virginia: Crossing Cultures in Early Colonial America." See his *Colonial Encounters* (London: Methuen, 1987). See also Michael Rogin, who refers to the differences between the "northern tribes which were smaller and more numerous than the five southern Indian confederations. They were less settled than the southern tribes, and never developed so large-scale an agriculture or so complexly stratified a social structure." To locate Cooper in a general moment of Indian removal, see Michael Rogin, *Fathers and Children: Andrew Jackson and the Subjugation of the American Indian* (New York: Knopf, 1975): 166–167.

32. His most ferocious critic was Juan Bautista Alberdi, one of the original members of the Generation of 1837, later called "Young Argentina." These romantic, rebellious youth had pledged themselves to overcoming the fratricidal antagonism between Europeanizing Centralists called Unitarians, based in Buenos Aires, and the more autochthonous Federalists who were then in control under the dictator Rosas. As the dictatorship turned to terror, practically all of the Generation of 1837 retreated to Unitarian sectarianism, except for Alberdi. And his criticism of Sarmiento's *Facundo* revives the principle of flexibility and conciliation. See his *Cartas quillotanas* where Alberdi objects to Sarmiento's binary formulation of city and country desert,

"an historical and empirical error, and source of artificial antipathy between sectors that need and complement each other." Quoted from *Historia de la literatura argentina/1* (Buenos Aires: Centro Editor de América Latina, 1967): 308.

Sarmiento, of course, knew he was being schematic. He admits, for example, that blacks have integrated well but also rejoices over their near extermination in the wars. See the suggestive essay by William H. Katra, "Reading *Facundo* as Historical Novel," *The Historical Novel in Latin America,* ed. Daniel Balderston (Gaithersburg, Md.: Ediciones Hispamérica, 1986): 31–46.

33. See Brook Thomas, *Cross-Examinations of Law and Literature: Cooper, Hawthorne, Stowe, and Melville* (Cambridge: Cambridge University Press): 23. "When Van Buren spoke against New York's 'aristocracy,' he was not making a claim for popular rule. The governing elite (to which Cooper belonged) was sustained by social position and family connection. Van Buren wanted to replace it with a new leadership of the rising powerful—the Albany Regency. The constitution that had ruled New York State from the Revolution until 1821 was an object of Van Buren's attack because it, along with residual elements of the old Dutch patroon system, protected the interests of what the Federalists called the 'guardian class.'"

34. Tompkins: 110.

35. Georg Lukács, *The Historical Novel,* trans. Hannah and Stanley Mitchell (Boston: Beacon Press, 1963). "Gorky's fine analysis of Cooper's novels . . . shows the divided attitude of the classics of the historical novel clearly. They have to affirm the downfall of the humanly noble Indian, the straightforwardly decent, straightforwardly heroic 'leather-stocking,' treating it as a necessary step of progress, and yet cannot help seeing and depicting the human inferiority of the victors. This is the necessary fate of every primitive culture with which capitalism comes into contact": 346.

Katra (39) then reads Lukács through Sarmiento and concludes rather hastily that both celebrated this "pitiless march of progress," when, in fact, Lukács tries to draw a distinction between classical historical novels and those of the Popular Front that can accommodate the "primitive communism." Compare Lukács: 347.

36. I am referring here to Michel Foucault's arguably schematic distinction in *The Order of Things: An Archaeology of the Human Sciences* (New York: Vintage Books, 1973).

37. See Sylvia Molloy's wonderfully probing discussion, p. 416.

38. Domingo Faustino Sarmiento, *Recuerdos de provincia* (Barcelona: Ramón Sopena, editor, 1931): 107–108. The passage contin-

ues: "That which we call plagiarism today was then erudition and enrichment."

39. Sarmiento, *Recuerdos*: 161.

40. William J. Nowak argues that the gesture to make himself representative of Argentina, the synecdoche for an entire country, meant that Sarmiento's self-portrait was purposefully impersonal. See "La personificación en *Recuerdos de provincia*: La despersonalización de D. F. Sarmiento," *Revista Iberoamericana*, no. 143 (April–June 1988): 585–601.

41. Carlos Altamirano and Beatriz Sarlo, "La estrategia de *Recuerdos de provincia*," in their *Literatura/Sociedad* (Buenos Aires: Hachette, 1983): 163–208; 165.

42. Sarmiento, *Recuerdos de Provincia*: 68. An extended quote appears in chap. 3, corresponding to endnote 26.

43. Jean Baudrillard, *Simulations*, trans. Paul Foss, Paul Patton, and Philip Beitchman (New York: Semiotext(e) Inc., Columbia University, 1983).

44. Baudrillard: 2.

45. Sarmiento, *Recuerdos*: 142.

46. Mario Vargas Llosa, *La tía Julia y el escribidor* (Barcelona: Seix Barral, 1977). Quoted from *Aunt Julia and the Scriptwriter*, trans. Helen R. Lane (London: Faber and Faber, 1983): 50.

47. Historians of the period, most notably Bartolomé Mitre, were also writing biography as one of the most compelling kinds of history.

48. Michel Foucault, *The History of Sexuality*, vol. 1. *An Introduction*, trans. Robert Hurley (New York: Vintage Books, 1980): 78.

49. See chap. 1, pt. 1, nn. 76–80.

50. Simón Bolívar, in *Pensamiento Político de la Emancipación*, ed. José Luis Romero (Caracas: Biblioteca Ayacucho, 1977): 114.

51. Henry Nash Smith, "The Dime Novel Heroine," in *Virgin Land: The American West as Symbol and Myth* (Cambridge: Harvard University Press, 1950): 126–135.

52. Baym picks up his point, p. 706.

53. For the definitive formulation of this idea see, Eve Kosofsky Sedgwick *Between Men: English Literature and Male Homosocial Desire* (New York: Columbia University Press, 1985).

54. See Carlos Altamirano and Beatriz Sarlo: 168.

55. Tulio Halperin Donghi, "Intelectuales, sociedad y vida pública en Hispanoamérica a través de la literatura autobiográfica," *El espejo de la historia: Problemas argentinos y perspectivas latinoamericanas:* 58. "Denounced for being of humble origins, Sarmiento exaggerates the accusation and tranforms it into a vindication. . . . A few years later,

the same Sarmiento would give a new account of himself in *Recuerdos de provincia*, and here the creation of his own works literally opens the book with a family tree: his effort now is to adapt the elite intellectual tradition to the social and ideological climate of republican times."

3. *AMALIA*: VALOR AT HEART AND HOME

1. José Mármol, *Amalia*, 5th ed. (Madrid: Espasa-Calpe, Colección Austral, 1978). Page references will appear parenthetically in the text and will refer first to this edition and second to the (notably shortened) translation: *Amalia: A Romance of the Argentine*, trans. Mary J. Serrano (New York: E. P. Dutton, 1919). Where only one page number appears, it refers to the Spanish text and indicates the lack of corresponding lines in Serrano's version.

2. Carlos Dámaso Martínez, "Nacimiento de la novela: José Mármol," *Cuadernos de la literatura argentina*, vol. 1. *La novela argentina traditional* (Buenos Aires; Centro Editor de América Latina, 1985): 265–288; 271.

3. See, for example, Myron I. Lichtblau, *The Argentine Novel in the Nineteenth Century* (New York: Hispanic Institute in the United States, 1959): 48–49.

4. Donna J. Guy notes that Unitarians showed some concern for women's education, and "Rivadavia's concern for the advancement of women augured a new era for family relations," dominated until then—and afterward—by the rule of father's right, *patria potestad*. See "Lower-Class Families, Women, and the Law in Nineteenth-Century Argentina," *Journal of Family History* (Fall, 1985): 318–331, esp. 324.

5. David Viñas, *De Sarmiento a Cortázar* (Buenos Aires: Ediciones Siglo Veinte, 1971): 17.

6. His cattleman's political economy, contemporary critics complained, concerned itself with selling meat, hides, and some grain, and turning the country into an outlet for England's manufacture. Jorge M. Mayer, *Alberdi y su tiempo*, 2 vols., 2d ed. (Buenos Aires: Biblioteca de la Academia Nacional de Derecho y Ciencias Sociales de Buenos Aires, 1973): 109.

7. Mayer, *Alberdi* . . . : 261–264, especially the meeting with Bouchet Martigny and letters between Alberdi and Mr. Baradere which were used to build a conspiratorial alliance.

8. See Adolfo Prieto, *Proyección del rosismo en la literatura argentina* (Rosario: Seminario del Instituto de Letras, Facultad de Filosofía y Letras, 1959); see also Enrique Anderson Imbert's standard *Historia de la literatura hispanoamericana* (México: Fondo de Cultura Econó-

mica, 1954), 2: 24. *Amalia,* he says, is Mármol's only enduring work. Several generations of Argentines learned its passionate vision of Rosas's terror. The story has also been popularized in two films, radio and television adaptations, and popular songs.

9. One important historical example of the advantage was General Paz's defeat during the Unitarian uprising on May 1, 1831. "The general's horse was faster than any of theirs, and for a moment it looked as if he might elude them. Then a gaucho who was proud of his skill with the Argentine bolas whirled this weapon around his head and let go at the legs of La Paz's horse. Horse and rider fell in a scrambled heap. . . . After that the unitarian cause was hopeless. A well-aimed bolas had cleared the last great obstacle from the path of Rosas." John A. Crow, *The Epic of Latin America,* 3d ed. (Berkeley, Los Angeles, London: University of California Press, 1980): 582.

10. Juan Bautista Alberdi, *Proceso a Sarmiento*: 33.

11. David Viñas, *Literatura argentina y realidad política* (Buenos Aires: Jorge Alvarez editor, 1964): 8. The contradiction in the Generation of 1837, he points out, was its literary Americanism and its political anti-Americanism.

12. Mayer, *Alberdi . . .* : 222. The quote is Alberdi's, very similar to Echeverría's statements.

13. James Scobie's *Argentina: A City and a Nation* (New York: Oxford University Press, 1964) acknowledges its borrowed title from René Marill's *Argentine, un monde, une ville* (Paris: Hachette, 1957).

14. Noé Jitrik, *Esteban Echeverría* (Buenos Aires: Centro editor de América Latina, 1967): 29.

15. See F. de La Mennais, *Words of a Believer* (translator not given) (New York: Henry Ludwig, Printer, 1834). In the Preface we learn that La Mennais began as a passionate monarchist and conservative during the Restoration but changed during the "three revolutionary days of July 1830": vii. After Pope Gregory XVI convinces the abbé to suppress publication of *L'Avenir,* radical feelings smolder and he publishes *Paroles d'un Croyant,* for which he is excommunicated. Especially interesting is his defense of a revolutionary Christ: "When thou seest a man conducted to prison or to execution, be not hasty to say: 'this is a wicked man who hath committed some crime against society'— . . . Eighteen centuries ago, in a city of the East, the chief priests and the kings of that day, nailed to a cross, after having beaten with rods, one whom they called seditious, and a blasphemer": 27–28.

16. Félix Weinberg, "La época de Rosas y el romanticismo," *Historia de la literatura argentina/1* (Buenos Aires: Centro Editor de América Latina, 1967): 169–216; 173.

17. Weinberg: 196.

18. Henrí Lefebvre gives this double meaning in "Toward a Leftist Cultural Politics: Remarks Occasioned by the Centenary of Marx's Death," a trans. David Reifman, *Marxism and the Interpretation of Culture*, ed. Cary Nelson and Lawrence Grossberg (Urbana: University of Illinois Press, 1988): 75–88; 78.

19. Mayer, *Alberdi . . .* : 196. The scant publication of four to six pages in fact replaces the Salon and is announced as *La Moda, gacetita semanaria de música, de poesía, de literatura, de costumbres, de modas, dedicada al bello mundo federal*.

20. I am very grateful to Prof. Tulio Halperín Donghi for this observation. Generously responding to my hunches about the period he writes, "The representation in the novel is fairly consistent with more personal testimonies. (Alberdi didn't hesitate to declare his entirely feminine character in letters to friends; this self-portrait didn't suppose a confession of sexual ambiguity. On the contrary he and his friends never pardoned Rivera Indarte's homosexuality, so extreme an infarction that they refer to it only vaguely.)" Letter of February 15, 1988. See also the strained relations with Rivera Indarte that Mayer records, *Alberdi y su tiempo*: 80, 277, 383, where he is called *perverso*: 404.

21. Weinberg: 175.

22. Jitrik: 30–31.

23. José Luis Lanuza, *Echeverría y sus amigos* (Buenos Aires: Paidós, 1967): 112.

24. Lanuza: 137.

25. Lanuza: 133.

26. I am grateful to Beatriz Sarlo for pointing out the resemblance. Sarmiento, *Recuerdos*: 68.

27. Even Rosas's own son collaborated with them. See Mayer, *Alberdi . . .* : 276.

28. Francine Masiello, "Texto, ley, transgresión: Especulación sobre la novela (feminista) de vanguardia," *Revista Iberoamericana*, nos. 132–133 (July–December 1985): 807–822. In the Argentine *mundonovista* canon, she points out, disobedience is disaster. Masiello has made the same type of argument for Manuel Gálvez's novels as she does here for West's: 809.

29. In general, as Mark D. Szuchman argues compellingly, Unitarians tended to be indeed as duplicitous and as "savage" as their Federalist counterparts. See his "Disorder and Social Control," *Journal of Interdisciplinary History* (Summer, 1984): 83–110, and in *Family, Order, and Community in Buenos Aires 1810–1860* (Palo Alto, Calif.: Stanford University Press, 1988).

30. In *Nuestra América* (Buenos Aires, 1918) Carlos Octavio

Bunge records this general observation about Rosas's verbal skill. "His speeches were never clear or straight to the point; they were diffuse, complicated with digressions and incidental phrases. His wordiness was obviously premeditated and aimed at confusing his interlocutor. It was, indeed, almost impossible to follow just what he had in mind. . . . Rosas would show himself in turn to be the consummate statesman, a very affable and sympathetic person, a fine dialectician, a vehement and impassioned orator. He was possessed in turn, and according to his mood, by raging anger, simplicity, or the utmost candor. He always spoke with the ulterior motive of intimidating, deceiving, or swaying his listener to accept his own point of view." Quoted in John A Crow: 589.

31. I am indebted here to Carlos Lizarralde's reading, which locates a similar textual restlessness in Sarmiento's description of General Paz.

32. Mayer summarizes, "Of course he wasn't a Federalist, he was a *porteño* and nothing more. 'Everyone says I'm a Federalist and I laugh,'" *Alberdi . . .* : 99.

33. After his loud arguments about spelling with Andrés Bello, Sarmiento had the satisfaction of winning *El Mercurio* of Santiago to his romantic and Americanist variations. But in 1844, recently emigrated Alberdi edited the paper and abandoned the innovations, the first of many dissenting gestures.

34. Mayer, *Alberdi . . .* : 420–422.

35. Juan María Gutiérrez, *Los poetas de la revolución* (Buenos Aires: Academia de Letras, 1951): 142.

36. See Tulio Halperin Donghi, "Una larga espera," chap. 3 of *Historia contemporánea de América Latina*: 134–206.

37. For this process see Reid Andrews, *The Afro-Argentines of Buenos Aires* (Madison: University of Wisconsin Press, 1980).

38. Elvira B. de Meyer, "El nacimiento de la novela: José Mármol," *Historia de la literatura argentina/1* (Buenos Aires: Centro Editor de América Latina, 1967): 216–239; 225. "Among his works prior to *Amalia*, is a short treatise titled: *Manuelita Rosas. Rasgos biográficos.* Three editions in one year prove its popularity . . . not only in Buenos Aires, but also in Europe." One curious circumstance of this book, originally published in 1850, is that Rosas himself saved the copy that Mármol dedicated to Manuelita.

39. I thank Mark D. Szuchman for pointing out Sarmiento's defense of "institutional forms of social exchange peculiar to British and North American societies," against even Alberdi's jurisprudent preference for "leaving Creoles to their customary habits, confident

that their excesses would be tempered by the benefits of economic federalism." Letter of May 23, 1988.

40. Mayer, *Alberdi* . . . : 244. Letter from Gutiérrez to Alberdi, no date.

41. José Luis Romero, *A History of Argentine Political Thought* (Palo Alto, Calif.: Stanford University Press, 1963): 86–87.

42. I owe this comparison and appreciation for the Arcadian cast of Tucumán to Tulio Halperín Donghi.

43. Mármol's first big break was to get third prize at the poetry contest in honor of Independence Day. Alberdi defended Mármol's disorderly exalted tone against Florencio Varela's classical bias; and Alberdi got the last word as editor and prologuist of the winning poems in *Certamen poético de Montevideo, 25 de mayo de 1841* (Imprenta Constitucional del P. F. Olave), 80 pp.

44. Mayer, *Alberdi* . . . : 379.

45. Mayer, *Alberdi* . . . : 39. "The field of my country's glory is also that of my childhood pleasures. We were both children: Argentina and I were the same age."

46. Later, Sarmiento could count the punishment against Rosas, *Recuerdos de provincia*: 37.

47. Mayer, *Alberdi* . . . : 466–467.

48. The historical narrative intrudes irresistibly as Mármol narrates Lavalle's advance on Rosas:

Ya estaban frente a frente.
Su voz se oía.
Sus armas se tocaban. . . . Entretanto la pluma del romancista se resiste, dejando al historiador esta tristísima tarea. (411)

[They were already face to face.
You could hear his voice.
Their armaments touched. . . . Meanwhile the novelist's pen gives out, leaving this sorrowful job for the historian.]

Pp. 421–430 record the official classifications of victims and explain in a footnote that these were added in 1855, after the tyranny's records became public.

For a sense of the international context of this crisis for Rosas, see Hernán Vidal, "*Amalia*: Melodrama y Dependencia," *Ideologies and Literature?*: 41–69.

49. Mayer, *Alberdi* . . . : 192. An undated letter to Alberdi.

50. Weinberg: 172.

51. Mayer, *Alberdi* . . . : 82. "Miguel Cané and I happened to sit to-

gether on the first bench, so close to the teacher's desk that he couldn't see us. One morning in the spring of 1829, he took a book out of his pocket, to see if we could entertain ourselves better than reading Virgilian verses. . . . After reading the first lines written in a style and about a subject until then unknown to my heart, my eyes were bathed in tears. The book was *Julie* by J. J. Rousseau; the Julie who kept my heart sunk in sweet illusions for four years."

52. Freedom of religion as a condition of immigration was evidently a legislative challenge for liberals throughout Latin America. See for example President Justo Rufino Barrios's declaration of 1873 in Guatemala, whose population by 1982 was 30 percent Protestant. Virginia Garrand Burnett, "Protestantism in Rural Guatemala, 1872–1954," *Latin American Research Review* 24, 2 (1989): 127–142.

53. Juan Bautista Alberdi, *Las "Bases" de Alberdi,* ed. Jorge M. Mayer (Buenos Aires: Editorial Sudamericana, 1969): 406 (my emphasis).

54. Jitrik: 25.

55. Elvira B. de Meyer: 252.

56. David Viñas, *Literatura argentina y realidad política:* 126–128.

57. Weinberg: 211.

58. Jitrik: 28.

59. Elvira B. de Meyer: 220.

60. Esteban Echeverría, *Prosa literaria,* ed. Roberto F. Giusti (Buenos Aires: Ediciones Estrada, 1955): 8.

61. See Lucía Guerra Cunningham, "La visión marginal en la narrativa de Juana Manuela Gorriti," *Ideologies & Literature,* New Series, 2, 2 (Fall, 1987): 59–76. But her simple summing up of Mármol's project (70) suggests that the opposition may be drawn too strongly.

62. Juana Manuela Gorriti, *Narraciones,* ed. W. G. Weyland (Silverio Boj) (Buenos Aires: Ediciones Estrada, 1958): 76–97.

63. Ibid., pp. 57–67.

64. Ibid., pp. 99–118.

65. For several other (in)versions of *Julie*'s fate in Argentina, see Elizabeth Garrels, "*La Nueva Heloísa* en América," *Nuevo Texto Crítico* 11, 4: 27–38.

66. See Elizabeth Garrels's excellent "El 'espíritu de la familia' en *La Novia del Hereje* de Vicente Fidel López," *Hispamérica* 16, 46–47 (April–August 1987): 3–24.

67. Mitre polemicized against fictional histories (and against López), paradoxically, in the folletín section of the newspaper. See "Uneven Modernities," paper presented by Julio Ramos at the April 1986 meeting of the ACLA in Atlanta.

68. Josefina Ludmer, *El género gauchesco*, details the literary maneuvers of elite poets who affect an esthetic (and political-economic) *Aufhebung* of gauchos.

69. He was forced into exile after the defeat and wrote his poem largely in Brazil. See Angel Rama, "Prólogo" to *La poesía gauchesca* (Caracas: Biblioteca Ayacucho, 1977): also 190.

70. I am indebted to Josefina Ludmer's work here, especially where she plays on the *género gauchesco* as a masculine engendering: 49–50.

71. See Rama's "Prólogo," *La Poesía Gauchesca*, where he refers to Lugones's appeal for a nationalist culture in 1913. See also Henríquez Ureña's *Literary Currents*: 147.

72. For example, Manuel Gálvez, *Vida de Don Juan Manuel de Rosas* (Buenos Aires: El Ateneo, 1940).

4. SAB C'EST MOI

1. A collection of essays in commemoration of Avellaneda represents the distinct claims upon her. *Homenaje a Gertrudis Gómez de Avellaneda*, ed. Rosa M. Cabrera and Gladys B. Zaldívar (Miami: Ediciones Universal, 1981), includes Severo Sarduy's emphasis on her quintessential Cubanness (reminiscent of Rafael María Merchán, *Patria y cultura* [Havana: Ministerio de Educación, Dirección de Cultura, 1948]: 116–121), others on her European roots, and a section on her feminism.

Among the growing number of essays on Avellaneda as feminist are: Mirta Aguirre, *Influencia de la mujer en Iberoamérica* (Havana: Servicio Femenino para la Defensa Civil, 1947): 20–26; Belkis Cuza Malé, "La Avellaneda: Una mujer con importancia," *Gaceta de Cuba*, no. 74 (1969): 28–29; Alberto J. Carlos, "La Avellaneda y la mujer," *Actas del Tercer Congreso Internacional de Hispanistas* (Mexico City: Colegio de México, 1970): 187–193, and "La conciencia feminista en dos ensayos; Sor Juana y la Avellaneda," Instituto de Literatura Iberoamericana, *El ensayo y la crítica en Iberoamérica* (Toronto: Universidad de Toronto, 1970): 33–41; Pedro Barreda Tomás, "Abolicionismo y feminismo en la Avellaneda: Lo negro como artificio narrativo en *Sab*," *Cuadernos Hispanoamericanos*, no. 342 (1978): 613–626; Beth Miller, "Avellaneda, Nineteenth Century Feminist," *Revista Interamericana* 4 (1974): 177–183; Nelly E. Santos, "Las ideas feministas de Gertrudis Gómez de Avellaneda," *Revista Interamericana* 5 (1975): 276–281; and Lucía Guerra, "Estrategias femeninas en la elaboración del sujeto romántico en la obra de Gertrudis Gómez de Avellaneda,"

Revista Iberoamericana 51, nos. 132–133 (July–December 1985): 707–722.

2. See Susan Kirkpatrick's chap. 4 of *Las Románticas: Women Writers and Subjectivity in Spain, 1835–1850* (Berkeley, Los Angeles, London: University of California Press, 1989). Also, Mary Cruz, "Gertrudis Gómez de Avellaneda y su novela *Sab,*" *Unión* (Havana) 12, 1 (1973): 116–149. "Since the appearance of her *Poesías* and *Sab* in 1841, Avellaneda's name began to appear in dictionaries, collections and biographical manuals . . .": 118. She quotes Avellaneda's Spanish contemporary Bretón de los Herreros as saying, memorably, "that woman is a lot of man": 127.

José Martí criticized her for the "masculinity" that seemed unnatural to him. See his comparison with Luisa Pérez Zambrana. José Martí, *Obras Completas* (Havana: Editora Nacional de Cuba, 1963) 8: 309–313.

José Zorrilla, by contrast, applauded nature's "mistake." "Because she was a beautiful woman, tall, shapely, with well-turned arms and a proud head crowned by abundant chestnut curls . . . [s]he was a woman, but she was one no doubt because of some mistake of nature, which, distracted, had put the soul of a man into a woman's body." See his *Recuerdos del tiempo viejo* (Madrid: Tipografía Gutenberg, 1882), 3: 131.

3. It is Carlota, the pampered mistress, rather than Sab, who offers a mimetic representation of Avellaneda. For that identification, based on autobiographical data, see Mildred V. Boyer, "Realidad y ficción en *Sab,*" *Homenaje a Gertrudis Gómez de Avellaneda*: 292–300. See also Lucía Guerra for whom Carlota becomes, retroactively, "the basic romantic subject" and therefore the novelist's representative: 709.

4. "Autobiografía de la Sra. Da. Gertrudis Gómez de Avellaneda," included as an appendix to *Sab* (Paris: Agencia General de Librería, 1920): 247–290. The letter is addressed to Ignacio de Cepeda y Alcalde and dated from July 23 to July 27, 1839.

5. For a summary and restatement see, Concepción T. Alzola, "El personaje Sab," *Homenaje a Gertrudis Gómez de Avellaneda*: 283–291.

6. Gertrudis Gómez de Avellaneda, *Sab*, "Prologue," Mary Cruz (Havana: Editorial Letras Cubanas, 1983). All quotes from the novel will refer to this edition and appear parenthetically in the essay. This passage hints at how much Avellaneda admired George Sand. Her trip through France, on the way to Spain, exposed Avellaneda to writers still unknown to many Americans.

7. The term *advenedizos* on p. 100 of the novel refers to the first

Spanish conquerors and, by extension, to contemporary English opportunists.

8. In the last chapter, I will again take up the strategy of Sor Juana Inés de la Cruz, seventeenth-century Mexico's brilliant and much-quoted poet and dramatist, who gives probably the earliest examples when she defended her right to write. See Margaret Sayers Peden translation, *A Woman of Genius: The Intellectual Autobiography of Sor Juana Inés de la Cruz* (Limerock, Conn.: Limerock Press, 1982): 81.

9. Lucía Guerra: 708–709.

10. Mary Cruz, "Prologue," *Sab* (Havana: Editorial Arte y Literatura, 1976): 56. "The date, during the heat of the War for Independence begun in '68, justifies our thinking that the novel was used as a far-reaching ideological tool."

11. In her Prologue, p. 9, Cruz surmises that Hugo's novel must have made an impact on Avellaneda, during her trip to France in 1836. In that very year, Félix Tanco was writing to Domingo del Monte: "And what do you say to *Bug-Jargal*? I'd like for us to write in the style of this little novel. Think about it. Blacks in the Island of Cuba are our Poetry, and that's that; but not the blacks alone, rather blacks with whites, all mixed together. . . . May our Victor Hugo be born, and may we know at long last what we are."

12. See the seminal article by Roberto Friol, "La novela cubana en el siglo XIX," *Unión* 6, 4 (Havana, 1968): 179–207.

13. Mary Cruz makes a convincing argument for Hugo's novel as the model for *Sab*. See her "Gertrudis Gómez de Avellaneda."

14. Other contemporary Cuban examples are "El niño Fernando" (published in 1925 in the journal *Cuba Contemporánea* 39: 255–288) by Félix Tanco Bosmoniel, *Francisco* by Anselmo Suárez y Romero, and later, *El negro Francisco* by Antonio Zambrana y Vázquez.

15. Mary Cruz, "Prologue": 11.

16. These powerful enclaves were made up of Spanish and creole capitalists. The former controlled the slave trade as well as financed the machinery needed in the sugar mills, while the latter constituted what was called the "sugarocracy," that is, owners of the mills, land, and slaves.

17. This shift from a local, historical issue, to the more general critique of binary and essentialist thinking has led at least a few readers to assume, or mistake, Avellaneda's romanticism as fundamentally apolitical. See, for example, Carmen Bravo-Villasante, *Una vida romántica: La Avellaneda* (Barcelona: Buenos Aires Editora Hispano Americana, 1967): 85. See also Allison Peers who had set this

tone, *Historia del movimiento romántico español,* 2d ed. (Madrid: Gredos, 1967) 2: 135, and Raimundo Lazo who emphasizes Sab's Platonic love: "More than an abolitionist narrative, it is a romantic embellishment of a slave." *La literatura cubana* (Mexico: UNAM, 1965): 86.

18. Manuel Moreno Fraginals, "Plantation Economies and Societies in the Spanish Caribbean, 1860–1930," *The Cambridge History of Latin America,* vol. 4. *c. 1870–1930,* ed. Leslie Bethell (Cambridge: Cambridge University Press, 1986): 187–232; 189.

19. Antonio Benítez Rojo and Eduardo González inform me that the popularity of the "zarzuela" was taken for familiarity with the book. But Benítez adds that the novel was indeed standard reading in schools, as was *Sab.*

20. For the differences, see for example the Prologue by Imeldo Alvarez García, in Cirilo Villaverde, *Cecilia Valdés,* 2 vols. (Havana: Editorial Letras Cubanas, 1981): 5–46. See also Roberto Friol: 178. Page references to the novel will appear parenthetically.

21. Imeldo Alvarez García: 14–15. In 1855 Villaverde marries Emilia Casanova, who forced her family to leave Cuba for New York, given her outspoken criticism of Spain. Later, he will write *Apuntes biográficos de Emilia Casanova de Villaverde* about her continuing political work, courage, intelligence.

22. Cirilo Villaverde, *Cecilia Valdés,* critical study by Raimundo Lazo (Mexico: Editorial Porrúa, 1979): 174. Page references to the novel will be to this edition. "She had no feminine softness, and it goes without saying, no voluptuousness. . . . The reason was obvious: horseback riding . . . swimming . . . almost daily long walks in the coffee plantation . . . had made her develop a robust constitution. . . . So that nothing would be lacking in her manly and determined looks, we should add that her expressive mouth had the shadow of a dark and silky fuz, which would surely have turned into a healthy mustache if it were shaved daily." On p. 88, Isabel's father proudly says that she's "quite a man," the mainstay of the plantation.

23. I owe this astute perception to Norman Holland.

24. The liberating possibilities of free markets in general are suggested when, for example, the slave María de Regla learns negotiations to everyone's advantage from a street vendor. Villaverde: 267.

25. The author gives the following footnote to pt. 2, chap. 3: 82, about a gala evening at the Philharmonic Society: "The following report is taken, practically verbatim from a weekly called *La Moda* published in Havana in 1830." [La relación que sigue la tomamos casi al pie de la letra de un semanario que se publicaba en La Habana en

1830, titulado *La Moda*.] The novel as well as those articles were dedicated to Cuban women.

26. I thank Enrico Mario Santí for this observation.

27. See Edith L. Kelly, "La Avellaneda's *Sab* and the Political Situation in Cuba," *The Americas* 1 (1945): 303–316. See also her "The Banning of *Sab* in Cuba: Documents from the Archivo Nacional de Cuba," *The Americas* 1 (1945): 350–353.

28. For a good study of Del Monte's influence on abolitionist literature, see Iván Schulman, "Reflections on Cuba and Its Antislavery Literature," *Annals of the Southeastern Conference on Latin American Studies* 7 (1976): 59–67.

29. For a succinct summary of the conflict, see Hugh Thomas, "Cuba from the middle of the eighteenth century to c. 1870," in *The Cambridge History of Latin America*, vol. 3. *From Independence to c. 1870* (Cambridge: Cambridge University Press, 1985): 277–298, esp. 286–287.

30. In Brazil, the conflict with England may have been even sharper because the same sectors were defending both sovereignty and slavery. See Leslie Bethell and José Murilo de Carvalho, "Brazil from Independence to the Middle of the Nineteenth Century," in *The Cambridge History of Latin America*, vol. 3. *From Independence to c. 1870* (Cambridge: Cambridge University Press, 1985): 679–746. See esp. 724–742.

31. Antonio Benítez Rojo establishes this distinction in "Poder/Azúcar/Texto: Triada de lo cubano," *Cruz Ansata* (Bayamón: Universidad Central de Bayamón, 1986), 9: 91–117.

5. *O GUARANÍ* AND *IRACEMA*: BRAZIL'S TWO-FACED INDIGENISM

1. Oswald de Andrade, *Revista de Antropofagia*, Sâo Paulo, 1, 1 (May 1928): 5. Translations throughout this chapter, unless otherwise noted, are mine.

2. See Manuel Cavalcanti Proença, *Roteiro de Macunaíma* (Sâo Paulo: Editora Anhembi, 1955).

3. Silviano Santiago pointed out this unavoidable pun on "to pee."

4. Roberto Schwarz, "Nacional por subtração" in *Que Horas Sâo?* (Sâo Paulo: Companhia das Letras, 1987): 29–48.

5. Fábio Freixiero, *Alencar: Os Bastidores e a Posteridade*, vol. 4 (Rio de Janeiro: Museu Histórico Nacional, Coleção "Estudos e Documentos," 1977): 35, 39.

6. *Miscelânea* (Rio de Janeiro, 1877), a collection of articles and speeches on the occasion of Alencar's death. Quoted in Freixiero: 37.

7. Ibid., p. 38.

8. Afrânio Coutinho, "Prefácio," in Freixiero, *Alencar: Os Bastidores*: xiv. "Alencar is not only the patriarch of Brazilian literature, the initiator of our modern novel. . . . He is also an example, a model for all of us to try to write literature in this country. He is the master, the guide, the conscience." See also his now-standard *A Tradiçâo Afortunada: (O Espírito de Nacionalidade na Crítica Brasileira)* (Rio: José Olympio Editora, 1968): 96–101; and his "A literatura como fator da nacionalizaçâo brasileira," *Revista Tempo Brasileiro*, nos. 33–34, (April–June 1973): 30: "Alencar wrote for the future, seeing correctly that Brazilian civilization is mestiza, neither white, nor black, nor indigenous, but mestiza, 'Brazilian,' something new with particular characteristics."

And according to David Miller Driver, *The Indian in Brazilian Literature* (New York: Hispanic Institute in the United States, 1942): 124: "The titles 'Father of the Brazilian novel' and 'Creator of a distinctive prose style' have so often been used with regard to Alencar that they have become the commonplace in studies of his works."

9. Silviano Santiago, "Liderança E Hierarquia em Alencar," *Vale Quanto Pesa* (Rio de Janeiro: Paz e Terra, 1982): 89–116.

10. Miller Driver: 80–81. His novels are: *O Guaraní* 1856 (in book form, 1857); *Cinco Minutos*, 1860; *A Viuvinha*, 1860; *Luciola*, 1862; *Diva*, 1864; *Iracema*, 1865; *As Minas de Prata*, 1866; *O Gaúcho*, 1870; *A Pata de Gazela*, 1870; *O Tronco de Ipé*, 1871; *A Guerra dos Mascates*, 1871; *Til*, 1872; *Sonhos d'Ouro*, 1872; *Alfarrabios*, three short novels, 1873; *Ubirajara*, 1875; *Senhora*, 1875; *O Sertanejo*, 1875; *Encarnaçâo*, 1877 (in book form, 1893); *Lembra-te-de-Mim*, posthumously, 1887.

11. Antônio Cândido, "Os três Alencares," *Formaçâo da Literatura Brasileira* (Sâo Paulo: Martins, 1964), vol. 2, chap. 5: 218–232. He refers specifically to *Senhora* and *Lucíola*. See also Valéria De Marco, *O Império da Cortesâ, Lucíola: Um perfil de Alencar* (Sâo Paulo: Martins, 1986).

12. Nelson Werneck Sodré, "O indianismo e a sociedade brasileira" in *Historia da Literatura Brasileira* (Rio: Civilizaçâo Brasileira, 4th ed., 1964): 272–294.

13. See Cleusa Aparecida Valin, "Escritores Brasileiros: Filmografía," in *Filme Cultura* 20 (May–June 1972): 42. After this article, Fauzi Mansur directed a new *Guaraní* in 1978, and a new *Iracema*, played by the porno star Helena Ramos and directed by Carlos Coimbra, came out a year later.

14. José Veríssimo begins to formalize the popular response, judging that *O Guaraní* is Alencar's first and best work. See *História da literatura brasileira*, 3d ed. (Rio: José Olympio, 1954): 223–234. A recent mention of the naming craze appeared on January 10, 1986, in a review of *Iracema* in French (trans. Ines Oseki-Dépré, UNESCO, 1986), titled "Les mythes fondateurs." "Depuis la premiére édition en 1865 jusqu'à nos jours, des milliers de Brésiliens ont reçu le prénom de leur ancêtre fictif, Moacir, le métis né de l'union passionnée entre l'héroine et le Portugais Martim." My favorite example is Moacyr Scliar, a contemporary novelist and the son of Hungarian Jewish immigrants.

15. Afrânio Coutinho, "Josê de Alencar na Literatura Brasileira," in *O Proceso de Descolonizaçâo Literaria* (Rio: Civilizaçao Brasileira, 1983): 73–76.

16. Raquel de Queiroz, "José de Alencar," first published in 1951 edition of *Iracema e Ubirajara*. Reprinted in centennial edition of *Iracema: Lenda do Ceará 1865–1965* (Rio: José Olympio, 1965): 251–253; 251.

17. José de Alencar, *O Guaraní* (Sâo Paulo: Editora Atica, 14th ed., 1988), a student edition with questions and exercises in a "Work Supplement" appended to the end. My references, prefaced with "1857," will be first to this text and then to the Spanish edition for the convenience of some readers. José de Alencar, *El Guaraní* (Havana: Casa de las Américas, 1983).

18. José de Alencar, *Iracema, Lenda do Ceará*, ed. Silviano Santiago (Rio de Janeiro: Francisco Alves, 1988). Parenthetical page references to this edition will follow an "1865." The second page reference will be to José de Alencar, *Iracema, The Honey-Lips: A Legend of Brazil*, trans. Isabel Burton (London: Bickers & Son, 1886; reprint New York: Howard Fertig Inc., 1976).

19. Samuel Putnam, *Marvelous Journey: A Survey of Four Centuries of Brazilian Writing* (New York: Alfred A. Knopf, 1948; reprint New York: Octagon Books, 1971); 147–148.

20. He was one of the few who published contemporary reviews praising Alencar's novels. See his pieces on *Iracema* and *O Guaraní* in Machado de Assis, *Critica Literaria* (Rio and Sâo Paulo: W. M. Jackson Inc. Editores, 1937): 64–76; 332–341.

21. Freixiero, 60.

22. Leslie Bethell, "The Independence of Brazil," *The Cambridge History of Latin America*, vol. 3. *From Independence to c. 1870* (Cambridge: Cambridge University Press, 1984): 157–196. See 162–163.

23. Silviano Santiago makes this point, p. 101.

24. Bethell: 178.

25. Ibid., p. 162.

26. Ibid., p. 192. The Confederation of the Equator, in the northeast, lasted for six months.

27. Ibid., p. 185.

28. Leslie Bethell, chap. 16, "Brazil from Independence to the Middle of the Nineteenth Century," *The Cambridge History of Latin America*, vol. 3. *From Independence to c. 1870* (Cambridge: Cambridge University Press, 1984): 679–794. See 702–704. Pará's was the first major provincial revolt of the 1830s. A Liberal president appointed by the Regency finally took office but was killed by radical liberals and the independence of Pará was proclaimed. The Regents appointed a new president, but in 1835 the rebel army—mostly blacks and *tapuios*—attacked, and war spread up the Amazon. Then General Andreia came from the capital; he was ruthless. "Violence and cruelty were widespread on both sides. Some people were seen proudly wearing rosaries made from the ears of dead *cabanos*. Around 4,000 *cabanos* died in prisons, ships and hospitals alone."

29. Bethell: 682.

30. Roberto Schwarz, "Misplaced Ideas: Literature and Society in Late Nineteenth-Century Brazil," *Comparative Civilizations Review* 5 (1979): 33–51.

31. José de Alencar, *Como e Porque Sou Romancista*, introduction by Afrânio Coutinho (Rio: Coleçâo Academia Brasileira, 1987; written in May 1873): 40.

32. Miller Driver: 14.

33. Ronald de Carvalho remarked on this in his *Pequena História da Literatura Brasileira* (Rio: Briguiet, 1919): 252. "His Indians do not express themselves like graduates of Coimbra; they speak the way Nature taught them to, they love, live and die like the plants and the lower animals of the earth."

34. Antônio Cândido, *Introducción a la literatura de Brasil* (Caracas: Monte Avila Editores, 1968): 27.

35. Renato de Mendonça in 1945, quoted in Freixiero: 58.

36. José de Alencar, *Obra Completa* (Rio de Janeiro: Editora José Aguilar Ltda, 1960), 4: 8–9, from Notes in Alencar archive for essays, no dates. And in "Questâo Filológica" (1874): 960, he makes a parallel with American English, quoting Webster, the first American lexicographer. Alencar also develops this position in a preface he wrote to defend this freedom for the second edition of *Iracema*.

37. Miller Driver: 78. "In 1872, the young novelist Franklin Silveira de Tavora assailed Alencar and his Indianist novels in a series

of articles called *Cartas a Cincinnato*. Cincinnato refers to the Portuguese poet Antonio de Castilho, with whom Tavora had nothing in common except the fact that Castilho was a bitter critic of Alencar's vocabulary and grammar."

38. The main difference between "Iracema e Atala" according to Antônio Soares Amora, *Revista de letras* (São Paulo) 3 (1962): 120–136, is the unproductive passion in Chateaubriand in contrast to the foundational love in Alencar. In one, self-sacrifice is merely suicide; in the other it is the condition of ideal (Heaven help us!) motherhood.

39. José de Alencar, *Como E Porque Sou Romancista*: 40. He goes on a bit defensively from p. 39 to p. 41. For a development of the parallel, see Renata R. Wasserman, "The Red and the White: The Indian Novels of José de Alencar," *PMLA* (October 1983); especially her "Re-Inventing the New World: Cooper and Alencar," *Comparative Literature* (Spring, 1984).

Afrânio Peixoto complained about this general tendency to copy and to deny: "We imitate European models while refusing to admit it and arrogantly pretending to originality. We have little imagination, whatever may be said to the contrary, and small power of reflection, but we do possess a great gift for showy verbal expression." See Afrânio Peixoto, *Noçoes de História da Literatura Brasileira* (Rio de Janeiro: Francisco Alves, 1931): 45–48.

40. Antônio Cândido, *Formaçâo da literatura brasileira*, 2: 324.

41. De Marco: 13.

42. Alencar, *Como e porque sou romancista*: 40.

43. José de Alencar, *Obras Completas*, 4: 913; 875.

44. Augusto Meyer, "Alencar," in *A Chave e a Máscara* (Rio: Ediçôes O Cruzeiro, 1964): 145–158. Reprinted in centennial edition of *Iracema: Lenda do Ceará 1865–1965*: 254–264.

45. Gilberto Freyre, *Sobrados e mucambos* (Rio: Livr. J. Olympio, 1936; reprint, 1968), 2: 590. Quoted in Luiz Costa Lima, *O Controle do Imaginário* (S. Paulo, Brasiliense, 1984): 134. See translation of Costa Lima, *Control of the Imaginary*, trans. Ronald W. Sousa (Minneapolis: University of Minnesota Press, 1988): 106.

46. Walnice Nogueira Galvâo, "Indianismo revisitado," *Esboço de Figura: Homenagem a Antônio Cândido* (Sâo Paulo: Duas Cidades, 1981): 379–389.

47. Bethell: 702–704.

48. Ibid., p. 787.

49. David H. Treece, "Victims, Allies, Rebels: Towards a New History of Nineteenth-Century Indianism in Brazil," *Portuguese Studies* 2 (London, 1986): 56–98.

50. Karl Friedrich Philipp von Martius, "How the History of Brazil Should Be Written," in *Perspectives on Brazilian History*, ed. E. Bradford Burns (New York: Columbia University Press, 1967): 21–41; 23.

51. Freixiero: 68.

52. See Manoel Luís Salgado Guimarâes, "Naçâo e civilizaçâo nos trópicos: O Instituto Histórico e Geográfico Brasileiro e o projeto de uma história nacional," *Estudos Históricos*, no. 1 (Rio, 1988): 5–27.

53. Martius: 24.

54. Martius: 25, 29.

55. Burns, Introduction: 21–22.

56. José de Alencar, "A língua portuguêsa no Brasil," *Obra Completa* (Rio de Janeiro: Editora José Aguilar Ltda, 1960), notes in Alencar archive for essays, no dates, 4: 8–9. In "Literatura Brasileira" (9–10), he follows von Martius about Brazilian character of history: "*Gênio*—Racial identity, but the soil, the climate, and Nature are different. Three elements: American, European, African; a new country. . . . Influence, amalgam, the fusion hasn't happened yet; it's evolving."

57. Gilberto Freyre, *The Masters and the Slaves (Casa-Grande & Senzala): A Study in the Development of Brazilian Civilization*, trans. Samuel Putnam (New York: Alfred A. Knopf, 1946): 69.

58. For Silviano Santiago, the indispensable text here is José Honório Rodrigues, "A Política de conciliaçâo: História cruenta e incruenta," in *Conciliaçâo e Reforma no Brazil* (Rio: Civilizaçâo Brasileira, 1975).

59. Quoted in Putnam: 144. The precise word an angry Peixoto used to refer to Indians is "bugres," literally buggers or sodomites.

See also Freyre, *Masters and the Slaves*: 65–66. "The lyric exaltation of the *caboclo*—that is to say, of the native Indian, which is common among us, or of the cross between Indian and white, a type in which certain persons would discover the purest exponent of the physical capacity, beauty, and even of moral resistance of the Brazilian racial strain—all this does not correspond to reality. . . . Wherever one turns, even in places where it is supposed that Amerindian blood or that of the Portuguese-Indian hybrid is preserved in its purest state, it will be found that the African has been there; in the very heart of the Amazon region, on the Serra do Norte, and in the backlands." Especially revealing is Freyre's assumption that Brazilians are all white, male, and served by darker people whose habits they cannot but absorb (255): "[W]e almost all of us bear the mark of that influence. Of the female slave or 'mammy' who rocked us to sleep. Who suckled us. Who fed us, mashing our food with her own hands. The influence of the old woman who told us our first tales of ghost and *bicho*. Of the mulatto girl who relieved us our first *bicho de pé*, of a pruriency that was so enjoyable. Who initiated us into physical love and, to the creaking of a canvas cot, gave us our first complete sensation of being a man. Of the Negro lad who was our first playmate."

And David Brookshaw, *Race and Color in Brazilian Literature* (Metuchen & London: Scarecrow Press, 1986): 10, where he says the Brazilian Indian "was a far more abstract figure than in most Spanish-speaking countries, given the fact that by the time of Independence, the only Indians left dwelt far from the nuclei of white settlements, and therefore outside the social structure of the nation."

60. José de Alencar, "Pós-escrito à segunda edição de *Iracema*," in *Obras Completas*, 3: 260.

61. Putnam: 27. And, for example, Afrânio Coutinho assured me that he did not speak Portuguese, but Brazilian, during a generous interview in July 1988.

62. Brookshaw: 23.

63. Brito Broca, "O drama político de Alencar," in José de Alencar, *Obra Completas*: 1039–1047; 1039–1040. It was probably his work as journalist, not novelist, that got him elected as deputy of Ceará in 1860. One Deputy Rapôso, from Rio Grande do Norte, began to taunt his opponent about *O Guaraní*, and asked two colleagues next to him, "What was that Indian's name?" Then he said, "that famous Peri-Peri" (1047).

64. Emir Rodríguez Monegal, "La novela histórica: Otra perspectiva," *Historia y ficción en la narrativa hispanoamericana: Coloquio de Yale*, ed. Roberto González Echevarría (Caracas: Monte Avila Editores, 1984): 169–183; 177. In 1922, Alencar's son Mário had probably alluded to this familial blemish when he accuses others, notably the Visconde do Rio Branco, of attacking his father with allusions to "the condition of his birth." See Mário de Alencar, "José de Alencar, o escritor e o político," in José de Alencar, *Obras Completas*: 13–23; 23.

65. Mirta Yáñez, "Prólogo," in José de Alencar, *El Guaraní* (Havana: Casa de las Américas, 1983): xvi.

66. De Marco: 46.

67. Broca: 1046.

68. Alencar, *Obras Completas*: 1060.

69. Bethell: 735.

70. Miller Driver: 77. " . . . his talent and his knowledge of jurisprudence gained him the post of Minister of Justice. Possibly due to some extent to his marriage to a Miss Cochrane, granddaughter of Admiral Dundonald, Alencar ardently advocated the ideas of the

British Conservative Party." For a characterization of Lord Cochrane, the future tenth Earl of Dundonald, see Leslie Bethell: 189. He was "Arrogant, ill-tempered, cantankerous, bellicose"; but he saved Brazilian sovereignty in 1823 from a Portuguese invasion.

71. Broca: 1042.

72. Bethell: 728.

73. Broca: 1042.

74. See De Marco: 62–70.

75. Raimundo de Magalhaês, *José de Alencar e Sua Epoca* (Sâo Paulo: Lisa—Livros Irradiantes, 1971): 253.

76. On the limits of Alencar's project, see De Marco: 62–70. On the limits of both projects, see Antônio Cândido's masterly "Literature and Underdevelopment," in *Latin America in Its Literature,* ed. Ivan Schulman, trans. Mary G. Berg (New York: Holmes & Meier, 1980): 263–282. And for Joaquim Nabuco's work, including a book titled *Abolition* (London, 1883), see Putnam: 124–127.

77. It was already a literary move for Gonçalves Dias (whose disenfranchised Indians were also disaffected whites) among others.

78. Treece: 62, 68, 70. The Liberal and abolitionist novelist Joaquim Manuel de Macedo had also written a popular play, *As Vítimas Algozes, Cobé* (1852) in which the race relations of African slavery are translated into a conflict between Indians and wicked conquerors.

79. I owe this observation to Roberto Schwarz, during a stimulating conversation of August 2, 1988.

80. Gilberto Freyre, *José de Alencar* (Rio: Ministry of Education and Health, 1952): 32, and *Reinterpretando José de Alencar* of 1955: 39.

81. Freyre, *The Masters and the Slaves*: 82. Miriam Moreira Leite pointed out to me that Southey, who was looking for lessons in subduing the Irish, never really went to Brazil, but to Portugal, and wrote his *History of Brazil* in England.

82. Freyre, *Masters and Slaves*: 159.

83. Putnam: 9. "In Brazil miscegenation has come to be viewed as the means of racial assimilation in the achievement of national unity, and this will account for the prominent part that the Indian and the Negro play in Literature. José de Alencar was not the only one to glorify the aborigine." Corresponding n. 12 reads: "The process of assimilation is sometimes known as 'Aryanization,' a term that does not have the same meaning in Brazil that it did in Hitler's Germany."

84. Putnam: 210. But on p. 12, he had already mentioned that Aranha would surely have preferred a clearer (unmixed) notion of Brazil than Alencar's.

85. Daniel da Cruz, "Preface" to *Iracema* by José de Alencar (New York: Longmans, 1943): v.

86. Putnam: 11.

87. Thomas Skidmore, *Black into White: Race and Nationality in Brazilian Thought* (New York: Oxford University Press, 1974); David Brookshaw, *Race and Color in Brazilian Literature* (Metuchen & London: Scarecrow Press, 1986); David Haberley *Three Sad Races: Racial Identity and National Consciousness in Brazilian Literature* (New York: Cambridge University Press, 1983).

88. This is the gist of Freyre's classic *Masters and Slaves*, a kind of anthropological celebration of syncretic Brazilianness in terms still dear to a Liberal elite and apparently written in response to eugenic puritans for whom the country was unredeemably corrupt racially.

89. In *Como e porque sou romanticista* (20, 24) Alencar recounts that as a teenager he helped his mother serve hot chocolate and cookies to the conspirators of the Maiorista revolt, who insisted on empowering Pedro II, and then of the popular revolt of 1842.

90. Justiniano José da Rocha, *O Brasil*, October 1842, quoted in Bethell: 735.

91. Treece yields to the same temptation: 76.

92. Treece: 70.

93. About the close ties between big house and slave shack, Freyre describes a situation familiar from Cuba's *Sab*. "The truth is that an extreme case of incest was not needed in order to scandalize him [Walsh in his travels]; those marriages, so common in our country since the first century of colonization, of uncle with niece and cousin with cousin were quite sufficient. These were marriages the obvious purpose of which was to prevent the dispersal of property and to preserve the purity of a blood-stream of noble or illustrious origin." *Masters and Slaves*: 310.

94. Ibid., pp. 13–14. "The singular predisposition of the Portuguese to the hybrid, slave-exploiting colonization of the tropics is to be explained in large part by the ethnic or, better, the cultural past of a people existing indeterminately between Europe and Africa and belonging uncompromisingly to neither one nor the other of the two continents; with the African influence seething beneath the European and giving a sharp relish to sexual life, to alimentation, and to religion; with Moorish or Negro blood running throughout a great light-skinned mulatto population, when it is not the predominant strain, and with the hot and oleous air of Africa mitigating the Germanic harshness of institution and cultural forms, corrupting

the doctrinal and moral rigidity of the medieval Church, drawing the bones from Christianity. . . . It was Europe reigning without governing; it was Africa that governed."

95. Ibid., p. 83.

96. This was first pointed out by Afrânio Peixoto, *Noçôes de História da Literatura Brasileira* (Rio: Francisco Alves, 1931): 75. Reference in Santiago: 99.

97. Sérgio Buarque de Hollanda, in *Raizes do Brasil,* quoted in Meyer: 153. The other suggestive book that Meyer mentions is *Suspiros Poéticos e Saudades,* by Gonçalves de Magalhâes.

6. *MARÍA'*S DISEASE: A NATIONAL ROMANCE (CON)FOUNDED

1. I would like to thank Allen Kaufman, Nancy Armstrong, Eduardo González, Angela Robledo, Marguerite Waller, and Mary Russo for their helpful criticism and generous suggestions for this chapter.

2. "National novel" is what Pedro Gómez Valderrama calls it in *"María en dos siglos,"* in *Manual de literatura colombiana,* ed. Gloria Zea (Bogotá: Planeta, 1988), 1: 369–394; 373.

3. See, Donald McGrady, "Introducción" to Jorge Isaacs, *María* (Barcelona: Editorial Labor, S.A., 1970): 8. And Roberto F. Giusti, "Prólogo," in Jorge Isaacs, *María* (Buenos Aires: Editorial Losada, novena ed., 1982): 7.

The pamphlet *100 Marías,* published by the Fondo Cultural Cafetero (Bogotá, 1985) informs us that "The Instituto Caro y Cuervo (in 1976) reports 164 editions of *María* in Spanish (Colombia, Mexico, Chile, Spain, Paris, Argentina, Uruguay, and Cuba)." *María on the Screen* made a debut in Mexico (1918), followed by *María, una película colombiana* (1922), another Mexican version (1938), one by Tito Davison (1972), and a television serial of that same year.

4. Jaime Mejía Duque, *Isaacs y María: El hombre y su novela* (Bogotá: La Carreta, Inéditos Ltda, 1979): 61–66. Nevertheless, Eduardo Camacho Guizado, writes that the period tended to be Conservative literarily and that a Liberal ideology was more often benevolently paternalist than subversive. See his "La literatura colombiana entre 1820 y 1900." *Manual de Historia de Colombia: Volúmen 2, Siglo XIX,* ed. Juan Gustavo Cobo Borda and Santiago Mutis Durán (Bogotá: Procultura, 2d ed., 1982): 615–693. Between these poles, one might place *Manuela* by Eugenio Díaz, for example. Its publication in *El Mosaico* during 1858 was sponsored by José María Vergara y Vergara who called it Colombia's "national novel." See Germán Colmenares, "Man-

uela, la novela de costumbres de Eugenio Díaz," *Manual de literatura colombiana* 1: 247–266; 249.

5. Jorge Isaacs, *María*, "Prólogo" by Roberto F. Giusti (Buenos Aires: Editorial Losada, novena ed., 1982). Parenthetical page references refer to this edition.

6. Jorge Isaacs, *María: A South American Romance*, trans. Rollo Ogden (New York: Harper and Brothers, 1890): 1. In the following quotes, the page numbers in parentheses will refer first to the Spanish edition and then to the corresponding page in English. When one number appears, it indicates a gap in the translation.

7. Sylvia Molloy gives by far the best development in "Paraíso perdido y economía terrenal en "María," *Sin Nombre* 14, 3 (April–June 1984): 36–55. She notes that the entire novel describes a series of returns that want desperately to keep the past intact. See also Enrique Anderson Imbert, "Prólogo," to Jorge Isaacs, *María* (Mexico: Fondo de Cultura Económica, 1951): xxix, where he alludes to "the foretaste of sadness."

Sharon Magnarelli's debatable conclusion is that nostalgia makes the title heroine "misleading," because, as in so many other Spanish American novels, the women who promise to be important really are not. *The Lost Rib: Female Characters in the Spanish-American Novel* (Lewisburg, P. A.: Bucknell University Press, 1985): 37.

8. His pose seems closer to the minor Colombian writers of his time who cultivated the vogue of *costumbrismo,* which Eduardo Camacho Guizado among others characterizes as almost always nostalgic and hardly ever socially critical. See his "La literatura colombiana."

9. McGrady (10) believes that *"Paul et Virginie* decisively influenced the conception of *María,* while the inspiration of *Atala* is perceptible only in the story of Nay y Sinar."

10. François-René de Chateaubriand, *Atala. René,* trans. Irving Putter (Berkeley: University of California Press, 1952; 8th printing 1974). Page references to this edition will be given parenthetically in the essay.

11. See Jorge Isaacs, *María*, Prólogo, Notas, and Cronología by Gustavo Mejía (Caracas: Biblioteca Ayacucho, 1978): 211. See also Alvaro Tirado Mejía, "El estado y la política en el siglo xix," *Manual de Historia de Colombia*: 327–384; 335–336.

12. Paul Oquist, *Violence, Conflict, and Politics in Colombia* (New York: Academic Press, 1980): 52. See also Alvaro Tirado Mejía, "El estado y la política en el siglo xix": esp. 334.

13. Germán Arciniegas, *Genio y figura de Jorge Isaacs* (Buenos Aires: Editorial Universitaria de Buenos Aires, 1967): 56–57.

14. Oquist: 55.

15. Anderson Imbert: viii; and Arciniegas: 21.

16. Jorge Isaacs, *María*: 252.

17. See Jorge Orlando Melo, "La evolución económica de Colombia 1830–1900," in *Manual de Historia de Colombia*: 135–207. See also Gustavo Mejía, "La novela de la decadencia de la clase latifundista: *María* de Jorge Isaacs," *Escritura* (July–December 1976): 261–278; 266.

18. Arciniegas: 37.

19. Oquist: 68.

20. See Tirado Mejía: 376–377; and Salomón Kalmanovitz, "El régimen agrario durante el siglo XIX en Colombia," in *Manual de Historia de Colombia*: 211–324; 243–244.

21. Mejía, "La novela de la decadencia . . . ": 275.

22. Mejía Duque: 57–58.

23. Sharon Magnarelli, in "*María* and History," *Hispanic Review* 49, 2 (Spring, 1981–Philadelphia): 209–217.

24. Arciniegas: 56–57.

25. Gustavo Mejía argues similarly in his "Prólogo" to *María*: x.

26. Arturo Capdevila, "La gran familia de los Efraínes y Marías," *Revista Iberoamericana* 1 (May and November 1939): 137–143; 143— ". . . very different Efraínes and Marías are what we need in America . . . they should love joyfully and marry and have healthy strong children."

27. Arciniegas: 56–57, and Jaime Concha, "Prólogo" to Alberto Blest Gana, *Martín Rivas (Novela de costumbres político-sociales)*. Prólogo, Notas, and Cronología by Jaime Concha (Caracas: Biblioteca Ayacucho, 1977): x.

28. Gustavo Mejía offers an excellent reading and a table of characters organized by class and fate on p. xii of his "Prólogo" to Isaacs, *María*.

29. Isaacs, *María*: 60. Emigdio complains about Carlos's father: "My father can't stand him since he's suing him about the boundaries of our property." Mariamercedes Carranza, in "Ubicación histórica de María," *Razón y fábula*, no. 8 (1968): 78–80, points out that this type of litigation was typical of the period.

30. See Margarita González, "Las rentas del estado": 388–410, and Salomón Kalmanovitz, "El régimen agrario durante el siglo xix en Colombia": 211–324, both in *Manual de Historia de Colombia*.

31. González and Kalmanovitz treat this issue, as does Oquist on p. 54.

32. Frank Safford, "Politics, Ideology and Society in Post-Indepen-

dence Spanish America." *The Cambridge History of Latin America*, vol. 3. *From Independence to c. 1870* (Cambridge: Cambridge University Press, 1985): 347–422; see 418. Jorge Melo points out that the problem of transportation did even more to retard national consolidation. Melo: 153.

33. Mejía, "La novela de decadencia . . . ": 261.

34. See Kalmanovitz: 243, where he discusses the devastating effects of the civil wars and also the political result, which was to prepare a rigidly centralized national government that ended any dream of relative autonomy for the southern states.

35. For a critique see Rogerio M. Velázquez, "La esclavitud en la *María* de Jorge Isaacs," *Universidad de Antioquia, Revista*, 33 (1957): 91–104.

36. Practically all the authors of the *Manual de Historia de Colombia* comment on the inflexible relations between latifundists and tenant farmers.

37. Emigdio's language echoes Rivera y Garrido's *Impresiones y recuerdos*, where the mayordomo "fell madly in love with an adorable Ñapanguita from Guadalajara, and even thought of marrying her, to which my father would *probably* not have objected" (51). The emphasis is Kalmanovitz's: 270.

38. See Velazco Madriñán, *Jorge Isaacs: El caballero de las lágrimas*: 150–151; 163. Also Mariano M. Sendoya, in "Apuntes sobre la libertad de los esclavos," *Boletín de la Academia de Historia del Valle del Cauca* (1962): 507–532, and Enrique Anderson Imbert, "Prólogo," to Jorge Isaacs, *María* (Mexico: Fondo de Cultura Económica, 1951): xxx.

39. Sylvia Molloy is right to emphasize the implied blame, which she locates in the father's authoritarian rule and his misfired bourgeois rationality.

40. Anderson Imbert: xxiv, suggests that María, and her parallel in Nay, represent the allegory of "la novia de la muerte" [Death's Bride], the impossible preservation of innocence.

41. See J. Lloyd Read, *The Mexican Historical Novel: 1826–1910* (New York: Instituto de las Españas en los Estados Unidos, 1939): 103–104.

42. Capdevila: 140.

43. Arciniegas: 37. Right after Isaacs's quip, "unforeseen enmities would develop. They practically scream Jew at him! And they remind him that he comes from an accursed race." (Notice how Arciniegas himself refers to the Jewish "race" as "accursed.") See also p. 64. "The crowds in Bogotá had repeated the injurious accusation: Jew. He again took up his study of the Old Testament." And p. 68. Isaacs

did ethnographic work in la Guajira, for which the Conservative censor, Don Miguel Antonio Caro (probably a converso) criticized him: The trouble with the Indians, he said, is the Jews' fault (74): "The Dutch Jews from Curazao have gotten control of the commerce in Riohacha, and with this key they have monopolized that of la Goajira . . . the trickery that the Israelites use to get a hold of Christians possessions."

44. I am thankful to Prof. María Teresa Cristina for pointing out this poem, as well as for her general work in preparing a definitive edition of all of Isaacs's work, to be published in seven volumes by the press of the National University in Bogotá.

45. Arciniegas: 16, 18.

46. This is a reference to Eve Kosofsky Sedgwick's masterful reading of Proust in *The Epistemology of the Closet* (Berkeley, Los Angeles, Oxford: University of California Press, 1990).

47. Luis Alberto Sánchez, *Nueva historia de la literatura americana* (Valparaíso: Ediciones Universitarias de Valparaíso, 1982): 285.

48. Daniel Mesa Bernal's *Polémica sobre el origen del pueblo antioqueño* (Bogotá: Ediciones Fondo Cultural Cafetero, 1988) reviews a century of romantic conjectures about Israel's American paradise, including a report by the International Health Board of the Rockefeller Institute, and far more phlegmatic denials, like Emilio Robledo's 1922 refutation of that report, incredulous that the rumor could be published officially and that it might seem flattering rather than insulting: 195.

49. An intriguing possible source might also have been Gustave de Beaumont's *Marie ou de l'Esclavage aux Etats Unis* (1836), a tragedy about an almost-white mulatta beloved who dies caught between her racial assignations.

50. I am indebted to Eduardo González for his observations on Disraeli's "philo-Hebraic version of Jewishness" in his romances.

51. "Memoir of the Earl of Beaconsfield": 4, an unsigned Afterword to Earl of Beaconsfield, in *Endymion* (London: Longmans, Green and Co. 1882).

52. See for example Disraeli's Preface to the fifth edition of *Coningsby*, written in May of 1849 (Oxford: Oxford University Press, 1931): xv–xvi.

53. I am grateful to Nancy Armstrong for detailing this parallel.

54. Disraeli, by the way, tried to fill the emptiness in his sister Sarah's life after her fiancé died. Among his strategies was to co-author a novel with her, *A Year at Hartlebury or The Election* (London: Saunders and Otley, 1834). In the Preface he writes: "Our *honeymoon*

being over, we have amused ourselves during the autumn by writing a novel" (my emphasis).

For a fascinating "defense" of a Jewish tradition that distinguishes between one family of human beings and others, a tradition that precisely guards against the general incest that results from considering all of humanity to be one family, see Marc Shell's "The Family Pet," *Representations* 15 (Summer, 1986): 121–153.

55. Alfonso López Michelsen, "Ensayo sobre la influencia semítica en *María*," *Revista de las Indias*, no. 62 (February 1944): 5–10; 6.

56. Sander L. Gilman, *Difference and Pathology: Stereotypes of Sexuality, Race, and Madness* (Ithaca, N.Y.: Cornell University Press, 1985): 110. See also his *Jewish Self-Hatred: Anti-Semitism and the Hidden Language of the Jews* (Baltimore: Johns Hopkins University Press, 1986) for the repeated overlapping between blacks and Jews in nineteenth-century discourse.

57. Sander L. Gilman, *Jewish Self-Hatred.* Throughout, esp. 286.

58. McGrady: 30–31. Luis Alberto Sánchez probably did a lot to raise readerly expectations about the "Jewish" quality of *María*, since 1937, when he first published *Historia de la Literatura Americana* (Santiago de Chile: Ercilla). See also José Padua Gómez, *Israel y la civilización* (Mexico: Ediciones Metrópolis, 1949), where the Sánchez passage is quoted at length. Even before this, Isaac Goldberg was seeking out "Jewish" elements and finding none in Isaacs, see "Jewish Writers in South America," *The Menorah Journal* 11, 5 (New York, October 1925): 479.

59. Ogden's translation misses the oxymoron of Jewish pride and "Christian virgin" by translating this last phrase to "pure and maiden soul."

60. Gilman, *Jewish Self-Hatred*: 6. The same passage is quoted in Gilman's *Difference and Pathology*: 30.

61. The entire first half of Gilman's *Difference and Pathology* details this sliding back and forth from sexual to racial stereotypes. See also Donna Guy's forthcoming book on white slavery in Argentina for the association of prostitution with Jewesses.

62. Isaacs's letter of June 22, 1880, to Alejandro Dorronsoro, quoted in Velazco Madriñán, *Jorge Isaacs: El caballero de las lágrimas*: 303.

63. Paul Roche, "*María* ou l'illusion chrétienne," in Claude Fell, ed., *Le roman romantique latino-américain et ses prolongements* (Paris: Editions L'Harmattan, 1984): 131–142; 136.

64. Sigmund Freud, "On the Psychical Mechanism of Hysterical Phenomena (In collaboration with Dr. Joseph Breuer, 1892)," in

Collected Papers: Volume 1, trans. Alix and James Strachey (New York: Basic Books, 1959): 24–41.

65. Janet Beizer makes this point in "The Doctors' Tale: Nineteenth-Century Medical Narratives of Hysteria," a manuscript she kindly allowed me to read.

66. Gilman, *Difference and Pathology*: 155. See also his *Jewish Self-Hatred*: 288.

67. Gilman, *Jewish Self-Hatred*: 286–287.

68. Nancy Armstrong develops this in her excellent manuscript essay, "When Alice Grows Up: Hysteria as History, 1857–1885," which she generously shared with me.

69. Armstrong, "When Alice Grows Up."

70. Gilman, *Difference and Pathology*: 184.

71. Claude Fell notices this too in "*María*, de Jorge Isaacs: L'utopie blanche," in Claude Fell, ed., *Le roman romantique latino-américain et ses prolongements*: 69–83; 75.

72. Sigmund Freud, "Notes Upon a Case of Obsessional Neurosis (1909)," in *Collected Papers: Volume 3,* trans. Alix and James Strachey (New York: Basic Books, 1959): 376.

73. Sigmund Freud, "Screen Memories (1899)," in *Collected Papers: Volume 5*: 52–53.

74. See McGrady for a detailed comparison.

75. Arciniegas: 68.

7. SOMETHING TO CELEBRATE: NATIONAL NUPTIALS IN CHILE AND MEXICO

1. First page numbers refer to Alberto Blest Gana, *Martín Rivas (Novela de costumbres político-sociales).* Prólogo, Notas, and Cronología by Jaime Concha (Caracas: Biblioteca Ayacucho, 1977). Second numbers refer to *Martín Rivas,* trans. Mrs. Charles Whitman (New York: Alfred A. Knopf, 1918).

2. Bernardo Subercaseaux reminds us that Scott was not yet the rage in Chile during the 1840s. "Filosofía de la Historia Novela y Sistema Expresivo en la Obra de J. V. Lastarria (1840–1848)," *Ideologies and Literature* 3, 11 (November–December 1979): 56–83; 75–76.

3. Gina Cánepa, "Folletines históricos del Chile independiente y su articulación con la novela naturalista," *Hispamérica* 50, (1988): 23–34. The serialized novels appealed to educated readers, eager not only for distraction but also for legitimation: 24–25.

4. Maurice Zeitlin, *The Civil Wars in Chile (Or the Bourgeois Revolutions That Never Were)* (Princeton: Princeton University Press, 1984):

24–27. In general this book is useful for appreciating the elite's ability to reach consensus, although the lasting and costly conflicts are sometimes understated. See William Sater's review in *Hispanic American Historical Review* 65, no. 3 (August 1985): 590–591.

5. See chap. 9 on Mexico's Liberal Reform in David Bushnell and Neill Macaulay, *The Emergence of Latin America in the Nineteenth Century* (Oxford and New York: Oxford University Press, 1988).

6. Alberto Blest Gana, "Literatura chilena: Algunas consideraciones sobre ella" (1861), inaugural address at university. Reprint in *El jefe de la familia*, Raúl Silva Castro, ed. (Santiago: Zig Zag, 1956): 455–472. Page references will appear parenthetically, and translations are mine.

7. See Iván Jaksić's *Academic Rebels in Chile: The Role of Philosophy in Higher Education and Politics* (Albany: SUNY Press, 1989): 21–34.

8. José Zamudio, *La novela histórica en Chile* (Santiago: Ediciones Flor Nacional, 1949): 49. "Lastarria's celebrated programmatic speech of May 3, 1842 at the Literary Society exhorts the assembled to write historical literature: 'Write for the people, educate them, . . . reminding them of heroic deeds, teaching them to venerate their religion and institutions.'"

9. Edelmira's reading habits were not the exception but the rule, even for Chile's "popular classes." See Zamudio: 34–40. Favorites included Hugo, Dumas, the ever-present Scott, Scott's Spanish imitators, and also Fenimore Cooper. Given this situation, Blest acknowledges how hard it is to replace these tastes with local books. But, he adds, this shouldn't deter us, especially since foreign novels are not helpful to Chileans.

10. Raúl Silva Castro, *Alberto Blest Gana (1830–1920): Estudio biográfico y crítico* (Santiago de Chile: Imprenta Universitaria, 1941): 337. "In 1848 Mitre publishes the second edition of *Soledad*, which had come out before in a Bolivian newspaper."

11. Zamudio: 68, notes that Blest Gana was typical of the Chilean writers who preferred not to write historical novels, even though they were all the rage in Europe and among Chile's readers. But a letter Blest wrote to Lastarria in 1864 shows that the cultural arbiter of the Liberals expected a serious, historical novel from Chile's best novelist. The result was *Durante la Conquista* (1897), considered Blest's only properly historical novel.

12. For a sense of that rage, see Gina Cánepa: 29–31. More popular than Blest Gana were Martín Palma, Daniel Barros Grez, Liborio E. Brieba, Ramón Pacheco, especially the last two, who specialized in long epics of military victory. Brieba's *Los Talaveras* and *El Capitán San*

Bruno celebrated Chile's heroic resistance during the Spanish reconquest of 1814. And Pacheco's *Episodios nacionales,* congratulated Chile
on winning the Guerra del Pacífico against the Peru-Bolivia coalition.
The first is about the province of Antofagasta, cast as woman desired
by Europe and then dominated by Bolivia.

13. Jorge Román-Lagunas, (Bibliografía anotada de y sobre Alberto Blest Gana," *Revista Iberoamericana,* nos. 112–113. (July–December 1980): 605–647; 606. The criticism on the influence of Balzac in
Blest Gana is legion. In his opinion it shows that the Chilean simply
imitated the French master.

Probably the best development of Balzac's importance (as a model
for combining literary traditions, appealing to a range of audiences)
is offered by Hernán Díaz Arrieta (Alone), *Don Alberto Blest Gana*
(Santiago: Editorial Nascimento, 1940): 118. See also Marguerite C.
Suárez-Murias, *La novela romantica en hispanoamérica* (New York: Hispanic Institute in the United States, 1963): 228.

14. Guillermo Araya, "Introducción" to Alberto Blest Gana, *Martín Rivas,* 2d ed. (Madrid: Cátedra, 1983): 16.

15. Ibid., p. 22. *"Martín Rivas* has been read by all Chileans who
went to high school and by many generations of foreigners who
are still interested in the novel despite the years." See also, Jorge
Román-Lagunas, "Bibliografía anotada de y sobre Alberto Blest
Gana," *Revista Iberoamericana,* nos. 112–113 (July–December 1980):
605–647.

16. Simon Collier, "Chile from Independence to the War of the
Pacific," *The Cambridge History of Latin America,* vol. 3. *From Independence to c. 1870* (Cambridge: Cambridge University Press, 1985): 583–
614; 591.

17. Collier: 584. "This relatively simple social structure was not
complicated by sharp cleavages of economic interest within the upper
class or by anything very much in the way of serious regional tension.
Santiago and its rich hinterland dominated the republic. The remoter
northern or southern provinces, whether disaffected or not, were
powerless to alter the balance in their own favour, as was shown very
clearly in the civil wars of 1851 and 1859."

18. Ibid., p. 584.

19. John Crow, *The Epic of Latin America,* 3d ed., expanded and
updated (Berkeley, Los Angeles, London: University of California
Press, 1980). This is his title for chap. 48 of this once-popular text
about Chile in the second half of the nineteenth century: 640–648.

20. Quoted in Collier: 583.

21. Víctor M. Valenzuela, *Chilean Society as Seen Through the Novel-*

istic World of Alberto Blest Gana (Santiago: Talleres Arancibia Hermanos, 1971).

22. The Literary Society, dedicated to fomenting a progressive culture, benefited from the sometimes heated debates with Argentine exiles, especially Sarmiento and Vicente Fidel López. In his inaugural address Lastarria advocated a particular "Chileanness" for Chilean literature. From Suárez-Murias: 103–104.

For Iván Jaksić, the religious question may have been the most volatile in these midcentury crisis years. Bushnell and Macaulay support this conclusion: 236–237.

23. Valenzuela: 75–76.

24. Collier: 590. See also Zeitlin: 26–30.

25. Vicente Fidel López, *La novia del hereje o la Inquisición de Lima* (Buenos Aires: La Cultura Argentina, 1917): 19. In opposition to Blest Gana, for whom detailed observation was the essence of good narrative, López argues in his "Carta-Prólogo" that since only great events are remembered, the novelist is free to invent domestic detail.

26. Hernán Díaz Arrieta (Alone), *Don Alberto Blest Gana* (Santiago: Editorial Nascimento, 1940): 161–162.

27. Raúl Silva Castro, *Alberto Blest Gana (1830–1920): Estudio biográfico y crítico* (Santiago de Chile: Imprenta Universitaria, 1941): 401.

28. Araya: 33.

29. See J. Lloyd Read, *The Mexican Historical Novel: 1826–1910* (New York: Instituto de las Españas en los Estados Unidos, 1939): 74. Read doesn't make the connection that I suggest; but it seems evident that the sentimental plot develops perhaps the major motivation for the revolution, to end the caste system. The revolution at the end of the narrative comes, then, as the logical solution for the frustration of love.

30. Suárez-Murias: 93.

31. Diego Barros Arana, a contemporary literary critic and historian, especially appreciated Blest's exposé and the general historical value of the novel. Quoted in Raúl Silva Castro: 405–406.

32. Román-Lagunas: 606. He observes that some critics point out that Blest Gana has little psychological depth in his characters and adds that this was not his purpose, nor that of Spanish American novels in general. His characters are stereotypical representatives of classes. "Martín Rivas *is* the middle class."

33. Zeitlin: 33.

34. Jaime Concha, Prólogo, Notas, and Cronología, in Alberto Blest Gana, *Martín Rivas (Novela de costumbres político-sociales)* (Caracas: Biblioteca Ayacucho, 1977).

35. Ibid., p. xxiv.

36. Renata R. Mautner Wasserman, "Reinventing the New World: Cooper and Alencar," *Comparative Literature* 36, no. 2 (1984): 130–145; 141.

37. Concha: xxvii. A similar distinction between politics and passion is assumed by Angel Flores, in *The Literature of Spanish America* (New York: Las Americas, 1976), 2: 225—". . . in his novel *Martín Rivas* (1862) he did try, despite its romantic afflatus, to look deep into the socio-political reality of Chile": 37.

38. Related to his defense of "philosophical" history against Andrés Bello's preference for narrative, Lastarria wrote novels in which appropriate sympathies would be unquestionable. Unlike Vicente Fidel López, who proposed and managed to portray a complex society in *La novia del hereje* (1845–1847), Lastarria preferred cleaner distinctions between colonial corruption and moral modernity. For the literary consequences of the polemic with Bello, see Bernardo Subercaseaux, "Filosofía de la Historia Novela y Sistema Expresivo en la Obra de J. V. Lastarria (1840–1848)": 71–72.

Alejandro Fuenzalida Grandón, in *Lastarria y su tiempo* (Santiago, 1911), 1: 91, writes this about *El mendigo* (1843), a novel about a frustrated love during the wars of Independence. Lastarria also wrote *Rosa* (1847), an amorous intrigue on the eve of the Battle of Chacabuco (1817) and the declaration of Independence (1818), and *El Alférez Alonso Díaz de Guzmán, Historia de 1612* (1848), based on the famous life of the Monja Alférez, Doña Catalina de Erauso. His later novels are usually described as "realist." See also Suárez-Murias: 109–110.

39. Blest Gana, *Martín Rivas*: 30; 29—"Doña Francisca Encina, his [Fidel's] wife, had some books and ventured to think for herself, thus violating the social principles of her husband, who looked upon every book as useless when it was not pernicious. As a blue-stocking, Doña Francisca Encina was liberal in politics and fomented this tendency in her brother [Dámaso]." On p. 179 (201), the narrator justifies Francisca and other women for enjoying respite from their husbands: "Doña Francisca saw him set out with the pleasure that many women feel when they find they can be free from their husbands for a few hours. There are a great number of marriages in which the husband is a cross which can be carried with patience, but is laid down with joy, and Don Fidel was a marital cross in the full extent of the word."

40. I translated directly. Mrs. Whitman's (in)version is: "Before love social equalities [*sic*] are of no value."

41. Jan Bazant, "Mexico from Independence to 1867," in *The*

Cambridge History of Latin America, vol. 3. *From Independence to c. 1870* (Cambridge: Cambridge University Press, 1985): 423–470; 426.

42. Some biographers emphasize his preference for German literature, but Juan Sánchez Azcona writes about Altamirano's contradictory love for the very Paris that produced Maximillian's occupation: "Actividad política de Altamirano," *Homenaje a Ignacio M. Altamirano: Conferencias, Estudios y Bibliografía* (Mexico: Universidad Nacional de México, 1935).

43. See, for example, José Luis Martínez, "El Maestro Altamirano," in his *La expresión nacional* (Mexico: Imprenta Universitaria, 1955): 55–122. For him, Altamirano's real calling was teaching (57). About the journal, *El Renacimiento,* it "managed to forge brotherly bonds among former enemies and promoted an entire epoch of splendor in Mexican literature": 58.

44. Read: 104, following many Mexican sources, says of Altamirano that he "indoctrinated Mexican writers in literary nationalism and became teacher and personal adviser to a whole generation of amateur novelists and poets." See José López Portillo y Rojas, *La novela: Breve ensayo* (Mexico: Tip. Vizcaíno y Viamonte, 1906): 46; Silvestre Moreno Cora, *La crítica literaria en México* (Vera Cruz: Tip. Artes y Oficio Teodoro A. Dehesa, 1907): 54; and Julio Jiménez Rueda—who calls Altamirano "Poet, novelist, *maestro* who had a decisive influence in the events of his time"—*Historia de la literatura mexicana* (Mexico: Editorial Cultura, 1928): 185. Finally, Carlos González Peña, *Historia de la literatura mexicana* (Mexico: Secretaría de Educación Pública, 1928): 381, agrees, " . . . he is the *maestro* of two generations" (my emphasis). His title of "maestro," conferred on him by his own teacher, Ignacio Ramírez, takes on its full meaning of master and teacher. See Francisco Monterde García Icazbalceta, "El maestro Altamirano, polígrafo." In his *Cultura mexicana: Aspectors literarios* (Mexico: Intercontinental, 1948): 213–223; 213.

45. See Mariano Azuela, *Cien años de Novela Mexicana* (Mexico: Edic. Botas, 1947), for whom the Revolution brought dusty nineteenth-century novels back into circulation: 75–76. But Azuela himself finds that the critical pendulum always swings too far; the praise is exaggerated for Payno, and especially for Altamirano who thought he was writing for "the people" but read his work in literary salons: 121.

46. See John A. Crow, chap. 51, "Porfirio Díaz: Bread or the Club": 668.

47. Henry Bamford Parkes, *A History of Mexico* (Boston: Houghton Mifflin, 1969; originally published 1939): 278–279.

48. Read: 98–99. "He held several responsible positions, includ-

ing . . . special envoy for his state in the conflict with the central government in 1841, *Consejero del Gobierno, Vocal de la Asamblea Departmental de Yucatán,* Deputy to the National Congress in 1852 and again in 1857, and President of the *Academia de Ciencias y Literatura de Mérida.* He took a prominent part in the opposition to Santa Anna's centralist pretensions. His name appears on the decree of January 1, 1846, declaring the independent sovereignty of Yucatán." Read's information is from, "Abreu Gómez, *Justo Sierra O'Reilly y la novela,*" an excellent article in *Contemporáneos,* no. 35 (April 1931): 39–73.

49. Bazant: 447.

50. See María del Carmen Millán, "Introducción," in Ignacio M. Altamirano, *El Zarco: Episodios de la vida mexicana en 1861–1863* (1st ed., Mexico, 1901; reprint, Mexico: Porrúa, 1982): ix, about the respect he commanded as a soldier in all these campaigns. Parkes, chap. 7 is a good summary of "The Revolution of Ayutla" against Santa Anna's authoritarian "feudal" centralism.

51. Read: 159. Altamirano was pure Indian-born and didn't speak Spanish until he was fourteen. See Parkes: 223. "Born in an Indian village in the mountains, unable even to speak Spanish until the age of twelve, Juárez had come to the city of Oaxaca as a household servant, had been given an education by a philanthropic creole, who had intended him to become a priest, and had finally graduated from the institute, opened a law office, and married the daughter of his first employer."

52. Rafael Heliodoro Valle (Altamirano's first bibliographer), "¿Desconfiaba de los indios Juárez? Una anécdota del gran zapoteca," *México al Día* 8, 139 (October 1, 1934): 19. Included in Ralph E. Warner, *Bibliografía de Ignacio Manuel Altamirano* (Mexico: Imprenta Universitaria, 1955). The article is about "Juárez's attitude in light of Altamirano's attacks published in *El Correo de México.*"

53. Parkes: 251. In January 1861 Juárez returned to México and declared an amnesty for all except a few of the Conservative generals. A new congress assembled in May. It was "a body of radical orators— Zarco and Ramírez and Sebastián Lerdo de Tejada and—the most eloquent of all—the young Ignacio Altamirano."

54. Salvador Reyes Nevares, "Prólogo," in Ignacio M. Altamirano, *Obras literarias completas* (Mexico: Ediciones Oasis, 1959): xv–xvi. "In 1867 he supported Díaz as defender of the Republic. . . . Later, around 1880, Altamirano breaks with Díaz, not for personal reasons, but because of something more important, the official positivism."

55. Read: 164. "In 1889 Altamirano was appointed Mexican Con-

sul General in Spain. Later he held the same post in France, having exchanged places with Manuel Payno."

56. Millán: xii. Altamirano is credited with applying the lessons learned from other American programs and literatures to Mexico, once the republic was reestablished in 1867.

57. I am grateful to Jean Franco for making this and other generous points on a draft of this chapter.

58. Parenthetical page references refer to Ignacio M. Altamirano, *El Zarco: Episodios de la vida mexicana en 1861–63*. Introduction by María del Carmen Millán (Mexico: Porrúa, 1982). Translations are my own.

59. Altamirano's own hometown was similarly in the State of Mexico, although now the area is Guerrero. See Reyes Nevares: xi— "he was born in Tixla . . . a small city in the mountainous region of the South, in a jurisdiction once in the State of Mexico, and now called Guerrero."

60. Altamirano, *El Zarco*: 78—"Martín Sánchez Chagollán, an absolutely historical character, as is Salomé Placencia, Zarco, and the bandits."

61. See for example, Millán: ix. Besides being a valiant and consistent soldier for the Liberal cause, Altamirano is remembered for "his parliamentary triumphs, especially his famous speech against the general amnesty." One aftermath of the debate on amnesty was the petition to remove Juárez, which lost by only one vote, fifty-one to fifty-two. See Parkes: 251.

62. Parkes: 285. "A Mixtec Indian with a little Spanish blood, half educated—to the end of his life he could not write Spanish correctly— and with the crude manners of a guerrilla chieftain, he had now allowed himself to be dominated by greed for power." P. 286: "Juárez had wished to lead Mexico towards democracy; Díaz proposed merely to enforce peace."

63. Azuela: 117–120. Altamirano evidently used Salomé Placencia, the most famous *plateado*, as his model for "Zarco." "Today there is still a popular tradition from Yautepec that celebrates Placencia for the valor, daring and even-temperedness that Altamirano denies him." See also Clementina Díaz y de Ovando, "La visión histórica de Ignacio Manuel Altamirano," *Anales del Instituto de Investigaciones Estéticas* (Mexico: Universidad Nacional, (1954), no. 22: 33–53; 52.

64. *Julia* (1870), considered a fragment, has the standard plot of unrequited love. The title heroine ignores the sensitive Indian engineer who adores her and throws herself on an indifferent and

calculating Englishman. Julia learns to distinguish between real virtue and superficial charm, and she rebels against the false values that had controlled her.

Antonia (1872), subtitled "Idylls and Elegies (Memoirs of an Imbecile)," is about a rejected lover who is about to lose his memory and his mind in general. The novel takes place during the North American intervention and is a critique of Santa Anna as well as of the people who didn't resist him. The particular lack of resistance that motivates the narrative is Antonia's, who ends her spontaneous love affair with the young hero once a dashing colonel arrives. Again, Altamirano offers his standard discourse on the errors of the woman who invariably chooses the handsome beau over the humble one, choosing at the same time the adventures associated with militarism over the domestic but monotonous joys of domesticity.

Atenea (1889), an unfinished novel written just before he left Mexico forever, is about an old, sick man's tragic love for a beautiful and cultivated woman, probably Adelaida Ristori, the most famous Italian actress of the century.

65. Ignacio M. Altamirano, "La literatura nacional" (1868), in *La literatura nacional,* edited and prologue by José Luis Martínez, México Edit (Mexico: Porrúa [Col. de Escritores Mexicanos, no. 52], 1949): 9–40. Page references from this essay appear parenthetically in the text.

66. This is Read's opinion: 76. Some examples are: *El nigromántico* by Manuel Pusalgas y Gerris (Barcelona, 1838); *Guatimozín* by Gertrudis Gómez de Avellaneda (Madrid, 1846; Santiago, 1851; Mexico, 1853 and 1857; English trans. by Blake, published in Mexico in 1898); *La conjuración de México o los hijos de Hernán Cortés* by Patricio de la Escosura (Madrid and Mexico, 1850).

67. See also Altamirano's "Prólogo" to *María* (Mexico: Tipografía Literaria, 1881): 5–13. Here he celebrates the novel's incredible success in Mexico. Unlike European imports that come with fanfare but don't resist a second reading, Isaacs's book "slipped humbly and imperceptibly in through newspaper serials which, at that time, lacked a large audience. By now there are five editions of *María*; this is the sixth and there will be still more."

68. Díaz y de Ovando: 36. Against any flights of fantasy in history, contemporaries stressed the need to historicize à la Leopold von Ranke (as if they could really write a history without interpretation). In Altamiranos's day, these assumptions had many more followers than today. To get beyond them, he took Herodotus as model for a history that admits local myths as narrative embryos and as marks of

authenticity: 37. But like his contemporaries, Altamirano preferred the "scientific documentation" of writers like Scott who gave the model for "impartial" narration.

69. Read. See pp. 73–74 about José Joaquín Pesado's *El inquisidor de México* (1835), whose title character had "condemned Sara and her lover along with other offenders. When all but Sara were burned and she was unconscious from the heat of the flames, the Inquisitor learned that she was his own daughter." She converts and her father renounces his office. P. 74: *El criollo* (1835) by J. R. Pacheco "has an interesting basis in the caste system of colonial times, . . . where a love affair between a Spanish girl and a creole son of highly respected Spanish parents came to a tragic end." On p. 76, Read does not consider that the plot of *Angela* (1838), by Mariano Navarro, may be an allegory of civil war. It "is the story of an army officer who, in the revolution of 1810, kidnapped, ravished and killed a girl who proved to be his own daughter. It is without interest." Pp. 103–104 summarize *La hija del judío* (in serial form in *El Fénix*, 1848–1850) by Justo Sierra (Padre), about a gentleman and his wife who had adopted María, "a little girl whose family had been exterminated and its property confiscated by the Inquisition on the charge that her father was a Jew." The Commissary of the Inquisition demanded that she enter a convent lest she claim her parents' fortune and take from that holy tribunal. But her lover's Jesuit confessor argues more convincingly for her freedom, "partly through humanitarian motives and partly for a share of the young lady's fortune." P. 113: "In 1845 Manuel Payno began the publication of *El fistol del diablo* in *La Revista Científica y Literaria*." It finally came to four long, rambling volumes whose greatest value is costumbrismo, not plot. There are similar descriptions in *Los bandidos de Río Frío* (Mexico and Buenos Aires: Maucci, n.d., probably 1927). See J. R. Spell, "The Literary Works of Manuel Payno," *Hispania* 12 (1929): 347–356.

70. Millán: xviii. For *Navidad en las montañas*, he uses similar ideas supporting the Leyes de Reforma to those of Nicolás Pizarro in his novel *El monedero* (1861), ten years earlier, except that (p. xix) Altamirano is more idealist and conciliatory than scientific.

71. J. S. Brushwood, in *The Romantic Novel in Mexico* (Columbia: University of Missouri Studies, 1954), seems to consider this lack of originality a fault or a deficiency rather than an opportune harnessing of the existing practice. See p. 40: "Altamirano's influence was mainly a matter of encouragement of processes that would have developed without him. He was no innovator. He did not introduce Realism, nor did he originate *costumbrismo*."

72. See Michael Davitt Bell, *The Development of American Romance: The Sacrifice of Relation* (Chicago: University of Chicago Press, 1980). José Luis Martínez sees this kind of contribution as far more positive than does Brushwood. "El maestro Altamirano," in his *La expresión nacional* (Mexico: Imprenta Universitaria, 1955): 55–122. On p. 61 Martínez writes that Altamirano combines two traditions in Mexican fiction for his programmatic fictions: a loose episodic costumbrismo and the tighter love stories that had almost nothing to do with Mexico.

73. Wondering why *El fistol* was not institutionalized. Read answers (126–127): "*El fistol del diablo* is lacking in the patriotic zeal that pervades much of the composition of Juan A. Mateos and Riva Palacio. . . . His consistent refusal to assume a fixed and fervid loyalty to any party left his judgment clear for objective evaluation of forces at play around him." P. 130: Payno's *Los bandidos del Río Frío* has the same unprogrammatic complexity.

74. See n. 44, also Azuela's reference to "*el maestro Altamirano*," even in a critical context: 148 (my emphasis). Among other numerous examples of this acknowledgment of intimacy and honor, the title appears in many articles dedicated to Altamirano. The earliest one may be by Justo Sierra, "El maestro Altamirano," *RNLC* 2 (1889): 161–167. Then there are: Manuel Gutiérrez Nájera, "Al maestro Altamirano: *Neniae*," in *Obras* (Mexico: Universidad Autónoma de México, 1959), 1: 485–488; and José Luis Martínez, "El maestro Altamirano," in his *La expresión nacional* (Mexico: Porrúa, 1949), 1: vii–xxiii.

8. STARTING FROM SCRATCH:
LATE BEGINNINGS AND EARLY (T)RACES
IN *ENRIQUILLO, CUMANDÁ,* AND *TABARÉ*

1. Manuel de Jesús Galván, *Enriquillo* "con un estudio de Concha Meléndez" (Mexico: Editorial Porrúa, 1976). First page references are to this text; the second are to Manuel de Jesús Galván, *The Sword and the Cross*, trans. Robert Graves (Bloomington: Indiana University Press, Unesco Collection of Representative works, 1954). In his intelligent "Translator's Note," xiii–xvii, Graves notes some of the omissions that cause "soft spots" or unconvincing transitions in the novel. This first quote adjusts Graves's far more elegant version to preserve the language of erasure.

2. I am thinking here of Andrew Parker's work on Karl Marx's compulsion to distinguish between poetry and philosophy, to deny his poetic past once he became a "marxist." See Parker's *Re-Marx*, forthcoming from the University of Wisconsin Press.

3. Bartolomé de las Casas began to champion the good only in 1515, after he had prospered by exploitation of Indians. As for his suggestions that blacks substitute for Indians, see his *Historia de las Indias,* "estudio preliminar de Lewis Hanke" (Mexico: Fondo de Cultura Económica, 1951) 3: 93–95. See also Jaime Concha's "La conversión de las Casas," *Casa de las Américas* (1989): xxix, n. 174; 33–44, for the politics of his conversion and for Las Casas's success in conciliating between Franciscans and Dominicans in their appeals to the court.

4. See Gordon Brotherston, "Ubirajara, Hiawatha, Cumandá: National Virtue from American Indian Literature," *Comparative Literature Studies* 9 (1972): 243–252, 244.

5. Page references are to Juan León Mera, *Cumandá, o un drama entre salvajes,* 5th ed., (Madrid: Espasa-Calpe, 1976).

6. For the mentorship, see, Julio Tobar Donoso, "Juan León Mera," an excellent biographical introduction to Juan León Mera, *La Dictadura y la Restauración en la República del Ecuador* (Obra inédita que se publica en conmemoración del primer Centenario del nacimiento de su Autor) (Quito: Editorial Ecuatoriana, 1932): v–xlv; see esp. pp. viii and x.

First published in Quito, *La emancipada* was reissued in Cuenca, 1983, with an introduction by Antonio Sacoto, who later wrote a piece on the general feminism of other Liberal novels, including *Carlota* (1900) by Manuel J. Calle, and *A la Costa* (1904) by Luis A. Martínez. See his "Mujer y sociedad en tres novelas ecuatorianas," in *La historia en la literatura iberoamericana: Memorias del XXVI Congreso del Instituto internacional de Literatura Iberoamericana,* ed. Raquel Chang-Rodríguez and Gabriella de Beer (Hanover: Ediciones del Norte, 1989): 213–223. Riofrío must have been too daring for García Moreno's orthodox taste. His novel is about a young woman, whose mother had died after giving her a Liberal "Lancasterian" education, who rebels against a traditionally tyrannical father who plans to marry her off to the highest bidder. Good Christians, says one of her friends, should be more advanced than those societies that treat women as merchandise or a plaything (33). After the inevitable wedding, Rosaura turns around and begins to walk out of the church alone. Her father stops her, but she reminds him that she is now "emancipada," an adult and free agent. She returns on horseback, packing two pistols and scoffing at her "husband." "When my husband wants me to follow him, he can go in front of me" (53). But because there is no room in society for her, or for the poor Indians she defends, Rosaura is forced into prostitution and an early, ignominious and grotesque death.

7. For these and other relevant details of Mera's political career, see Tobar Donoso, esp. xi and xvii.

8. See Hernán Vidal, "*Cumandá*: In Defense of the Theocratic State," in *Ideologies and Literature* 3 (1981): 57–74. Originally appeared as "*Cumandá*: Apología del estado teocrático," in a special issue on indigenism in *Revista Latinoamericana de Crítica Literaria* (Lima) 6 (1980): 199–212.

9. Tobar Donoso: xx–xxi.

10. Agustín Cueva calls the novel a guilt-ridden apologia for a Christianity trying to erase its feudal, latifundist past with good works. *La literatura ecuatoriana* (Buenos Aires: Centro Editor de América Latina, 1968): 37.

11. Regina Harrison wonders why this is the setting for the highland writer who knew his own territory far better than the forest. For conversations about Cumandá, I am grateful to Elizabeth Garrels, Efraín Barradas, Neil Larsen, and Roger Zapata.

12. About the 1599 rebellion of the Jíbaros, see Juan de Velasco, *Historia del Reino de Quito en la América Meridional,* vol. 3, pt. 3 of *La historia moderna* (Quito: Imprenta del gobierno, 1842), also cited in Michael Harner, *The Jívaro: People of the Sacred Waterfalls* (New York: Doubleday, 1972). For an account of the rebellions in that tropical forest zone, see Segundo Moreno Yáñez, *Sublevaciones indígenas en la Audiencia de Quito* (Quito: Ediciones de la Universidad Católica, 1985).

13. He began with *Brenda* (1886), published serially in *La Nación* of Buenos Aires, followed by *Soledad* (1894), a rural idyll. But Acevedo Díaz, later ambassador to various countries and a historian, is best remembered for a series of "realist" historical novels including *Ismael* (1888) about Artigas's campaign, *Nativa* (1890) about the Cisplatine Province period, and *Grito de Gloria* (1893) about final independence.

14. Juan Valera, in letter dated May 17, 1886, to the director of the Academia Ecuatoriana. See, "Estudio preliminar," by Antonio Seluja Cecín, in Juan Zorrilla de San Martín, *Tabaré*: 32.

15. Quoted in Seluja Cecín: 42. For Mera's version, "I will continue to be Spanish and American," see Alfonso M. Escudero, O.S.A., "Datos para la biografía," in Juan León Mera, *Cumandá: O Un drama entre salvajes,* 5th ed. (Madrid: Espasa-Calpe, Colección Austral, 1976): 22.

16. For its careful historical documentation, and the subtle connections that make an enormous amount of information very readable, see Hugo Achúgar's excellent study of *Poesía y sociedad (Uruguay 1880–1911)* (Montevideo: Arca, 1985).

17. Galván's paper was *La razón,* founded in 1862 as the official

organ of the Spanish annexationist government. Mera founded *La Civilización católica* in 1876; and Zorrilla, *El Bien Público* in 1878. For their greater political designs, see Tobar Donoso and Mario Cayota's review of Zorrilla's Catholic Democratic politics in a special feature of *Opción*, Year 1, no. 3 (November 10, 1986): 15–25, commemorating the fiftieth anniversary of Zorrilla's death.

18. See Lily Litvak, *El Jardín de Aláh: Temas del exotismo musulmán en España, (1880–1913)* (Granada: Don Quijote, 1987).

19. Juan Zorrilla de San Martín, *El Libreto de Tabaré* (Montevideo: C. García, 1936), records the performances. Also, from letters to Zorrilla by Bretón in the archive on *Tabaré* in the Biblioteca Nacional of Montevideo. My thanks to Mireya Callejas, archivist.

20. Enrique Méndez Vives, *Historia Uruguaya, tomo 5. El Uruguay de la Modernización 1876–1904,* 7th ed. (Montevideo: Ediciones de la Banda Oriental, 1987): 44.

21. Méndez Vives: 44. See also León Pomer, *El soldado criollo* (Buenos Aires: CEAL, *La historia popular* 22, 1971); Alfonso Fernández Cabrelli, *Los orientales,* vol. 2 (Montevideo: Grito de Asencio, 1974); Washington Reyes Abadie, *Artigas y el federalismo en el Río de la Plata* (Buenos Aries: Hispamérica, 1986). These historians agree that Artigas's politics benefited the rural masses and that he incorporated gauchos and Indians into the army. He apparently suffered no serious desertions, in great contrast to the Argentine troops. The references are cited in Ludmer: 28.

22. Mario Cayota, "Zorrilla y la 'raza decrépita,'" *Aquí,* Year 3, no. 164 (March 29, 1986): 18. In contrast to Sarmiento's recommendation to Mitre at the battle of Pavón, "Don't try to skimp on gaucho blood, it's the only thing they have that's human. . . . Zorrilla de San Martín breaks abruptly with this judgment."

23. See D. A. G. Waddell, "International Politics and Latin American Independence," *The Cambridge History of Latin America,* vol 3. *From Independence to c. 1870* (Cambridge: Cambridge University Press, 1984): 197–228.

24. John Lynch, "The River Plate Republics from Independence to the Paraguayan War," *The Cambridge History of Latin America*: 615–678.

25. Méndez Vives: 45.

26. This is perhaps an ironic twist on Brazilian Roberto Schwarz's "Nacional por subtraçâo," in *Que Horas Sâo?* (Sâo Paulo: Companhia das Letras, 1987): 29–48.

27. Juan Zorrilla de San Martín, *Tabaré,* "Edición crítica, estudio preliminar," Antonio Seluja Cecín (Montevideo: Universidad de la Repúblic, 1984). References are to line numbers in this edition.

28. Achúgar: 93.

29. Clorinda Matto de Turner, *Aves sin nido* (Lima: Ediciones Peisa, 1984): 9. In her "Proemio" she writes, "If history is the mirror where future generations will contemplate the image of generations past, the novel should be the photograph that renders a people's vices and virtues as stereotypes and elicits the concomitant moral judgments."
Aves sin nido is a frustrated romance between a very decent white youth and a just as charming Indian girl. She has been adopted by a courageously liberal couple from the capital after her parents die trying to defend themselves from brutal whites. Finally discouraged from failed attempts to oblige the provincial mayor, magistrate, and priest to behave legally and humanely, the couple, their ward, and her beloved move back to the city. There they discover that the romance is doomed. Both lovers had the same lecherous priest of a father. Innocently in love, they are a brother and a sister barely saved from incest. And unlike the apparently similar obstacle between Cumandá and Carlos, these lovers are the victims of a priest's abuse. In *Cumandá*, whites bring pain to themselves by abusing others; in *Aves sin nido*, whites cause pain to Indians. Cumandá is lovable because she is really white; Margarita is a lovely mestiza. Institutionalized religion saves (souls) in *Cumandá*; it deforms and destroys the lives of Matto de Turner's *Aves sin nido*.
For a study of the general dialogue between novels and social reform in Peru, see Efraín Kristal, *The Andes Viewed from the City: Literary and Political Discourse on the Indian in Peru, 1848–1930* (New York: Peter Lang, 1987).

30. Some of Galván's "ponderous" and "serenely classical" style that Pedro Mir admires is evidently lost in translation. See Pedro Mir, *Tres Leyendas de Colores* (Santo Domingo: Editora Nacional, 1969; reprint, Santo Domingo: Taller, 1978): 167.

31. Concha Meléndez, "La tradición indianista en Santo Domingo," in Manuel de Jesús Galván, *Enriquillo* "con un estudio de Concha Meléndez" (Mexico: Editorial Porrúa, 1976): xii.

32. See Franc Báez Evertsz, *Azúcar y dependencia en la República Dominicana* (Santo Domingo: UASD, 1978), esp. 21–22, where he discusses the transformation of commercial to industrial (sugar) capital.

33. Independence in 1844 was opposed by many landholders who saw the effort as a disagreeable repetition of Núñez de Cáceres's proclamation of liberty twenty-one years before, a hasty move that invited the Haitian invasion. And others were concerned that La Trinitaria, a secret organization founded in 1838 to break with Haiti, would reestablish slavery, as Núñez de Cáceres did. See Frank Moya

Pons, *Manual de historia dominicana* (Santiago: UCMM, 1978): 269, and Josefina de la Cruz, *La sociedad dominicana de fines de siglo a través de la novela* (Santo Domingo: Cosmos, 1978): 31. As for Núñez's justified worries about racial sympathy, see Piero Gleijeses, *The Dominican Crisis: The 1965 Constitutional Revolt and American Intervention* (Baltimore: Johns Hopkins University Press, 1978): 5.

34. Malcolm Deas, "Venezuela, Colombia and Ecuador: The First Half-Century of Independence," *The Cambridge History of Latin America*, vol. 3. *From Independence to c. 1870* (Cambridge: Cambridge University Press, 1984): 507–538; 535. Flores planned to lead a Spanish-backed expedition of reconquest after his forced departure in 1845.

35. Quoted from the article on Galván in the *Diccionario biográfico-histórico dominicano* by Rufino Martínez (Santo Domingo: UASD, 1971): 187.

36. Compare Bartolomé de Las Casas, *Historia de las Indias*, chap. 127 (Madrid: Biblioteca de autores españoles, 1957): 483; with Gonzalo Fernández de Oviedo y Valdés, *Historia general y natural de Las Indias*, chap. 7 (Madrid: Biblioteca de autores españoles, 1959): 130.

37. The "Italian fashions" are Graves's embroidery on this text, as is the taunting parenthesis about (Galván's?) overly classical style that follows: "Later, severity returned and smothered artistry."

38. Franklin J. Franco, *Trujillismo: Génesis y rehabilitación* (Santo Domingo: Editora Cultural Dominicana, 1971): 67.

39. Oviedo: 125.

40. See chap. 1, pt. 1, n. 30. In a letter to Galván dated September 1884, which has since appeared as a preface to the novel, Martí writes, "This is no historical legend, but rather a brand-new and enchanting way to write our American history."

And Henríquez Ureña would second him in an article published in *La Nación*, Buenos Aires, January 13, 1935, and reprinted in *Ensayos*, ed. José Rodríguez Feo (Havana: Casa de las Américas, 1973): 371. "And so, this vast portrait of the beginnings of the new life in post-conquest America is an image of the truth, superior to the complaints of those who dispute it. Virtue and error, prayer and protest are unified in a concert of final harmony in which Spaniards and Indians make their peace and deliver themselves to faith and hope."

41. Franklin J. Franco: 67. "Elevated since the past century to the level of required reading in the public school system, it fulfilled its role as an ideological bridge that allowed for the rehabilitation of Hispanophilia. . . . For us, despite all the highly positive qualities that the indigenist literary movement had in other latitudes, this shameful

Enriquillo—I say it boldly—was no more than a perfect instrument of ideological manipulation."

Pedro Conde's *Notas sobre el Enriquillo* (Santo Domingo: Taller, 1978) is similarly critical of the book's ideological manipulations.

42. Oviedo: 125–126.

43. Adriana García de Aldridge, "De la teoría a la práctica en la novela histórica hispanoamericana," unpublished doctoral thesis, University of Illinois, Urbana, 1972: 137.

44. See, for example, Moya Pons: 371–378.

45. Moya Pons: 418.

46. Andrée Collard, "Translator's Note," in Bartolomé de Las Casas, *History of the Indies* (New York: Harper and Row, 1971): xxii.

47. Although much of the *Historia* is written with the dauntless optimism of a man who continues to have faith in God and the king, claiming that their will could be done *if* covetousness ended, Las Casas was not unaffected by the hard knocks of experience. As the colonists continued to disregard both their heavenly and their temporal monarchs, Las Casas became increasingly disillusioned with his utopian project of winning souls for Christ and Caesar. See vol. 3, chap. 138.

In a letter of 1544 to the future Felipe II, Las Casas practically recommends that all Spaniards abandon the New World. But despite the murder of priests by unconverted or ungrateful Indians, and despite the incessant usurpation of "freed" Indians by unrepenting *encomenderos,* Las Casas was always reluctant to consider his own colonizing scheme faulty or unrealizable. See Lewis Hanke, *The Spanish Struggle for Justice in the Conquest of America* (Philadelphia: University of Pennsylvania Press, 1949), chap. 5.

48. Fray Cipriano de Utrera, *Polémica de Enriquillo,* "Prefacio" by E. Rodríguez Demorizi (Santo Domingo: Editora del Caribe, 1973): 445.

49. Utrera: 448.

50. Utrera: 478.

51. On the 1937 massacre in Dajabón, see Jesús de Galíndez's classic *La era de Trujillo* (Santiago: Editorial del Pacífico, 1956).

52. E. Rodríguez Demorizi, "Prefacio," in Cipriano de Utrera, *Polémica de Enriquillo*: 5.

9. LOVE *OF* COUNTRY: POPULISM'S REVISED ROMANCE IN *LA VORAGINE* AND *DOÑA BÁRBARA*

1. José Eustasio Rivera, *La vorágine* (Buenos Aires: Losada, 1971). All references to the novel are from this edition.

2. José Eustasio Rivera, *The Vortex,* trans. Earle K. James (New

York: G. P. Putnam's Sons, 1935). Subsequent page references in parentheses refer consistently first to the Spanish version, then to the translation.

3. For a more developed discussion of the gendered terms of populist culture, see my *One Master for Another: Populism as Patriarchal Rhetoric in Dominican Novels* (Lanham, Md.: University Press of America, 1984).

4. John A. Crow, *The Epic of Latin America*, 3d ed. (Berkeley, Los Angeles, London: University of California Press, 1980): 682.

5. Quoted in Ibid., p. 682.

6. The Mexican writer Luis Quintanilla gives this account in his *A Latin American Speaks*. Reference in Crow: 686–687.

7. Pedro Henríquez Ureña reviews that literature in *Literary Currents in Hispanic America* (Cambridge: Harvard University Press, 1945). After chap. 7, "Pure Literature: 1890–1920" (161–184), on the *modernismo* and literary vanguards that these writers reacted against, follows chap. 8, "Problems of Today: 1920–1940" (185–204). It gives an overview of socially concerned novelists that included, among others, Rivera, Gallegos, Mexico's Mariano Azuela and Gregorio López y Fuentes, Bolivia's Alcides Arguedas, Ecuador's Jorge Icaza, Peru's Ciro Alegría, and Argentina's Ricardo Güiraldes and Eduardo Mallea. Roberto González Echevarría gives an excellent review of this genre, which proposed to be distinctly and originally American by capturing the autochthonous qualities of American life, in the country rather than in Europeanized cities. "The *novela de la tierra* elaborates a new Latin American literary reality, and it is precisely for this reason that it is so important today. It is the ground, the foundation, on which the present-day Latin American novel is erected." See Roberto González Echevarría, *The Voice of the Masters: Writing and Authority in Modern Latin American Literature* (Austin: University of Texas Press, 1985): 44–46.

8. Henríquez himself mentions their ties to populist parties such as APRA in Peru and the Partido Nacionalista and Partido Popular Democrático in Puerto Rico: 188.

9. R. Gutiérrez Girardot accuses Latin American elites of becoming used to sitting back and "letting them [usually the United States] rule." Rafael Gutiérrez Girardot, "Prólogo" to Pedro Henríquez Ureña, *La utopía de América* (Biblioteca Ayacucho: Caracas, 1978): xiv.

10. Rivera's first draft apparently had even more unacknowledged modernist verse—which came so easily to the sonneteer of *Tierra de Promisión* (1921)—according to his friend, Miguel Rasch Isla, who argued that much of the poetry should stay. See "Cómo escribió Rivera *La vorágine*," in *La vorágine: Textos críticos*, edited with introduc-

tion by Montserrat Ordóñez Vila (Bogotá: Alianza Editorial Colombiana, 1987): 83–88.

11. This characterization of both writer and writing is indebted, along with several other observations to follow, to Sylvia Molloy's brilliant essay, "Contagio narrativo y gesticulación retórica en *La vorágine*," in Ordóñez, *Textos críticos*: 489–513.

12. About the 1599 rebellion of the Jívaros, see Juan de Velasco, *Historia del Reino de Quito en la América Meridional*, vol. 3, pt. 3 of *1930*, ed. Leslie Bethell (Cambridge: Cambridge University Press, 1986): 121–151. "The rubber boom attracted Brazilians towards the Amazon. . . . The population of the Amazon region increased by 65.7 percent between 1877 and 1890 and by 40 percent in the last decade of the century. The opulent city of Manaus was the flourishing center of this boom between 1890 and 1920, but it also had repercussions in the eastern territories of Colombia, Peru and Bolivia, through which the fortune seekers spread" (147).

13. José Eustacio Rivera, "*La vorágine* y sus críticos," *El Tiempo*, November 25, 1926, in Ordóñez, *Textos críticos*: 63–76. In his response to Luis Trigueros' objections to the book's presumed irrelevance and inelegance, Rivera wrote a public letter that turns the accusations around.

14. Eduardo Neale-Silva, "The Factual Bases of *La vorágine*," *PMLA* 54 (1939): 316–331; 316.

15. Eduardo Castillo, "La vorágine," in Ordóñez, *Textos críticos*: 41–47. This was a review published in *El Tiempo*, January 18, 1925.

16. Montserrat Ordóñez, "*La vorágine*: La voz rota de Arturo Cova," in *Manual de literatura colombiana*, ed. Gloria Zea (Bogotá: Procultura y Planeta Colombiana Editorial, 1988): 434–518. Ordóñez herself seems to strain between this tradition of taking the voice for the man, whose assumptions of racial and gender privilege provoke more outrage than admiration in her rereading, and an insistence on the textual fissures that can produce the outrage.

17. Ordóñez cleverly glosses, "rumberos y rumberas menos clementes aún seguirán ampliando sentidos y posibilidades de interpretación." "La voz rota . . . ": 514.

18. James R. Scobie, "The Growth of Latin American Cities, 1870–1930," in *The Cambridge History of Latin America*, vol. 4, *c. 1870 to 1930*: 233–265; 254.

19. José Eustacio Rivera, "*La vorágine* y sus críticos," *El Tiempo*, November 25, 1926, in Ordóñez, *Textos críticos*: 63–76.

20. Hildebrando Fuentes, *Loreto: Apuntes geográficos, históricos, estadísticos, políticos y sociales* (Lima, 1908), 2: 113. Quoted in Neale-Silva: 322.

21. Neale-Silva: 317.

22. For a more "constructive" analysis of Rivera's treatment of populism, see David Viñas, "*La vorágine:* Crisis, populismo y mirada," *Hispamérica* 3, 8 (1974): 3–21.

23. See Meyra Jehlen, "Archimedes and the Paradox of Feminist Criticism," *Feminist Theory: A Critique of Ideology,* ed. Nannerl O. Keohane, Michelle Z. Rosaldo, and Barbara C. Gelpi (Chicago: University of Chicago Press, 1982): 189–216.

24. Ernesto Porras Collantes, "Hacia una interpretación estructural de *La vorágine,*" *Thesaurus* 23, 2 (1968): 241–271; 249.

25. Rivera himself explains the dynamic to his benighted critic Trigueros: "Any warm-blooded man knows well enough that you can't remain indifferent to a woman as soon as another man desires her. . . . The man is piqued, not so much as a lover, but as a man, and he insists on avenging himself on the rival." "*La vorágine* y sus críticos": 67. For the seminal discussion of triangulated desire see René Girard, *Deceit, Desire, and the Novel* (Baltimore: Johns Hopkins University Press, 1965); and for its application to "homosocial desire," see Eve Kosofsky Segwick, *Between Men: English Literature and Male Homosocial Desire* (New York: Columbia University Press, 1985).

26. See Luce Irigaray, "Any Theory of the 'Subject' Has Always Been Appropriated by the 'Masculine,'" in *Speculum of the Other Woman,* trans. Gillian C. Gill (Ithaca, N.Y.: Cornell University Press, 1985): 133–146.

27. The first, equally conflicting reviews spurred lively responses by Rivera himself. See Ordóñez, *Textos críticos:* 63–76.

28. Molloy: 501.

29. Luis Carlos Herrera, S.J., "Introducción," in José Eustasio Rivera, *La vorágine* (Bogotá: Editorial Pax, 1974): 11–47.

30. See Sharon Magnarelli, *The Lost Rib* (Lewiston, P. A.: Bucknell University Press, 1985).

31. Rivera, "*La vorágine* y sus críticos": 69.

32. Jorge Añez, *De "La vorágine" a "Doña Bárbara"* (Bogotá: Imprenta del Departamento, 1944). Añez begins by recording Gallegos's denial of influence. In an interview of 1942, Gallegos told a Mexican journalist that he had read *La vorágine* just after finishing *La trepadora* (1925) and while writing *Doña Bárbara.* The denial was repeated, but Añez is convinced of the plagiarism: 21–22.

33. This edition was by Editorial Araluce, Barcelona. A smaller edition was also published by Editorial Elite, Caracas. When he was asked in 1936 if the book had not been censored in Venezuela, Gallegos admitted that "the justified rumor about *Doña Bárbara* representing Gomecismo reached Maracay, and began to foment a hostile

atmosphere for me. But I enclosed myself in the life of teacher and writer, to dream about the next book." Quoted in Añez: 19.

Juan Liscano, *Rómulo Gallegos y su tiempo* (Caracas: Universidad Central de Venezuela, 1961): 113–127, writes that, in fact, the novel was largely composed in Europe, during the last months of 1928 and the first part of 1929.

34. Although they continued to regard him as their intellectual mentor, the leaders were really Gallegos's ex-students. He had long been a high school teacher and, from 1922, the director of the Liceo Caracas.

35. See Mario Torrealba Lossi, *Los años de la ira: Una interpretación de los sucesos del 28* (Caracas: Editoria Ateneo de Caracas, 1979): 21 and passim for an account of the celebration turned rebellion. Gómez was paternal enough—and sufficiently wise—to bow to the elite's outrage and initially to release the students, who by now numbered over 250 and represented most of the university body. But the troublemakers soon joined a failed army rebellion, and that's when Gómez cracked down. I am indebted to Julie Skurski's doctoral dissertation "The Civilizing Mission: The Representation of the Pueblo and the Bourgeoisie in Venezuela," Department of Anthropology, The University of Chicago, 1991.

36. Steven Ellner, "Populism in Venezuela, 1935–48: Betancourt and Acción Democrática," in *Latin American Populism in Comparative Perspective*, ed. Michael Conniff (Albuquerque: University of New Mexico Press, 1982): 135–149; 136–137.

37. Ellner: 138–139.

38. See John Beverley, *Del Lazarillo al Sandinismo: Estudios sobre la función ideológica de la literature española e hispanoamericana* (Minneapolis: Institute for the Study of Ideologies and Literature, 1987): 108.

39. Torrealba Lossi writes of the Generation of 1928, "When in 1929 *Doña Bárbara* appears and separates the country in two broad typologies,—the Luzardos and the Bárbaras—many of those youths felt themselves personified in the first": 174.

40. For an excellent review of Venezuelan literature, see John Beverley, "Venezuela," in *Handbook of Latin American Literature*, comp. David William Foster (New York: Garland Press, 1987): 559–577.

41. Gonzalo Picón Febres: *Le literatura venezolana en el siglo XIX* (Caracas: El Cojo, 1906): 127. Quoted in Marguerite C. Suárez-Murias, *La novela romántica en Hispanoamérica* (New York: Hispanic Institute of the United States, 1963): 154.

See also Jesús Semprún, "Una novela criolla" (1920), reprinted in

Rómulo Gallegos ante la crítica, ed. Pedro Díaz Seijas (Caracas: Monte Avila Editores, 1980): 11–18; Orlando Araujo, *Lengua y creación en la obra de Rómulo Gallegos* (Buenos Aires: Editorial Nova, 1955): 92, who agrees with others that Gallegos marks a "transition from a false and evasive 'criollismo' . . . to a responsible literature"; and Felipe Massiani, *El hombre y la naturaleza en Rómulo Gallegos* (Caracas: Ediciones del Ministerio de Educación, 1964): 22.

42. Massiani: 29, for example, writes, "A few years had passed in this century when a novel appears in America with a real American shape, its own accent, and all those qualities that will convince Europe of the maturity attained by the creole novel."

43. Araujo: 94. Gallegos's techniques "Brought the national novel to the attention of people in America and Europe."

44. First page references to the novel are from Rómulo Gallegos, *Doña Bárbara,* 32d ed. (Buenos Aires: Colección Austral, 1975); the second number refers to the corresponding page of *Doña Bárbara,* trans. Robert Malloy (New York: Peter Smith, 1948; originally published in 1931).

45. See José Luis Romero, "Prólogo," in *Pensamiento político de la Emancipación* (Caracas: Biblioteca Ayacucho, 1977): xxvii. "This basic conviction [that privileges had to be abolished] raised the most difficult post-revolutionary problem: the confrontation between the old colonial capitals and the interior regions of each viceroyalty."

46. José Antonio Páez suppressed the last serious separatist revolt. See John V. Lombardi, *Venezuela: The Search for Order, the Dream of Progress* (New York: Oxford University Press, 1982): 163–178.

47. "Cómo nació *Doña Bárbara?*" asked Luis Enrique Osorio, in an article published in Bogotá's *Acción Liberal* of November 1936. "She was born on a ranch owned by Juan Vicente Gómez, the Candelaria. There I took in that smell of cattle and dung that fills my novel. I also felt there the aura of barbarism that afflicted my country. Instinctively, I pursued the symbol, and the protagonist appeared in all her strength." Quoted in Añez: 18–19.

48. The leading ideologue was Laureano Vallenilla Lanz, whose *Cesarismo democrático* (1919) argued that the Venezuelan masses were an unfinished amalgam of primitive races who could be brought to civilization only through a dictator's strong guiding hand.

49. Rómulo Gallegos, "La pura mujer sobre la tierra," in *Una posición en la vida* (Mexico: Ediciones Humanismo, 1954): 414.

50. Juan Liscano: 109.

51. Rómulo Gallegos, "Necesidad de valores culturales" (1912), *Una posición en la vida:* 101–102.

52. Arturo Rioseco, "Novelistas contemporáneos de América Rómulo Gallegos," *Gallegos ante la crítica*: 63—"Gallegos es dueño de un estilo clásico, y entendemos por clásico un estilo racial, con esa sencillez, esa claridad, esa robustez, esa fuerza, propias de *Lazarillo de Tormes* y *Novelas ejemplares*." [When Gallegos uses the expressions of his country, the colloquial idioms (mastranto, totumo, merecure, talisayo, paraulata, güiriríes, hatajos), he is justifying the richness of our languge, impoverished by other writers.] Quote from p. 85 of first edition.

53. V. I. Lenin, cited in Andrzej Walicki, "Russia," in *Populism: Its Meaning and National Characteristics*, ed. Ghita Ionescu and Ernest Gellner (New York: Macmillan, 1969): 186–191.

54. Gallegos reveals that Santos and Marisela are the only characters in the novel who are not modeled after historical people. Both Bárbara and her dissolute ex-lover, Lorenzo Barquero, are adaptations from life. But to make their story into a future project he had to add Santos, "the civilizing idea and will," and Marisela, "the innocent product." See Gallegos, *Una posición . . .* : 415.

55. González Echevarría: 49–50.

56. González Echevarría: 54. "Lorenzo represents the defeat of language as well as its triumph; the defeat because it leads to no self-revelation, except to a negative understanding; the triumph because meaning, even if it is a series of lies, can only dwell in language itself."

57. See the essays in *Rómulo Gallegos ante la crítica*, ed. Pedro Díaz Seijas (Caracas: Monte Avila Editores, 1980), especially, Jesús Semprún, "Una novela criolla" (11–18), Julio Planchart, "Reflexiones sobre novelas venezolanas con motivo de *La trepadora*" (19–52), and Juan Liscano, "Ciclos y constantes galleguianos" (111–166).

58. As a figure for Gómez, Bárbara's literary dissemination is rather apt. It spends itself as indiscriminately as Gómez's more literal dissemination. Julie Skurski notes that "he administered offers and threats through his agents to young women of every class and origin whom he wished to conquer, either briefly or as a mistress. (He had over 100 children . . .) Yet what distinguished him from other rulers who have similary expressed their power, was his refusal both to marry and to cohabit with a woman . . . he constructed his identity as a ruler who stood above all ordinary human bonds of sentiment or reciprocity." "Courting 'El Pueblo'": 7.

10. "IT'S WRONG TO BE RIGHT":
MAMÁ BLANCA ON FATHERLY FOUNDATIONS

1. Teresa de la Parra, *Las memorias de Mamá Blanca* (Caracas: Monte Avila Editores, 1985). References will be made to this edition. Second

page numbers refer to Teresa de la Parra, *Mamá Blanca's Souvenirs,* trans. Harriet de Onís (Washington, D.C.: Pan American Union, 1959), which I cite here with an occasional adjustment.

2. Luis Sánchez-Trincado, a Spanish critic, called *Mamá Blanca* a "novela-album," explaining that these "viñetas folk-lóricas" are typical of children's literature with which Parra's work is often associated. "Teresa de la Parra y la creación de caracteres," in *Revista Nacional de Cultura* 2, 22 (Caracas, September 1940): 38–54; 47.

3. For an excellent study of *Las memorias,* which includes a suggestive comparison with *Doña Bárbara,* see Elizabeth Garrels, *Las grietas de la ternura: Nueva lectura de Teresa de la Parra* (Caracas: Monte Avila Editores, 1986). Another perceptive comparison, more generally between feminism and "mundonovismo," appears in an essay by Francine Masiello: "Texto, ley, transgresión: Especulación sobre la novela (feminista) de vanguardia," *Revista Iberoamericana,* nos. 132–133 (July–December 1985): 807–822.

4. If a case had to be made for the prevalence of stereotypes like Gallegos's, many writers could be mentioned, among them the very popular José Rafael Pocaterra. The heroine of his aptly and allegorically titled novel *Tierra del Sol amada* is described like this: "she encarnates the great spiritual *patria,* which gives herself over, offers herself entirely, whose body flourishes and then disintegrates, self-denying, like the dark roots of a race." Quoted in Pedro Díaz Seijas, *La antigua y la moderna literatura venezolana* (Caracas: Ediciones Armitano, 1966): 494. Of Teresa de la Parra's work, the same critic will say it is less objective, more inductive and feminine.

5. Their literary "collaboration" dates at least from 1920, when Parra published "Diario de una caraqueña por el Lejano Oriente" in the magazine *Actualidades,* edited by Gallegos. See the Chronology at the end of Teresa de la Parra, *Obras completas "Narrative, ensayos, cartas),* "Selección, Estudio Crítico y Cronología by Velia Bosch" (Caracas: Biblioteca Ayacucho, 1982): 696.

6. For the contrast see Bella Brodzki and Celeste Schenck, "Introduction" to *Life/Lines: Theorizing Women's Autobiography* (Ithaca, N.Y.: Cornell University Press, 1988): 7.

7. de Onís translates, more literally, "No hay que tener razón," as "There is no need to be right."

8. See Luce Irigaray's discussion of the imaginary as a male "Blindspot," that space that separates the boy from his mother while positing a primal unity. "The Blind Spot of an Old Dream of Symmetry," in *Speculum of the Other Woman,* trans. Gillian C. Gill (Ithaca, N.Y.: Cornell University Press, 1985): 87–89. Also "Questions," in *This Sex Which Is Not One* (Ithaca, N.Y.: Cornell University Press,

1985): 164: "I am trying, . . . to go back through the masculine imaginary, to interpret the way it has reduced us to silence, to muteness, to mimicry . . . "

Also Patricia Yaegar, *Honey-Mad Women* (New York: Columbia University Press, 1987), on playful strategies as against a French feminist idea that language is always alienated.

9. Teresa de la Parra, *Ifigenia: Diario de una señorita que escribió porque se fastidiaba,* published in 1924. For a fine reading, see Julieta Fombona, "Teresa de la Parra: Las voces de la palabra," in de la Parra, *Obras completas*: ix–xxvi; but I evidently quibble with the contrast she suggests between this first novel (where words are obstacles to meaning) and *Memorias* (where words fit meanings perfectly): xxii.

10. Arturo Uslar-Pietri appreciated Parra's writing for similar reasons. His essay called "El testimonio de Teresa de la Parra" begins, "There was a time, marvelously imprecise and static . . . " Although, to judge from his quick overview, he misses much of the slow-motion detail: "In *Mamá Blanca* Teresa painted the portrait of our grandmothers. A world devoted to security, resigned to pain." See *Letras y hombres de Venezuela* (Mexico: Fondo de Cultura Económica, 1948): 148–153.

11. This is my more literal translation of "el roce de mis manos sobre las huellas de las manos ausentes."

12. Sandra Gilbert and Susan Gubar, *The Madwoman in the Attic: The Woman Writer and the Nineteenth-Century Literary Imagination* (New Haven: Yale University Press, 1979): 37. "The real story begins when the Queen, having become a mother, metamorphoses also into a witch—that is, into a wicked 'step' mother: ' . . . when the child was born, the Queen died,' and 'After a year had passed the King took to himself another wife.'"

13. Nancy Choderow, *The Reproduction of Mothering: Psychoanalysis and the Sociology of Gender* (Berkeley, Los Angeles, London: University of California Press, 1978). The relationship is not always a happy one, of course, because the daughter's only recourse for limiting her mother's consuming power is to submit to paternal authority.

14. I refer to the distinction made by M. M. Bakhtin in "Epic and Novel," in *The Dialogic Imagination,* trans. Caryl Emerson and Michael Holquist (Austin: University of Texas Press, 1981): 3–40.

15. Gallegos, *Doña Bárbara*: 178–179.

16. For a more developed discussion, see my *One Master for Another.*

17. Teresa de la Parra, "Influencia de las mujeres en la formación del alma americana," in *Obras completas*: 474. She defends women's rights to careers, "fitting for women with fair pay. . . . I don't want,

as a consequence of my tone and argument, to be considered a suffragist. I neither defend or object to suffragism for the simple reason that I don't understand it. The fact of knowing that it raises its voice to win for women the same attributions and political responsibilities that men have frightens and disburbs me so that I could never manage to hear out what suffragism has to say. And this is because I generally believe, in contrast to suffragists, that we women should thank men for resigning themselves to take on all the political work. It seems to me that, next to that of coal miners, it is the most difficult and least cleanly work that exists. Why demand it?

"My feminism is moderate."

18. In the second of three talks she gave on the "Influencia de las mujeres en la formación del alma americana," Parra corrected, or responded defensively to, a common (mis)perception: "My affection for the Colony would never bring me to say, as some do in lyrical moments, that I would have preferred being born then. No, I am quite happy in my epoch and I admire it." *Obras completas*: 490.

For a lovingly written evocation of de la Parra, the creole Circe, see Mariano Picón Salas's review of her published letters in *Estudios de literature venezolana* (Madrid: Ediciones Edime, 1961): 265–270—" . . . so beautiful a woman, who could be seen at all the parties with her splendid eyes and her bearing of a young Spanish Marquise who dressed in Paris, could tell us about episodes and anecdotes that dated back a century, because she had heard them from grandmothers and from old servant women": 266–267.

19. Of course, one may choose to draw connections between Teresa de la Parra's ideological position and the bald manipulations justified by the socialist rhetoric that she admires in Daniel (148):

> En el corralón, sobre la república de las vacas, por elección y voluntad soberana de ellas . . . todo sabiduría y buen gobierno, imperaba Daniel, Daniel era el vaquero . . .
>
> El orden reinante era perfecto: era el orden de la ideal ciudad futura. Al pleno aire, pleno cielo y pleno sol, cada vaca estaba contenta y en su casa, es decir atada a su árbol. . . . Nadie se quejaba ni nadie se ensoberbecía, nada de comunismos. Satisfecha cada cual con lo que se le daba, daba en correspondencia cuanto tenía. Por todas partes conformidad, dulzura y mucha paz. (142–143)

> [The ruler of the republic of the cows, by their choice and sovereign will— do not laugh, you will see that this is true—, all wisdom, all good government, was Daniel, the cowherd.
>
> When we made our appearance in the city of the cows, Daniel, who had been up since four in the morning, had already, with the assistance of

a stable boy, filled many buckets of milk. The order which existed was perfect: the order of the ideal future city. In the open air, under the sky and sun, each cow was happy and in its house, that is to say, tied to a tree or a post. . . . Nobody complained and nobody was resentful; there was no class warfare. To each according to her needs, from each according to her ability. All was peace, all was light.] (102)

But this praise occurs in a novel where other systems of organization or disorganization receive equal applause. And if one thinks of the liberties the girls take with everyone, or of Juancho's flagrant failures and the other's anachronistically poetic posturing, among other practices, it may be seen that Daniel's government represents one point of this portrait, if not a delicate scoffing at the "future city."

20. Parra, *Obras completas*: 503.

21. Although Julia Kristeva assumes woman's challenge to symbolization differently from Parra's performance (as a presymbolic "semiosis," an "archaic, instinctual, and maternal territory" of language that challenges meaning by cultivating meaningless phonic and rhythmic, poetic, excesses), Mamá is subversive, not because she's indifferent to meaning, but because she competes by exaggerating its opacity. Nevertheless, Parra's evocation of Cochoco's style does respond to Kristeva's celebration of semiosis. "From One Identity to Another," in *Desire in Language: A Semiotic Approach to Literature and Art* (New York: Columbia University Press, 1980): 124–147. For a useful review see also Deborah Cameron, *Feminism and Linguistic Theory* (New York: St. Martin's Press, 1985).

22. Regarding "author-ity," the editor of the memoirs comes "to the melancholy conclusion that this compelling need to sign a book may not be the manifestation of talent, but perhaps, a weakness of the auto-critical faculty" (24; 12–13).

23. This and other references to Argentine women's claims for sexual equality come from Francine Masiello's very informative essay, "Between Civilization and Barbarism: Women, Family, and Literary Culture in Mid-Nineteenth-Century Argentina," in *Cultural and Historical Grounding for Hispanic and Luso-Brazilian Feminist Literary Criticism*, ed. Hernán Vidal (Minneapolis: Institute for the Study of Ideologies and Literature, 1989): 517–566; 530.

24. Masiello, "Between Civilization and Barbarism": 535.

25. For the best narrative I know of this fascinating triangulated power play between two men over an apparently defenseless woman, see Octavio Paz, *Sor Juana Inés de la Cruz: Las trampas de la fe* (Barcelona: Seix Barral, 1982), trans. Margaret Sayers Peden (Cambridge, Mass.: Belknap Press, 1988).

26. There is Saint Paula, for example, whom Jerome, the patron of Juana's Carmelite order, repeatedly honors for her sanctity and her learning. On the next page is Hypatia, the Alexandrine mathematician and astrologer whom the church fathers ran out of town for improprieties of doctrine, and perhaps of gender too.

27. Sor Juana Inés de la Cruz, *Respuesta a Sor Filotea,* translated in a bilingual edition as *A Woman of Genius: The Intellectual Autobiography of Sor Juana Inés de la Cruz* by Maragret Sayers Peden (Lime Rock, Conn.: Lime Rock Press, 1982): 80–81.

28. See P. Paul Jouon, *Grammaire de l'ebreu Biblique* (Rome: Institut Biblique Pontifical, 1923). On pp. 148–149 there are several examples: e.g., Gen. 31: 5, 6 is feminine and Gen. 31: 9 masculine. Ruth 1: 9*a* and 1: 9*b*. See also *Journal of Biblical Literature* 105 (1986): 614.

29. Sor Juana, *Respuesta*: 98–99.

30. *Me llamo Rigoberta Menchú* (Havana: Casa de las Americas, 1983): 42. *I, Rigoberta Menchú: An Indian Woman in Guatemala,* edited and introduced by Elisabeth Burgos-Debray, trans. Ann Wright (London: Verso, 1984): 9.

31. Menchú: 377; trans., 247.

32. Irigaray, in "La mechanique des fluids," *Ce sexe* (108), where she turns around Lacan's privileging of metaphor over (continuous) metonymy.

Index

Permission to reprint has been generously given for the following illustrations: "Latin America in 1830" appeared originally in *Latin American History: A Teaching Atlas*, by Cathryn L. Lombardi and John V. Lombardi with K. Lynn Stoner (Madison: University of Wisconsin Press, 1983):49; reprinted with the permission of University of Wisconsin Press. Portrait of *María*, now in El Paraíso, Cali; photo courtesy Juan Carlos Benoit. Illustration for children's edition of *María*, originally published by Ariel Juvenil (Guayaquil, Quito); reproduced in *100 Marías* (Bogota: Fondo Cultural Cafetero, 1985):11. *The abduction of a captive girl*, reproduced in *Mauricio Rugendas*, by Bonifacio del Carril (Buenos Aires: Academia Nacional de Bellas Artes, 1966).

Enriquillo and Las Casas appeared in *Historia gráfica de la República Dominicana*, by José Ramón Estella (Santo Domingo: Editora Taller, 1986):37. Student worksheet, from *O Guarani*, 14th ed., by José de Alencar (Sao Paulo: Editora ática s.a.); © 1988 by Editora ática s.a. *José Francisco*, reproduced in *Pintura española y cubana y litografías y grabados cubanos del siglo XIX* (Havana: Ministerio de Cultura, Derección General de Bellas Artes y Archivos, 1983):62, pl. 51. Film still from Doña Bárbara, reproduced in *Foreign and American Feature Films* (Chicago: Trans-World Films, Inc.):37. Ink drawing of Teresa de la Parra, reproduced in *Teresa de la Parra*, edited by Velia Bosch (Caracas: Documentos de la Biblioteca Ayacucho, 1984):111. *La plaza mayor de Lima*, reproduced in *El Perú Romántico del siglo XIX: Juan Mauricio Rugendas*, edited by José Flores Araoz (Lima: Editor Carlos Milla Batres, 1975):pl. 61; reproduced here with permission of Felipe Benavides.

Other illustrations appeared in the following: *La Coqueta, La China*, and *El Ranchero*, in a facsimile of an 1855 edition of *Los mexicano pintados por sí mismos*, by Hilarión Frías y Soto et al. (Mexico: Porrua, 1974):90, 136, 192. *Juárez's Triumphal Entry into Mexico City in 1861*, in *Historia de México* (Mexico: Salvat Editores de México, 1974):294. *Baptism of Camila O'Gorman's Unborn Child*, reproduced in *Cuadernos de la literatura argentina*, vol. 1 of *La novela argentina traditional* (Buenos Aires: Centro Editor de América Latin, 1985):299. Film still from *Amalia*, reproduced in an announcement for *Jornadas de cine mudo argentino* (Buenos Aires: Museo del Cine, 1981). *Disembarking in Buenos Aires*, reproduced in *Mauricio Rugendas*, by Bonifacio del Carril (Buenos Aires: Academia Nacional de Bellas Artes, 1966):pl. 135.

Tabaré and the Monk, in *Tabaré*, by Juan Zorrilla de San Martín (Montevideo: Editora de la Universidad de La República, 1984):213. Portrait of Gertrudis Gómez de Avellaneda, reproduced in *La Avellaneda y sus Obras*, by Emilio Cotarelo y Mori (Madrid: Tipografía de Archivos, 1930):193. *La Vorágine*, reproduced on the cover of *José Eustasio Rivera, 1888–1988* (Bogota: Colcultura—Biblioteca Nacional, 1988). Photograph of de la Parra's family, reproduced in *Esta pobre lengua viva: Relectura de la obra de Teresa de la Parra*, by Velia Bosch (Caracas: Ediciones de la Presidencia de la República, 1979).

Designer:	U.C. Press Staff
Compositor:	Prestige Typography
Text:	11/13 Baskerville
Display:	Baskerville
Printer:	Princeton Univ. Press/Printing
Binder:	Princeton Univ. Press/Printing